This book has many faults, but where it shines, it shines because of you. Thank you for sharing your knowledge of early modern France and your editorial expertise with me. I'll always appreciate and benefit from the time you put into improving what appears of the pages that follow.

Merci Mille Fois

Henry IV and the Towns

The Pursuit of Legitimacy in French Urban Society, 1589–1610

This book is the first serious study of Henry IV's relationship with the towns of France, and offers an in-depth analysis of a crucial aspect of his craft of kingship. Set in the context of the later Wars of Religion, it examines Henry's achievement in reforging an alliance with the towns by comparing his relationship with Catholic League, royalist and Protestant towns.

    Annette Finley-Croswhite focuses on the symbiosis of three key issues: legitimacy, clientage, and absolutism. Henry's pursuit of political legitimacy and his success at winning the support of his urban subjects is traced over the course of his reign. Clientage is examined to show how Henry used patron–client relations to win over the towns and promote acceptance of his rule. By restoring legitimacy to the monarchy, Henry not only ended the religious wars but also strengthened the authority of the crown and laid the foundations of absolutism.

S. ANNETTE FINLEY-CROSWHITE is Associate Professor of History, Old Dominion University, Norfolk, Virginia

CAMBRIDGE STUDIES IN EARLY MODERN HISTORY

Edited by Professor Sir John Elliott, University of Oxford
Professor Olwen Hufton, University of Oxford
Professor H. G. Koenigsberger, University of London
Dr H. M. Scott, University of St Andrews

The idea of an 'early modern' period of European history from the fifteenth to the late eighteenth century is now widely accepted among historians. The purpose of Cambridge Studies in Early Modern History is to publish monographs and studies which illuminate the character of the period as a whole, and in particular focus attention on a dominant theme within it, the interplay of continuity and change as they are presented by the continuity of medieval ideas, political and social organization, and by the impact of new ideas, new methods and new demands on the traditional structure.

For a list of titles published in the series, please see end of book

Henry IV and the Towns

The Pursuit of Legitimacy in French Urban Society, 1589–1610

S. ANNETTE FINLEY-CROSWHITE

CAMBRIDGE
UNIVERSITY PRESS

PUBLISHED BY THE PRESS SYNDICATE OF THE UNIVERSITY OF CAMBRIDGE
The Pitt Building, Trumpington Street, Cambridge CB2 1RP, United Kingdom

CAMBRIDGE UNIVERSITY PRESS
The Edinburgh Building, Cambridge, CB2 2RU, United Kingdom
http://www.cup.cam.ac.uk
40 West 20th Street, New York, NY 10011–4211, USA   http://www.cup.org
10 Stamford Road, Oakleigh, Melbourne 3166, Australia

© S. Annette Finley-Croswhite 1999

First published 1999

Printed in the United Kingdom at the University Press, Cambridge

Typeset in Postscript Ehrhardt 10/12 pt [VN]

A catalogue record for this book is available from the British Library

Library of Congress Cataloguing in Publication data
Finley-Croswhite, S. Annette
Henry IV and the towns: the pursuit of legitimacy in French urban society, 1589–1610 /
S. Annette Finley-Croswhite.
p.   cm. – (Cambridge studies in early modern history)
Includes bibliographical references.
ISBN 0 521 62017 1 (hardback)
1. Henry IV, King of France, 1553–1610.   2. Urban policy – France – History – 16th
century.   3. Monarchy — France — History – 16th century.   4. Religion and politics –
France – History - 16th century.   I. Title.   II. Series.
DC122.3.F56   1999
944'.031'092–dc21   98–38098   CIP

ISBN 0 521 62017 1 hardback

For John R. Rilling and
in memory of
J. Russell Major

Primi studiorum duces et primae faces

Contents

Illustrations

Tables

Acknowledgements

Rien n'est simple, Emmanuel Le Roy Ladurie once commented in reference to Henry IV's reign, and I borrow the phrase to emphasize that neither is the writing of a book about his municipal politics. In the course of its long years of production, beginning as a doctoral dissertation at Emory University and ending many years later in 1998, I have incurred enormous debts to scholars, institutions, friends, and family, in both the United States and France. The generosity of the many has been truly humbling.

I owe my conceptualization of *Henry IV and the Towns* to the works of and conversations with Mack Holt, Bill Beik, Gayle Brunelle, Sharon Kettering, Barbara Diefendorf, Philip Benedict, Stuart Carroll, Mark Greengrass, Richard Bonney, Orest Ranum, J. H. M. Salmon, Jim Collins, Chris Stocker, Rondo Cameron, Penny Roberts, Mark Konnart, Ron Love, Kevin Robbins, Michael Wolfe, Julie Hardwick, Brad Smith, and Kathy Pearson. Jeff Hamilton helped with the Latin translations in chapter three, Philip Benedict graciously read chapter five, Steve Finley gave advice on an early version of chapter seven, and Maura Hametz edited chapter eight. In France Jean-Pierre Babelon, Janine Garrisson, Bernard Barbiche, Pierre Tucoo-Chala, Marcel Lachiver and, the late, Roland Mousnier opened many doors for me. I would particularly like to thank Jacques Perot, director of the Musée de l'Armée in Paris, who took an interest in me as a young graduate student. Thanks to him I was invited to an international conference on Henry IV in 1989 where I met a multitude of sixteenth- and seventeenth-century historians, most notably Robert Descimon and Denis Crouzet.

In the course of researching this book I travelled from one end of France to the other. I thank all the directors and staff of the many libraries and archives where I worked. I would especially like to thank the personnel at the *Archives Départementales de la Somme* and the *Archives Municipales* in Amiens, Dijon, and Lyons for their courteous service and helpful advice.

The National Endowment for the Humanities, the Society for French Historical Studies, the Committee on Research in Economic History, Phi Alpha Theta, the National History Honor Society, the Atlanta branch of the English Speaking Union, Emory University, and Old Dominion University all provided funding for my research. I owe special thanks to my former dean, Charles O. Burgess, who enthusiastically found money for me even in the worst of financial times in Virginia,

Acknowledgements

and to a very generous colleague, Carl Boyd, who allowed me to tap into some surplus research monies which helped with my revisions. Debbie Miller in the Graphics Department was wonderfully helpful in devising the graphics in chapter two. Three students, Scott Becker, Brian Crim, and Jan Rives challenged me in the classroom to rethink many of my ideas, and another student, Catherine Cardon, helped with some of the French translations. Finally, many years ago Ted Llewellen tried to impart to me the thinking of an anthropologist. Those lessons have served me well ever since.

I additionally wish to thank Richard Fisher for opening the door for me at Cambridge University Press, William Davies, my editor, for offering encouragement and advice, and Rachel Coldicutt, my copy-editor, for making many helpful suggestions in improving the text.

I also have incurred debts of a very personal nature. In Atlanta, Georgia Jonathan Prude and Rosemary Eberel, Rick and Shana Elliott, and Dick and Barbara Baker all gave me free lodging and friendship during the writing of the dissertation. The support of Laura Mackail and Jody Aud has been unending. In France, Marika Neoschil, Hélène Bourdon, Anne-Marie Chevais, Dennis and Janey Barton, and Bernard and Christel Teisseire all took me into their homes and provided me with family. The Teisseires in particular showered me with southern French hospitality and charm and made me an honorary *citoyenne* of Foix.

I extend special thanks to Sharon Kettering. She poured over the manuscript for many long hours and tirelessly read and reread chapters and offered advice. Her generosity and friendship are extraordinary, and her insight improved the book immeasurably. My debt to her is great.

Three friends also stand out above the rest and deserve special mention. Mack P. Holt has acted for me like a sixteenth-century patron. He has written numerous letters of recommendation, commented on the book, and extended never-ending encouragement. Gayle Brunelle made the whole process enjoyable. The best parts of this book stem from the many conversations we had during our summer research trips to France. Finally, Philippe Andrau offered boundless enthusiasm for the project and made many a relevant comment along the way.

The thanks I extend to my family seems hardly adequate. My husband, Chip Croswhite, never went on a research trip or took any notes for me and had to make do with postcards during my many long absences. Yet he bore up amazingly well competing for my attention with a king who has been dead for nearly four hundred years. He is a walking lexicon and has saved me from many embarrassing mistakes. My parents, Clyde and Eula Finley, have deep pockets and big hearts. They helped to support my research as a graduate student in 1987 and again as a new professor in 1993. But their agape love is what sustained me.

Finally, I wish to thank my two mentors, John R. Rilling and J. Russell Major. Rilling was my undergraduate academic advisor at the University of Richmond. To him above all others I owe my life as a scholar – such is the life-changing power of

Acknowledgements

teaching at its very best. The idea of *Henry IV and the Towns* belonged to my dissertation director, J. Russell Major. It's humbling to think that he conceived the project before I was ever born. Sadly, he did not live to see the completion of this project; however, his guidance proved essential, and his patience and wisdom knew no limits. All mistakes and errors of judgement are wholly my own, but the work remains part of Russell Major's intellectual legacy. To these two great men of history, this book is respectfully dedicated.

Introduction

The aim of this book is to examine the relationship that Henry IV cultivated with urban France in order to explore how he acquired power and strengthened the French state. The work continues the general effort made by revisionary historians to explain what the term 'absolute' meant in practice to rulers and subjects as opposed to what it meant in theory to jurists and dogmatists.[1] This book is not a biographical assessment of Henry IV, but rather a case study of his interactions with selected towns. It attempts to discover how the balance between royal authority and urban autonomy was negotiated in the late sixteenth century. Henry IV mastered urban France with a policy of lenient pacification that emphasized his clemency. By easing internal strife after the religious wars, he re-opened lines of communication between the Crown and the towns. The re-establishment of communication strengthened the state by promoting cooperation between the king and his urban subjects and encouraging their compliance.

In the pages that follow two key concepts appear many times, legitimacy and clientage. In fact, the two terms are linked in explaining how Henry secured his realm and restored peace to France. The idea of a 'legitimate' king is one that appears often in the literature on early modern kingship, but legitimacy is a concept seldom defined by historians.[2] This book relies on Orlando Patterson's definition of legitimacy as a process that incorporates power relations into a moral order ultimately defining right and wrong.[3] Legitimation, the action of establishing

---

[1] For the historiography of absolutism see William Beik, *Absolutism and Society in Seventeenth-Century France, State Power and Provincial Aristocracy in Languedoc* (New York: Cambridge University Press, 1985), 3–33; Richard Bonney, 'Absolutism: What's in a Name?', *French History*, 1 (1987), 93–117; Nicholas Henshall, *The Myth of Absolutism: Change and Continuity in Early Modern European History* (London: Longman, 1992).

[2] For an exception see, Reinhard Bendix, *Kings or People: Power and the Mandate to Rule* (Berkeley: University of California Press, 1978), 8–9.

[3] Orlando Patterson, *Slavery and Social Death: A Comparative Study* (Cambridge, Massachusetts: Harvard University Press, 1982). Patterson does not address 'legitimacy' as a separate topic, but he does discuss it in relation to authority. His conceptualization is close to Jean-Jacques Rousseau's belief that legitimacy is grounded in human agency expressed through conventions or customs that validate it. Jean-Jacques Rousseau, *The Social Contract*, ed. Charles Frankel (New York: Hafner Publishing Company, 1947), 8; William Connolly, 'Introduction: Legitimacy and Modernity', in *Legitimacy and the State*, ed. William Connolly (New York: New York University Press, 1984), 4–7; Ronald Cohen, 'Introduction', in *State Formation and Political Legitimacy 6: Political Anthropology*, eds. Ronald Cohen and Judith Toland (New Brunswick, New Jersey: Transaction Books, 1988), 3.

legitimacy, is an important part of all political processes and can be conceptualized in the early modern period as a dialogue between rulers and subjects. In the premodern context legitimacy was circumscribed by Christianity so that rulers were divinely sanctioned. As Johann Huizinga put it, monarchies were thought to be ordained by God as good and perverted by humans as bad, but people never contemplated 'reforming' what was divinely inspired.[4] The Wars of Religion complicated this view of kingship when France first faced a series of weak kings and then an unacceptable Protestant one. The effects caused political thinkers to question divine right rule and introduce the idea of natural law; some even advocated the overthrow of tyrants and heretics.[5] Legitimation was thus a key issue confronted by the last Valois and the first Bourbon.

Henry IV's position in 1589 was uncertain. Under normal circumstances a king acquired his right to rule at the death of his predecessor.[6] When Henry III lay dying, however, his last thoughts were on the unsure succession. He mumbled over and over to the circle of nobles around him to accept his cousin, Henry of Navarre, as the legitimate king of France. Legitimacy under the Salic law meant tracing a blood alliance through the male line back to the thirteenth century. Twenty-two degrees of cousinage separated Henry III and Henry IV. Yet this distant familial link would not have been an issue if Henry of Navarre had been Catholic. But Navarre claimed the throne as a Protestant and delegitimized himself to most of France. He faced not only a kingdom torn apart by religious warfare, but also one in which the majority of cities and towns refused to recognize his kingship.[7] The pivotal moment of Henry IV's reign was his abjuration on 25 July 1593 when he formally took on his role as France's 'most Christian [Catholic] king'.[8] Certainly this 'perilous leap' made Henry *legitimus* to many, but it also alienated him from his former Protestant allies and never really convinced his most zealous Catholic subjects of his sincerity.

The subtitle of this book, *The Pursuit of Legitimacy*, best describes the trajectory of Henry's reign. The central point hinges on the distinction between Henry's clear *de jure* legitimacy based on Salic law and his lifelong pursuit of political legitimation. Legitimation, Reinhard Bendix has explained, realizes what power alone

---

[4] Johann Huizinga, *The Waning of the Middle Ages* (New York: Double Day Anchor Books, 1954) 38; Connolly, 'Introduction', 3.

[5] See for example Kathleen Parrow, *From Defense to Resistance: Justification of Violence during the French Wars of Religion* (Philadelphia: The American Philosophical Society, 1993) Transactions of the American Philosophical Society, vol. 83, part 6 ; Frederic J. Baumgartner, *Radical Reactionaries: the Political Thought of the French Catholic League* (Geneva: Droz, 1976); J. H. M. Salmon, *Renaissance and Revolt, Essays in the Intellectual and Social History of Early Modern France* (New York: St Martin's Press, 1987).

[6] Frederic J. Baumgartner, *France in the Sixteenth Century* (New York: St Martin's Press, 1995), 235–6.

[7] Jean-Pierre Babelon, *Henri IV* (Paris: Fayard, 1982), 317–21. Henry III was descended from Saint Louis's oldest son, Philip the Hardy, while Henry IV was descended from Louis's youngest son, Robert of Clermont.

[8] Michael Wolfe, *The Conversion of Henri IV: Politics, Power and Religious Belief in Early Modern France* (Cambridge, Massachusetts: Harvard University Press, 1993).

cannot because it promotes acceptance in the rightness of rule.[9] My concept of legitimacy is based on Jean-Jacques Rousseau's notion of a social contract in which people give their consent to be governed, an idea that Henry never would have recognized, although the belief that legitimacy was tied to popular support became increasingly prevalent during the sixteenth century.[10] Henry secured his throne through battle, bribery, diplomacy, and negotiation. Eventually he won his people's consent, although his assassination in 1610 proves his legitimacy as king was never universally accepted.[11]

Ronald Cohen has argued that acquiring legitimacy involves 'changing capabilities (i.e. power) into culturally sanctioned rights.'[12] In this context legitimacy and clientage can be linked. Clientage humanizes power by involving human agents in the struggle for consent.[13] Clientage also provides the historical context in which to consider legitimacy. Clients sanction power by giving their consent to be ruled, thereby recognizing a ruler as legitimate. More importantly, clients often open the dialogue that brings together rulers and ruled.

Sharon Kettering has studied the complex realities of the patron–client system in early modern France and defined key words like patron, client, broker, clientelism, and fidelity.[14] I use her definition of clientage as 'a voluntary relationship based on a reciprocal exchange between participants who are unequal in status' and accept her scepticism of Roland Mousnier's argument defining patron–client relations as *maître-fidèle* relationships denoted by absolute loyalty in the man-to-man tie.[15] Like Stuart Carroll, I believe such a model exaggerates the strength of vertical links uniting nobles and their clienteles.[16] Like Robert Harding I see many different kinds of clientage relationships, some motivated by self-interest, most more fragile than ties of complete devotion, and more easily severed.[17] Finally, I agree with

[9] Bendix, *Kings or People* 17.
[10] Ibid., 8–9.
[11] For a good summary of the history of the idea of legitimacy, see Tilo Schabert, 'Power Legitimacy and Truth: Reflections on the Impossibility to Legitimise Legitimations of Political Order': *Legitimacy/Légitimité Proceedings of the Conference held in Florence June 3 and 4, 1982* (Berlin: Walter de Gruyter, 1985), 96–104; Connolly, 'Introduction', 1–19.
[12] Cohen, 'Introduction', 3.
[13] On 'consent' see Schabert, 'Power, Legitimacy and Truth'.
[14] For example, Sharon Kettering, *Patrons, Brokers and Clients in Seventeenth-Century France* (Oxford: Oxford University Press, 1986); 'Clientage during the French Wars of Religion' *Sixteenth Century Journal*, 20 (1989), 68–87; 'Friendship and Clientage in Early Modern France', *French History*, 6 (1992), 139–58; 'The Historical Development of Political Clientelism', *Journal of Interdisciplinary History*, 18 (1988), 419–47; 'Patronage in Early Modern Europe', *French Historical Studies*, 17 (1992), 839–62; 'Political Parties at Aix-en-Provence in 1589', *European History Quarterly*, 24 (1994), 181–211. Kettering also surveys the literature on clientage. See in particular 'Patronage in Early Modern Europe'.
[15] Kettering, *Patrons, Brokers, and Clients*, 33.
[16] Stuart Carroll, 'The Guise Affinity and Popular Protest During the Wars of Religion', *French History*, 9 (1995), 126.
[17] Robert Harding, *Anatomy of a Power Elite: The Provincial Governors of Early Modern France* (New Haven: Yale University Press, 1978), 36–7.

Sharon Kettering that the word 'affinity', preferred by Mark Greengrass and Stuart Carroll in describing client networks, is too ambiguous.[18] 'Affinity' perhaps better denotes the wide range of personal relationships that included clienteles. Client, clientage, and clientelism give a more precise indication of the patron–client system to the English speaker.[19]

An objective of this study is to explore the ways in which the patron–client system operated in an urban setting. The extent to which vertical ties reaching down from the Crown penetrated into French cities and towns is unknown because no serious study of Crown–town patronage has been made.[20] Accumulating the documentation to pursue such research has been an obstacle for historians because no tidy set of documents exists in one location, and constant travel between national and local archives is necessary. Municipal magistrates, unlike robe and sword nobles, rarely left memoirs, and almost none of their personal correspondence has survived. The historian, therefore, must painstakingly sift through state papers, municipal documents, deputy-to-court letters, wills, marriage registers, godparentage records, property transfers, notarial acts, inventories after death, appointments to offices, and the occasional rare memoir in a frustrating and often abortive attempt to reconstruct kinship networks and clienteles. Not surprisingly, there is very little literature on Henry IV and the towns, and when the issue is addressed the same examples are used over and over.

One essential argument of this book asserts that Henry IV's pursuit of legitimacy among his urban subjects involved the effective use of the patron–client system. In short, clientage was one means Henry employed to increase his legitimacy as king of France. In dealing with the towns, Henry sought their loyalty and secured peace by placing his clients in municipal office. Royal clients were rewarded with favour, gifts, and increased status, and their reciprocal duty was to provide the king with peaceful, cooperative, and well-administered towns. Kettering believes that patrons disseminated their ideas to their clients. 'A patron's personal and political goals become the collective goals of his clientele.'[21] Since municipal elites were patrons who had their own clientele networks, Henry's use of patronage helped to ensure the acceptance of his legitimacy among nameless subjects he never saw. His employment of the patron–client system refutes Robert Harding's belief that there was a failure of patronage during the religious wars. In fact, Henry's pursuit of legitimacy made the patron–client system all the more relevant.[22]

---

[18] Mark Greengrass, 'Noble Affinities in Early Modern France: The Case of Henri I de Montmorency, Constable of France', *European History Quarterly*, 16 (1986), 275–311; Carroll, 'The Guise Affinity'.

[19] See Kettering's excellent discussion of the terminology of clientelism in 'Patronage in Early Modern France', 839–71, see especially, 850–1.

[20] Kettering points out the problem of the scarcity of evidence in 'Patronage in Early Modern Europe', 842. [21] Kettering, *Patrons, Brokers, and Clients*, 69.

[22] See Kettering's criticism of Robert Harding who argued in favour of a failure of clientage during the French Wars of Religion. Kettering, 'Clientage During the French Wars of Religion'; Harding, *Anatomy of a Power Elite*, 68–87.

It is in relation to power that the symbiosis of legitimacy, clientage, and absolutism was achieved during Henry's reign. Power is embedded within society. A community of people achieves power by acting in concert; their power reflects a coalescence of opinions and beliefs. Power has no independent justification. It takes its justification from the community, and it is the community that endows rulers and institutions with political legitimacy.[23] Rulers possess legitimacy when they adopt and promote the common beliefs of the group. The success of rulers in projecting acceptance of shared beliefs reinforces their legitimacy.[24] Belief in their legitimacy also enhances their authority while the possession of authority, legitimizes their power.[25] The distribution of power also involves the circulation of knowledge. Henry used clientage to promote his legitimacy and urge townspeople to accept his rule. It was Henry's clients in the towns who spoke out for his clemency and re-incorporated him into the spiritual and moral order of the day by voicing their consent to his authority through the cry, *Vive le Roi!* If power in its most rudimentary form incorporates the ability of someone to get someone else to do what he or she wants, the king's clients were crucial in re-establishing stability in France.[26] The process was not simple because clienteles were not easily controlled. Power was fragmented among competing clienteles, and loyalties changed over time. Even so, clients aided the king by serving as avenues of human access to the towns.[27] Legitimacy is a quality of power, and clientage served Henry to buttress his legitimacy.

In the context of legitimacy my statement on absolutism is a simple one. Henry pursued legitimacy and in the process strengthened Bourbon rule, although he never envisioned becoming an 'absolute' king. Looking at the way he acquired legitimacy and hence power allows us to reassess the political achievements of his reign. Frederic Baumgartner states, 'His contribution to absolutism was restoring the efficiency of the government so that it was again responsive to the king's will.'[28] He also restored legitimacy to the monarchy as a force able to exert its will and bring about the desired response. Consent is seldom universal in any political setting, and in Henry's case it was never complete, but he won the active support of his people so that his government proved effective. Re-establishing the alliance and dialogue between the Crown and the towns enjoyed by earlier kings was one of Henry's successes.

[23] Richard Flathman, *The Practice of Political Authority, Authority and the Authoritative* (Chicago: University of Chicago Press, 1980), 152–3; Hannah Arendt, *On Violence* (London: Allen Lane, Penguin Books, 1970), 46; Barry Barnes, *The Nature of Power* (Urbana, Illinois: University of Illinois Press, 1988), 61.

[24] R. B. Friedman, 'On the Concept of Authority in Political Philosophy', *Authority*, ed. Joseph Raz (New York: New York University Press, 1990), 58; Emile Durkheim, *The Elementary Forms of the Religious Life*, trans. Joseph Swain (New York: Free Press, 1965), 236–45; Barnes, *The Nature of Power*, 58–63.

[25] Carl J. Friedrich, *Tradition and Authority* (New York: Praeger Publishers, 1972), 94.

[26] Kenneth E. Boulding, *Three Faces of Power* (Newbury Park, California: Sage Publications, 1989), 15.

[27] Carroll, 'The Guise Affinity', 150.   [28] Baumgartner, *France*, 234.

Henry IV and the Towns

Henry IV has attracted many biographers and historians. Scholars before the 1970s who studied his reign interpreted his actions using a top-down model in which the king forced his will on the towns and imposed royal directives from above. Henry's intervention in municipal politics caused many historians to decide that he had intended to destroy municipal privileges. Jean Mariéjol and Gabriel Hanotaux, for example, argued in the early twentieth century that Henry perceived town privileges as threats to his authority and wanted to discontinue their use.[29] Mariéjol called Henry an 'enemy of the franchises of the towns'.[30] Paul Robiquet likewise argued that when the king re-established order after the religious wars, he destroyed municipal privileges to punish the Catholic League.[31] Georges Pagès, however, disagreed with his contemporaries. Rather than threatening urban autonomy, Pagès believed Henry IV simply accommodated himself to existing municipal institutions.[32]

In the late 1940s scholars began incorporating Henry IV into the growing literature on absolutism. Gaston Zeller and Roger Doucet, for example, saw Henry as a founder of absolutism. Zeller placed Henry at the head of municipal reform and contended that no other king intervened more often in municipal affairs. Doucet saw Henry as an innovator and wrote that 'the absolutist reaction [that had] begun with the reign of Henry IV' contributed to 'the ruin of the [municipal] institutions'.[33] For some historians, the real issue was the growing trend toward centralization of government. Robert Trullinger investigated Henry's attempts to oversee financial matters in the towns of Brittany. He concluded that Henry succeeded in extending Crown control over matters formally handled by municipalities. 'By the end of the reign', he states, 'the king and his government had established an organized and centralized structure for the control of the financial administration of the towns.'[34] Henry's determination to weaken the towns and end municipal independence was also the interpretation emphasized by two biographers of the king, Jean-Pierre Babelon and Janine Garrisson, who published works in the early 1980s.[35] Babelon went so far as to subtitle his discussion of Henry's municipal policy, 'La mainmise sur les villes'.[36]

[29] Jean Mariéjol, *Histoire de France 6: Henri IV and Louis XIII*, ed. Ernest Lavisse (Paris: Hachette, 1911), 33–5; Gabriel Hanotaux, *Sur les Chemins de l'histoire* (Paris: Edouard Champion, 1924), 44–5.
[30] Mariéjol, *Histoire de France*, 34.
[31] Paul Robiquet, *Histoire municipale de Paris* (Paris: Hachette, 1904), vol. 3, 196–9. For more arguments along these lines see, August Poirson, *Histoire du Règne de Henri IV* (Paris: Didier, 1862), vol. 3, 29–30; François Bourçier, 'Le Régime Municipal à Dijon sous Henry IV', *Revue d'Histoire Moderne*, 4 (1935), 118.
[32] Georges Pagès, *La Monarchie d'Ancien Régime en France de Henri IV à Louis XVI* (Paris: Armand Colin, 1928), 58–9.
[33] Roger Doucet, *Les Institutions de la France au XVI Siècle 1: Les Cadres géographiques, les institutions centrales et locales* (Paris: A. and J. Picard, 1948), 393. See also, Gaston Zeller, *Les Institutions de la France au XVI siècle* (Paris: Presses Universitaires de France, 1949), 38.
[34] Robert Trullinger, 'The Royal Administration of Bretagne Under Henri IV (1589–1610)', (Ph. D. thesis, Vanderbilt University, 1972), 317.
[35] Babelon, *Henri IV*, 792–6; Janine Garrisson, *Henri IV* (Paris: Editions du Seuil, 1984), 260–2.

By the 1980s, however, several historians began to advise caution in judging Henry's relationship with the towns. J. Russell Major saw Henry as a founder of absolutism but recognized that it was easy to exaggerate his ability to control the towns. He wrote, 'As a whole they [the towns] remained quite capable of thwarting the royal will by their delaying tactics and in some instances of putting up stout defenses against the royal army, as the following reign was to prove.'[37] This sentiment was echoed by David Buisseret who felt Henry's intervention in the towns was sporadic. He emphasized that the king interfered in town politics only when the requirements of military necessity, civil order, and fiscal needs forced his hand. 'Outside these limits', Buisseret observed, 'his intervention was rare.'[38]

Finally, Robert Descimon in 1988 published an intensive study of Henry's interference in Parisian elections. He argued that the king and the municipal magistrates reached a compromise designed to maintain the appearance of free elections while ensuring the king's participation in the events. Henry frequently nominated the city's *prévôt des marchands*, but Descimon found that he rarely interfered in the election of *échevins*. When the king did recommend a royal candidate for senior office, he generally confirmed a choice the electors had already made. Henry thus rubber-stamped the popular voice as kings had often done before him and sealed the collusion between the state and the municipal oligarchy. Descimon asserted, 'To sum up, the attitude of Henry IV referred to the most archaic possible political framework, far from all centralizing, modernizing, or absolutist will.'[39]

William Beik has made scholars aware in recent years of the shortcomings of traditional political history by uncovering an alliance in seventeenth-century Languedoc between provincial elites and the Crown that was profitable to both.[40] Micro-histories of towns, published with increasing frequency since the 1960s, have also underscored the complexities of urban life and revealed the wide diversity of the urban experience in early modern France.[41] Recent monographs on towns during the Wars of Religion, for instance, those by Philip Benedict, Robert Descimon, and Penny Roberts, have exposed the complex rivalries that existed

[36] Babelon, *Henri IV*, 792.
[37] J. Russell Major, *Representative Government in Early Modern France* (New Haven: Yale University Press, 1980), 380.
[38] David Buisseret, *Henry IV* (London: George Allen and Unwin, 1984), 169.
[39] Robert Descimon, 'L'Echevinage Parisien sous Henri IV (1594–1609). Autonomie urbaine, conflits politiques et exclusives sociales', *La Ville la bourgeoisie et al Genèse de L'Etat* (Paris: Editions du CNRS, 1988), 150. For more background see, Sharon Kettering, 'State Control and Municipal Authority in France', in *Edo and Paris: Urban Life and the State in the Early Modern Era*, eds. James McClain, John Merriman, and Ugawa Kaoru (Ithaca: Cornell University Press, 1994), 86–101.
[40] Beik, *Absolutism and Society*.
[41] For example, Pierre Goubert, *Beauvais et les Beauvaisis de 1600 à 1730* (Paris: SEVPEN, 1960); Pierre Deyon, *Amiens, capitale provinciale, étude sur la société urbaine au 17e siècle* (Paris: Mouton, 1967); Richard Gascon, *Grand commerce et vie urbaine au XVIe siècle: Lyon et ses marchands (environs de 1520–environs de 1580* (Paris: SEVPEN, 1971); Robert Schneider, *Public Life in Toulouse, 1463–1789: From Municipal Republic to Cosmopolitan City* (Ithaca: Cornell University Press, 1989).

inside urban power structures.[42] The following pages examine the interplay between urban elites and the Crown, and several chapters use a micro-history approach by focusing on a few urban examples. Substantial case studies are made of Amiens, Abbeville, Limoges, and Lyons. Other chapters, specifically four and five, consider Henry's interaction with the towns more broadly. By using these two approaches, both in-depth and comparative analyses and top-down and bottom-up models are developed of Henry IV's relationship with his towns. Finally, while this book makes no attempt to engage in the current debate among scholars about the place of religion in the Wars of Religion, the importance of religion in the lives of sixteenth-century people is endorsed completely as part of the backdrop to Henry's reign.[43]

To eliminate confusion in the text, the reader should note that municipal governments came in all shapes and sizes in the sixteenth century. The *corps de ville* numbered four at Blois, five at Paris, six at Narbonne, eight at Toulouse, twenty at Dijon, and twenty-four at Poitiers. A varying degree of advisory bodies could boost the number of municipal councillors in any given town to over one hundred, as in the case of La Rochelle, although this was rare. Terminology was not uniform either. Mayors headed most municipal governments in northern and central France, but this position equalled that of *vicomte-mayeur* in Dijon, *prévôt des marchands* in Paris and Lyons, and *lieutenant du capitaine* in Reims. Aiding these important officials were burghers for the most part known as *échevins*. Governing councils in the south of France were known as consulates. Consuls shared equal power and prestige whereas mayors outranked *échevins*, although sometimes a *premier consul* was named. A few towns acquired unique titles for their municipal officers. There were *gouverneurs* at Senlis, *jurats* at Bordeaux, and *capitouls* at Toulouse.[44]

After a short introduction that places French early modern towns in historical context, chapter two on patronage and clientage in Amiens demonstrates how Henry used his clients to broker his clemency for capitulation and to secure the town from within as the Catholic League fell apart in Picardy. Chapter three looks at ceremonial entries and the imaginative way Henry turned former Catholic League towns into institutional clients. Chapters four and five explore Henry's relationship with former Catholic League, royalist, and Protestant towns and underscore his use of clientage to negotiate with the towns. Chapter six discusses

[42] Philip Benedict, *Rouen During the Wars of Religion* (Cambridge: Cambridge University Press, 1981); Robert Descimon, *Qui Etaient Les Seize? Mythes et réalités de la Ligue parisienne (1585–1594)* (Paris: Klincksieck, 1983); Penny Roberts, *A city in conflict: Troyes during the French Wars of Religion* (Manchester: Manchester University Press, 1996).

[43] Mack P. Holt, 'Putting Religion Back in the Wars of Religion', *French Historical Studies*, 18 (1993), 524–51.

[44] Doucet, *Les institutions de la France*, vol. 1, 370; Albert Babeau, *La Ville sous l'Ancien Régime* (Paris: Didier, 1880), 75–6. For more on municipal magistrates and their duties, see William Beik, *Urban Protest in Seventeenth-Century France, The Culture of Retribution* (Cambridge: Cambridge University Press, 1997), 73–94.

the clients Henry placed in municipal office. Chapter seven examines two tax riots Henry faced and argues that his responses to these crises helped to resolve ongoing problems related to the religious wars. Chapter eight investigates the issue of post-war debt liquidation and reveals how Henry and his financial minister Sully used the debt issue to increase the Crown's authority. A short conclusion summarizes the relationship between town politics and absolutism. The chapters move chronologically from 1589 to 1610, but most of the book centres around the years 1593 to 1598 when the towns of France capitulated to the king and the religious wars came to an end. All translations are my own and original spellings have been maintained from the document sources.

The respect and influence enjoyed by urban elites and their control over town patronage made them exceedingly important to Henry IV. The Wars of Religion created a situation in which the king had to placate the towns in order to pacify France. Yet in rebuilding a royal alliance with the towns, Henry IV also took every opportunity to strengthen his royal authority. The success of his kingship cannot be fully understood without reference to his achievement with the towns.

France in the 1580s and 1590s

To many historians, and especially to Fernand Braudel, the part French towns played in the religious civil wars, and in particular their support of the Catholic League, marked a return to the age of medieval urban independence.[1] French medieval towns had exhibited a republican spirit that included pride in their urban autonomy, but increasingly during the sixteenth century their hallowed liberties and privileges came under attack.[2] Louis XI, Charles VIII, Louis XII, Francis I, Henry II, Charles IX, and Henry III all interfered in municipal elections on a sporadic basis and passed a variety of laws designed to increase royal involvement in town politics and finances. Francis I's Edict of Crémieu ordered bailiffs from the local royal courts to observe all municipal general assemblies and elections while Charles IX's Ordonnance of Orléans instructed all towns to submit their financial records to royal officials for auditing. In 1547 Henry II enacted legislation that made municipal offices incompatible with royal ones and ordered municipal offices on town councils reserved for merchants and bourgeois notables. In 1566 Charles IX passed the Ordonnance of Moulins which restricted municipal jurisdiction to criminal affairs and matters of police and delegated all civil suits to royal judges. What these laws had in common was that they threatened municipal independence, although they were operated for the Crown more as fiscal expedients but were rarely enforced. Towns with healthy treasuries and wealthy citizens paid fees to buy exemptions from their restrictions.[3] Thus while Crown control of municipal

---

[1] Fernand Braudel, *The Mediterranean and the Mediterranean World in the Age of Philip II*, trans. Sian Reynolds (New York: Harper and Row), 1215–16.

[2] For more background on Crown interference in urban government before the reign of Henry IV see Annette Finley-Croswhite, 'Henry IV and the Towns: Royal Authority and Municipal Autonomy, 1589–1610' (Ph.D. thesis, Emory University, 1991), 26–76.

[3] Roger Doucet, *Les Institutions de la France au XVIe siècle* (Paris: A and J Picard, 1948), vol. 1, 366–7, vol. 2, 501; Gaston Zeller, *Les institutions de la France au XVIe Siècle* (Paris: Presses Universitaires de France, 1949), 43; Émile Chénon, *Histoire générale du droit Français public et privé des origines à 1815 1: période Gallo-Romaine, période franke, période féodale et coutumière* (Paris: Société Anonyme du Receuil Sueiy, 1926), 388; Nora Temple, 'The Control and Exploitation of French Towns during the Ancien Regime', *History*, 51 (1966), 17; François Isambert, ed., *Recueil général des anciennes lois françaises dépuis l'an 420 jusqu'à la Révolution de 1789 8: Henri II* (Paris: Plon Frère, 1822–33), 35; Georges Testaud, *Des juridictions municipales en France des origines jusqu'à l'Ordonnance de Moulins 1566* (Paris: Librairie de la Société du Recueil Général de Lois et des Arrêts, 1901), 5–10, 216–19.

life was both incomplete and ineffective in the last half of the sixteenth century, many towns began to perceive the slow infiltration of royal designs and royal officials into their administrations, and the sense existed that municipal life as experienced in the past was threatened. Within the towns urban life was changing as well. Municipal governments became more oligarchic in the sixteenth century, and internal animosities destroyed the solidarity of the idealized medieval commune. Even so, town-dwellers continued to hold their liberties and privileges with high regard. This was the situation in 1584–5 when a rejuvenated Catholic League came into existence.[4]

The Catholic League has been described as the final phase of the ideological struggle of the religious wars and a reflection of the collective panic generated by the religious fervour and eschatological angst many early modern French men and women felt in times of crisis.[5] It had its largest impact in the towns. Paris was the crucible of the League where it was established clandestinely in 1584 by an officer of the Bishop of Paris and three zealous clerics. Over the next few years the radical League council, the Sixteen, won adherents throughout the city and penetrated all of the capital's major institutions. Driven by religious passion, Leaguers were united by the desire to exterminate Protestant heresy and preserve a Catholic monarchy in France. During 1587–9, the Sixteen dispatched agents and preachers to key towns throughout France to try and increase the number of urban members. Before the Day of the Barricades approximately three hundred towns of moderate size had joined the League, but after the assassinations at Blois in December 1588, the majority of the major non-Protestant towns in France adopted its cause. The largest and most important Catholic League cities and towns were: Paris (250,000), Rouen (60,000), Marseilles (55,000), Toulouse (400,000), Orléans (37,500), Lyons (32,500), Troyes (25,000), Nantes (25,000), Reims (22,500), and Dijon (14,000).[6]

The period of the Catholic League is often portrayed as one in which the advances made by Renaissance monarchs to bring the towns under tighter Crown control were halted as the towns reasserted their urban independence. According to Fernand Braudel, Bernard Chevalier, Pierre Deyon, Robert Descimon, and J. Russell Major, the League marked a return to municipal autonomy and a medieval

---

[4] Ultra-zealous noble Catholics formed a Catholic League in 1576 to exterminate heresy. The rejuvenated League took shape in 1584 and 1585 and was dominated by the Guise family. Mark Greengrass, *France in the Age of Henri IV, the Struggle for Stability* (1995; London: Longman, 1984), 42–72.
[5] Ibid., 42; Denis Crouzet, *Les guerriers de Dieu: La Violence au temps des troubles de religion, vers 1515–vers 1610*, 2 vols. (Seyssel: Champ Vallon, 1990).
[6] Philip Benedict, 'French Cities from the Sixteenth Century to the Revolution: An Overview', in *Cities and Social Change in Early Modern France*, ed. Philip Benedict (London: Unwin Hyman, 1989), 24–5; Gerald Fox, *Three-Thousand Years of Urban Growth* (New York: Academic Press, 1974), 108–10, 114–20, 122; Greengrass, *France in the Age of Henry IV*, 43–55; Mack P. Holt, *The French Wars of Religion, 1562–1629*, (Cambridge: Cambridge University Press, 1995), 122–3.

past that the monarchy had fought to overcome.[7] These scholars believe that League enthusiasm was coupled with a strong desire to recreate the ideal medieval commune by defending municipal privileges and ending Crown infiltration of municipal administrations. Most of the towns were administered and policed by merchants, lawyers, and middle-ranking officeholders. It is argued that the spirit of republicanism arose from these middle-level burghers who joined the League as a means of recovering lost urban autonomy.[8]

Initially League towns did enjoy a renewed independence, at least from royal supervision, but many soon found themselves obeying the dictates of powerful nobles and magistrates who controlled them through their urban clienteles. A few, Marseilles, Saint-Malo, and Morlaix established independent republics, but most towns simply traded royally appointed masters for League appointed ones. Peter Ascoli and Yves Durand have urged caution in associating the Catholic League with municipal independence. Ascoli believes there were varying degrees of independence, and many townspeople actually found themselves with fewer liberties during the League because some governors and mayors wielded dictatorial powers and even forced towns to support hated garrisons, despite their privileged exemptions from billeting troops.[9] Yves Durand points to the reign of terror that characterized the republics of Marseilles and Saint-Malo where factional fighting included the torture and mutilation of suspect inhabitants as well as the confiscation of their goods. These tactics were practised by many towns during the religious wars, but they seem to have been particularly severe in Marseilles.[10]

One aspect of Catholic League history that is usually associated with its urban focus was the creation of the General Council of Union in Paris. Following the Guise murders, the Sixteen urged the creation of a federated union of councils throughout France in which member towns would send delegates to the main council in Paris. Provincial councils were erected in twenty-two cities and towns including Amiens, Dijon, Rouen, Le Mans, Nantes, Bourges, Riom, Agen, Troyes, Poitiers, Lyons, Mâcon, and Toulouse. These key cities became centres of regional alliances affiliated to greater and lesser degrees with the General Council in Paris.

[7] Braudel, *The Mediterranean 1215–16*; Bernard Chevalier, *Les Bonnes villes de France du XIVe au XVIe siècle* (Paris: Aubier Montaigne, 1982), 111; Robert Descimon, *Qui Etait les seize? Mythes et réalities de la ligue parisienne (1585–1594)* (Paris: Fédération des Sociétés Historiques et Archéologiques de Paris et de L'Ile-de-France, 1983), 62–5, 295–96; Pierre Deyon, *L'Etat face au pouvoir local* (Paris: Editions Locales de France, 1996), 60–2; J. Russell Major, *From Renaissance Monarchy to Absolute Monarchy, French Kings, Nobles, and Estates* (Baltimore: The Johns Hopkins University Press, 1994), 121.
[8] Holt, *The French Wars of Religion*, 134–5; Major, *From Renaissance Monarchy to Absolute Monarchy*, 121; J. H. M. Salmon, *Society in Crisis, France in the Sixteenth Century* (New York: St Martin's Press, 1975), 252; Mark Konnart argues against this idea in 'Civic Rivalry and the Boundaries of Civil Identity in the French Wars of Religion: Châlons-sur-Marne and the Towns of Champagne', *Renaissance and Reformation/Renaissance et Réforme*, 21, 1 (1997), 20.
[9] Peter Ascoli, 'French Provincial Cities and the Catholic League', *Occasional Papers of the American Society for Reformation Research*, 1 (December 1977), 15–37.
[10] Yves Durand, 'Les Républiques urbaines in France à la fin du XVIe siècle', *Société d'histoire et d'Archéologie de l'Arrondissement de Saint-Malo, annales 1990* (1990), 227–30.

The men who sat on these councils usually included nobles, officeholders, municipal magistrates, town notables, and church officials and represented the leading families in the towns. The councils tried to coordinate military operations, and in some cases finances in the provinces, but their history is not well known. In 1953 Henri Drouot published a short survey of the foundation of several provincial councils, but their breakdown of authority has never been seriously examined. Few of the provincial councils endured for long, however, or were able to create any real unity in the provinces. Their fate was sealed in December 1589 when the duke of Mayenne dissolved the General Council of Union in Paris because it had escaped his control and become a tool of the Sixteen.[11]

The case of Amiens offers a typical example of a short-lived council. City leaders founded a provincial alliance of towns in Picardy's capital at the end of 1588. Known as the *Chambre des Etats de Picardie*, its members agreed to cooperate with the General Council of Union in Paris, and they invited all Picard towns to join the urban alliance. The authority of the *Chambre* disintegrated quickly, however, when Picardy's leaders quarrelled over finances. Outfitting noble armies and urban militias and supporting member towns proved too large a task for the *Chambre*. The Catholic League duke of Aumale hoped to use the *Chambre* in Amiens to collect taxes through his clients in member towns, but the leaders in neighbouring Abbeville refused to send monies to Amiens, and jurisdictional jealousies throughout Picardy doomed the *Chambre* to a life of only nine months. During its brief existence, the *Chambre* emptied Amiens's treasury and increased the city's indebtedness which already stood in 1588 at 250,000 *livres*.

The league-affiliated regional alliances never functioned effectively, and their ultimate failure suggests that the Catholic League was never as strong in the provinces as many scholars have believed. Urban particularism and devotion to self-interest inhibited regional cooperation during the League while families, noble clienteles, and city populations exhibited a chameleon-like ability to switch sides on political issues. League ideology, especially, after Henry IV's reconversion to Catholicism, failed to offer enough cohesion to supersede urban self-interest. A key component of the Catholic League's demise, therefore, pivoted on the fact that in failing to create a political framework capable of serving as an alternative to monarchy, the League remained a collection of disunited urban cells.[12]

---

[11] Ascoli, 'French Provincial Cities', 18; Greengrass, *France in the Age of Henri IV*, 69; Mark Greengrass, 'The Sainte Union in the Provinces: The Case of Toulouse', *Sixteenth Century Journal*, 14 (Fall 1983), 469–96; Annette Finley-Croswhite, 'Confederates and Rivals: Picard Urban Alliances during the Catholic League, 1588–1594', *Canadian Journal of History / Annales canadiennes d'histoire*, 31 (December, 1996), 359–76; Robert Harding, *The Anatomy of a Power Elite: The Provincial Governors of Early Modern France* (New Haven, Connecticut: Yale University Press, 1978), 89–97.
[12] This paragraph is taken from Finley-Croswhite, 'Confederates and Rivals', 362.

ECONOMIC AND EPIDEMIOLOGICAL CRISES

The greatest catastrophes occurred in early modern European society when war, crop failure, and epidemic disease struck simultaneously.[13] Such was the case for France in the 1580s and 1590s. The first half of the sixteenth century had been marked throughout western Europe by population growth.[14] This demographic trend came to an end around 1560, and the downturn was particularly pronounced in France because of the calamities produced by the civil wars.[15] Bad weather contributed to the problem as winters became harsher, springs cooler, and summers wetter causing poor harvests and rising prices. In Languedoc, Emmanual Le Roy Ladurie has shown that grain prices between 1585 and 1600 sextupled, wages did not keep up with price rises, textile production fell off, and the standard of living declined.[16] In the 1580s price curves attained their highest levels of the century while taxes rose and exacerbated the depressed economy.[17] 1586–7 was a particularly bad year when nearly all of France suffered a crisis of subsistence and wheat prices rose in the north by nearly seven hundred per cent. This disaster was followed in 1590 by another year of famine in northern France. The south was also hard hit. In Aix corn prices soared in 1591–2 to reach their highest levels for the period 1570–1700.[18]

Between 1589 and 1592 military engagements became most intense in the north of France between the Loire and the lower Seine rivers and particularly around Paris. The fighting moved south and west after 1595 into Britanny and Burgundy and culminated along the border with the Spanish Netherlands in 1598.[19] Urban indebtedness also increased, while towns bolstered their defences, outfitted troops, and provisioned passing armies to avert pillage. Troop movements disrupted production, intensified food shortages, and fuelled high prices while sieges decimated urban populations and left survivors frail. Cutting-off trade routes, the wars stymied communications and hindered efforts to send grain shipments to famine-

---

[13] Myron P. Gutmann, *War and Rural Life in the Early Modern Low Countries* (Princeton: Princeton University Press, 1980), 4; Henri Hauser, *Recherches et documents sur l'historie des prix en France de 1500–1800* (Paris: Les Presses Modernes, 1936); Pierre Goubert, *Beauvais et le Beauvaisis de 1600 à 1730. Contribution à l'histoire sociale de la France du XVIIe siècle* (Paris: SEVPEN, 1960); Andrew B. Appleby, 'Grain Prices and Subsistence Crises in England and France, 1590–1740', *The Journal of Economic History*, 39 (1979), 865–87; Pierre Deyon, *Amiens capitale provinciale étude sur la société urbaine au 17e siècle* (Paris: Mouton, 1967); Emmanuel Le Roy Ladurie, *The Peasants of Languedoc*, tr. John Day (Chicago: University of Illinois Press, 1974).
[14] Le Roy Ladurie, *The Peasants of Languedoc*, 45–9.   [15] Ibid., 53–83.   [16] Ibid., 107.
[17] Martin Wolfe, *The Fiscal System of Renaissance France* (New Haven: Yale University Press, 1972), 137–84.
[18] Peter Clark, 'Introduction' in *The European Crisis of the 1590s, Essays in Comparative History*, ed. Peter Clark (London: George Allen and Unwin, 1985), 8.
[19] Jean Jacquart, *La Crise Rurale en Ile-de-France 1550–1670* (Paris: Armand Colin, 1974), 179–87; Philip Benedict, 'Civil War and Natural Disaster in Northern France', *The European Crisis of the 1590s*, 84–105; Mark Greengrass, 'The Later Wars of Religion in the French Midi', *The European Crisis of the 1590s*, 106–34; Holt, *The French Wars of Religion*, 193–203.

stricken areas. As markets collapsed, commercial activity also declined.[20] Gayle Brunelle contends that in Rouen commercial traffic fell steadily after 1585 and slowed to a virtual stop in 1589 after the foreign merchant community abandoned the city.[21]

Philip Benedict has examined the demographic impact of the wars and shown that during and after the 1591–2 siege of Rouen, mortality rose dramatically and conceptions did not again surpass deaths until well into 1593.[22] In referring to this mortality crisis, Benedict notes, 'Virtually all were casualties not of fighting but of the famine and plague provoked by siege.'[23] The ravaging of the countryside along with bad weather contributed to the fact that the 1590s witnessed the lowest agricultural yields of the century. 'By about 1580–90', Le Roy Ladurie has noted, 'the poor man's bread was black bread, and the poor man's wine was cheap piquette.'[24] Chronic undernourishment meant that in the last two decades of the sixteenth century the French urban and rural poor were likely to have suffered from micronutrient and vitamin deficiencies that left their bodies weak, their immune systems depressed, and in some cases their mental health impaired.[25] Contemporaries reflected on the sad state of the starving peasants who poured into the cities and towns hoping to find food and work. In 1595 one observer in Senlis recorded seeing, 'men and women, young and old, shivering in the streets, skin hanging and stomachs swollen, others stretched out breathing their last sighs, the grass sticking out of their mouths.'[26]

Epidemic diseases accompanied famine and the movement of armies and homeless peasants. Wherever one looks in western Europe in the late sixteenth century there is evidence of widespread bubonic plague epidemics. Human suffering during the period also included the increased prevalence of fevers, influenza, whooping

---

[20] Clark, 'Introduction', 3–15; R. J. Knecht, *The French Wars of Religion, 1559–1598* (1996; London and New York: Longman, 1989), 90–6.

[21] Gayle K. Brunelle, *The New World Merchants of Rouen, 1559–1630*, (Kirksville, Missouri: Sixteenth Century Journal Publishers, 1991), 25–6.

[22] Philip Benedict, *Rouen during the Wars of Religion* (Cambridge: Cambridge University Press, 1981), 221. [23] Ibid., 222. [24] Le Roy Ladurie, *The Peasants of Languedoc*, 106.

[25] There is not space here to discuss in detail the impact of famine and disease on human health. For insight into this issue see: Fernand Braudel, *Civilization and Capitalism, 15th–18th Century 1: The Structures of Everyday Life, The Limits of the Possible*, trans. Sian Reynolds (New York: Harper and Row, 1981), 187–265; Robert Rotberg & Theodore Rabb, *Hunger and History: The Impact of Changing Food Production and Consumption Patterns in Society* (New York: Cambridge University Press, 1983); Peter J. Morgaine, Robert Austin-LaFrance, 'Prenatal Malnutrition and Development of the Brain', *Neuroscience and Biobehavioral Review*, 17 (1993), 91–128; Alfred Sommer, 'Vitamin A: Its effect on Childhood Sight and Life', *Nutrition Reviews*, 52 (February, 1994), 60–6; Henry Ricciuti, 'Nutrition and Mental Development', *Psychological Science*, 2 (1993), 43–46; Lindsay Allen, 'Iron-Deficiency Anemia Increases Risk of Preterm Delivery', *Nutrition Reviews*, 51 (1993), 49–52; Ernesto Pollitt, 'Timing and Vulnerability in Research on Malnutrition and Cognition', *Nutrition Reviews*, 54 (1996), 49–55; Oswald Roels, 'Vitamin A Physiology', *Journal of the American Medical Association*, 214 (1970), 1097–102; Ann Carmichael, 'Infection, Hidden Hunger, and History', *Journal of Interdisciplinary History*, 14 (1983), 249–64.

[26] Quoted in Henry Kamen, *European Society 1500–1700* (1996; London and New York: Routledge, 1984), 37.

cough, smallpox, and tuberculosis and the appearance of the new diseases scurvy, rickets, typhus, and scarlet fever.[27] In France a revived religious consciousness seeking divine aid in difficult times accompanied epidemic outbreaks that were interpreted as manifestations of God's anger. Many believed the outriders of the apocalypse had been let loose. Religious processions in the 1590s were often staged in reaction to rampant disease while confraternities took on new vigour.[28] The religious resurgence of the Catholic League can be explained in part by these epidemics and the apocalyptic fear they engendered.[29]

One of the towns hardest hit by plague during the period was Marseilles in 1580. This epidemic is rarely discussed although it killed nearly as many inhabitants (around 25,000) as the more famous plague epidemic of 1720. Beaune suffered successive outbreaks in 1568, 1569, 1573, 1577, 1581, 1585, 1596, and 1597, while Dijon endured ten years of seasonal plague outbreaks between 1585 and 1595. 1595–96 were particularly bad years in Burgundy. Chalon-sur-Saône actually capitulated to Henry IV in the middle of a terrible epidemic, having lost one-third of its population. Nor was the rest of the country immune. All major cities in the Midi experienced at least one plague outbreak between 1580 and 1598 just as all major towns in Picardy endured plague epidemics in 1596–7.[30] Most plague data, moreover, is related to urban disasters in which the records have been preserved. Epidemiologists have recently proven, however, that heavy losses from plague outbreaks are also incurred in rural areas surrounding large cities.[31] Urban environments actually produce lower morbidity rates relative to population size than rural communities during plague epidemics.[32] This data supports Jean Jacquart's description of rural France during 1589 to 1594 as 'les années terribles'.[33]

Reaction to plague epidemics was similar everywhere and tended to foster the breakdown of communal bonds and loyalties.[34] Those that could fled the plague stifled city, and in the worst cases this included churchmen and women, members of the medical community, and city leaders. Many cities turned out their poor in visual displays of what some felt was moral indignation. Commerce was affected by the suspension of fairs and markets. Governments collapsed and lawlessness

[27] Ann Carmichael, 'Diseases of the Renaissance and Early Modern Europe', in *The Cambridge World History of Human Disease*, ed. Kenneth Kiple (Cambridge: Cambridge University Press, 1993), 279–86. [28] Victor Fouque, *Histoire de Chalon-sur-Sôane* (Marseilles: Laffitte Reprints, 1975), 154.
[29] For example, Henri Bon, *Essai historique sur les epidémies en Bourgogne depuis l'établissement des Bourgondes en Gaule jusqu'à la Révolution* (Dijon: Paul Bertheir, n.d.), 70; Wolfgang Kaiser, *Marseille au Temps des Troubles, Morphologie sociale et luttes de factions 1559–1596*, trans. Florence Chaix (Paris: École de Hautes Études, 1992), 243–57; Clark, 'Introduction', 14–15.
[30] Greengrass, 'The Later Wars of Religion in the French Midi', 112–13.
[31] Carmichael, 'Diseases of the Renaissance and Early Modern Europe', 281: O. J. Benedictow, 'Morbidity in Historical Plague Epidemics', *Population Studies*, 41 (1987), 401–31, esp. 421.
[32] Benedictow, 'Morbidity in Historical Plague Epidemics', 422.
[33] Jacquart, *La Crise Rurale*, 179–87.
[34] Alan Dyer, 'Influence of Bubonic Plague in England, 1500–1667', *Medical History*, 22 (1978), 308–36.

prevailed after town notables fled. In Marseilles in 1580 the municipal deliberations show that the town council rarely met during the plague epidemic.[35] In Nîmes during an epidemic in 1587 all of the city government fled except one man, Balthazar Fournier, who heroically remained in the city and tried to maintain some order while seven-thousand inhabitants died.[36] In 1596 while plague raged in Amiens, the ramparts fell into disrepair, the guard was irregularly kept, and several of the city's magistrates were fined for abandoning the city.[37]

Plague epidemics encouraged social conflict in a number of ways. Alan Dyer believes they eroded the bonds that held early modern society together by destroying instincts of sociability in which friends and families relied on each other for mutual assistance.[38] Not only did the rich abandon their Christian duties, but their actions stimulated resentment on the part of the populace left behind. Quarantine systems were objectionable and aroused bitterness and fear. Anguish, horror, and grief created a nervous environment that ate away at social cohesiveness and drove people to suspect and distrust those around them.[39] Subsistence crises and epidemics greatly increased the social misery of the times and added to the problems that the Catholic League could not solve.

URBAN DISCONTENT AND THE CATHOLIC LEAGUE'S DISINTEGRATION

Enthusiasm for the Catholic League diminished slowly as Henry won battles, decreased markedly after his abjuration in July 1593, and plummeted following his coronation at Chartres in February 1594. The submission of Paris on 22 March 1594 served as a catalyst for other towns on the verge of reconciling, especially those unwilling to accept the Catholic League proposal of a Spanish heir for the French throne. One month after the reduction of Paris, the municipal magistrates in the city recognized that their submission had inspired Troyes, Auxerre, Sens, Chaumont, Bar-sur-Seine, Rouen, Verneuil, Le Havre, Péronne, Montdidier, and Abbeville to accept Henry IV.[40] Northern French municipalities in 1593–4 ceased to be dominated by Catholic League majorities. Municipal magistrates who had originally cooperated with the League for religious reasons and self-preservation now advocated accepting the newly Catholic Henry IV. In many cases, town leaders grew disgruntled as League promises failed to materialize and royalist enticements became irresistible. The king's manoeuvring weakened the League's hold over urban governments as he played upon the towns' desire for peace. By the time of his abjuration, most towns had grown weary of the suffering caused by marauding

[35] Kaiser, *Marseille au temps des troubles*, 246.
[36] Victorin Laval, *Des grandes épidémies qui ont régné à Nîmes depuis le VIe siècle jusqu'à nos jours* (Nîmes: Clavel-Ballivet, 1876), 80.   [37] *Archives Municipales*, Amiens, (hereafter AMA) BB55, fols., 21–4.
[38] Dyer, 'Influence of Bubonic Plague', 319.   [39] Ibid., 319–20.
[40] Alexandre Tuetey (ed.), *Registres des Délibérations du Bureau de la Ville de Paris 11: 1594–1598* (Paris: Imprimerie Nationale, 1902), 9.

troops and siege warfare.[41] Once Henry had abjured, there seemed little reason to support the League. The inhabitants of Riom in Auvergne summarized this sentiment well in a published manifesto issued at the town's capitulation. They acknowledged joining the Catholic League because they had rejected the king's Calvinist faith. Because his abjuration had rendered this reason null and void, they willingly recognized his kingship.[42]

Most large towns left the League after royalists gained control of town governments. Some town councillors voluntarily accepted Henry IV, but in other cases a royalist coup was necessary. Smaller towns were conquered or forced into submission.[43] Henry besieged Laon in June and July of 1594, and the city capitulated once supplies of food and munitions were exhausted. The urban militia then joined the populace in demanding a settlement with the king.[44] The siege of Laon influenced the capitulation of towns in Picardy and the Ile-de-France whose inhabitants feared a repeat performance by the king and his army.[45]

Determining the right moment to switch allegiance was crucial. A miscalculation in staging a royalist coup by Dijon's mayor, Jacques La Verne, resulted in his arrest and decapitation by the city government in 1594.[46] Yet, one year later his replacement as mayor, René Fleutelot, successfully orchestrated the city's capitulation.[47] Urban populations between 1592 and 1594 lost their enthusiasm for the League and fell out with League leaders. Contemporary accounts record the changing tide of emotions. A master carpenter of Reims, Jean Pussot, left a journal describing his slow transformation from an earnest Leaguer to a pragmatic royalist. Angry with League nobles and preachers, he wrote in 1594 that the duke of Guise 'accumulates great treasure and riches from the traffic in merchandise and the pillage of war . . .

---

[41] Asoli, 'French Provincial Cities', 35–6; Greengrass, *France in the Reign of Henri IV*, 58–62; *Archives de la Société des Antiquaires de la Picardie, Musée de Picardie*, CB6, 'Manuscrits originaux ou oeuvres de M. Claude Le Mâtre, siegneur de Hardicourt, citoyen, et échevin d'Amiens concernant la defense de cette ville pendant la Ligue, 1597', and 'Harangue de M. le maieur Augustin de Louvencourt, 12 Août 1595'.
[42] Auguste Poirson, *Histoire du Règne de Henri IV* (Paris: Didier et Cie., Libraires-Editeurs, 1862), vol. 4, 576.
[43] Ascoli, 'French Provincial Cities,' 35–36.
[44] Anthoine Richart, *Mémoires sur la ligue dans le Laonnais* (Paris: Didron-Neveu, 1869), 465–7.
[45] Jean Gaillard, *Les derniers temps de la ligue à Beauvais* (Beauvais: Imprimerie du Moniteur de l'Oise, 1900), 30.
[46] M. de Gouvenais (ed.), *Inventaire-sommaire des Archives Communales antérieures à 1790, ville de Dijon* (Paris: Imprimerie et Librairie Administratives de Paul Dupont, 1867), vol. 1, 111; Henri Drouot, *Un épisode de la ligue à Dijon, l'affaire La Verne (1594)* (Dijon: Revue Bourguignonne and l'Université de Dijon), vol. 20, 1910; Holt, *The French Wars of Religion*, 145–7. La Verne was ambitious and used political allegiances to further his political legitimacy. Involved in factional politics, he opted for the royalist cause only after his dictatorial power began to slip in Dijon as townspeople grew critical of the League.
[47] Henri Drouot, 'Henri IV et les officiers de la milice dijonnaise, 1595', *Equisses 1573–1600, Etudes Bourguignones sur le XVIe siècle* (Dijon: Bernigaud et Privat, 1937), 71.

all at the expense of poor people'.[48] Pussot participated in a secret coup to deliver Reims to Henry IV, and eventually reflected on the Catholic League as 'a time of terrible calamities and miserable wars and intrigues'.[49] Women also voiced anti-League sentiments and influenced events. In Dijon, Madeleine Hennequin, wife of the parlement's first president, grew dissatisfied with League leadership in 1594. She badgered Dijon's mayor, René Fleutelot, to capitulate one year before the city's actual surrender. Hennequin argued that Dijon's inhabitants wanted to accept Henry IV, but a powerful few, tainted by their League affiliation, resisted submission. Her words stirred protest within the city and several prominent League leaders were hanged in effigy.[50]

Renouncing the League was often the result of popular protest. Weavers in Amiens, wine-growers in Dijon, and militia captains in Lyons demanded capitulation from their municipal leaders in 1594 and 1595.[51] On 8 February 1594, Lyons's inhabitants jettisoned their green scarves symbolizing the Catholic League and replaced them with white scarves associated with the royalist cause. At the end of the day a militia captain erected a large portrait of Henry IV in front of the *Hôtel de Ville*, and the next day Alphonse d'Ornano marched into Lyons and accepted the city's capitulation.[52]

Circulars sent from newly won Paris, royalist propaganda, and letters from the king convinced many to submit. By 1594 Henry had already proven himself a clement conqueror. On the battlefield, he was one of only a few early modern commanders who tried to prevent pillage, rape and wanton destruction by his troops.[53] Mark Greengrass emphasizes that the king sought to win 'his subjects' hearts as well as their minds'.[54] Henry revealed his magnanimity and compassion by allowing three-thousand starving peasants to leave Paris during the siege of 1590 and by freeing prisoners after the 1590 battle of Ivry.[55] Clearly he preferred negotiation and settlement over combat and offered generous terms to the van-

---

[48] Edouard Henry (ed.), 'Mémoires ou journalier de Jean Pussot', *Travaux de l'Académie Impériale de Reims*, 25 (1857), 25. Pussot wrote that Guise 'accumule grands trésors et richesse thant de trafiques de marchandise que des pillages de la guerre, d'rançons, tailles, subsides, péages, que pentions de tout aux dépense des pauvres gens'.

[49] Edouard Henry (ed.), 'Journalier ou Mémoires de Jehan Pussot, Notices biographique et bibliographique', *Travaux de l'Académie Impériale de Reims*, 23 (1855), 128. Pussot wrote of 'temps d'effroyables calamites de miserables guerres et intrigues'.

[50] M. de la Cuisine, *Le Parlement de Bourgogne* (Dijon: J-E Rabutot, 1864), 2, 223–5; Annette Finley-Croswhite, 'Engendering the Wars of Religions: Female Agency during the Catholic League in Dijon', *French Historical Studies*, 20 (1997), 127–54.   [51] Ascoli, 'French Provincial Cities', 36.

[52] Jean H. Mariéjol, *Charles-Emmanuel de Savoie duc de Nemours, Govverneur du Lyonnais, Beaujolais, et Forez (1567–1595)* (Paris: Hachette, 1935), 226–8.

[53] T. W. Loveridge, 'Henri IV as Military Commander', unpublished paper, 11. The author thanks Mr. Loveridge for a copy of the paper.   [54] Greengrass, *France in the Age of Henri IV*, 75.

[55] Ibid.; 'Brief traité des misères de la ville de Paris', in *Archives Curieuses de l'Histoire de France depuis Louis XI jusqu'à Louis XVIII*, eds. M. L. Cimber and F. Danjou (Paris: Membres de l'Institut Historique, 1837), 278.

quished. He wrote to the municipal government of Dijon shortly before the town's capitulation in 1595 extolling his legitimacy and benevolence.

We are assured that you will never agree to such a lamentable felony [accepting Spanish tyranny], and that you retain sparks of the vehement zeal with which your predecessors embraced the sweet subjection to this Crown. We write to you, therefore, to invite you to quit suffering and depriving yourselves of the peace and contentment that God is preparing for this realm. He wishes and commands you to conform. In the meantime, we believe you cannot ignore the authority and royal power His divine goodness put in our hands and extends to you by grace and miraculous advancement.[56]

The king promised his subjects mercy and forgiveness and deployed his own agents to the towns to publicize his clemency. In 1594 he sent one of his secretaries, Nicolas du Fren, on a successful mission as an undercover emissary to Abbeville to try and sway the town's mayor, Jean de Maupin, to capitulate.[57] Méric de Vic worked more openly for Henry IV in Languedoc and wrote to him from Albi in 1595 stating, 'We have offered all of the important towns the benevolence and protection of Your Majesty, [and] sent them your letters.'[58]

Much of the responsibility for the towns' submissions fell upon the mayors and other city leaders. In Troyes, for example, the *premier échevin*, Jean Paillot, adopted the royalist cause in 1593–4 and thereafter acted as the king's agent to encourage his fellow magistrates and townspeople to abandon the League.[59] In Beauvais, a lawyer, Léonard Driot, urged city leaders to make peace with the king by emphasizing their desperate situation in the summer of 1594: 'We are surrounded not only by enemy forces but also by rival towns [who have already capitulated], and the inhabitants for the most part do not want to expose themselves to the dangers of a siege.'[60] After negotiations were completed and capitulation treaties were signed, mayors and

---

[56] Printed in Henri Drouot, 'Cinq lettres de Henri IV sur le fin de la Ligue en Bourgogne (1594–1595)', *Mémoires de l'Académie de Dijon* (1924), section 2, 264–5. 'L'asseurance que nous avons que ne consentirés jamais à une si lasche felonnie, et qu'il vous reste encores quelque estincelle de ceste vehemente ardeur [avec] laquelle voz predecesseurs ont embrassé la douce subjection de ceste Couronne, nous faict vous escrire la presente, pour vous convier, sure la fidelité que vous nous devés, que vous ne souffriés plus longuement vous priver du bien, repos et contentement, que vous voyés que Dieu prepare à tout nostre Royaume, à la volonté et commandement duquel il vous convient conformer: et cependant, de l'auctorité et puissance Royalle, que sa Divine bonté nous a mis en main, et donnee sur vous successivement, et confirmee par tant de graces et advancement miraculeux que vous ne pouvés ignorer.' For royalist propaganda see, Greengrass, *France in the Age of Henri IV*, 73–88.
[57] *Archives Municipales*, Abbeville, MS 310, heading 'Jean de Maupin'. Du Fren was a native of Abbeville and presumably used this fact to disguise his reason for visiting the town.
[58] BN, MSS fr. 23195, fol. 179v. 'Nous avons offrer à toutes les villes plus importantes la bienveillance et protection de vostre Majesté, leur envoiant de vos lettres.'
[59] Théophile Boutiot, *Histoire de la ville de Troyes et de la Champagne méridionale* (Troyes: Dufey-Robert, 1873), vol. 4, 234–5.
[60] Quoted in Gaillard, *Les derniers temps de la ligue*, 39. 'Nous sommes environnés non seulement de forces ennemies mais aussi de villes contraires, et vos habitants pour la plupart ne se veulent exposer aux dangers d'un siège.'

magistrates concluded the surrender process by personally unlocking their town gates and permitting the royalists to enter. In Paris, the leading *échevin*, Martin Langlois, opened the Porte Saint-Denis to begin the city's formal surrender.[61] Municipal councillors who had aided in the submission of their towns usually won special favours from the king, which sometimes took the form of letters of *annoblissement*. The most compromised Leaguer leaders suffered imprisonment or exile once their town had capitulated although most of these men were eventually forgiven by Henry IV and allowed to return home.[62]

Town and provincial governors influenced both the timing and the success of submissions. Louis de L'Hôpital, baron of Vitry and governor of Meaux, recognized Henry IV in late-1593 and persuaded the people of Meaux to do likewise; the city gates were opened to the king on 4 January 1594.[63] Abbeville was persuaded to capitulate by the persistence of the duke of Longueville, governor for the king in Picardy. Town governors who aided the surrender were paid handsomely for their services. A former League noble, the sieur of Saisseval, governor of Beauvais, received a share of 2,600 *écus* for assisting in the capitulation of his city.[64] Great regional magnates guaranteed the surrender of key towns in their provinces upon settling with, or rather selling their loyalties to Henry. Claude de la Châtre, governor and lieutenant general of Berry, made peace with Henry in early 1594 and earned for himself 250,000 *écus* by bringing the cities of Bourges and Orléans into the king's camp.[65]

Towns, however, did not need to wait for their provincial governors to be reconciled with Henry. Municipal leaders in Amiens submitted years before the duke of Mayenne and against the wishes of their League governor, the duke of Aumale.[66] Similarly, when Troyes decided to make peace with the king, the bourgeois militia forced their governor and League chief, Claude of Lorraine, the prince of Joinville, to leave the town.[67] Municipal leaders in Lyons never enjoyed good relations with their League governor, the duke of Nemours, and actually imprisoned him in 1593 after his troops ravaged the countryside, raping and killing those allied with the League.[68]

The Catholic League came to an end in the various treaties of capitulation negotiated with towns and nobles between 1593 and 1598. While each capitulation

[61] David Buisseret, *Henry IV* (London: George Allen and Unwin, 1984), 51.
[62] See for example Ponson Bernard, 'Journal de Ponson Bernard', ed. F. Rolle, *Revue du Lyonnais*, 30 (1865), 444.
[63] Michael Wolfe, '"Paris is Worth a Mass" Reconsidered: Henri IV and the Leaguer Capital, March 1594', paper presented at the Society for French Historical Studies conference, Wilmington, Delaware, March 1994, p. 4. I thank Dr. Wolfe for giving me a copy of his paper; Jean-Pierre Babelon, *Henri IV* (Paris: Fayard, 1982), 568. [64] BN MSS fr., 16216, fol. 114r.
[65] Pierre de L'Estoile, *Journal de L'Estoile pour le Règne de Henri IV*, ed. L. Lefevre (Paris: Gallimard, 1948), 393.
[66] Révérend Père Daire, *Histoire de la ville d'Amiens depuis son origine jusqu'à présent* (Paris: Chez-la-veuve de Laguette, 1757), 328–9. [67] Poirson, *Histoire du Règne*, vol. 4, 575.
[68] Mariéjol, *Charles-Emmanuel de Savoie duke of Nemours*, 165–98.

treaty was unique, they did share certain similarities. Articles generally acknowledged that only the Catholic religion would be practised inside the town, although some treaties allowed for the practice of Calvinist worship in a nearby location. Other clauses reaffirmed privileges and franchises, addressed municipal taxes and extended *octrois*, or stated that key institutions such as a parlement or a *bureau des finances* would be maintained. Nobles, churchmen, gentlemen, magistrates, and inhabitants who had joined the League were pardoned while royal officials were confirmed in their positions and promised back wages. Most treaties also addressed specific matters. In Amiens's treaty of capitulation, the king formally forgave the magistrates who had imprisoned the royalist duke of Longueville's mother in the city for several years in the early 1590s. The treaty also guaranteed the Leaguer duke of Aumale a passport in the form of a letter of safe conduct from the king to leave Amiens.

Most treaties were also similar in emphasizing forgiveness and the importance of forgetting the past. The molestation of clergy and secular leaders over wrongs committed during the League was prohibited, and townspeople were instructed to live in peace. Just as Henry had forgiven his rebellious subjects, he encouraged all French men and women to follow his reconciliatory lead and work for greater harmony, the merits of which he promised would return prosperity to France.[69] Mark Greengrass states, 'The rest of the reign would be devoted to attempting to confirm the benefits which could accompany stability.'[70] The part played by the towns in the civil wars had led to the disintegration of France. Henry IV's achievement can be seen in his reconstruction of the urban political framework of his country into a united whole that recognized his legitimate authority and the political authority of the French monarchy. Chapter two begins the discussion of this achievement by examining in-depth the 1594 capitulation of Amiens.

[69] Copies of treaties can be found in DeVic and Vaissete, *Histoire général de Languedoc* (Toulouse: Privat, 1889), col. 1553–64; 'Articles de la capitulation arrêtes à Champmaillot entre les Députés de la Ville et le Maréchal de Biron', and 'Confirmation de ces articles par le roi Henri IV', *Archives Municipales*, Dijon, B119, fols. 6v–9v; AMA, BB53, fols. 166–71rv; B9, fol. 347, 26–7 May 1585; Augustin Thierry, *Recueil des monuments inédits de l'histoire du Tiers-Etat* (Paris: Firmin Didot, 1856), vol. 2, 1059–69. [70] Greengrass, *France in the Age of Henri IV*, 88.

2

Brokering clemency in 1594: the case of Amiens

The 1594 capitulation of Amiens is a good example of how Henry IV used political patronage to defeat the Catholic League. From 25 June to 9 August 1594 factional conflict turned Amiens into an armed camp. The Catholic League came to an end in a political confrontation between factions and families over the exercise of power in the city. Henry IV's clients played a major role in this struggle and succeeded in securing positions of power for themselves as a result. Their success was based on their ability to undermine the League's credibility and refocus political dialogue on the recognition of Henry IV as France's legitimate king. During the weeks leading to the capitulation, the king's clients reiterated his desire for peace and his willingness to treat his foes with leniency. In this way, they convinced influential Leaguers to switch sides. In return, compromised members of the elite were allowed to remain in Amiens and retain familial authority. Brokers arranged exchanges of resources, such as patronage and offices, in exchange for something for themselves.[1] As a reward for brokering his clemency, Henry's clients were given positions of authority in the city.[2]

Henry IV did not begin constructing urban clienteles in Catholic League cities in 1594. Rather at the beginning of his reign in 1589 he had channelled monies to Bourbon family clients to secure local support for his kingship. These clients

[1] Sharon Kettering, *Patrons, Brokers, and Clients in Seventeenth-Century France* (Oxford: Oxford University Press, 1986), 40–67, 98–140; Kettering, 'Brokerage at the Court of Louis XIV', *The Historical Journal*, 36, 1 (1993), 69–87.
[2] David Cressy, 'Kinship and Kin Interaction in Early Modern England', *Past and Present*, 113 (1986), 38–69; Sharon Kettering, 'Friendship and Clientage in Early Modern France', *French History* 6 (1992), 139–58; 'Clientage during the French Wars of Religion', *Sixteenth Century Journal* 20 (1989), 68–87; 'Patronage in Early Modern Europe', *French Historical Studies*, 17 (1992), 839–62; Mark Greengrass, 'Noble Affinities in Early Modern France: The Case of Henri I de Montmorency, Constable of France', *European History Quarterly* 16 (1986), 275–311; Philip Curtin, *Cross-Cultural Trade in World History* (Cambridge: Cambridge University Press, 1984); Yves Durand, *Hommage à Roland Mousnier: clientèles et fidélités en Europe à l'époque Moderne* (Paris: Presses Universitaires de France, 1981). David Warren Sabean, *Power in the Blood: Popular Culture and Village Discourse in Early Modern Germany* (Cambridge: Cambridge University Press, 1984); William Beik, *Urban Protest in Seventeenth-Century France: The Culture of Retribution* (Cambridge and New York: Cambridge University Press, 1997), 199–218; William Beik, 'Urban Factions and the Social Order during the Minority of Louis XIV', *French Historical Studies*, 15 (1987), 36–67; Sidney Tarrow, *Power in Movement. Social Movements, Collective Action and Politics* (Cambridge and New York: Cambridge University Press, 1994), 88–9; Robert Harding, 'Revolution and Reform in the Holy League: Angers, Rennes, Nantes', *Journal of Modern History*, 53 (1981), 379–416.

helped to preserve royal authority in Amiens where the king's legitimacy was not officially recognized after 1589, and they helped restore the king to power in 1594. Henry's clients, and the web of men and women who encircled them, contributed to the defeat of the League by negotiating a shift in power inside Amiens.[3] This process reveals that urban political clientelism was less formally structured than noble clientelism, but it easily mobilized neighbourhood and business ties, kinship networks, friendships, and even social acquaintances to accomplish political change. Royalist clemency brokers activated many roles and kinship ties simultaneously as they mediated the city's capitulation.[4]

Municipal governments during the years of the League were a jumble of divided loyalties. At no time during the six years of the League in Picardy was Amiens's *échevinage* entirely Leaguer or royalist. The municipal elite came from families with long records of public service, and many influential *Amiénois* were linked historically and financially to the municipal government.[5] Wealthy merchant families, for example, regularly made large loans to the city government. A family's politics, even in a period of religious warfare, did not always tarnish its reputation or weaken its influence. Overlapping layers of family, clientage, and business ties characterized this elite, ties that predated and outlasted the Wars of Religion. Elite families lacking strong kinship ties may have opted for neutrality during the wars simply because their power and influence was not as strong as those whose kinfolk had served the city for generations.[6]

Henry III made a list in 1588 of the clientage affiliations of Amiens's elite so that he could influence the results of upcoming municipal elections.[7] The list specified clientage affiliation with either the duke of Aumale or with the king. It reveals that Leaguer and royalist lines, clearly drawn in 1588, changed little thereafter, even with the ascension of Henry IV. The list indicates that between 1588 and 1594 the king had a solid base of royalist supporters within the municipal elite, and their numbers increased as religious enthusiasm for the League waned and the economic situation worsened. Most League leaders in Amiens remained loyal to the League and their patrons until 1594 when the capitulation forced them and the neutrals to become realists about their futures. Henry IV acquired many of the clients of his predecessor and strengthened his ties to them and his other clients after 1594 by rewarding them with stipends, ennoblement, and offices.

[3] *Archives Nationales*, 120, AP12, 'Dons du Roi, 1589–1596'.
[4] Andrejs Plakans, *Kinship in the Past. An Anthropology of European Family Life 1500–1900* (London: Basil Blackwell, 1984), 85–96; Alex Weingrod, 'Patronage and Power', *Patrons and Clients in Mediterranean Societies*, eds. Ernest Gellner and John Waterbury (London: Duckworth & Company, 1977), 41–52; Jeremy Boissevain, *Friends of Friends Networks, Manipulators and Coalitions* (Oxford: Basil Blackwell, 1974); Hans Medick & David Warren Sabean, *Interest and Emotion. Essays on the Study of Family and Kinship* (Cambridge: Cambridge University Press, 1984).
[5] Christopher Friedrichs, 'Urban Politics and Urban Social Structure in the Seventeenth Century', *European History*, 22 (1992), 192.
[6] Kettering, 'Political Parties at Aix-en-Provence in 1589', *European History Quarterly*, 24 (1994), 181–211.   [7] BN, MSS fr. 3411, fols. 133–8.

Bourbon patronage in Picardy had a dual basis. As dukes of Vendôme, the Bourbons possessed land holdings in the province around La Fère. In addition, Louis I of Bourbon, prince of Condé, was governor of Picardy during the 1570s and Henry of Bourbon, duke of Longueville during the 1590s. But Bourbon resources in the province were limited. Longueville's clientele was strong in La Fère and Saint-Quentin, but weak in Amiens, which explains why Saint-Quentin never joined the League: the city's leaders had sworn an oath to Longueville to oppose all persons who supported the League. Longueville could depend on Charles of Humières, governor of Compiègne who was his lieutenant-general in Picardy, and on Antoine of Estrées, a Bourbon family client who was governor of La Fère. Although Humières and Estrées both loaned him money, Longueville did not have access to the wealth that the dukes of Mayenne and Aumale enjoyed through their Spanish connections in Flanders. Lack of money limited his patronage and weakened the Bourbon clientele. As a result, the majority of Picardy's nobility declared for the League including Michel of Estourmel, governor of Péronne, and Jean of Monluc, seigneur of Balagny, governor of Cambrai, the duke of Aumale's lieutenant-general in the province.[8] Strong League patronage among Picardy's nobility explains why the majority of the towns in Picardy declared for the League as well.

THE ROYALIST CLIENTS IN AMIENS: THE LOUVENCOURT NETWORK

Henry IV did not know many *Amiénois* personally and could count on only a few *fidèles* in the city loyal to him until death.[9] Nonetheless, his key clients were influential men, and their circle of kin, allies, and friends widened his base of support. Henry's clientele in Amiens branched out from Nicholas de Lan, one of the highest-ranking royal officials in the city. Amiens had no parlement, and royal justice was dispensed through the *bailliage* and *siège présidial*. Several *élections* existed in Picardy, and Amiens had its own *bureau des finances*.[10] De Lan became a *trésorier général* in 1581, and held the position until his death in 1616, when the

[8] Ibid., fr. 13071, 20 February 1589; Xavier de Bonnault d'Houët, *Compiègne pendant les guerres de religion et la ligue* (Compiègne: Imprimerie du Progrès de l'Oise, 1910), 204–9; Baron A. Calonne, *Histoire de la Ville d'Amiens* (Amiens: Piteux Frères, 1900), vol. 3, 58–9; 72–91. *Archives Municipales*, Saint-Quentin, coll. 151, letters from the duke of Longueville to Saint-Quentin; F6, 23 November 1589, 12 February 1591.

[9] Roland Mousnier, *Les institutions de la France sous la monarchie absolue, 1598–1789* (Paris: Presses Universitaires de France, 1974), vol. 1, 83–93. Mousnier used the word *fidèle* to characterize the strong bonds of extreme loyalty that bound patrons and clients. Sharon Kettering, Mack Holt, and others, however, have criticized the definition as too narrow. Not all clients were *fidèles*. Sharon Kettering, 'Clientage during the French Wars of Religion', *Sixteenth Century Journal*, 20 (1989), 221–39; Mack P. Holt, 'Patterns of Clientèles and Economic Opportunity at Court during the Wars of Religion: The Household of François, duke of Anjou', *French Historical Studies*, 18 (1984), 306.

[10] David Potter, *War and Government in the French Provinces, 1470–1560* (London and New York: Cambridge University Press, 1993), 15–17; E. Lambert, 'Les Limites de la Picardie', *Société archéologique, historique, et scientifique de Noyon: Comptes rendus et mémoires* 34 (1972), 53–65.

office passed to François de Louvencourt, his wife's nephew.[11] Few details about De Lan have survived. He was imprisoned by one of the first acts of the *Chambre des Etats de Picardie*, the Catholic League's provincial council, on 3 January 1589. This was immediately after League leaders had created a *Chambre des finances* and named the duke of Aumale's client, Antoine de Berny, *receveur général*. De Berny was charged with collecting revenue from the League *élections* in Picardy. The *Chambre* replaced De Lan after identifying him as a loyal supporter of Henry III.[12] It is unclear how long De Lan was in prison, but he must have remained in Amiens because he was present at the baptism of twin sons in 1591, and at the baptism of another son in 1593.[13] In the summer of 1594, De Lan participated in the royalist overthrow of the League in Amiens.[14] As a reward he was ennobled by Henry IV, named a *conseiller du roi*, and given at least 1,600 *écus* from the king.[15]

De Lan was tied by family and political opinion to the wealthy cloth merchant, Augustin de Louvencourt. The two men were brothers-in-law; De Lan had married Louvencourt's sister, Jeanne. Augustin de Louvencourt was Henry IV's most trusted client in Amiens and from him radiated a circle of royalists. De Lan, as a royal official, enjoyed a higher social rank than Louvencourt, but this wealthy merchant was at the centre of the king's political clientele in Amiens. Louvencourt's business ties extended throughout the city, and his political influence was immense. He served in the *échevinage* fourteen times between 1586 and 1626, either as *prévôt*, *échevin*, *premier échevin*, or mayor. He was descended from a secondary branch of a noble family prominent in Amiens since the 1470s with a long history of service to the *Hôtel de Ville*. League leaders regarded Augustin de Louvencourt as a royalist and ordered him imprisoned briefly in March of 1594 for participation in an anti-League conspiracy. Five months later he led royalist street fighting to overturn the League. Henry IV ennobled him in 1594 as a reward for his loyal service.[16]

[11] BN, MSS fr. Pièces Originales, 1633; MSS fr. 28117; Collection de Picardie, 74, fols. 26–105. De Lan was married to Jeanne de Louvencourt whose brother, Jehan de Louvencourt, was the father of François de Louvencourt. De Lan was ousted from his position as *trésorier général* during the Catholic League but was reinstated in 1594.

[12] Calonne, *Histoire d'Amiens*, vol. 2, 85.

[13] *Archives of the Church of Jesus Christ of the Latter Day Saints*, (hereafter ACJCLDS), 'Registres des Paroisses,' 1552622, Amiens, St Firmin à la Porte, 1590–5, entry dated 25 October 1591 and 7 October 1593.

[14] *Archives Municipales*, Amiens, (hereafter AMA), BB53, fol. 147 v. De Lan was expelled by the duke of Mayenne on 28 June 1594 as a royalist.

[15] F. Pouy, *La Chambre du Conseil des Etats de Picardie pendant la ligue* (Amiens: Delatte, 1882), 43; AN 120 AP12 'Dons du Roi, 1589–1596', 138r, 167; AMA, FF647, 21 May 1616; FF665, 25 January 1618. Robert Harding, 'Corruption and the Moral Boundaries of Patronage in the Renaissance', *Patronage in the Renaissance*, eds. Guy Lythe and Stephen Orgel (Princeton, New Jersey: Princeton University Press, 1981), 62.

[16] AMA, BB53, fols. 123–4, 134 v; Janvier, *Livre d'or de la municipalité d'Amiens* (Paris: Picard, 1893), 227, 232–4, 239, 240, 242, 245–6; Louis L'Orgnier, *Un homme à la mode, François de Louvencourt, siegneur de Vauchelles et de Bourseville, poète, romancier et historien, Président-Trésorier de France en Picardie, Premier Échevin d'Amiens: La vie amiénoise à l'époque de la Ligue d'Henri IV et de Louis XIII*

Brokering clemency in 1594: the case of Amiens

Kinship played a vital role in motivating political behaviour. Numerous Louvencourt family members belonged to the Bourbon clientele in Amiens. Augustin's
nephew, François de Louvencourt, seigneur of Vauchelles was an important
royalist in Amiens and Paris.[17] Augustin's cousin, Florent de Louvencourt, was also
a respected city leader who served as *échevin* eleven times between 1592 and 1613
and *premier échevin* in 1607.[18] Florent's cousin, Charles de Louvencourt, married
his daughter to Jean d'Aguesseau, seigneur of Ignaucourt, *receveur générale des
finances* in Picardy. Jean's older brother, François d'Aguesseau, served as *échevin* in
1593. François de Louvencourt acted as godfather to Jean d'Aguesseau's only
daughter, Marie. Henry IV ennobled both D'Aguesseau brothers for their loyalty.[19]
In addition, Charles de Louvencourt had married Catherine du Bos, whose two
brothers, Philippe and Nicholas, were royalist *trésoriers généraux* in Picardy. Philippe died in 1594, but Nicholas took over his brother's office in the *bureau des
finances* that year, and was ennobled by Henry IV.[20]

Augustin de Louvencourt's circle of kin and allies formed the backbone of the
king's clientele in Amiens. Robert Correur, a rich cloth merchant and one of Henry
IV's most faithful clients in the city, was linked to Louvencourt through business
and family ties. A former client of the prince of Condé, Correur lost his position as
garde de l'artillerie in Amiens in 1588, and spent most of the next six years either in
prison or under house-arrest because of his royalist politics.[21] He was a well-known
Protestant who refused to lend the city 400 *écus* in May of 1589. Correur's name
appears on every list of taxes imposed on suspected royalists throughout the period
of the League. He organized a failed coup in 1590 to deliver the city to the royalists,
earning himself a reputation as a dangerous man. Under constant surveillance by
League authorities, he paid a bond of 2,000 *écus* to the municipal government in the
winter of 1594, so that he could attend the funeral of his son. He participated in
another failed royalist conspiracy in March 1594, and fought side-by-side with
Louvencourt in the uprising that delivered the city to the king later that year.
Henry IV ennobled Correur in 1594, and made him a *chevalier de la companie du roi*
as well as a *captaine de la guet* in Amiens.[22]

(Amiens: Société des Antiquaires de Picardie, 1942), 44, 25–9; BN, MSS fr. Pièces Originales 1762,
fol. 53; MSS fr. Cabinet d'Hozier, 218; MSS fr. Dossiers bleus 408.
[17] L'Orgnier, *Un homme à la mode*; BN, MSS fr. Cabinet d'Hozier, 218.
[18] BN, MSS fr. Pièces Originales, 56. Janvier, *Livre d'or*, 232–4, 238–43; L'Orgnier, *Un homme à la
mode*, 16. Florent de Louvencourt was Augustin's cousin in the sixth degree. Augustin's father,
Pierre, had a cousin named Nicolas, and Florent was Nicolas's son.
[19] Alcius Ledieu, 'Livres de Raison de Deux Seigneurs Picards (1559–1692)', *Le cabinet historique de
L'Artois et de La Picardie*, 7 (1892), 321–8 and 8 (1893), 11–20, 82–6; L'Orgnier, *Un homme à la mode*,
12–13, 15–16.   [20] L'Orgnier, *Un homme à la mode*, 12–13; Pouy, *La Chambre des Etats*, 43.
[21] AMA EE156, entry dated 3 February 1588.
[22] BN, MSS fr. Pièces Originales 886; *Archives Départementales*, Somme (hereafter cited as ADS),
1B1720, entry dated 8 February 1588; E30644, fol. 192; AMA BB50, fol. 23–24rv, 29 v; BB53, fol.
123, 126; CC807; FF545, 26 September 1598; *Archives Municipales*, Abbeville, (hereafter AMAV),
MSS 647 bis, genealogy of Robert Correur; Roger Rodière, *Epitaphier de Picardie* (Paris: Picard,
1925), 200.

Marriages were used to cement clientele networks in early modern society, and the importance of marriage alliances in expanding Louvencourt's and Correur's networks of clients underscores Sharon Kettering's belief that historians have overlooked the importance of matrilineal kinship ties in securing patronage and building clienteles.[23] For example, the affluent Pingré family was allied by marriage to Augustin de Louvencourt and Robert Correur. The Pingré included the merchant Guillaume and his brothers Antoine and Pierre. Antoine Pingré had married Robert Correur's daughter, and Guillaume Pingré married Augustin de Louvencourt's sister. Guillaume married his daughter, Isabeau, to a distant cousin of Augustin, Antoine de Louvencourt.[24] Multi-generational marriage ties also united the Louvencourt and Pingré clans. When Augustin's father, Pierre, died in 1557, his mother, Isabeau Lamy, remarried Antoine Pingré, whose son participated in the royalist uprising of 1594. This meant that Guillaume, Antoine, and Pierre Pingré and Augustin de Louvencourt were step-brothers. The Pingré brothers also had a great uncle, Henry Pingré, who held the office of *trésorier général en Picardie*. He was ennobled by Henry IV in 1594 for his fidelity during Amiens's capitulation.[25]

The Louvencourt and their kin were linked to other royalists in the city through ties of marriage, business, neighbourhood, and godparentage. For example, Augustin married his daughter, Françoise, to Antoine Trudaine, seigneur of Oissy, a royalist *échevin* in 1589 and 1590, who became a *trésorier général*.[26] Augustin de Louvencourt's neighbour, Vincent Voiture, was a substantial merchant who imported wine from the south of France in partnership with the Pingré family. He joined the royalist cause in Amiens with his Louvencourt neighbour and ally. Voiture's son, Vincent, was also the godson of Louvencourt's brother-in-law, Nicholas de Lan.[27]

Many of Augustin de Louvencourt's family ties linked him to men who had initially joined the Catholic League, but had abandoned it before 1594. We may speculate that Augustin's influence swayed many of his relatives and business associates as their dissatisfaction with the League grew. One such tie was with Antoine Gougier, an *échevin* loyal to the League who later switched his allegiance and was ennobled for his loyalty in 1594. Gougier's daughter, Hélène, married Antoine de Louvencourt, who then married Isabeau Pingré upon Hélène's death.[28]

[23] Kettering, 'Patronage and Kinship in Early Modern France', *French Historical Studies*, 16 (1989), 420–9.

[24] Augustin's father, Pierre de Louvencourt, had a cousin named Charles de Louvencourt, *écuyer*, seigneur de Brétencourt, who was *prévot royal* in Amiens in 1566. Charles's son, Antoine de Louvencourt married Augustin's sister, Marie. L'Orgnier, *Un homme à la mode*, 5, 8–10.

[25] L'Orgnier, *Un homme à la mode*, 8–10; AMAV MSS 647 bis. genealogy of the Pingré family; AMA FF566 8 January 1604; AMA, FF11372, fols. 178–82; BN, MSS fr. Collection de Picardie 133, fols. 291, 301; Pouy, *La chambre des Etats*, 43; BN, MSS fr. Pièces Originales, fol. 2284; MSS fr. Dossiers bleus; fol. 525; MSS fr. Carnès d'Hozier, fol. 497. Henry Pingré had not entered the War of the Catholic League as a client of Henry IV. He belonged to the League from 1589 to 1591 and thereafter changed allegiances.   [26] L'Orgnier, *Un homme à la mode*, 28.

[27] A. Dubois, *Recherches sur la maison ou Naquit à Amiens Vincent Voiture* (Amiens: Lemer, 1866), 3–4.

[28] ADS, 1B72, fols. 69rv.

Gougier's royalist family ties may have been crucial in his decision to abandon the League by 1593. He had married into the Aux Cousteaux family, unrelated to the Louvencourts but supporters of the royalist cause from 1588 to 1594. Augustin de Louvencourt's sister, Adrienne, moreover, had married Antoine Scourion, seigneur of Bégueudet, a *procureur* in the *bailliage*. Scourion supported the League enthusiastically in 1588–9, but eventually allied himself with the king and had his nobility reconfirmed in 1594. He died shortly before the capitulation, but Henry IV granted his widow a yearly pension of 300 *livres* in recognition of his service in 1594. The incorporation of disgruntled Leaguers into Louvencourt's clientele reveals how royalist factions were able to expand before 1594.[29]

Augustin de Louvencourt was linked to other men who were not his kin, but who helped him overthrow the League in 1594. These ties were more tenuous because these men had supported the League for almost six years, and probably switched sides in 1594 for reasons of self-interest. For example, Henry IV ennobled the wealthy cloth merchant Louis de Villers in 1594. Both Louvencourt and Villers belonged to the *Confrérie du Puy* associated with the city's Notre Dame cathedral. The Villers did business with Vincent Voiture, and were allied by marriage to the Sachy merchant family of Amiens. The Sachy also belonged to the *Confrérie du Puy*, and had marriage ties with the Postel and Du Fresne merchant families. The Villers, Sachy, Du Fresne, and Postel families all supported the Catholic League, but they switched sides in 1594. Postel did so in time to earn himself ennoblement from Henry IV and a stipend of 300 *livres*.[30] (Louvencourt's network of allies is outlined concisely in figure 1 and more extensively in figure 2.)

THE CATHOLIC LEAGUE CLIENTS IN AMIENS: THE LE ROY NETWORK

The clientele of Charles of Lorraine, duke of Aumale, helped the League to control the city government of Amiens from 1588 to 1594. The duke's clientele centered around Vincent Le Roy, a *lieutenant général* in the *siège présidial*. Contemporary documents describe him as an ally of Aumale and the League chief, the duke of Mayenne. One of the most powerful Leaguers in the city, Le Roy met frequently with Aumale as a member of his private council. His brother, Jean Le Roy, a canon at the Cathedral of Notre Dame and a member of the League, was a client of the cathedral's bishop, Geoffrey de la Martonnie, who was a zealous Leaguer. Vincent Le Roy switched his political allegiance to the king at the eleventh hour, and was

[29] ADS, E30644, fol. 169; L'Orgnier, *Un homme à la mode*, 23–4; BN, MSS fr. 3411, fol. 133.
[30] AN, AP120 12, fol. 131 v; AMAV MSS 647 bis, genealogy of the Sachy family; AMA, FF1372, fols. 5–8; F. Pouy, *La chambre des Etats*, 44; Du Bois, *Recherches sur Vincent Voiture*, 3–4; Robert Richard, 'Art et Poèsie: Les Puys d'Amiens et d'Abbeville', *Plaisir de France*, no. 428 (1975), 28–33; Robert Guerlin, *Notes sur les tableaux offerts à la Confrérie de Notre-Dame du Puy à Amiens*, (Paris: E. Plon, 1898), 6–10.

Figure 1   Augustin de Louvencourt's network of allies

ennobled by Henry IV as a reward. He became a *conseiller d'Etat* and received a gift of 6,000 *écus* at the capitulation.[31]

Le Roy was connected to other Leaguers in the city. The *lieutenant particulier* of the *siège présidial*, for example, Adrien Picquet, was his paternal cousin as well as a representative of the presidial court in the League council, the *Chambre des Etats de Picardie*. Le Roy's clientele, like Louvencourt's, grew in size through marriage alliances.[32] Le Roy's sister, for example, Marie Le Roy, had married Nicolas Nibat, seigneur de Belleviller, a former mayor who was Aumale's client. Nibat sat in the *Chambre des Etats de Picardie* as a representative of the bourgeoisie. Henry III's advisors had described him as 'very pernicious' in their 1588 political evaluation of the city's elites. In addition, the *procureur* and Leaguer, Antoine Scourion, was Le Roy's uncle. Neither Nibat, Picquet, Scourion or Le Roy were related by blood or marriage to the lawyer, Godefroy de Baillon, but the five are lumped together in the documents as powerful Leaguers.[33]

Claude Pécoul, a lawyer in the presidial court, was another client of Aumale. Pécoul received at least 6,000 *livres* from Aumale during the League years. He was *receveur* for Aumale's barony of Boves, sat on his council, and was known as an agent of the Spanish. Pécoul held the office of *échevin* in 1589, 1592, and 1593 and went on several missions in Picardy for the Catholic League. Claude's brothers, André, a *procureur*, and Adrien, a canon of the cathedral, were other influential adherents of the League.[34]

Claude Pécoul had married the daughter of Guillaume de Lattre, a prominent merchant and League chief who had sworn an oath of loyalty to the Spanish king, Philip II. De Lattre's two merchant brothers, Robert and Jehan, supported the League, as did other family members who held offices in the cathedral. Kinship ties bound Claude Pécoul to Pierre de Famechon, a lawyer and *échevin* whose mother was a Pécoul; the two families had many business dealings. Famechon eventually joined the royalists while Pécoul and Guillaume de Lattre remained loyal to the League. Henry IV ennobled Famechon in 1594, but banished Pécoul and de Lattre from the city.[35]

---

[31] Pouy, *La Chambre des Etats*, 43–4; AMA, FF640, 21 March 1616; FF665, 25 January 1618; BN, MSS fr. 32444, fol. 201; M. Haudicquer de Blancourt, *Nobiliaire de Picardie* (Paris, 1695), 470.

[32] Kettering, 'Patronage and Kinship', 421–2.

[33] BN, MSS fr., 3411, fol. 133; Pouy, *Les chambre des Etats*, 3; AMA, FF498, 12 January 1593; FF492, 20 January 1593; Stuart Carroll, 'The Guise Affinity and Popular Protest During the Wars of Religion', *French History* 9 (1995), 147–8.

[34] ADS, E30576, 19 April 1589; AMA, FF503, 27 February 1595; Janvier, *Livre d'or*, 403–4; Annette Finley-Croswhite, 'Urban Identity and Transitional Politics: The Transformation of Political Authority Inside Amiens Before and After the City's 1594 Capitulation to Henry IV', *Proceedings of the Annual Meeting of the Western Society for French History*, 20 (1993), 55.

[35] For Famechon see, BN, MSS fr. Pièces Originales 1098; MSS fr. Dossiers bleus 260; MSS fr. Cabinet d'Hozier 134; MSS fr. Nov. Acq. 22227, fol. 541–3rv; ADS, E28825, 26 April 1607; 1B15, fols. 46–7rv; AMA, FF503, 27 February 1595; FF660, 13 December 1617; *Société des Antiquaires de Picardie*, Archives, CB129, piece dated 24 January 1599. For De Lattre see, Edmond Soyez, 'Adrien

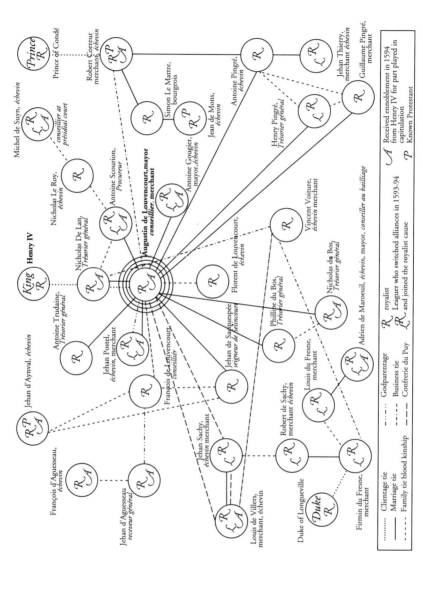

Figure 2 Clientage and family connections of prominent Amiénois belonging to the royalist cause, 1588–1594

Prince of Condé

Michel de Suyn, *échevin*

Robert Corteur merchant, *échevin*

Simon Le Mattre, *bourgeois*

Jean de Mons, *échevin*

Antoine Pingré, *échevin*

Jehan Thierry, merchant *échevin*

Guillaume Pingré, merchant

Henry Pingré, *Trésorier général*

Nicholas Le Roy, *échevin*

conseiller at présidial court

Antoine Scourion, *Procureur*

Augustin de Louvencourt, mayor *conseiller, merchant*

Antoine Gougier, mayor, *échevin*

Nicholas De Lan, *Trésorier général*

King Henry IV

Antoine Trudaine, *Trésorier général*

Jehan d'Aynval, *échevin*

Florent de Louvencourt, *échevin*

Vincent Voiture, *échevin* merchant

Nicholas du Bos, *Trésorier général*

Jehan Postel, *échevin*, merchant

François d'Aguesseau, *échevin*

Phillibe du Bos, *Trésorier général*

François de Louvencourt, *conseiller*

Jehan de Sacquespée *seigneur de Selincourt*

Adrien de Maroeuil, *échevin, mayor, conseiller au bailliage*

royalist
Leaguer who switched alliances in 1593–94
and joined the royalist cause

Jehan Sachy, *échevin* merchant

Louis du Fresne, merchant

Jehan d'Aguesseau, *receveur général*

Robert de Sachy, merchant *échevin*

Louis de Villers, merchant, *échevin*

Duke of Longueville

Firmin du Fresne, merchant

Duke

Received ennoblement in 1594 from Henry IV for part played in capitulation
Known Protestant

...... Clientage tie
——— Marriage tie
-·-·- Family tie blood kinship

······ Godparentage
- - - - Business tie
-- -- Confrerie du Puy

32

Claude Pécoul had a cousin, Michel Randon, an enthusiastic Leaguer and successful merchant. Randon had frequently served as an *échevin* in the 1580s as had his grandfather and fellow Leaguer, Nicholas Randon. Etienne Boullet, another *échevin* and Leaguer, was connected to the Randons through marriage, and Michel Randon was allied to the zealous League lawyer and former *Amiénois* mayor, François Gauguier, through marriage to his daughter. Gauguier's brother, Jehan, was a canon of the cathedral and a Leaguer. François Gauguier worked for the Spanish and was expelled from the city by Henry IV in 1594.[36] Godparentage tied François Gauguier to another League *échevin*, François Bigant. Gauguier and Vincent Le Roy became godfathers to Bigant's daughter, Anne, in 1575. In addition, neighbourhood ties united the Leaguers. François Bigant, for example, lived near the Leaguers Guillaume de Lattre, Philippe du Béguin, and Jehan Potel in the parish of St Rémy.[37] (A brief version of Vincent Le Roy's network of allies is shown in figure 3.)

Aumale had three other important clients in Amiens, Jehan de Cordelois, François de Castelet, and Antoine de Berny. Cordelois abandoned the League, receiving ennoblement from Henry IV in 1594 as a reward, but his nephew, Jehan Le Pot, and his uncle, Jehan Sagnier, remained ardent Leaguers. Sagnier served the Spanish as an agent of Philip II. Castelet held the offices of mayor and *échevin* of Amiens during the League and was expelled from the city by Henry IV in 1594. Aumale named his client, Antoine de Berny, mayor in 1593. De Berny took an oath of loyalty to Henry IV under duress in August of 1594 but fled the city with Aumale thereafter. Henry III's 1588 report on Amiens had described Antoine de Berny as 'the most ambitious man in the city'.[38] (A more complex drawing of Catholic League clientage is shown in figure 4.)

Because of alliances among the elite that predated the Catholic League, most *Amiénois* had blood or fictive kinship ties in the opposite camp. Firmin du Fresne, for example, had connections through his wife to the royalist duke of Longueville. Even so, he supplied Aumale with cannon, guns, and powder in 1589.[39] Royalists, Leaguers, and neutrals shared family connections, and clientage ties were extremely unstable toward the end of the religious wars as League patronage failed. Kinship and clientage ties overlapped in complex webs of interdependencies. Thus while

de la Morlière, Historien d'Amiens', *Mémoires de la société des antiquaires de Picardie*, 32 (1894), 453. Soyez mentions the De Lattre family. Claude Pécoul was married to Claire de Lattre.
[36] ADS, 1B12, fol. 130; 1B2078, 16 November 1597; AMA, FF702, 13 December 1622; FF578, 30 December 1606; FF1249, fol. 33rv. Michel Randon was married to Françoise Gauguier.
[37] BN, MSS fr. 3411, fol. 137v. AMA, FF497, 17 February 1593; ACJCLDS 'Registres des Paroisses', Amiens, St Remy 1348781, 25 August 1575.
[38] Finley-Croswhite, 'Urban Identity', 55; Augustin Thierry, *Recueil des monuments inédits de l'histoire du Tiers-Etat* (Paris: Firmin Didot, 1856), vol. 2, 1043–5; BN, MSS fr. 3411, fols. 133–8; AMA, FF484, 25 June 1591; FF1249, fol. 30; FF576, 576, 21 July 1606.
[39] AMA, FF629, 7 November 1608. Firmin du Fresne's wife is mentioned as a lady-in-waiting to the duke of Longueville's mother, Marie de Bourbon, who was held hostage and imprisoned during much of the Catholic League period in Amiens.

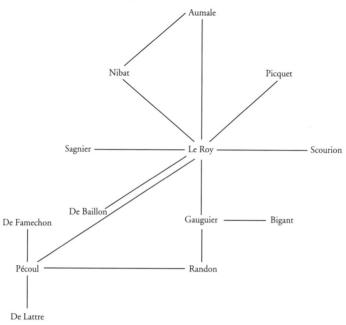

Figure 3   Vincent Le Roy's network of allies

Michel and Nicolas Randon served the League, they were also allied by marriage to the Louvencourt family. Nicolas's daughter, Marie Randon, was married to Augustin de Louvencourt's cousin, Florent. The interconnections of these royalist and League families explain why the Louvencourts helped to clear the Randon name after the fall of the League. The Louvencourts were linked by marriage to the Leaguer François Castelet.[40] They were also linked by marriage to the Leaguer Le Picard family. François de Louvencourt's father, Jehan, died in 1569, and his mother, Jeanne de Sacquespée, remarried Jacques Le Picard. Le Picard served as *lieutenant-civil et criminel* at the presidial court in Amiens from 1587 to 1601. He also represented that court in the *Chambre des Etats de Picardie* in 1589. Thus, while François de Louvencourt was allied with the royalists, his step-father was an important League leader.[41] Le Picard, moreover, had a daughter married to Jehan d'Aynval, a lawyer and ardent royalist whom Henry IV ennobled at the capitulation.[42] Not surprisingly, Le Picard ended the War of the Catholic League on the

---

[40] A. Janvier records that François Castelet was married to a Jeanne de Louvencourt. I have been unable to ascertain what branch of the Louvencourt family this 'Jeanne' belonged to. Janvier, *Livre d'or*, 399.

[41] Ledieu, 'Livres de Raison', 8, 11–20.

[42] BN, MSS fr. Cabinet d'Hosiers, fol. 3; MS fr. Dossiers bleus, fol. 48. Jehan d'Aynval was married to Marie Le Picard.

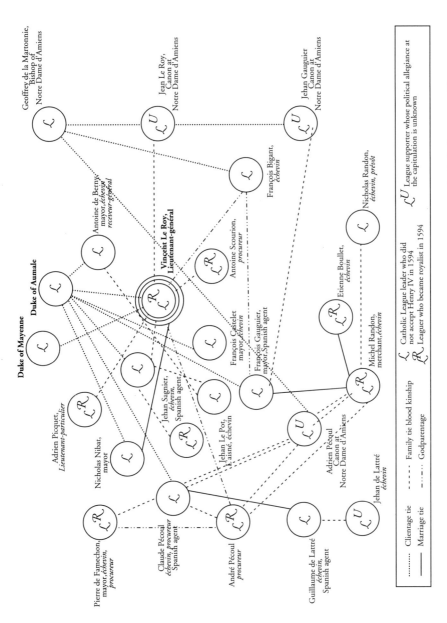

Figure 4   Clientage and family connections of prominent *Amiénois* belonging to the Catholic League, 1588–1594

Geoffrey de la Martonnie, Bishop of Notre Dame d'Amiens

Jean Le Roy, Canon at Notre Dame d'Amiens

Jehan Gauguier Canon at Notre Dame d'Amiens

Antoine de Berny, mayor, *échevin* *receveur-général*

François Bigant, *échevin*

Duke of Aumale

Vincent Le Roy, Lieutenant-général

Antoine Scourion, *procureur*

Duke of Mayenne

Nicholas Randon, *échevin, prévôt*

François Castelet mayor, *échevin*

François Gauguier, mayor, Spanish agent

Etienne Boullet, *échevin*

Adrien Picquet, *Lieutenant-particulier*

Jehan Sagnier, *échevin*, Spanish agent

Michel Randon, merchant, *échevin*

Nicholas Nibat, mayor

Jehan Le Pot, l'aisné, *échevin*

Adrien Pécoul Canon at Notre Dame d'Amiens

Pierre de Famechon, mayor, *échevin*, *procureur*

Claude Pécoul *échevin, procureur* Spanish agent

André Pécoul *procureur*

Jehan de Lattré *échevin*

Guillaume de Lattré *échevin*, Spanish agent

.... Clientage tie   ------ Family tie blood kinship $\mathcal{L}$ Catholic League leader who did not accept Henry IV in 1594 $\mathcal{L}^U$ League supporter whose political allegiance at the capitulation is unknown

——— Marriage tie   –·–·– Godparentage $\mathcal{R}\atop\mathcal{L}$ Leaguer who became royalist in 1594

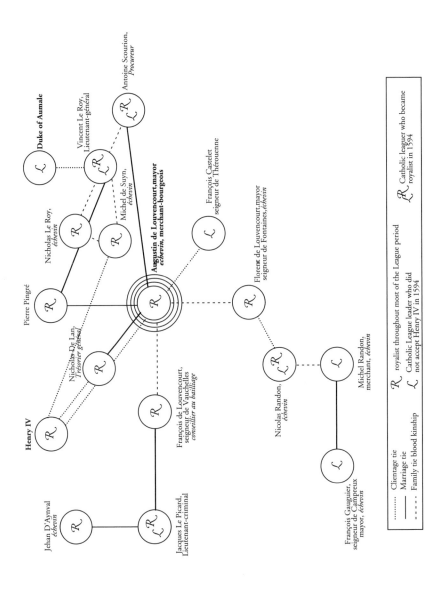

Figure 5 Familial connections of royalist and Catholic League leaders in Amiens, 1588–1594, using the example of Augustin de Louvencourt

The figure contains the following labels:

Duke of Aumale

Antoine Scourion, *Procureur*

Vincent Le Roy, Lieutenant-général

$\mathcal{L}$

Nicholas Le Roy, *échevin*

Michel de Suyn, *échevin*

Augustin de Louvencourt, mayor *échevin, merchant-bourgeois*

Pierre Pingré

François Castelet seigneur de Thérouenne

Florent de Louvencourt, mayor seigneur de Fontaines, *échevin*

Nicholas De Lan, *Trésorier général*

Henry IV

François de Louvencourt, seigneur de Vauchelles *conseiller au bailliage*

Nicolas Randon, *échevin*

Michel Randon, merchant, *échevin*

Jehan D'Aynval *échevin*

Jacques Le Picard, Lieutenant-criminal

François Gauguier, seigneur de Campreux mayor, *échevin*

.... Clientage tie
——— Marriage tie
- - - - - Family tie blood kinship

$\mathcal{R}$ royalist throughout most of the League period
$\mathcal{L}$ Catholic League leader who did not accept Henry IV in 1594

$\mathcal{R}$ Catholic leaguer who became royalist in 1594

36

royalist side. Although the Le Roy family traditionally served Guise patrons, Vincent Le Roy was related to Antoine Scourion, who was a kinsman of Henry's client, Augustin de Louvencourt. Le Roy also possessed kinship ties with the royalist Suyn and Pingré families. Vincent's son Nicolas joined the Catholic League briefly in 1588, but thereafter served the king's cause, meaning Vincent's own nuclear family was split, perhaps in an astute political attempt to place family members in both political camps. (The political and familial ties linking important royalist and League families are outlined in figure 5.)

Urban clientage ties in the sixteenth century were fragile. Families implemented strategies meant to preserve family power and minimize political misconduct, and in the process often weakened or severed clientage ties. Urban conflict caused men to abandon their patrons and search for new ones in an effort to keep their positions of authority. As the League fell apart, the royalists of Amiens offered their assistance to their Leaguer kin who had begun to talk of reconciling with the king. Their political transformation played into Henry IV's hands since he had already sent messages promising clemency. Because few *Amiénois* had direct access to the king, his clients brokered the peace of 1594. They used their personal ties to convince important Leaguers to accept the king.

In the spring and summer of 1594, a rift developed between Amiens's inhabitants and the Catholic League chiefs. When the League began to lose power, especially after Henry IV's abjuration, its sources of wealth and patronage dried up. Mayenne, the League chief, soon had little largesse to distribute, making it difficult for him to retain control of the *échevinage*. To keep control of the city, Mayenne and Aumale ran roughshod over the privileges and franchises of the *Amiénois*, alienating the general population and upsetting the League supporters.[43] The October 1593 mayoral election illustrates the turning tide of allegiances within Amiens. Incumbent magistrates nominated three candidates to fill the mayor's office, François Gauguier, François Castelet, and Antoine de Berny, all clients of Aumale. But when the city's bourgeois arrived at the town hall to cast their ballots, the populace learned of these three candidates, and they demanded the re-election of the city's incumbent mayor, Antoine Gougier, a former Leaguer turned royalist. The diarist, Jehan Patte, clearly states that Amiens's

[43] AMA, BB50, fols. 85; 115–16. It was rumoured that Antoine de Berny gave Amiens's tax monies as personal gifts to his patron, Aumale. De Berny denied the claim, but it appears that in July of 1589 he gave Aumale 800 *écus* from *Amiénois* taxes. Two months later the *échevinage* acknowledged that the provincial League council, the *Chambre des Etats de Picardie* existed in name only as the townspeople refused to recognize its authority. S. Annette Finley-Croswhite, 'Confederates and Rivals: Picard Urban Alliances during the Catholic League, 1588–1594', *Canadian Journal of History/Annales canadiennes d'histoire*, 31 (1996), 370–1.

populace disrupted the election, and that those supporting Gougier were royalists and Protestants.[44]

Political tensions mounted when Gougier took the oath of office on the morning of 28 October. He was forced to give up the office late that afternoon, however, when Aumale installed his own client, Berny, as mayor for the 1593–4 term. The Amiénois criticized Aumale for refusing to respect their wishes with regard to Gougier, and became more upset when the duke's followers brought firearms into the town hall. They interpreted Aumale's actions as an infringement of their privileges. In his journal, Jehan Cornet, a wealthy merchant, who was disillusioned by the event, equated municipal service with the whims of great nobles. He wrote that the election increased divisions in the city.[45] The incident reveals an important urban dynamic that incorporated popular protest during elections into the vocalization of political dissent. It shows that the factional contest for power between Leaguers and royalists that would culminate in the capitulation had already begun as each side tried to enlist the support of Amiens's inhabitants. By the end of 1593, the Catholic League no longer enjoyed the support of Amiens's inhabitants.[46]

Royalists used the perception that League leaders and their clients had ignored the city's traditional privileges to their advantage. Henry IV emphasized this point in letters he sent to the League towns throughout France. He argued that the League chiefs had abused the very municipal privileges he sought to honour.[47] Concern for urban privileges had always been uppermost in the minds of Amiens's elite. Jehan de Collemont, mayor of Amiens in 1588, joined the Catholic League but warned his fellow magistrates that supporting the League might one day lead to the destruction of their municipal privileges.[48] His warning became reality in 1594 when Mayenne could only retain Amiens by bringing more troops into the city. Rumour had it that the duke intended to use Spanish troops to augment his forces as he had done in nearby Beauvais and St Riquier. Amiens's municipal charter contained an exemption from billeting troops. Royalists repeated this rumour, asserting that Aumale and his supporters were nothing but a *'cabale espagnole'*.[49] The royalists incited the populace by saying that Mayenne and Aumale intended to deliver Amiens to the Spanish. This talk stirred the townspeople who feared the

[44] Jehan Patte, *Journal Historique de Jehan Patte, 1587–1617*, ed. M. J. Garnier (Amiens: Lemer Aîné, 1863), 75–6.
[45] AMA, BB53, fol. 105rv; Thierry, *Recueil des monuments du Tiers-Etat*, vol. 2, 1042–3.
[46] Mack Holt, 'Popular Political Culture and Mayoral Elections', in *Society and Institutions in Early Modern France*, ed. Mack P. Holt, (Athens: University of Georgia Press, 1991), 98–116.
[47] See for example the letter Henry IV wrote to Abbeville in 1594 in Ernest Prarond, *La Ligue à Abbeville, 1576–1594*, (Paris: Champion, 1873), vol. 3, 116.
[48] Georges Durand, ed. *Inventaire Sommaire des Archives Communales Antérieures à 1790, Ville de Amiens* (Amiens: Charles Beton, 1925), vol. 7, 310–11. This entry refers to AMA, FF805, fol. 38.
[49] Jehan Pagès, *Manuscrits de Pagès Marchand d'Amiens*, ed. Louis Douchet (Amiens: Libraires de la Picardie, 1859), 71; Finley-Croswhite, 'Urban Identity and Transitional Politics', 56; Finley-Croswhite, 'Confederates and Rivals', 374.

horrors of Spanish domination. The royalists staged personal confrontations in the streets and plotted behind the scenes to demolish the League.[50]

Discontent bubbled beneath the surface from March to May, and then erupted into revolt in June 1594. On 15 March, two of the king's clients, Augustin de Louvencourt and Robert Correur, were discovered in a plot to seize the Porte de Montrescu. They intended to open the city to royalist troops under the command of Henry's lieutenant-general in Picardy, the duke of Humières. One week later news reached Amiens of Henry IV's entry into Paris, and on 5 April letters arrived from the king promising a complete pardon if the city abandoned the League. In mid-April the *Amiénois* learned that their neighbours in Abbeville had capitulated. Henry IV's siege of Laon aroused more fear about Amiens's future. On 31 May the mayor, Berny, discovered that someone inside the city had sent Henry IV a list of more than eight-hundred supposedly royalist *Amiénois*, who were awaiting his arrival in the city. About the same time, placards and broadsides appeared attacking prominent Leaguers. A new oath of union, issued by the municipal government on 1 June, did little to quell the discontent. De Berny suggested that a meeting of leading citizens be called on 6 June to discuss the situation, but Mayenne vetoed the idea because he feared a pro-royalist demonstration.[51]

During June artisans and labourers protested that grain was in short supply and that people throughout Picardy were starving. The *échevins* admitted during their deliberations on 21 June that no one could earn a living in the city anymore.[52] When the Spanish captain Charles de Mansfeld arrived in Picardy with his army, townspeople began roaming Amiens's streets crying, '*Point d'espagnols*'.[53] Barricades went up throughout the city on 25 June, and later that day a royalist *échevin* named Mathieu Certain was mortally wounded when he tried to pass through the parish of St Martin on his way to the *Hôtel de Ville*. Angry inhabitants shot and killed him on the rue des Lombarts.[54] The attack on Certain confirmed that the *Amiénois* were in open revolt. The balance of power was shifting, but for the time being the Catholic League remained in control.

Trying to retain his authority the duke of Mayenne exacerbated tensions in June and July. He issued a new oath of loyalty that many refused to take. He insinuated that he would soon bolster Amiens's internal defences with more of his own troops, and he began expelling prominent royalists including Nicholas de Lan, Antoine Scourion, and Guillaume Pingré. Their brother-in-law, the *échevin*, Augustin de Louvencourt, could do nothing to save them. The city's most influential men declared angrily that Mayenne did not possess the authority to expel bourgeois

---

[50] Pages, *Manuscrits*, 77.
[51] A. Dubois, *La ligue: Documents relatifs à la Picardie* (Amiens: Typographie E. Yvert, 1859), 84–8.
[52] AMA, BB53, fol. 136.   [53] Dubois, *La ligue*, 90.
[54] Jehan Patte, *Journal Historique de Jehan Patte, 1587–1617*, ed. M. J. Garnier (Amiens: Lemer Ainé, 1863), 81; Pages, *Manuscrits*, 72; Certain was shot in the shoulder on 25 July and died eleven days later.

elites. The duke responded by issuing five-hundred more letters of expulsion on 26 July.[55]

On 27 July Mayenne's troops mustered at the Porte de Beauvais. The inhabitants feared they would enter the city, and several *échevins* met with the duke and asked him to send his troops away. Mayenne refused and informed the magistrates that if they troubled him, he would burn Amiens to the ground.[56] This was a major turning point because the *échevins* ordered all militia captains to arm the men of their *quartiers*. They issued letters of recall to all banished bourgeois, and ordered the expulsion of all Mayenne's soldiers inside the city.[57] More barricades went up: Mayenne and his soldiers held the *Grande Marché*, and the royalists and their allies commanded the *Petite Marché*. The city remained in arms and barricaded until 9 August. Royalists incited the townspeople against Mayenne and Aumale, and many inhabitants left the *Grande Marché* and went over to the *Petite Marché*. When word came that Henry IV had conquered Laon, Mayenne fled Amiens on 27 July. His departure set off a scramble among his clients, who realized the political necessity of changing patrons. In desperation, the *échevins* stationed troops around the *Hôtel de Ville* to protect themselves from the angry populace.[58]

Aumale and his dwindling band of supporters struggled to keep Amiens loyal to the League, but food and money were in short supply.[59] On 8 August, Amiens's weavers and woolcombers demonstrated in front of the *Hôtel de Ville* crying: 'We're starving, give us work, we want peace!'[60] The mayor promised them bread, but as night fell the demonstrators grew angry, egged on by the royalists. A number of League *échevins* took refuge in the *Hôtel de Ville* after being stoned by the crowd. Aumale and a small force of two-hundred-and-fifty soldiers barricaded themselves in the square in front of the cathedral. The parish of St Leu joined the revolt as did the parish of St Martin. Barricades also went up on the Place de la Belle Croix not far from the *Hôtel de Ville*. Augustin de Louvencourt, Robert Correur, Antoine Scourior, Jean and François d'Aguesseau, and Vincent Voiture commanded the royalist barricade in St Martin that strategically blocked Aumale's access to the town hall. Documents note that these royalists were supported by their kinsmen and allies on this night of fighting. Louvencourt and Correur were the key figures in the royalist camp, and their importance grew during the tumult. They moved through the city, urging the townspeople to accept the peace offered by the king and opening channels of communication to the politically compromised members of the urban elite. They also engaged the general populace in a dialogue

---

[55] Pagès, *Manuscrits*, 74.   [56] AMA, BB53, fol. 158r.
[57] Ibid., fols. 158v–161r. City officials knew that Mayenne had troops stationed in Amiens disguised as peasants.
[58] Calonne, *Histoire d'Amiens*, 3, 125–6; Pagès, *Manuscrits*, 75–8; Patte, *Journal historique*, 86–7.
[59] AMA, BB53, fol. 163v.
[60] Quoted in Calonne, *Histoire d'Amiens*, vol. 3, 126. Calonne reports the *sayeterus* cried, 'Nous mourons de faim! donnez-nous du travail! nous voulons la paix! la paix!'

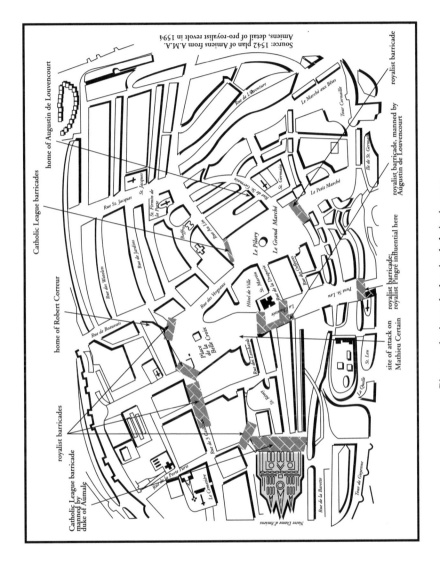

Catholic League barricades

home of Augustin de Louvencourt

Catholic League barricade
manned by
duke of Aumale

home of Robert Correur

royalist barricades

Source: 1542 plan of Amiens from A.M.A.
Amiens, detail of pro-royalist revolt in 1594

Rue de L'Aventure

Le Marché aux Bêtes

Tour Corneille

Rue St. Jacques

St. Jacques

St. Firmin de la Place

Rue du St. Germain

St. Germain

Île de St. Germain

royalist barricade

royalist barricade, manned by
Augustin de Louvencourt

Le Petit Marché

Rue de Jardins

Beffroy

Le Pilory

Le Grand Marché

Le Petit Marché

Rue du Vieu

Rue des Wadelets

Rue des Vergeaux

Hôtel de Ville

St. Martin

La Motette

Rue des Orfèvres

Pont St. Leu

royalist barricade;
royalist Pingré influential here

Rue de Beauvais

Place de la Belle Croix

Rue des Lombards

Rue de la Dragerie

St. Leu

site of attack on
Mathieu Certain

Rue de 3 Cailloux

St. Remy

La Coille

Rue la Porte Paris

Le Courtier

Rue la Corderie

Tour de Gayerne

Notre Dame d'Amiens

Rue de la Barette

Plan 1   Amiens, the barricaded city in 1594

and tried to win their support in this contest for power.[61] (The barricaded city is pictured in plan 1.)

Influential men like Louvencourt undoubtedly swayed their kin, neighbours, and allies to switch sides during the night of fighting that delivered Amiens to the king. Neighbourhoods represented the physical spaces in which factions and clienteles existed. Henry's client, Augustin de Louvencourt, lived in the parish of St Germain on the rue St Germain where he owned much property. His status as a wealthy cloth merchant meant that he had contacts throughout the city, especially in the parish of St Jacques, heavily populated by weavers. His authority in his own *quartier* extended throughout the blocks surrounding the *Petite Marché*, the *Marché aux Bêtes*, and onto the Ile St Germain. Henry's key man, Robert Correur, lived near the *Marché au Ble*.

The royalist concentration on the rue de Beauvais, leading out from the *marché*, was significant: Correur had strong ties with the merchant Caron family, also royalists, who lived around the *Porte de Beauvais* and enjoyed influence on the streets surrounding this important city gate. The royalist Pingré lived in St Leu, another parish dominated by merchants and artisans. St Leu was strongly pro-League, although important pockets of royalist allegiance existed there in alliance with the Pingré and Louvencourt. Louvencourt–Pingré influence was strong around the parish church of St Leu, the *donjon* behind it, and on the bridge just in front of the church.[62] (Neighbourhood concentrations of royalists, Leaguers, and areas of mixed allegiances, are specified in plan 2.)

A large number of League supporters existed in the wealthier parishes of St Rémy, St Firmin-à-la Porte, St Firmin-le-Confesseur, and St Michel. Affluent St Rémy was the home of the Leaguer Pécoul, Famechon, and De Lattre families. The merchant Randon family enjoyed influence in St Jacques where Michel Randon lived. The Randon's influence extended into the heart of Amiens because most of the family members lived on the rue des Orfèvres, a street that led into the *Grande Marché*. Other merchant families allied with the League controlled the *Grand Marché* and the rue de la Draperie leading into the market square. The Du Fresne, for example, supported the League and lived in a house that fronted the *Grande Marché*. Poorer sections of the city around the Porte de Montrescu and the parish of St Sulpice, where artisans, labourers, and many urban poor lived, were known as pockets of allegiance to Aumale.[63]

Models and static pictures, however, cannot express the complexity of the religious/political cleavages that divided Amiens in the summer of 1594. Factions changed constantly as Leaguers weighed their options and gradually came over to

---

[61] Carroll, 'The Guise Affinity', 129.
[62] AN KK1213, 12; AMA, FF545, 26 September 1598; L'Orgnier, *Un homme à la mode*, 27–8; FF1372, fols. 178–82; ADS, E29713, 29 October 1619.
[63] AMA, FF572, 29 October 1605; FF702, 13 December 1622; FF501, 7 December 1594; FF485, 7 January 1592; FF503 27 February 1595; FF629, 7 November 1608; GG302 (St Remy), fols. 36v, 66v; Gabriel de Sachy de Fourdrinoy, *Historique de la Famille de Sachy de Fourdrinoy* (Blois: Editions Linages, 1991); AD Somme, B386, fol. 16.

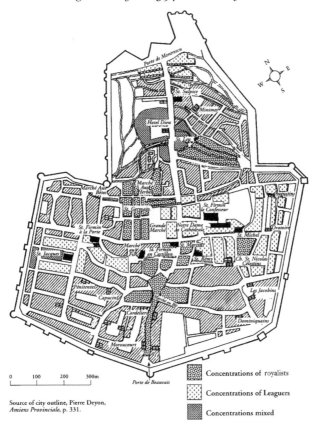

Plan 2   Concentrations of royalists and Catholic League supporters on
8–9 August 1594, Amiens

the royalist side. Parishes did not always fight as a united whole, and many streets
were divided in their loyalties. The rue des Vergeaux located behind the *Hôtel de
Ville*, for example, was consistently identified as a royalist street in Amiens's
municipal deliberations.[64] But François Castelet, Philippe Matissart, and Jehan
Hémart, all wealthy Leaguers, lived on this street. Similarly, the rue de la Draperie
was known as a League street, but royalists lived there too.[65] Divided streets
represented divided loyalties, with Leaguer strength diminishing as influential
Leaguers changed sides and encouraged their neighbours to do likewise.

Henry IV's forces captured Amiens during the early morning hours of 9 August,
although the king was not physically present. Elites loyal to Aumale, obviously
shaken by Mayenne's departure, began to defect before midnight on the 8th. An

---

[64] AMA, BB50, fol. 82v.
[65] AMA, FF576, 21 July 1606; FF473, 12 April 1589; FF467 26 February 1588; AD Somme, 1B12, fol.
161r.

important League noble, the seigneur of Saisseval, and Amiens's *vidame*, Emmanuel d'Ailly, switched allegiances, signalling to their followers to join them. This brought the parish of St Firmin-à-la-Porte, in which Saisseval controlled entire streets, into the royalist camp. The news of their defections caused street fighters near the Pont de St Leu and the Place de la Belle Croix to lay down their arms and change sides. The League leader, Vincent Le Roy, abandoned the League, and immediately began encouraging his former League colleagues to do the same. Aumale still held strategic streets around the cathedral, but his support in the *Grand Marché* was gone. When he marched on the town hall, one of his own captains began crying out '*Vive Le Roi*', and was allowed behind the royalist barricade at St Martin.[66]

By the night of 8–9 August, Aumale's clientele in Amiens had disintegrated. Leaguers were encouraged by Henry's clients to leave the Holy Union, and when they did so, they roamed through the streets urging their former League allies to join them. When Aumale's own troops fell into disarray, the Catholic League became a lost cause in Amiens, and all remaining resistors gave up their support of the League. At that moment the royalists took control; Augustin de Louvencourt entered the *Hôtel de Ville* with articles of capitulation signed by Henry IV; and the inhabitants encircled the building, chanting the king's name. It took just a few more hours to convince the remaining League elites and churchmen to abandon the 'Holy Union' and accept the legitimate king of France, Henry IV. Near dawn on 9 August, a herald was sent to all the main intersections of the city to announce the ascension of Henry IV to the throne of France. The duke of Humières entered Amiens later that day and claimed the city for the king.[67]

CAPTURING A TOWN FROM WITHIN: HENRY IV AND URBAN CLIENTAGE

It is likely that the behaviour of Catholic League clients in Picardy's capital was repeated in other large cities throughout France.[68] Reconstructing urban clienteles, however, is a difficult task. Henry was quick to open his purse to buy off prominent League leaders, but tracing the distribution of his gifts always proves tedious and usually impossible. Gifts to great nobles appear in capitulation documents, but the way in which these gifts trickled down to urban leaders remains obscure. The capitulation of Picardy supposedly cost Henry 1,261,880 *livres*, but whether his non-noble urban clients in Amiens received any of this money is unknown. Henry's list of *Dons du roi*, kept by his finance minister, Sully, records cash gifts to important royalists. Henry's gifts to Nicholas de Lan, a treasurer-general in

---

[66] Pagès, *Manuscrits*, 82; Patte, *Journal Historique*, 90–1; Père Daire, *Histoire de la ville d'Amiens depuis son origine jusqu'à present* (Paris: Chez La Veuve de Laguette, 1757), 328–39.

[67] AMA, Amiens, 159–166rv; Pagès, *Manuscrits*, 82–6; Patte, *Journal Historique*, 90–1; Calonne, *Histoire d'Amiens*, vol. 3, 131; Daire, *Histoire d'Amiens*, 328–39.

[68] For an excellent example of the uses of family and patronage during political crisis see Kevin Robbins, 'The Social Mechanisms of Urban Rebellion: A Case Study of Leadership in the 1614 Revolt of La Rochelle', *French Historical Studies*, 19 (1995), 559–90.

Picardy, for example, are listed in the *Dons*, as are gifts to other prominent men from all over France. Even so, the names of men below the rank of sword and robe nobles seldom appear in the document: The merchant Augustin de Louvencourt is not listed in the *Dons* although he played a major role in negotiating Amiens's capitulation.[69] Henry knew Louvencourt personally and trusted him enough to request his presence at the Assembly of Notables held in Rouen in 1596. Louvencourt's importance is visible in Amiens's archives, but not apparent in documentation found in Paris.[70]

The demise of the Catholic League in Amiens demonstrates the importance of clientage in delivering League cities to Henry IV and validates Sharon Kettering's belief that clientage thrived during the Wars of Religion.[71] Far from causing a failure of clientage as Robert Harding has suggested, the religious wars created many new patron–client opportunities for nobles, elites, townspeople, and the king.[72] Personal bonds influenced the course of the religious wars and the timing of capitulations. The king's clients were not always nobles or *fidèles*, but included important merchants like Louvencourt who connected Henry to networks of wealthy elites and city dwellers of middle or low status. Henry's reconversion to Catholicism earned him acceptance and legitimacy throughout France, but as the League fell apart his legitimacy often had to be established in the streets. Capitulations occurred when Henry's clients won the support of the urban population, who realized that continued opposition was pointless.[73] A complex dialogue ensued uniting the entire urban population in collective action. The outcome determined the matter of kingship.

The revolt in Amiens can be interpreted as a kind of signalling behaviour that occurs when political elites vie for power. It fits into the pattern of factional struggles among urban elites that William Beik and other historians have analyzed.[74] The power and influence of urban factions was determined by the strength of their urban supporters. Heads of factions signalled as patrons to those who agreed to follow them in the hope of receiving rewards, and in response clientele networks grew and shrank.[75] Henry's clients were already patrons within the city, and their political success meant that they would soon control the distribution of an increased supply of goods and resources, which meant more clients and more power. Their authority was increased in 1594 because they associated themselves with the influence of a leader outside their city, Henry IV.[76] Once the reputation of Mayenne and Aumale as potential sources of patronage was undermined, the townspeople turned to the king's clients and their kin for patronage.

[69] AN, 120 AP12.   [70] AMA, BB54, fols. 52, 91, BB55, fols. 20, 49.

[71] Kettering, 'Clientage during the French Wars of Religion', 221–39.

[72] Robert Harding, *The Anatomy of a Power Elite The Provincial Governors of Early Modern France* (New Haven: Yale University Press, 1978), 64–7.

[73] Barry Barnes, *The Nature of Power* (Chicago: University of Chicago Press, 1988), 123.

[74] Beik, *Urban Protest*, 173–218, see in particular 199.

[75] Weingrod, 'Patronage and power', 41–52, esp. pp. 50–1.

[76] For the importance of princely leaders see Beik, *Urban Protest*, 199–200.

The case of Amiens demonstrates a crucial aspect of how Henry IV won the religious wars through the use of his clients and their clienteles. His success did not come all at once; he had supporters in Amiens who organized resistance and recruited popular support throughout the period. The king touched the backstreets and alley ways of Amiens through men like Augustin de Louvencourt, Robert Correur, and Antoine Pingré. His clients acted as middlemen connecting him to both the municipal elites and the politically disenfranchised. Henry's clients transformed him in the eyes of most *Amiénois* from an abstract symbol into an actual man who could protect life, privileges, and the Catholic faith. The king acquired power through the support of men like Louvencourt and Correur. Like a financial investment, the power that he invested in these men grew over time, and in 1594 the political return on his investment ensured his success.[77]

Henry's clients also served him as brokers in re-establishing social cohesion within Amiens as the League disintegrated. The great significance of the city's League revolt is that Henry's client-brokers were able to mediate between the Crown and Amiens's Leaguers. When League leaders lost their sources of patronage, the king's clients had commodities superior to cash with which they could bargain – royal clemency and royal patronage. Had Henry refused to accommodate Leaguers by refusing clemency, he would have harmed his supporters more than his enemies. Instead, he extended clemency and patronage to his clients to broker on his behalf.

During July and August of 1594, Leaguers argued bitterly about the political ramifications of Amiens's capitulation while the king's clients maintained a discourse based on mediation. Influential *Amiénois* like Vincent Le Roy had been seriously compromised by their League loyalties. But Le Roy and others like him possessed kin loyal to the king whom they mobilized to help them, using them as brokers and go-betweens. Kinship achieved new meaning in this time of political crisis. Augustin de Louvencourt's brother-in-law, Antoine Scourion, for example, was Vincent Le Roy's uncle. Louvencourt's step-brother, Pierre Pingré, was also Le Roy's son-in-law. These kinship ties became Le Roy's entrée to Henry IV. Acting as social integrators, Henry's client-brokers persuaded League leaders and neutrals to realign themselves with the king. When compromised Leaguers recognized the power shift inside Amiens they cast their lot with Henry IV.[78] By brokering clemency, Henry's clients re-established an urban discourse focused on loyalty to the Crown. This dialogue realigned the city's political leadership with Henry IV and allowed many Leaguers to survive politically. The use of patronage thus reduced capitulation anxiety, restored peace and harmony to Amiens, and maintained the city's traditional elites in positions of authority.

---

[77] Barnes, *The Nature of Power*, 17.
[78] Ronald Cohen, 'Introduction', in *State Formation and Political Legitimacy, Political Anthropology*, vol. 6, eds. Ronald Cohen and Judith Toland (New Brunswick, New Jersey: Transaction Books, 1988), 3.

3

Henry IV's ceremonial entries: the remaking
of a king

Henry made ample use of individual clients during his struggle to end the war of
the League, but once capitulation treaties had been signed, the king was anxious to
remake his formerly rebellious towns into institutional clients and re-establish a
harmonious relationship between the Crown and the towns. He accomplished this
task by using the royal entry to take formal possession of select cities and towns. A
medieval spectacle, the royal entry developed during the Renaissance as an arena
for the dramatization of political ideas and the symbolic expression of the relationship between the monarchy and the towns. French kings used entries to emphasize
their roles as heads of state, guarantors of civic liberties, and protectors of the peace.
Entries created opportunities for dialogue between ruler and subjects as well.
Edward Muir argues that these civic ceremonies re-ordered civic space and time
and allowed participants to calculate their effect.[1] Town leaders organized the
spectacles and used them to emphasize their own positions and power, and to
obtain a confirmation or augmentation of municipal liberties and privileges granted
by earlier kings. These welcoming ceremonies encouraged kings to take special
interest in their towns and promoted good relations. Royal entries thus became
self-serving. They united kings and subjects in an understanding of expectations
and created a site for negotiating the meaning of kingship and royal authority.[2]

---

[1] Edward Muir, *Civic Ritual in Renaissance Venice* (Princeton, New Jersey: Princeton University Press,
1981), 241.
[2] Ibid.; Barbara Hanawalt and Kathryn Reyerson, eds., *City and Spectacle in Medieval Europe* (Min-
neapolis: University of Minnesota Press, 1994); Roy C. Strong, *Art and Power, Renaissance Festivals
1450–1650* (Berkeley: University of California Press, 1973), 85; Lawrence Bryant, 'Parliamentary
Political Theory in the Parisian Royal Entry Ceremony', *The Sixteenth Century Journal*, 7 (April
1976), 15; Bernerd Guenée, Françoise Lehoux, *Les entrées royales Françaises de 1328 à 1515* (Paris:
Editions du Centre Nationale de la Recherche Scientifique, 1968), 8–9. For more information on royal
entries see: Lawrence Bryant, *The King and the City in the Parisian Royal Entry Ceremony: Politics,
Ritual, and Art in the Renaissance* (Geneva: Droz, 1986); Jean Jacquot (ed.), *Les Fêtes de la Renaissance*
(Paris: Centre Nationale de la Recherche Scientifique, 1956), 3 vols. Sydney Anglo, *Spectacle
Pageantry, and Early Tudor Policy* (Oxford: Clarendon Press, 1969); Jean-Marie Apostolides, *Les
Roi-Machine, Spectacle et Politique au Temps de Louis XIV* (Paris: Les Editions de Minuit, 1981);
Richard A. Jackson, *Vive le Roi! A History of the French Coronation from Charles V to Charles X*
(Chapel Hill: University of North Carolina Press, 1984). Kings were not the only important figures to
participate in entries. Powerful nobles and queens also participated in entries.

Henry IV's royal entries form an interesting chapter in the evolution of Renaissance rituals because they contained a unique aspect not present in the entries of other kings. Entries usually took place soon after a king had ascended the throne. Henry's kingship was disputed, however, so his entries into Catholic League towns were made in the 1590s as part of their submissions. Henry's entries served to reunite the monarchy with estranged towns and heralded a reconciliation between the king and his urban subjects, but scholars seldom discuss this point in the abundant literature devoted to royal entries.[3] Only Ruth Kaufman has addressed the idea of ceremonial reconciliation in Henry's entries although her analysis is confined to an 1817 painting representing his entry into Paris.[4] As the religious wars drew to a close, Henry's royal entries emphasized the return of peace and harmony made possible by his greatness. At no time was the reconciliation motif as important as during his reign.[5]

This chapter explores ritual in the form of the ceremonial entry as both a symbol of power and a means by which Henry IV acquired authority and legitimacy. Ritual played an important role in times of political change. Henry used ritual to identify with powerful cultural symbols and project his legitimacy. Henry's entries marked the final demonstrative display of the submission process and announced the beginning of a new age. As lavish rites of passage, they purified a war-weary society with a rebirth of structure based on a new understanding of fidelity. Henry's entries

---

[3] Robert Hodge and Gunther Kress, *Social Semiotics* (Ithaca: Cornell University Press, 1988), 55; David Sless, *In Search of Semiotics* (Totowa, New Jersey: Barnes and Noble Books, 1986), 48–62; Yuri Lotman, *Universe of the Mind A Semiotic Theory of Culture*, trans. Ann Shukman (Bloomington: Indiana University Press, 1990), 102–19; Roland Barthes, *Mythologies*, trans. Annette Lavers (New York: Hill and Wang, 1972); Arthur Asa Berger, 'Semiotics and TV', *Understanding Television, Essays on Television as a Social and Culture Force*, ed. Richard P. Adler (New York: Praeger, 1981), 91–114. Reference to this last article may not be easily appreciated, but Berger offers an excellent analysis and summary of the meaning and application of semiotics.

[4] Ruth Kaufman, 'François Gérard's Entry of Henry IV into Paris, The Iconography of Constitutional Monarchy', *The Burlington Magazine*, 117 (1975), 790–802.

[5] For Henry's entries see: Théodore Godefroy, *Le cérémonial françois contenant les cérémonies observées en France aux sacres et couronnements du roys et reynes de quelques anciens duke of Normandie, d'Aquitaine, et de Bretagne* (Paris: Sebastien Cramoisy, 1649), vol. 1, 930–59; J. Félix (ed.), *Entrée à Rouen de Roi Henry IV en 1596* (Rouen: Imprimerie de Esperance Cagniard, 1887); Albert Babeau, *Henri IV à Troyes* (Troyes: DuFour-Bouquot, 1879); Pierre Matthieu, *L'Entrée de trèsgrand Prince Henry III en sa bonne ville de Lyon* (Lyon: s.d.). The best work I know of on Henry's entries is an unpublished paper by Michael Wolfe. Michael Wolfe, '"Paris is Worth a Mass" Reconsidered: Henri IV and the Leaguer Capital, March 1594', paper presented at the Society for French Historical Studies, Wilmington, Delaware, March 1994; abundant recent literature exists concerning Henry II's royal entries. See for example, I. D. MacFarland, *The Entry of Henry II into Paris, 16 June 1549* (Binghamton, New York: Medieval and Renaissance Texts and Studies, 1982); Margaret M. McGowan, *L'Entrée de Henry II à Rouen en 1550* (Amsterdam: Theatrum Orbis Terrarum, 1970); Denis Gluck, 'Les entrées provinciales de Henri II', *L'Information d'histoire de l'art* 10 (November–December 1965), 215–19; V. L. Saulnier, 'L'Entrée de Henri II à Paris et La Revolution Poëtique de 1550', in Jacquot, *Les Fêtes de la Renaissance*, vol. 1, 31–59. More recent works on entries include: Jean Boutier, Alain Dewerpe, and Daniel Nordman, *Un tour de France royal, le voyage de Charles IX (1564–1566)* (Paris: Editions Aubier Montaigne, 1984); Marina Valensis, 'Le Sacre du Roi: Stratégie Symbolique et Doctrine Politique de la Monarchie Française', *Annales economies, sociétés, civilisations*, 41 (1986), 543–77.

brought together individuals from all levels of society and emphasized comradeship and community.[6]

The focus of inquiry will begin with Henry's royal entry into the former League stronghold of Abbeville in Picardy, and this event will be compared with other entries later in the chapter. Abbeville left the Catholic League in April 1594. In that month the town magistrates secured a treaty from Henry IV maintaining their town charter and confirming their municipal privileges. Henry's entry occurred in December of that same year while he was touring the province of Picardy.

HENRY IV'S ROYAL ENTRY INTO ABBEVILLE

Shortly before noon on 18 December 1594, the mayor, magistrates, and bourgeois leaders of Abbeville rode out into the countryside beyond the walls to bid their new king welcome. As representatives of Abbeville, their authority was reflected in their robes of office. The mayor and *échevins* wore red robes of damask and taffeta with purple bands across the sleeves while the junior officials were clothed in the colours of the town, their robes divided equally between tan and purple. The group stood atop a hill, and along the road behind them, eight companies of armed militia joined them. Henry had not asked for a lavish display, but the town intended to impress their king nevertheless.[7]

Abbeville's representatives met up with the king and his entourage on the outskirts of the town. Picardy's governor, the duke of Longueville, directed the mayor of Abbeville, Jean de Maupin, toward the king. When Maupin saw Henry, he dismounted and fell to his knees. The act of kneeling was customary when a subject met his king. This particular gesture, however, had special significance because Abbeville had so recently denied the king's legitimacy. Maupin recognized Henry's power by kneeling, and lowered himself in the presence of a superior as a physical sign of the capitulation.[8]

---

[6] Victor Turner, *The Ritual Process. Structure and Anti-Structure* (Chicago: Aldine Publishing, 1969), 95; Louise Olga Fradenburg, *City, Marriage, Tournament, Arts of Rule in Late Medieval Scotland* (Madison, Wisconsin: University of Wisconsin Press, 1991), 74; David Kertzer, *Ritual, Politics, and Power* (New Haven: Yale University Press, 1988), 38–40; Amélie Kuhrt, 'Usurpation, Conquest and Ceremonial: From Babylon to Persia', in *Rituals of Royalty Power and Ceremonial in Traditional Societies*, eds. David Cannadine and Simon Price (Cambridge: Cambridge University Press, 1987), 20–55.

[7] BN, MSS fr. 91 *Collection de Picardie*, 'Entrée et réception du roi Henri IV à Abbeville le 18 decembre 1594', fol. 183r. The deliberations of the municipality of Abbeville were destroyed in a fire in the twentieth century, but an eighteenth-century copy of some of the deliberations can be found in BN, MSS fr. 91, fols. 183r–191r. The text of the entry I analyze comes from the eighteenth-century record. It reads very much like a word for word copy of the original except that quotes are given in third person instead of first. An account with little analysis of Henry's entry into Abbeville can also be found in Ernest Prarond, *La ligue à Abbeville 1576–1594* (Paris: Dumoulin Libraire, 1873), vol. III, 210–45. Other accounts of the ceremonial entry can be found in Pau, *Bibliothèque du Château de Pau* (hereafter B.C.P.), BP 6841.C, 'Texcte de la harangue de Henri IV en réponse au maire Jean de Maupin', and in Abbeville, *Archives Municipales*, Abbeville (hereafter AMAV), MSS 20.088, 'Manuscript de Pierre Waigart.'

[8] Hodge and Kress, *Social Semiotics*, 57.

Maupin then addressed the king and voiced Abbeville's recognition of his kingship and gratitude for his clemency.

Your very humble, loyal, and obedient subjects, the mayor, *échevins*, inhabitants, and community of your town of Abbeville are very pleased today because God has saved us from Spanish domination and returned us to our duty in recognizing His Very Christian Majesty. We can now enjoy the effects of your clemency and receive your good graces . . .[9]

The mayor rendered homage to the king in the name of the town and declared an ardent affection for him. As an indication of the town's loyalty, Maupin reminded Henry that Abbeville's surrender had been voluntary. He asked Henry to take pity on the poor people left homeless in the countryside and above all to maintain the town in its liberties and privileges. He requested that the king uphold the Roman Catholic faith, and after his closing remarks, he removed the keys to the town from a purple purse hanging from a white taffeta cord and gave them to the king. The keys symbolically represented the town, and Maupin used ritual to give Abbeville to Henry. The gates that had once been closed to the king were now his to open.[10]

Maupin thus completed his important part in the ceremonial entry. He had formally surrendered Abbeville to Henry, and at the same time had reminded the king of his duties toward the town. All of this occurred before Henry entered Abbeville. When the king finally rode into the town, he did so as a victor: Abbeville was symbolically and actually his. Henry responded to Maupin with a short acknowledgement. He connected himself historically with the town by mentioning that he had been conceived in Abbeville and promised to reign as a good king.

Your town is the first in the province to submit and I therefore wanted to visit it . . . Two motives compelled me to come here. First to extend my good will, and second because I was conceived here . . . I will be your good king so that you will continue to honour and love me.[11]

[9] BN, MSS fr. 91, fols. 183v–84r. The mayor said, 'Vos trez humbles, trez loiaulx et trez obeissans subjets les maieur, eschevins, habitans et communauté de vostre ville d'Abbeville ont receu ung trez grand plaisir et contentement en leurs ames depuis que Dieu leur a fait la grace de s'estre garantis de la domination espagnolle pour rentrer en leur debvoir et recongnoissans Vostre Majesté trez chrestienne et gousté les effets de sa clémence en les recevant en ses bonnes graces . . .' I have taken the liberty of translating this quote in first person instead of third.

[10] Ibid.

[11] Ibid., fol. 183v; Prarond, *La ligue à Abbeville*, vol. 3, 221–2. The person who transcribed this speech gave the king's response in the third person. See also, A. Janvier, *Petite histoire de Picardie, simple récits* (Amiens: Hecquet, Libraire-Editeur, 1880), 224. The secretary who recorded Henry's entry in the municipal deliberations of Abbeville's town government that were transcribed in the eighteenth century gave great detail on the entry from the town's point of view, but was slight concerning Henry's comments. Henry was conceived in Abbeville in 1552 or 1553. BCP., BP 6841.C, 'Texcte de la harangue de Henri IV en réponse au maire Jean de Maupin'; AMAV, MSS 20.088, manuscript of Pierre Waignart, 2, 630–1. Waignart also gives the king's responses in the third person, but I have translated the quote in first person. Waignart writes, 'Ayant fin le roy luy respondit que la ville d'Abbeville avoit esté la première de ceste province qui s'estoit réduicte; que, dès lors, il avoit désiré de nous voir, meais que ses affaires l'avoient tiré ailleurs; que, sy tost qu'il a peu soustraire ung jour de temps, il l'avoit donné pour nous visiter; que Dieu sembloit avoir favorisé, aiant adoucvi l'inclémence du temps; qu'il avoit volontiers entrepris son voiage pour deux obligations qui l'y convoient, sa

When Henry had finished, the crowd cried aloud in a great oral shattering of League allegiance, 'Vive le roi'.[12]

Royal entries provided towns with unique opportunities to express their desires to the king, and Maupin was not alone in haranguing Henry during his entry into Abbeville. In fact, Henry heard three speeches delivered by the most important leaders of Abbeville, the mayor, the lieutenant general, and a canon from Abbeville's cathedral acting in the dean's stead. All three speeches were similar. The men thanked Henry for gracing Abbeville with his presence; they swore loyalty to the Crown and rendered homage to the king. And they expressed a common anxiety by using dramatically Catholic language to emphasize Henry's role as the *Catholic* king of France. This emphasis is revealing since Henry had not yet been absolved by the pope. Jean de Maupin recognized Henry as the legitimate issue of Louis IX and called on the saint to bless the new king and the realm.[13] Jacques Bernard, lieutenant general in the *sénéchaussée* of Ponthieu, reminded the king of his title, *très chrètienne*: 'It is the most beautiful mark, the diadem, the richest banner that your predecessor kings have carried, and as fervent Christians none of them failed this very Christian tradition'.[14] The canon, Jehan Belloy, spoke of the importance of having a true faith in Jesus Christ that would enable the king to carry out his duties as protector of the faith, father of his people, and defender of justice.[15] Apprehensive over Henry's recent re-conversion to Catholicism, these men all indicated in polite language that they desired a Catholic king.

Dialogue, however, was not the only means that a town used to communicate its wishes to a king. Visual imagery was an integral part of medieval and Renaissance entries. A *châpeau de triomphe* made of ivy and tinsel, for instance, hung over Abbeville's main gate bearing the coats of arms of France and Navarre united by a crown. Paintings, banners, friezes, and tapestries referring to Henry's greatness and his victories over the Catholic League lined the parade route. Poems and inscriptions in Greek, Latin, and French written for the occasion were displayed on plaques and banners strategically placed around the town. The writers and artists in Abbeville thus used symbolism and allegory to represent the king and the community, accommodate the past with the future, and reconcile the town as a child with the king as father.[16] Two stanzas from a poem displayed in Henry's lodging for the night in Abbeville aptly supports this point.

---

qualité premièrement, y pour ce qu'il avoit esté engendré en cest ville . . . qu'il nous seroit ung bon roy, et que l'on continuât de l'honorer et de l'aimer.'
[12] BN, MSS fr., 91, fol. 183v.
[13] Ibid., fols. 183rv.
[14] BN, MSS fr. 91, fol. 184r; Prarond, *La ligue à Abbeville*, 3, 223. Bernard stated, 'C'est la bellemarque, le diadème et le riche bandeau qu'ont tousjours porté vos prédécesseurs Roys, et comme très-chrestiens aucuns d'icuex ont aussi pris et eu ceste devise très-chrestienne'.
[15] BN, MSS fr., 91, fols. 188rv.
[16] Ibid., fols. 183r-191r.

But our Hercules – Monster chaser of Gaul
Has triumphantly sent the enemies to retreat
Has Geryon and his race blackened.
And pulled the victim to him out of reach
Has suffocated the designs of the Spanish
And made their châteaux go up in smoke.[17]

Abbeville, once a defender of the Catholic League, now rejoiced in its allegiance to Henry. Spain and the League were associated with the hideous monster Geryon, and Henry as the mythical Hercules was the protector and saviour of France. In this way the League was vilified and turned into a monster, an 'Other'. Abbeville's inhabitants symbolically disengaged themselves from their former ally as good and evil were clearly defined. The entry created its own myth in the way Roland Barthes has noted of myths in general: complex realities were displayed in simple and easily understood terms.[18]

Royal entries always included the participation of an entire community. As a king entered a town, he joined a parade made up of many inhabitants. Such processions were carefully orchestrated events with each individual and group assigned a particular place in the parade formation. It was common for elites to argue over places of precedence. The parade was an important part of the collective effort of the entry since the king and the community were united in this way: the ceremony bound the king to his subjects and his subjects to him. In this instance the *Abbevillois* no longer saw their king as an abstraction, and the king no longer regarded them as faceless subjects. The entry thus allowed Henry and his subjects

[17] Ibid., fol. 188v. In the complete poem all original spellings have been maintained. The *échevins* and other municipal leaders of Abbeville wrote all of the poems and Latin and Greek inscriptions for the entry. Since they were not professional scholars, some of their Latin translations were bizarre, and their poems were unpolished.

> L'Iberian en sa creuse cervelle
> Edifiant des fantasques chesteaux
> Tenoit desja les palais les plus beaux
> (Ce luy sembloit) de la France plus belle.
>
> Avec ses chefs déguisés d'un feint zèle
> Par ses supports (de france les fléaux)
> Et à main forte avoit les plus féaux
> Fainct mutiner d'un courage rebelle.
>
> Mais notre Hercule, chasse-monstre gaulois
> A, triomphant, faict rendre les abois
> A Geryon et sa race enfumée
> Et, luy tirant la proye hors les mains,
> A de l'Ibère etouffe les desseings
> Et les Chasteaux faict resoundre en fumée.

[18] Roland Barthes, *Mythologies*, 143. 'Myth does not deny things, on the contrary, its function is to talk about them; simply, it purifies them, it makes them innocent, it gives them a natural and eternal justification, it gives them a clarity which is not that of an explanation but that of a statement of fact ... In passing from history to nature, myth acts economically: it abolishes the complexity of human acts, its gives them the simplicity of essences, it does away with all dialectics, with any going beyond what is immediately visible, it organizes a world which is without contradictions because it is without depth, a world wide open and wallowing in the evident, it establishes a blissful clarity: things appear to mean something by themselves.'

to identify with each other and re-establish a healthy body politic. While it is not clear what percentage of a town actually participated in the processional parade, those excluded joined in the celebration as spectators. When Abbeville's procession began, trumpets sounded, church bells rang, muskets and cannons went off, and the crowd shouted 'Vive le roi!'[19]

Henry marched into Abbeville beneath a white satin canopy from Bruges, upheld by silver batons carried by four of the town's *échevins*.[20] At the Saint-Gilles gate he saw the first of many symbolic representations of reconciliation. Before his eyes on the drawbridge hung a banner made of orange satin with a silver border on which two kings dressed in Roman robes were painted in the centre. Each king carried in one hand a sword intersected by a Crown, and their other hand rested on a shield standing between them engraved with the arms of France. Above the shield two nymphs representing Fortune and Virtue were locked arm in arm. A Latin inscription read, 'DESTINY AND VIRTUE UNITED TOGETHER IN ONE'.[21]

The painting was rich in meaning. The two kings represented Clovis, the first Christian king of France, and Henry IV, the first re-converted king of France. Both kings had taken the 'perilous leap' and adopted Catholicism.[22] Metaphorically, the banner acknowledged re-inheriting Henry and united the king's two bodies. It joined Henry's perishable and personal body with his mystical and immortal one.[23] The succession from Clovis to Henry and the linking of the natural body with the body politic was expressed by each king touching the French coat of arms. The message revealed Henry as divinely chosen to ascend the throne of France just as Clovis had been. Poems appeared on the painting praising the valour and goodness of Henry. By depicting Henry and Clovis together the *Abbevillois* represented both kings as legitimate defenders of France.[24] Denis Crouzet believes that the message embedded in the emphasis on destiny in Henry's entries projected the image of a

---

[19] BN, MSS fr. 91, fol. 184v. Prarond, *La Ligue à Abbeville*, vol. 3, 226. Amid the excitement an artillery guard named Nicolas Le Moictié was accidently killed.

[20] BN, MSS fr. 91, fol. 184v.

[21] Ibid., fol. 187r, SORS ET VIRTUS MISCENTUR IN UNUM

[22] 'Perilous leap' were the words Henry himself used to describe his re-conversion to Catholicism. David Buisseret, *Henry IV* (London: George Allen and Unwin, 1984), 44–55.

[23] Ernst Kantorowicz, *The King's Two Bodies* (Princeton, New Jersey: Princeton University Press, 1957), 9; Thomas Greene, 'The King's One Body in the *Balet Comique de la Royne*', *Yale French Studies*, 86 (1994), 87.

[24] BN, MSS fr. 91, fol. 187r. The poem read:

 1. Ces roy oincts de grace divine,
   Doués de vertu et bonheur,
   Ont conservé par leur valeur
   Le beau champ où le lys domine.

 2. Clovis, le premier de nos rois
   Abjurant la secte paienne,
   Enta la piété chrèstienne
   Sur l'estoc roial des François.

 3. Henry le Grand, vray exemplaire
   De bonté, de gloire et valeur,
   Aux ennemys est en terreur
   Et aux siens doux et debonnaire.

king with superhuman abilities who would fulfill a predestined purpose and establish a Golden Age of happiness for all of France.[25]

Proceeding through the Saint-Gilles gate and into the city, Henry and the parade marched through the streets to arrive at a triumphal arch adorned with elaborate moldings. The iconographic message of the arch was re-inheritance and confirmation. Posed atop this 7–foot-high arch was a Herculean equestrian figure wearing a Crown and carrying a mace-like sceptre. He was Antoine de Bourbon, Henry's father, who had been governor of Picardy.[26] On the ledge beneath the figure appeared the Latin phrase from Virgil's twelfth book of the *Aeneid*, 'Learn, youth, virtue from me, and truth, labour, and fortune, from others.'[27] The arch referred to Henry's ties with Picardy and to the fact that he had been conceived in Abbeville in 1552 or 1553. In this manner Abbeville re-integrated Henry and the Bourbon dynasty into the town's history. Two poems inscribed on the arch declared the lasting importance that Henry would have to the townspeople.[28]

The procession continued, arrived in the market place and faced the town hall. A cloth of green satin bordered with silver fringe draped the building. On it were painted the arms of France, Navarre, Picardy, and Abbeville. Originally it had been intended to include an oval picture beneath the coats of arms portraying Henry as Hercules victorious over lions, snakes, and all manner of monsters representing Spain and the Catholic League. The artists given the job, however, failed to complete the work before Henry's arrival.[29]

Once through the market place, the parade neared the cathedral, and Henry passed beneath one more triumphal arch embellished with moulding, friezes, and Corinthian columns. Positioned on top of the arch was a nymph dressed in Roman robes, wearing a laurel wreath, and holding three keys in her right hand and a sickle in her left. She was flanked on either side by laurel wreaths. The symbolic message of this arch was the most important. The sickle referred to the richness of the earth, and the three keys represented France, Brittany, and Flanders. Abbeville fancied itself the heartland of France and the gateway to Brittany and the Spanish

[25] Denis Crouzet, 'Henry IV, King of Reason?', in *From Valois to Bourbon, Dynasty, State and Society in Early Modern France*, ed. Keith Cameron (Exeter: University of Exeter Press, 1989), 89–91.
[26] BN, MSS fr. 91, fol. 187v. Henry IV was conceived in Abbeville in late 1552 or early 1553 while his mother, Jeanne d'Albret, was following her husband, Antoine de Bourbon, the duke of Vendôme during his campaigns in Picardy.
[27] *Ibid.*, DISCE, PUER, VIRTUTEM EX ME, VERUMQUE, LABOREM, FORTUNAME EX ALLIS
[28] Ibid. The poem read:

> Ce Vêndosmis, qui a aimé
> Nos pères d'amour paternelle,
> De soi la Mémoire eternelle
> Dedans nos coeurs a enfermé.

The one in Latin read:

> Nostratum Rector, Dux hic Vindocimus ad se
> Corda pius longo traxit amore sui,
> Sed cum, Rex magnum te protulit, Enrice, Gallis,
> Gallia eum merito, totus et orbis amat.

[29] Ibid., fol. 187v.

Netherlands.[30] The significance, certainly optimistic, was that of conquest. If the first banner Henry saw linking himself and Clovis had been a pictorial re-iteration of the theme 'under this sign, conquer', here was the proof.[31] In 1594 Brittany remained under the control of the Catholic League, and although most of Picardy had recently capitulated to Henry, Spanish troops continued to threaten the area. A Latin inscription on the triumphal arch read:

> Fruitful king, the three keys are relinquished to you,
> Which unlock the three doors for you.
> The first your French, the second the
> Flemish rebels,
> And the third throws open the divided
> fields of the world.
> It is right to receive the gifts of Saint Genetrice
> Which you once united under your foreign sceptre.[32]

Saint Genetrice was the patron saint of Abbeville, and the keys were a gift from the town to the king. Abbeville was the first town in Picardy to surrender to Henry, and this action inspired the submission of other towns in the region during 1594. Thus Abbeville represented the king's key to Picardy. The *Abbevillois* exalted Henry as being destined for even greater victories over the Spanish. He was a Messianic ruler foreordained to conquer and rule.[33]

Passing beneath this arch, Henry came to the end of his journey, arriving at the portal of the cathedral of Saint Vulfran to be met by the canon Belloy. The canon asked Henry to take Moses, Abraham, Isaac, Jacob (Israel), Job, and David as his models of leadership, strength, wisdom, dedication, patience, and valour.[34] Henry then knelt before the canon, took a cross from him, and kissed it for all the town to see. He went into the church and knelt again before the altar while a *Te Deum* was

---

[30] Ibid., fols. 187v–188r.
[31] This pictorial representation was first suggested to me by Ron Love. See, Ron Love, 'Commentary on the Papers by Finley-Croswhite and Kim', in *Proceedings of the Annual Meeting of the Western Society for French History*, 17 (1990), 114.
[32] BN, MSS fr. 91, fol. 187v. The entire inscription is printed here.
> Belgica cum pandas castella, sinusque Britannos,
> Tutaque sint vallo celtica sceptra tuo;
> Cumque colant regi addicti tus maenia cives,
> Num merito nomen clavis et urbin habes
> Jure clues igitur foetus regalis alumna
> Henrico officiis chara Abbavilla tribus.
>
> Frugifera, en tibi, Rex ternas Abbavilla resignat
> Claves, quae reserant ostia trina tibi.
> Prima tuos Francois, Flandrosque secunda rebelles,
> Tertia divisos orbe recludit agros.
> Macte, igitur, divae genitricis suscipe dona
> Queis olim jungas extera sceptra tuis.
[33] For more on the semiotics of Henry's entries see Denis Crouzet, *Les guerriers de Dieu, la violence au temps des troubles de religion vers 1525–vers 1610*, (Paris: Champ Vallon, 1990), vol. 2, 569–84.
[34] Prarond, *La ligue à Abbeville*, vol. 3, 237.

sung.[35] This act held immense meaning because the community came together before God to witness Henry in his role as the most Christian king of France. For those who had doubted Henry's conversion, this was visual proof of his sincerity. In the town's holiest of places, Henry's subjects could judge the king's earnestness for themselves. Real or feigned, Henry made his conversion and his commitment to the Catholic church visible before the whole of Abbeville. In the cathedral, moreover, the king and his subjects physically embodied the idea of 'one king, one faith, one law'. This communal solidarity based on a religious ideal was a product of the reconciliation ceremony. The harmony of the metamorphic moment stressed religious orthodoxy and fidelity to the Crown.

During the entry, Henry's authority and legitimacy were confirmed by a ritualized display of both royal power and municipal devotion. His entry complete, the king retired to his lodging to eat and receive gifts from the town. There he made new friends and further cemented his alliance with the municipality. And these acts went beyond mere politeness and entertainment. Gerard Nijsten has shown that the act of eating together after a formal entry emphasized shared goals. 'Both parties', he states, 'derived power from these convivial shows of unity.'[36] The *Abbevillois* were honoured to have the king at their table. Henry and his subjects broke bread together and celebrated the dawning of a more peaceful age.[37]

ROYAL ENTRIES AND THEIR PLACE IN THE RECONCILIATION PROCESS

How typical was Abbeville's entry? It paled in comparison with those staged in major urban centres like Lyons, Rouen, and Paris. The splendour of an entry reflected the town's wealth, and Abbeville could not compete with larger cities like these. In Lyons, for example, in 1595 Henry marched beneath five triumphal arches past statues and obelisks, and at least one fountain constructed for the event.[38] We do not know how much the municipality spent on the entry into Abbeville, but it could not have equalled the entry into Rouen which cost 37,500 *livres*. The Rouen entry in 1596 had coincided with the signing of a treaty with England, the convocation of the Assembly of Notables, and the reception of the papal legate, Alexandre de Medicis. It was attended by dignitaries from France, England, the Netherlands, Spain, Italy, and the Vatican.[39]

The allegorical trappings and symbolism used in Henry's entries differed in type

---

[35] BN, MSS fr. 91, fols. 188rv.
[36] Gerard Nijsten, 'The Duke and His Towns The Power of Ceremonies, Feasts, and Public Amusement in the Duchy of Guelders (East Netherlands) in the Fourteenth and Fifteenth Centuries', in Reyerson and Hanawalt, eds., *City and Spectacle in Medieval Europe*, 245.
[37] BN, MSS fr. 91, fol. 191r. The king was given three casks of wine, three roast beefs, and three barrels of oats. The next morning he was given twelve *quennes* of Hypocras (his favourite wine). Prarond, *La Ligue à Abbeville*, vol. 3, 240, 243.
[38] Pierre Matthieu, *L'Entrée de très grand Prince Henri IIII en sa bonne ville de Lyon* (Lyons, s.d.).
[39] Félix, *Entrée à Rouen*, vii–xiv.

though seldom in meaning. Towns usually portrayed the king interchangeably as Hercules, Alexander, Caesar, Apollo, Jupiter, or Samson to represent his destiny and greatness. During the entries into Lyons and Rouen, for example, Henry saw representations of himself as the Gallic Hercules with chains extending from his mouth to representations of his subjects. This imagery endowed Henry with the power of persuasion and the ability to conquer through his words and wisdom.[40] Yet Denis Crouzet believes that the use of the Renaissance Gallic Hercules was overshadowed in Henry's entries with the image of Henry as the Hercules, victorious over violence and evil. Crouzet argues that this second Hercules reflects a psychological turning point and endowed Henry with absolute power to save his people from the horrors of the League.[41] Henry was also represented as a Messiah in entries to underscore his similarities to Christ and his willingness to forgive and suffer for his subjects.[42] The association of Henry with mythical and religious heros revealed that he was ideally suited to return stability to France. The implications, Crouzet perceives, aimed at the return of strong monarchy strengthened by the dutiful obedience of faithful subjects.[43]

Entries into royalist towns were stylistically different, emphasizing fidelity rather than reconciliation. The 1603 entry into Caen accentuated the town's long record of loyalty to the Crown, especially during the recent religious wars.[44] Henry often told his royalist towns that he preferred less elaborate affairs, and in some instances he ordered them to forego staging an entry. When he came to Rennes in May 1598, for example, he forbade the town to decorate the streets or carry a canopy for him to march under.[45] Henry seems to have felt entries were expensive, and from royalist towns he preferred gifts and promises of money instead of spectacles. In the case of Rennes he solicited 200,000 *écus* for the maintenance of his army in lieu of an entry.[46] The fact that Henry never made a royal entry into a major Protestant town such as La Rochelle, Montauban, or Nîmes demonstrates that his entries into former League towns were used to re-establish trust and stability. He already enjoyed the loyalty of his royalist towns, and he did not want to agitate his Protestant ones with the issue of his re-conversion.

In the former League towns all the royal entries staged after their capitulations

[40] For more on the Gallic Hercules see, Strong, *Art and Power*, 24–5, 71, 171; C. Vivanti, 'Henry IV, The Gallic Hercules', *Journal of the Warburg and Courtauld Institutes* 30 (1967), 176–97.
[41] Crouzet, 'Henry IV, King of Reason?', 92–3.   [42] Strong, *Art and Power*, 171.
[43] Crouzet, *Les Guerriers de Dieu*, vol. 2, 541–603; Crouzet, 'Henry IV, King of Reason?', 80, 86. Crouzet argues that during Henry's reign royalist propaganda shaped neo-Stoic philosophy into a new political ideology that resacralised the monarchy and reinforced absolutism.
[44] M. Beaullart, Sieur de Maizet, *Discours de l'entrée faicte par très haut et très puissance Prince Henri III, roi de France et de Navarre, et très illustré Princesse Marie Medicis, la royne son espouse en leur Ville de Caen au mois de septembre 1603* (Caen: Mancel Librairie-Editeur, 1842).
[45] *Archives Municipales*, Rennes, reg. 474, fol. 50.
[46] Jules Berger de Xivrey, ed., *Receuil des lettres missives de Henri IV* (Paris: Imprimerie Nationale, 1848), vol. 4, 1066, 1068. Henry arrived in Rennes on 12 May, and the Estates of Brittany opened a few days later on 16 May. Henry wanted 200,000 *écus* from the Estates, 50,000 of which was expected from Rennes.

shared a similar purpose and design: they were exciting and exposed the senses to a variety of pleasures. Townspeople covered the streets with sweet smelling herbs and flowers and decorated house fronts along processional routes with tapestries and banners.[47] Colour added to the visual delight of entries as the towns alternately displayed their own colours and those of the king. In Abbeville the coats of arms of the king and the town were used to express re-unification. In Troyes during Henry's 1594 entry, he rode into town on a horse draped in a red, white, and blue saddle blanket, the colours of the town. Seated on a horse in this way he looked every bit a conqueror, but the gesture also implied that the town had been re-united with the realm through its king, Henry IV.[48]

A more direct expression of municipal loyalty, one that particularly pleased Henry, was the gift of money. Abbeville's sparse records do not indicate whether the king was offered anything more than food and wine, but most larger towns and cities made sizeable donations to the king's purse, and one can speculate that Abbeville's elite probably made some monetary gift to the king as well. In Troyes Henry received 20,000 *écus* in the form of a loan from its wealthiest citizens.[49] The gift of the town's keys was always a part of a royal entry, but other gifts were more elaborate. In Troyes, beautiful young girls offered the king a golden heart as a symbol of the town's affectionate loyalty.[50] Youths played a significant role in most royal entries, as in Henry's royal entry into Lyons in 1596. Young men noted for their grace and dexterity, wearing grey satin and white plumes in their caps, marched before the king while their captain announced: 'Sire, these young men could have no greater favour in heaven or honour on earth, than to prostrate themselves at the feet of Your Majesty, and offer you their hearts, fortunes, and lives.'[51] The young men pledged their futures to the king in an act symbolizing youthful devotion to the Crown.

Henry took advantage of royal entries to dramatize the merits of fidelity. He rode into towns with repentant former Leaguers by his side, thus visually emphasizing his clemency. When he entered Dijon, he was flanked by marshall Biron on his right and the mayor of Dijon, René Fleutelot, on his left. Fleutelot had belonged to the League and served Guise patrons, but he renounced the League in 1595 to help orchestrate Dijon's capitulation.[52] Here was proof for all to see that the king's clemency was genuine. Henry's longtime allies were also encouraged to emulate their king and his willingness to forgive.[53]

---

[47] As an example see the case of Amiens in Père Daire, *Histoire de la Ville d'Amiens depuis son Origine jusqu'a Présent* (Amiens: Chez la Veuve de Laguette, 1757), vol. 1, 336.

[48] Albert Babeau, *Henri IV à Troyes* (Troyes: Dufour-Bouquot, 1879), 9.   [49] Ibid., 14.   [50] Ibid., 11.

[51] Godefroy, *Le Ceremonial François* 1, 941. The captain of the youth stated, 'Sire, cette ieunesse ne pouuoit esperer ny desirer plus grande faueur du Ciel, plus grand honneur en la terre, que de se voir prosternée aux pieds de vostre Maiesté, pour luy offrir son coeur, ses fortunes, et sa vie.'

[52] Girault, 'Henry IV à Dijon', 92.

[53] Michael Wolfe provides a nice contemporary observation of the unification theme in his paper. Wolfe, 'Paris is Worth a Mass', 16. Wolfe quotes one anonymous writer as saying, 'All good Leaguers became good Royalists, and all good Royalists became good Leaguers, at the festivities attending this

Henry used entries to reconfirm the offices of loyal servants and to distribute rewards to them for fidelity. He reconfirmed town charters and municipal privileges while demonstrating his authority. By granting gifts and favours, he acquired individual clients and turned former enemies into clients. Formerly rebellious towns were remade into institutional clients and the medieval alliance between the king and his towns was reforged.[54] To win the affection of townspeople Henry sometimes augmented municipal privileges or at least made reference to the fact that he intended to increase them. This is what he told the people of Meaux during his entry on 1 January 1594.[55] In Amiens in 1594, he was moved to say: 'I have forgotten the past, and intend to conserve the privileges, franchises, and liberties of the town of Amiens, and even augment them if I am able.'[56]

Henry's entries also emphasized the idea that he had been chosen by God to rule. During his entry into Limoges, a royalist town with a strong League party, a child dressed as an angel was lowered from above Henry's head by a system of pulleys to present him with the keys to the town. Henry's divine right to rule was symbolically depicted as he received the keys, it seemed, directly from Heaven.[57] When Henry rode into Lyons on 4 September 1595, the city magistrates presented him with palm leaves, symbolizing both Christ and victory: Henry crossed triumphantly into his town as the new Messianic king of Catholic France.[58]

The feature linking all Henry's entries into former League towns was their dramatic endings in churches or cathedrals. Henry had not only made peace with the towns but with the Church and God as well. These services magnified the king's new Catholic persona and were meant to discredit the rumours circulating about his reconversion. In Abbeville Henry did not actually participate in a Mass celebrating the eucharist, but he dramatized his new Catholic orthodoxy by kissing the cross. This aspect of the entry was repeated over and over again in town after town. Henry kissed his rosary and holy relics as well. The king's participation in Catholic ritual represented a visual testimonial to his rejection of Calvinist doctrine

great day of peace . . .' I thank Professor Wolfe for sharing this paper with me. Mack Holt also cites Wolfe and this quote, Holt, *The French Wars of Religion, 1562–1629* (Cambridge: Cambridge University Press, 1995), 160.
[54] For more on institutional clientage see Laurie Nussdorfer, *Civic Politics in the Rome of Urban VIII* (Princeton, New Jersey: Princeton University Press, 1992), 173.
[55] Antoine-Etienne Carro, *Histoire de Meaux* (Paris: Res Universis, 1989), 294.
[56] *Archives Municipales*, Amiens, BB53, fol. 174. Henry stated, 'J'oublie le passé et j'entends conserver les privilèges, franchises et libertés des habitants; même je les augmenterai si je puis.' Henry did not always agree to the augmentation of privileges and generally referred such matters to his council. See A. Précigou, 'Entrée d'Henri IV à Limoges en 1605 (Suite et Fin)', *Bulletin de la Société les Amis des Sciences et Arts de Rochechouart*, 6 (1896), 12.   [57] Précigou, 'Entrée d'Henri IV à Limoges,' 126.
[58] H. J. Martin, *Entrées royales et fêtes populaires à Lyon du xve au xviiie siècles* (Lyon: Bibliothèque de Lyon, 1970), 83. The association of palm leaves and victory can be found in Leviticus 23:40 when they were carried during Passover. 1 Maccabees 13:51 also mentions that when Simon Maccabeus saved Jerusalem his entry included palm branches. John 12:13 recounts Jesus's entry into Jerusalem in which palm leaves were used as an emblem of victory. Charles Patrick Roney, *Commentary on the Harmony of the Gospels* (Grand Rapids, Michigan: Eerdmans Publishing, 1948), 359. I thank Rev. C. L. Finley for this reference.

and his acceptance of the Catholic faith. Thus during his entry into Dijon on 4 June 1595, observers remarked that Henry had proclaimed in a loud, clear voice his readiness to live and die in the Catholic faith.[59]

Henry's most important entry was the one made into his capital on 22 March 1594. He entered by the Porte-Neuvre, the same gate through which Henry III had left nearly six years before. He then went straight to Notre Dame to attend Mass in a ritual act linking the king, the Crown and the church.[60] Through ritual Henry demonstrated that the legitimate king of France had returned home with God's blessing. Crowds of Parisians poured into the cathedral to worship with him, and he was joined at the Mass by nobles, city leaders, church officials, and influential elites who revealed to the public their acceptance of him as king. By taking Mass Henry dramatically reunited the body politic with the body of Christ. He stayed in Paris for one week and emphasized the sincerity of his reconversion in numerous ways. He prayed in all the city's parish churches, visited the sick in the *Hôtel Dieu*, and touched hundreds of scrofula victims. In his dealings with former enemies, he spoke Christlike of mercy rather than vengeance. His convergence with Christ was all the more relevant since his entry was orchestrated during Holy Week and ended on the greatest of all Christian feast days, Easter Sunday.[61]

Henry took many opportunities to stress the sincerity of his conversion during these reconciliation rituals. Shortly after his entry into Dijon, for example, Henry participated in a procession of the *Sainte-Hostie* on 2 July 1595. He wore a black taffeta robe setting off a magnificent collar he wore around his neck identifying him as the head of the sacred order of *Saint-Esprit*. Beneath a canopy of gold cloth supported by four *échevins*, he marched along with Dijon's lay and clerical elite who were arrayed in festive dress. They paraded through the city and then entered the *Sainte-Chapelle* to hear Mass.[62]

During this event Henry's power and authority were represented visually by his dress, the canopy, and the seat of honour he took inside the chapel. His actions were iconoclastic for many who saw him wearing the cross of the *Saint-Esprit* and eating the body of Christ in Catholic fashion. The procession consisted of former Leaguers and former royalists now reunited as faithful subjects of the king. Forgiveness and reconciliation characterized this event enacted for the whole city of Dijon.

---

[59] M. Girault, 'Henri IV à Dijon', *Compte rendu des travaux de l'Académie de Dijon* (text housed at the Bibliothèque Municipale de Dijon, s.d.), 92. *Archives Municipales*, Dijon, B232, fol. 284.
[60] Pierre de L'Estoile, *Mémoires-journaux*, ed. Paul Bonnefon (Paris: Alphonse Lemèrre, 1888), 4, 332–3.
[61] Wolfe, 'Paris is Worth a Mass', 8–9; Holt, *The French Wars of Religion*, 160.
[62] BN, MSS fr. 8351, fols. 43–4rv; Joseph Garnier, ed., *Correspondance de la Mairie de Dijon, extraite des Archives de Cette Ville* (Dijon: Rabutot, 1870), 3, 5.

CONCLUSION: HENRY IV'S ROYAL ENTRIES

Henry used ceremonial entries into former Catholic League strongholds to re-fashion his image. By taking the body and the blood of Christ, he wiped away the stain of Protestantism and initiated a new age based on orthodox Catholicism and reconciliation. The Mass and other Catholic ritual transformed him into a new Catholic Christian and represented a rite of passage in inaugurating general acceptance of his rule. Of all France's kings, Henry was the most self-created: he inherited his kingship by his blood, won it on the battlefield, forged it with his clemency, and mythologized it in ceremonial entries.

The entries engaged the selves of both Henry and his subjects as they captured the hearts of his kingdom. They exposed the transformative power that resided not only in the king's touch but also in his gaze. Henry's gaze held a potent, creative force that could change Leaguers into royalists and doubters into believers. This power was not just one-sided, for the king's subjects caught his eyes and returned the gaze, transforming in that magical moment, a heretic into a saint, a usurper into a king. Henry's gaze thus allowed his subjects to re-envision their king.[63] During his entry into Nantes in 1598, as pictured on the cover of this book, Henry gazes squarely on his subjects as they gaze back lovingly at him. Many messages were exchanged in those looks as the process of seeing and thinking came together. Such an awe inspiring communitarian experience is the way Louise Fradenburg believes power makes love. The fertility of the union, she argues, produced loyal subjects and clients of the king.[64] The entry also created moments of viewer projection as the selves of the spectators merged with the king. Replacing alienation with adoration, the king's gaze removed Catholic League infection and restored Bourbon health to the body politic.

The ceremonial entry was in many ways a ritualized cleansing of a sick realm. In the symbolic refashioning of ruler and subject, the king's authority and legitimacy were accepted and his power augmented. Henry dramatized a Catholic identity and a readiness to rule while he spoke of forgiveness. That forgiveness allowed for the recreation of subjects as new individuals united in peace and ready to honour their king. By proving his Catholic orthodoxy, Henry offered his subjects a way to free themselves from the taint of treason and symbolically baptized them through his gaze in sovereign love and mercy.[65]

---

[63] John Orr, *Cinema and Modernity* (Cambridge: Polity Press, 1993), 59–84; I thank Robert Butler for discussing with me his ideas on viewer projection.

[64] Fradenburg, *City, Marriage, Tournament*, 74. Fradenburg uses the phrase 'power makes love' to explain the broad dynamics of communitarian rituals in general in her discussion of ceremony and kingship. She argues that communitarian rituals refashion subjects to identify with and desire authority. '[C]ommunitarian experience can do essential work for sovereign love; it is a way of securing the desire for hierarchy.'

[65] Ibid., 74–5, 243, 264. The paragraph is based on Fradenburg. She states 'In enacting himself, then, the sovereign uses the selves of other people as well as his own, and over those other selves, as well as his own, he tries to exert a power of change' (p. xi). Tony Wilson, *Watching Television: Hermeneutics,*

When the ceremonial entry ended, normal time resumed. With signed treaties, sworn oaths, and formal ceremonies completed, the king and his towns settled down into a working relationship. Both sides had seen what they had wanted to see; a Catholic king, a repentant town. The entry had remade the king and his subjects and prepared them to live in a newly reconstructed world. The wars were ending, the country was becoming re-united. Many townspeople now held memories of a king they felt they personally knew. It appeared that the Catholic League was dead. Indeed, Henry wrote to the governor of Paris, François d'O, just after his royal entry into Amiens: 'You have never seen a people so affectionate [towards me] or so hateful of the League.'[66] Royal entries marked a major event in the lives of townspeople that would be recalled and discussed in the years to come. The events dispelled conflict and displayed magnanimously the theme of reconciliation by demonstrating Henry's clemency. The entries did not satisfy everyone, but they helped to convince a majority of former Leaguers of the Bourbon king's legitimacy. They represent one way Henry IV increased his authority by ritually forging a unified realm of subjects devoted to his rule. The more pragmatic and tangible ways that Henry extended his authority over urban France are discussed in the next two chapters.[67]

Reception and Popular Culture (Cambridge: Polity Press, 1993), 51–2; Ron Burnett, *Cultures of Vision, Images, Media & the Imaginary* (Bloomington: Indiana University Press, 1995), 8–15.

[66] Berger de Xivrey, *Recueil des Lettres Missives*, vol. 4, 208. Henry wrote, 'Vous n'avés jamais veu peuple si affectionné, et detestant si fort la Ligue que cestuy-cy.'

[67] I do not imply that all participants in rituals understood or accepted all messages used in entries. Nor do I believe that entries converted all doubters into believers or were the main reason behind Henry's success in gaining acceptance to his rule. I have discussed only my interpretation of the meaning and form of Henry's entries and suggest that they were one of many ways he used to re-establish peace in the realm and his legitimacy on the throne. Orlando Patterson states, 'Mythic and ritual processes by nature are multivocal, ambiguous, diffuse, and sometimes downright incomprehensible. Within a given cultural domain, however, a dominant symbol – a major mythic theme, a key ritual act – stands out as pivotal. By its emergence it makes possible an internal interpretation of the symbolic process on both the intellectual and the social level.' Orlando Patterson, *Slavery and Social Death A Comparative Study* (Cambridge, Massachusetts: Harvard University Press, 1982), 37.

4

Henry IV and municipal franchises in Catholic League towns

To pacify his realm by ensuring that individuals loyal to the Crown held municipal offices, Henry IV interfered in municipal elections. From 1594 to 1598 many towns remained divided between royalists and Leaguers, and the king relied on electoral intervention to help prevent social unrest. Not surprisingly, Henry most often influenced the outcome of elections in former League towns, and in a few cases he reduced the size of their municipal governments. During the first half of the twentieth century, historians interpreted these actions as a policy intended to destroy municipal privileges. Henry IV was portrayed as the founder of absolutism with a municipal policy meant to centralize royal government and weaken municipalities. But this interpretation is misleading because it exaggerates Henry's efforts by failing to consider the number of towns he left alone and by associating electoral intervention with absolutism. In fact, the king's actions were more probably meant to secure stability after the long years of civil war.

Confirming municipal privileges demonstrated Henry's benevolence and legitimated his new kingship. In making peace with the towns, he restored municipal privileges with fatherly kindness. On a visit to Amiens in 1594, he told the townspeople that no king who truly loved his subjects would ruin them.[1] He knew the *Amiénois* associated privileges with their well-being: 'Your ruin is my ruin', he declared.[2] Henry understood that dismantling municipal governments or tampering with their charters threatened the fragile support of former Catholic League towns. Thus in 1594 Henry gave little thought to changing municipal governments because he urgently wanted the towns to accept his kingship.

As League towns were subdued, however, Henry discovered that he needed men loyal to him sitting on town councils. He also confronted the fact that townspeople jealously guarded their right to free elections and often interpreted royal intervention as a general attack on municipal liberties, especially since the Crown had a long history of electoral intervention. Examples of Henry IV's interventions in municipal politics will be explored below in an attempt to evaluate his motives. It will be shown that the king actually intervened in municipal affairs infrequently. When he

---

[1] *Archives Municipales*, Amiens (hereafter cited as AMA), BB54, fol. 24.   [2] Ibid.

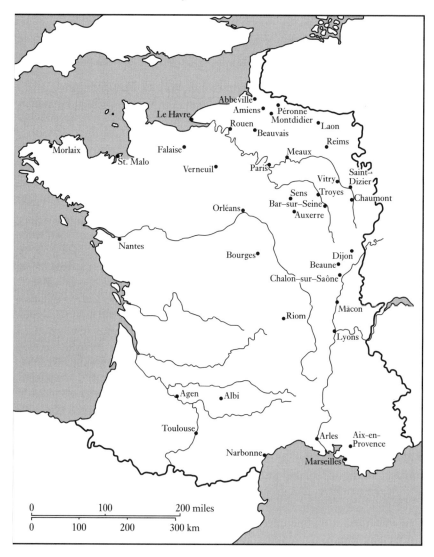

Map 1   Catholic League towns mentioned in the text

did so it was for a good reason, usually an attempt to settle a specific problem or to place his client(s) in municipal office(s). Only former League towns will be considered here because Henry focused most of his attention on them.

Within two years of pacifying Amiens, Henry IV intervened in municipal elections and broke a promise in the capitulation treaty to respect municipal franchises. Amiens received its copy of the published accord made between it and the king in September 1594, and by the terms of the accord, Henry placed the government of the town in the hands of the mayor and *échevins*. He stated that he would not change, alter, or revise any of Amiens's established privileges.[3] A subtle indication that this might not be the case, however, occurred one month later during the October elections of 1594. Just before the event, he wrote to the town councillors and admonished them 'to elect magistrates affectionate to my service.'[4] The *Amiénois* responded to the king's request with a letter stating, 'All of the magistrates are His Majesty's very affectionate servants.'[5] The statement was true because most of Amiens's notorious Leaguers had been banished after the city's capitulation. A list of the newly elected municipal officials was enclosed in the letter for the king's perusal.

Elections the following year proceeded without any unusual occurrences, but in 1596 Henry intervened directly. On 26 October, a few days before annual elections were to take place on the feast of Saint Simon and Saint Jude, Vincent Le Roy, lieutenant general in the *bailliage* of Amiens, appeared before the town council and read letters from the king forbidding the election of new *échevins*. The king ordered that the twenty-four incumbents retain their posts another year. As for the mayor, the king allowed the magistrates their choice of either continuing him in office or replacing him for the coming term.[6]

Surprised by Henry's orders, the town did not know how to react. At first, town leaders believed the incumbent *échevins* had solicited letters of continuation from the king. But under oath they swore this was not the case and offered to relinquish their offices if the king agreed. Two days later on the day that the elections were usually held, news of the king's order reached the inhabitants. A mob gathered

---

[3] Augustin Thierry, *Recueil des monuments inédits de l'histoire du Tiers-Etat*, vol. 3 *Les Pièces relative à l'histoire municipale de la ville d'Amiens dépuis le XVIIe siècles jusqu'en 1789* (Paris: Firmin Didot Frères, 1856), 1059–68.

[4] AMA, BB54, fol. 3. The document states that it is necessary 'd'elisre des magistras affectionnez à mon service'.   [5] Ibid. The magistrates wrote, 'tous Messieurs sont ses très affectionnez serviteurs'.

[6] Ibid., fol.45v; *Archives Départementales de la Somme* (hereafter cited as ADS), 1B13, fol. 183. At first the king ordered the continuation of the *échevinage* only until the end of 1596. On December 20, 1596, however, the king sent *lettres patentes* to Amiens saying that he wished the group to remain in office until the normal elections scheduled for October 1597. ADS 1B14, fol. 9v.

outside the *Hôtel de Ville* and shouted that the elections should take place as scheduled.[7] Angry townspeople blamed lieutenant general Le Roy for the delay, denouncing him verbally and on placards. He placed guards at the entrance to the town hall and ordered the election of a new mayor but not of the *échevins* until he had further word from the king. Amiens's *échevins* nominated three candidates for the office of mayor and waited while those with suffrage rights cast their ballots. Pierre Famechon won the mayor's seat, and when negotiations with the king for a new election of the *échevinage* broke down, the *échevins* of 1595 were formally continued for another term on 24 November 1596. The town elected four new *échevins* to replace four who had died during the past year, but maintained obediently the other twenty by the king's decree.[8]

Henry's intervention had occurred sooner in Nantes than in Amiens. Nantes was the last League stronghold to settle with Henry IV, capitulating in February 1598. Two months later during a visit to the city, the king informed the municipal government that he intended to alter the normal election procedures and change the date of the elections from 28 December to 1 May. Beginning immediately, he commanded the town to send him a list of three candidates for the office of mayor and a list of eighteen candidates for the six *échevin* slots to be filled. From these names he would appoint the new mayor and two of the six *échevins*.[9] A few days later on 1 May Henry chose Charles de Harouys, sieur de Lépinay, president in the *présidial* court, as the new mayor of Nantes. Harouys took the oath of office before the king and seemed to enjoy the support of the populace.[10]

The next year in preparation for a new election Henry sent a letter to Nantes on 22 April informing the magistrates that they should prepare a list of possible mayoral candidates. Henry also told the town leaders that he wished to see the name of Gabriel Hux, sieur de la Bouchetière on the list. He wrote:

We would find it very agreeable that you name the sieur de Bouchetière, for we have proof of his commitment to establish our affairs, and also of his willingness to maintain our city and subjects in union, friendship, peace, and tranquility.[11]

---

[7] Thierry, *Recueil des Monuments Inédits*, vol. 3, 1073–82.

[8] AMA, BB55, fol. 74v. The municipal government of Amiens consisted of one mayor and twenty-four *échevins*. Every year on 28 October, twelve *échevins* were also elected. These were known as the *échevins du jour*. The next day these twelve selected twelve others to serve in the municipal government known as the *échevins de lendemain*. The former outranked the latter.

[9] Archives de Bretagne, *Recueil d'Actes de Chroniques et de Documents Historiques ou inédites publié par la Société des Bibliophiles Bretons 1: Privilèges de la Ville de Nantes*, ed. Stéphan de la Nicollière-Teijeiro (Nantes: Société des Bibliophiles Breton et de L'Histoire de Bretagne, 1883), 15.

[10] Alexandre Perthuis and Stéphan de la Nicollière-Teijeiro, *Le Livre d'Oré de L'Hôtel de Ville de Nantes avec les Armoires et les Jetons des Maires* (Nantes: Jules Brinsard, 1873), vol. 1, 192.

[11] Cited in ibid., 195. 'Entre ceulx-là, nous aurons fort agréable que le sieur de Bouchetière nous soit par vous nommé, pour avoir beaucoup de bonnes preuves et assurances de sa fidellité au bien et establissement de nos affaires, et non moins d'affection à la manutention de notre dite ville et subjectz d'icelle en union, amityé, repos et tranquillité.'

Henry closed the letter by stating, 'We are assured you will conform, knowing it is our pleasure.'[12]

Nantes responded unfavourably to the king's command. Grudgingly, Bouchetière's name was put on the candidate list, but during the election he failed to receive a single vote.[13] Faced with a dilemma, the *Nantais* magistrates dispatched a deputy to the court to plead with the king, complaining that his decision left the municipality with 'no liberty'. The deputy offered the king a list of three candidates approved for nomination by the city's electors, and suggested continuing Harouys in office as a compromise.[14]

Nantes's insubordination angered Henry, who immediately responded with a threatening letter.

I find it very strange that in prejudice to what I have written concerning the election of my very faithful servant the sieur de la Bouchetière as mayor in the city of Nantes for the present year, that some among you are willing to oppose me and name others whom I do not want as mayor. I am writing this letter to you in my own hand so that the sieur de la Bouchetière will be elected. He has no fault, and I will be obeyed. If not, I will find ways to make myself obeyed.[15]

These were strong words coming from the king, and they did not go unheeded. Nantes's leaders conceded, and Henry officially named Bouchetière mayor of Nantes by letters patent on 13 May 1599. The next year the city government sent deputies to court to try and persuade the king to allow Nantes to return to the pre-1598 electoral format. Henry denied the request.[16]

Occurring in the wake of League capitulations, Henry's motivation seems obvious. Resurgence of the 'Holy Union' was a valid concern during the 1590s, and the king could not risk free elections returning committed Leaguers to municipal governments in important cities. To deny Leaguers access to local offices, he

---

[12] Ibid., 'A quoy nous assurons que vous conformerez sachant que tel est notre plaisir.'

[13] Nantes had a much larger electorate than most cities and towns. All male heads of households were allowed to cast their votes in elections for the city mayor. Nantes had a population of around 25,000 in 1600 so that several thousand people generally participated in *Nantais* elections. Thus, the fact that Bouchetière received no votes is quite significant. Guy Saupin, 'Les Elections Municipales à Nantes Sous l'Ancien Régime', *Centre Généalogique de l'Ouest*, 35 (1983), 89.

[14] L'Abbé Travers, *Histoire Civile, Politique et Religieuse de la Ville du Comté de Nantes* (Nantes: Forest Imprimeur-Libraire, 1841), vol. 3, 125.

[15] Quoted in, Perthuis and Nicollière-Teijeiro, *Le Livre D'Oré*, vol. 1, 196. 'Je trouve fort estrange de ce que, au préjudice de ce que je vous ay cy-devant escript pour eslire marie de ma ville de Nantes, pour la présente année, le sieur de la Bouchetière, lequel j'ay tousiours recogneu pour mon très-fidelle serviteur, il y en ait eu quelques-uns d'entre vous si hardiz de sy opposer, et d'en nommer d'aultres que je ne le veulx qui le soient cette année. C'est pourquoy je vous fais ce mot de ma main, par lequel vous saurez que ma volonté étant telle, que le sieur de la Bouchetière soit eslu et nommé, qu'il ny ait auculne faute, et que je sois obey en cela, autrement j'aurais occasion de rechercher les moyens de me faire obeyr.'

[16] Travers, *Histoire de Nantes*, 126. The election of Bouchetière was a very entangled and complicated event. There were more reasons involved behind the dispute than just ex-Leaguer versus ex-royalist. Some problems could have been related to his financial dealings, but this is uncertain.

manipulated elections to his own advantage. In this way he ensured the continuation of his reign and of peace.

Henry's fears about a revival of the League were justified. The municipal deliberations of many of the major League towns contain numerous references to League activity and anti-royalist demonstrations for several years after peace was restored. In Amiens, for example, between 1594 and 1597, the town government discovered several plots to re-establish the League; there was much negative sentiment towards the Bourbon king. Late in 1594, for example, the *Amiénois* magistrates ordered the locks changed on all the city gates to prevent expelled Leaguers from returning and stirring up trouble. Conspiracies were discovered throughout 1595, and rumours of League resurgence in 1596 caused Henry to ask the magistrates for a list of all persons residing in the city.[17] Early the next year several magistrates were incriminated in a plot, and the municipal government was forced to send deputies to court to deny rumours that they planned to ally with Spain against the French Crown. Amiens fell to the Spanish two months later.[18]

Considering Henry's position in the early years of his reign, his motives with regard to elections are clear. In Amiens and Nantes, Henry kept or placed men in municipal office whom he knew he could trust. In Amiens, Henry's decision was based on the emergency the city faced in 1596. Amiens was a strategically important frontier city, and in 1595–6 Henry was stockpiling munitions there as part of his war effort against Spain.[19] In addition, an outburst of bubonic plague disrupted the city in the autumn of 1595, and by the next autumn it was raging out of control. Over two-thousand people died in a six week period.[20]

Even more serious for Henry was the fact that the plague caused those who could to abandon Amiens in an effort to escape the disease. Consequently, over half the *échevinage* fled the city in 1596, and those remaining could not find sufficient men to fill the urban militia. Reports circulated that a faction within the city planned to turn Picardy's capital over to Spain.[21] Henry had already lost Doullens to the Spanish in 1595. Given this, the king felt it best to continue the *échevins* in their offices rather than risk a new election returning disloyal or incompetent men to

---

[17] AMA, FF54, fols. 7, 10, 11, 62; BB55, fols. 5, 10v. On 10 November 1594 the town government voted to change all locks on all city gates. On 22 November 1594 all town inhabitants were prohibited from leaving Amiens for three months without permission from the municipal government. The municipality decided on 29 April 1595 that anyone caught blaspheming the king would be punished. A conspiracy against the king was discovered on 24 November 1594 at the abbey of Saint John, and another conspiracy was exposed on 24 April 1596.

[18] AMA, BB55, fols. 94rv. Abbeville was also connected with this conspiracy to ally with Spain. See the letter Henry wrote to Abbeville after receiving deputies from the town denying their participation in the plot. Jules Berger de Xivrey, *Recueil des Lettres Missives de Henri IV* (Paris: Imprimerie Nationale, 1848), vol. 4, 681–82.

[19] Roger Apache, 'Images du siège d'Amiens de 1597 ou l'emphémère célébrité du malheur', *Terre Picardie*, 9 (1985), 32–40.

[20] AMA, AA17, fol. 168; BB55, fols. 24, 57v. 76; Baron A. Calonne, *Histoire de la Ville d'Amiens* (Amiens: Piteux Frères, 1900), vol. 2, 146–8. [21] AMA, BB55, fols. 42rv, 47rv, 49rv, 57v.

power. Since incumbent *échevins* participated in the co-optation of new *échevins* in the election process, any election would have been difficult to hold because of the number of absent magistrates. If an election had been held, the normal procedure could not have been followed. The king explained his actions by saying that because 'the principal families of our town . . . are absent and do not dare return, the election cannot take place with the number of voices, suffrages, and with the degree of solemnity that is custom.'[22] Thus, Henry's ruling to continue the *échevinage* of 1595 for another year was not an extreme measure attacking Amiens's privileges but rather a means of ensuring that standard procedures would be followed when elections did take place. Instead of breaking with custom, Henry enforced it. Since the elections of 1595 had produced a largely pro-royalist *échevinage*, Henry was confident enough in their ability to maintain order in the very difficult 1596–7 term. He also allowed the *Amiénois* to elect a new mayor, offering further proof that his intervention was not designed as an attack on privileges.

In Nantes, as elsewhere, Henry's motives stemmed from the need to place loyal clients in municipal office. The duke and duchess of Mercoeur had a large Catholic League clientele in Brittany, and Henry could not risk a resurgence of League sentiment. Thus he changed the election procedure in 1598 to gain more control over the process, and even changed the date of the elections so that they could be held while he was in Nantes. He established a compromise arrangement that he already enjoyed with other cities such as Paris in which he appointed to office one of three candidates suggested by the town. Generally, in these situations, Henry chose the man who had won the most votes in a normal election. The atmosphere in Nantes, however, was of enough concern that Henry felt he had to place a royalist client in the mayor's seat. The mayor in Nantes commanded the urban militia and held the title *colonel de la milice bourgeois*. This was a position of importance and endowed the mayor with patronage to dispense.[23] Since the militia policed the city, it was vital for Henry to have a trusted man in this office. Appointing the mayor in Nantes was Henry's way of destroying League authority not municipal privileges.

In 1598 Henry chose Charles de Harouys as the mayor of Nantes, a man he knew well. Harouys was an enemy of the duchess of Mercoeur. The duchess had had him removed from the mayor's office in 1589, and thrown into prison when the League

---

[22] ADS, 1B13, fol. 183. Henry wrote, 'le temps du renouvellement des magistratz de nostredicte ville est proche, et ne voions parmy les desorders que le guerre continuelle de la frontiere et la contagion quy ne cesse en icelle, que commodément l'on puisse à present proceder à nouvelle eslection de magistratz, les principalles famille de notredicte ville, la pluspart de noz officiers et en general la plus apparente et notable partie des habitans d'icelle ville s'estans absentez et n'osans encore y retourner, ne permettent que ladicte eslection se face avecq les voix et suffrages et telle solempnité que l'on a accoustumé . . . ordonnant en conséqence que les échevins seront continués.' *Inventaire Sommaire des Archives Départementales Antérieures à 1790*, ed. Georges Durand (Amiens: Imprimerie du Progrés de la Somme, 1920), 160.

[23] Guy Saupin, 'La vie municipale à Nantes sous l'Ancien Régime, 1565–1789', (Thèse 3ème cycle, Université de Nantes, 1981), vol. 1, 22.

took power because of his royalist politics.[24] When Henry put Harouys in office, he superbly returned urban authority to the man who had held it before the League took over. The king's dispute with Nantes over the election of Bouchetière was even more pointedly an attempt to keep his client in office. Henry knew Bouchetière personally, and the man enjoyed a royal pension because of his loyalty during the War of the League. He had spent some time during the League in Rennes, and had met with the king in 1590 to discuss ways of maintaining royal authority in Britanny. Henry obviously had confidence in Bouchetière and insisted on his election in 1599. Bouchetière remained mayor of Nantes until 1601.[25]

Henry liked to appoint the leading official in key cities. He learned from his experiences with the capital city of Paris in which he participated in many municipal elections. Henry normally selected the highest ranking magisterial official in the Parisian *échevinage* known as the *prévôt des marchands*. Even so, Robert Descimon argues that Henry's relationship with the capital city was archaic and predictable. Descimon shows that when Henry selected a *prévôt* he gave royal approval to an election that had already taken place. Henry normally appointed the man who had earned the most votes in the regular election. He acknowledged candidates who had been elected by the municipality.[26] For Descimon this protocol represents a compromise worked out between the Crown and the capital city. Henry tried to enforce the same compromise in Nantes.

Paris was not indifferent to Henry's compromise. As in the case of all other municipalities, the city leaders resented royal intervention. In August 1596, Henry prohibited a new election in the capital for the office of *prévôt des marchands* and two of the four offices of the *échevinage*. He stipulated that he wanted the incumbent, Martin Langlois, to continue as *prévôt* for another year. An election was held and Langlois won by the slight majority of thirty-one votes to twenty-eight.[27] He was then confirmed in the office by Henry. Langlois's election reflected the voice of the people and the will of the king.[28] The election had aroused conflict, however, and

[24] The dispute between Harouys and the duchess de Mercoeur occurred in the spring of 1589. Philippe-Emmanuel de Lorraine, the duke of Mercoeur, wanted to station his troops in the city of Nantes and impose a tax on the city to pay for their maintenance. The magistrates discussed taxing those individuals absent from Nantes as a way of raising the money. But Harouys was opposed and acted as mayor for the last time in 1589 on 4 April. The duchess ordered his arrest three days later, and the poor man spent two years in a cell in the Château de Nantes before paying a ransom of 3000 *écus* to obtain his release in 1591. *Archives Municipales*, Nantes, BB21, fols. 212–27. I thank Gayle Brunelle for this citation.

[25] Bouchetière was *receveur des fouages de l'evêché de Saint-Malo* and *trésorier des Etats de Bretagne*. Perthuis and Nicollière-Teijeiro, *Le Livre Doré*, vol. 1, 197.

[26] Robert Desçimon, 'L'Echevinage Parisien sous Henri IV (1594–1610) Autonomie urbaine, conflits politiques et exclusives sociales', in *La Ville, La Bourgeoisie et La Genèse de L'Etat Moderne (XIIe-XVIIIe Siècles)* (Paris: Editions du C.N.R.S., 1988), 150.

[27] Ibid., 129; David Buisseret, *Henry IV* (London: George Allen and Unwin, 1984). 165. Henry intervened in elections in Paris in 1596, 1598, 1600, 1602, and 1604.

[28] Alexandre Tuetey, ed. *Registres des Délibérations du Bureau de la Ville de Paris*, vol. 11 *1594–1598* (Paris: Imprimerie Nationale, 1902), 302.

was held in direct defiance of the king's original order forbidding an electoral assembly. Of the fifty-nine persons participating in the election, twenty-eight voted against the Crown, demonstrating that Henry's municipal orders did not meet with general approval. The Parisian magistrates had voiced serious objections to what they perceived as an attack on their privileges.[29] The most important aspect of Henry's intervention in Paris is that he selected Martin Langlois as *prévôt des marchands*. Henry knew Langlois well. The *échevin* had opened the Porte-Saint-Denis to him in 1594 during the city's capitulation, and afterwards he negotiated the submission of other towns to the king, including Montdidier in Picardy.[30]

It is doubtful Henry IV ever envisaged a post-League plan to destroy municipal privileges, but he did need to consolidate his authority and increase his legitimacy. The best way to do this was to maintain his clients in office. In 1594, the king received a letter offering advice on how to defeat the League in Lyons. The anonymous author of this piece suggested, 'Re-establish the king's servants in their charges and replace Leaguers with persons loyal to the service of the king.'[31] The author warned, 'Oversee carefully the creation of *échevins* because on them depend the peace and security of the town . . .'[32] These words would have been sound advice in any of the former Catholic League towns. In the 1590s the most important quality Henry needed in his municipal magistrates was loyalty to him.

ELECTORAL SCANDAL AND CROWN INTERVENTION

Municipal officials were quick to associate royal inteference in town politics with an attack on their privileges, so when the king intervened, he usually offered some sort of explanation for his actions. The rationale he frequently gave was that normal orderly procedures had been subverted by scandals and corruption which had led to the election of the wrong kind of 'ill-willed' officials who allowed 'disorder, division, and dissension' to ruin his towns.[33] Sixteenth-century municipal history indicates that factional disputes and vote-buying were common enough occurrences during elections, and they were usually accompanied by elaborate bouts of

---

[29] Ibid., 294–303.

[30] Buisseret, *Henry IV*, 51; V. de Beauvillé, *Histoire de Montdidier* (Amiens: Jaunet, 1859), 260.

[31] BN, MSS fr. 16661, fol. 422. The document reads, 'Restablir les serviteurs du Roy en leurs charges et au lieu des Ligueurs qui seront demis, creer aux charges personnes assidez au service du Roy. Ce sera un moyen pour entretenir et conserver se peuple en l'obeissance du Roy.'

[32] Ibid., fol. 424. The writer continues, 'Prendre garde à la Creation des Eschevins parce que d'eux depend le repos et seurté de la ville . . .'

[33] This statement reflects a letter Henry sent from Fontainebleau on 23 May 1599 explaining his decision to choose henceforth the mayors and *échevins* in Nantes from lists submitted to him by the municipal government. Referring to municipal personnel he wrote, ' . . . leur négligence, mauvaise volonté ou autres deffaultz y ont autrefois laissé glisser le désordre, et la division et dissension tant ruineuse et perilleuse qui s'y est venu ces derniers troubles.' Remarking on elections he continued, ' . . . que les choses ne s'y sont passées avec l'ordre que nous eussions bien désiré.' Quoted in *Archives de Bretagne Recueil d'Actes de Chroniques et de Documents Historiques ou inédites publié par la Société des Bibliophiles Bretons et de L'histoire de Bretagne* (Nantes: Société des Bibliophiles Breton, 1883), 15.

drinking and revelry which sometimes led to violence. Influential families vied with rivals for control of municipal governments, and conflicts characterized elections during and after the religious wars. Every election had the potential for causing social unrest.[34] In Bourges former Leaguers managed to retain their hold on municipal office during the elections of 1594, but were deposed in the next year's elections. Fierce public protest and civil strife accompanied both events.[35]

Henry stressed that his interventions were meant to decrease election strife by increasing royal participation in urban affairs. The king's actions suggest that he was distressed by the kinds of violence elections triggered. He often criticized towns for electoral conflict and repeatedly warned them to take measures to prevent violence.[36] In 1609 he summoned to court two deputies from the town of Poitiers to give an accounting of elections in their town. The deputies told the king about bribes of food, wine, and money used to buy votes. They disclosed that rival candidates accompanied by friends and family solicited votes from door to door. When one group encountered the other in the streets, fighting erupted. The deputies explained to the king that if bribery did not sway elections, tampering with the returns did. The number of votes in magisterial elections, they stated, rarely matched the number of voters.[37]

Electoral corruption was a recurring problem all over France during the early modern period. Monitoring the municipal government in Lyons, for example, the sieur d'Escoussieu wrote to his father, the chancellor Bellièvre, and questioned the wisdom of holding an election in 1605.

I find myself frustrated over the election three weeks from now for the *prévôt des marchands* and two *échevins* who will serve the next two years. Scandals are so widespread and extraordinary that I do not think it would be good for the king or the public to proceed with this kind of election . . .'[38]

During the same period in Dijon, scandals were equally troublesome, and to promote order the Parlement de Dijon tried to supervise the events. In 1605 the parlement changed the traditional inauguration oath so that anyone elected to municipal office had to swear that he had not won his post by dishonest means.[39]

[34] André Chédevilles, Jacques Le Goff, Emmanuel Le Roy Ladurie, eds., *Histoire de la France Urbaine 3: La Ville Classique de la Renaissance aux Révolutions* (Paris: Seuil, 1981), 167, 177–8.
[35] Louis Raynal, *Histoire du Berry depuis les Temps les plus anciens jusqu'en 1789* (Bourges: Devermeil, 1847), vol. 4, 214–15; M. Baudouin-Lalondre, *Le Maréchal Claude de la Chastre* (Bourges: M. Sire, 1895), 188.   [36] Baudouin-Lalondre, *Le Maréchal*, 330.
[37] Henri Ouvré, *Essai sur l'histoire de Poitiers depuis la fin de la Ligue jusqu'a la prise de La Rochelle* (Poitiers: A. Dupré, 1856), 29–30. Henry's transformation of the municipal government in Poitiers is discussed in chapter 7.
[38] BN, MSS fr. 15900, vol. 2, fol. 667. M. d'Escoussieu wrote 'Jeme trouve fort empesché pour la prochaine eslection qui se doibt faire dans trois sepmaines du prevost des marchands et de deux eschevins qui doibvent servir les deux annees suivants parce que les brigues sont si grandes et se fort si extraordinaires que Jene scaurois croire que se soit pour zele du service du Roy et bien publicq, qu'on y procede de ceste sorte . . .'
[39] François Bourçier, 'Le régime municipal à Dijon sous Henri IV', *Revue d'Histoire Moderne*, 8 (1935), 115–16.

Election days thus involved town-dwellers in more complicated behaviour than town charters would suggest.[40] How widespread election scandals were in France is hard to determine because the losers often went to the king with complaints of corruption. Factional fighting was a normal part of the electoral process. Henry regarded electoral abuses as dangerous to the public good and attempted to combat the problem in formal pronouncements. After learning about election disputes in Troyes in 1600 he announced:

[W]e expressly move, order, and state, that before the declaration and nomination of the mayor . . . you will send us the name of three councilors who have received the greatest number of votes . . . and we will give the charge of Mayor to the one we judge to be the most worthy and capable.'[41]

Henry ordered the townspeople to 'cease their wrong doing' and to elect officials capable of 'faithfully' performing the tasks associated with their offices.[42] When the elections took place, the king selected Jehan d'Aultry from a list of three to serve as Troyes's new mayor. Henry knew d'Aultry personally as a man who had already proven his loyalty to him. D'Aultry had been mayor of Troyes in the crucial year of 1594, and had helped arrange that city's capitulation to the king.

To supervise municipal elections, Henry IV relied on royal officials, commissioners, and provincial governors. Governors were attached to key towns in a province by patron–client relationships and frequently acted as mediators between the king and these towns. Towns showered their governors with gifts in hopes of persuading them to support their cause with the king. In Bourges, for example, in 1609 the annual elections produced chaos and turmoil, and Henry IV sent the governor of Berry, Claude de la Châtre, to rectify the situation. 'Tell them that I find these scandals damaging, and order them to never allow them again in the future', Henry wrote.[43] The governor decided to forego holding a new election, and continued the incumbent magistrates in their posts for another year.[44]

---

[40] Mack P. Holt, 'Popular Political Culture and Mayoral Elections in Sixteenth-Century Dijon', in *Society and Institutions in Early Modern France*, ed. Mack P. Holt (Athens: University of Georgia Press, 1991), 98–116. Holt argues that 'elections had a dynamic all their own' (p. 99).

[41] Berger de Xivrey, *Recueil des lettres missives*, vol. 8, 767. See editor's comment in n. 2, page 767. 'A quoy desormais nous sommes bien resoluz de copper cours de nous reserver, ainsi qu'en la pluspart des autres bonnes villes de nostre royaulme la cognoissance et establissement de ceux qui auront esté choisiz pour estre admis esdictes charges. Pour cest effect et plusieurs autres importantes considérations à ce nous mouvons vous mandons ordonnons & enjoignons tres expressement qu avant que passer plus avant à la declaration et nomination du maire qui doibt estre renouvelle au jour de St Barnabé prochain vous nous envoyez les noms de troys conseillers qui auront eu le plus de voix pour estre faictz maire. Affin que selon quil s'est observé du vivant du feu Roy decedé nostre très cher sieur et frere que Dieu absolve des troys nous en choisissions lun et luy donnions la charge de maire selon que nous l'en jugerons et cognoistrons plus digne et capable.'

[42] Jacques Paton, *Le Corps de Ville de Troyes (1470–1790)* (Troyes: Paton Imprimeur-Editeur, 1939), 115.

[43] Raynal, *Histoire du Berry*, vol. 4, 215. Henry wrote, 'Dites-leur que je ne trouve pas bon ces monopoles, et qu'ils donnent order que cela n'arrive à l'advenir.'

[44] Ibid.

Henry IV handled Marseilles in much the same way as Troyes. Marseilles ended the Wars of Religion heavily in debt. The debt reached 1,554,000 *livres* in 1598, but the largest part of this sum, or 972,000 *livres* had been incurred between 1589 and 1596 while the League dominated the city. After Marseilles capitulated, the city government developed a plan to liquidate the debt. Not everyone agreed with the decision, however, and until well into the reign of Louis XIII two factions struggled for control of the municipal government. One group wanted to amortized the debt as rapidly as possible while the other group denied the legality of repaying debts assumed during the League.[45]

To help administer Marseilles, Henry in 1596 named a special commissioner to the city, Guillaume du Vair, who was president of the Parlement of Provence and a faithful servant of the king.[46] Du Vair regularly wrote to Henry and kept him informed about political events in a provincial city so far from Paris. He steadfastly gave the king advice and warned him 'to police the town council and establish order there'.[47] He believed that if Henry could suppress election scandals he would 'target the source of quarrels that bring division and trouble the repose of the town.'[48] Following Du Vair's counsel, Henry intervened in Marseilles's affairs often. In 1604 he prohibited new elections and continued the past year's incumbents in office. Following the king's orders in 1605, the provincial governor, the duke of Guise, appointed the municipal council. In 1607, Henry postponed the elections altogether, and when the city held them, he vetoed their results. He eventually named the municipal officials of 1607 himself. He also reserved the right to designate the city's magistrates through 1611.[49]

Conflict over urban authority caused municipal elections to become violent, and the king was called in to mediate. In Dijon Henry intervened to settle a dispute between the Parlement of Dijon and the municipal government. This situation was not unusual. During the sixteenth century provincial parlements were expanding

[45] René Pillorget, 'Luttes de factions et intérèts économiques à Marseille de 1598 à 1618', *Annales Economies Sociétés Civilisations* 27 (1972), 705–30; René Pillorget, *Les Mouvements insurrectionnels de Provence entre 1596 et 1715* (Paris: A Pedone, 1975). For more on the liquidation of municipal debt during Henry's reign, see below, chapter 7.
[46] René Radouant, *Guillaume du Vair L'Homme et L'Orateur* (Paris: Société Français d'Imprimerie et de Librairie, 1907). Wolfgang Kaiser, *Marseille au Temps des Troubles, Morphologie sociale et luttes de factions 1559–1596*, trans. Florence Chaix (Paris: Ecoles des Hautes Etudes en Sciences Sociales, 1992), 348. In 1603 Henry IV gave Du Vair the *évêché de Marseille* as a reward for his loyalty.
[47] BN, MSS fr. 16656, fol. 18. There are numerous letters throughout BN, MSS fr. 23195–8 concerning election scandals and social unrest in Marseilles. Du Vair told the king to 'policier la maison de ville et y establire l'ordre porté par les reiglements.'
[48] BN, MSS fr. 16656, fol. 18v. Du Vair wrote, 'Si on gaigne ce point on tar(blank space)t la source des querelles qui peuvent porter de la division et troubler le repos de ceste ville.'
[49] Pillorget, 'Luttes de factions', 705–30; Gustave Fagniez, 'Douze lettres inédites de Henry IV concernant les Affaires de Marseille', *Revue Henry IV*, 3 (1909), 1–16; Edouard Baratier, ed., *Histoire de Marseille* (Toulouse: Privat, 1973), 171–2; Philippe Tamizey de Larroque, *Lettres Inédites de Guillaume du Vair* (Paris: Auguste Aubrey, 1873).

their power bases and challenging town governments for control of local politics.[50] The rivalry between the Parlement of Dijon and the *Chambre de Ville* was especially pronounced because of the polarization of allegiances during the League. A majority of the parlementaires had become royalists by 1591 while the municipal government had remained a staunchly Leaguer body filled with the duke of Mayenne's clients until the capitulation.[51]

Once the Catholic League had been overthrown a struggle for authority between the parlement and the municipality resumed, paving the way for Henry's intervention.[52] Angry that their candidates frequently lost elections, the Parlement of Dijon established a ten-man commission in 1598 to investigate electoral problems. Dijon possessed a wide electorate. On average between one thousand and fifteen hundred voters turned out for municipal elections in the city during Henry's reign.[53] Such a large voting body caused steep competition between candidates, and the parlement planned to reform elections in a way that guaranteed their professional supervision of the events.[54] Their actions sparked a private war with the *Chambre de Ville* that outlasted Henry IV's reign.

Hostility between the two foci of urban authority heightened after the parlement's commission went to work.[55] On 21 May 1599 the sovereign court passed an act abolishing the city's medieval suffrage customs and in their place imposed a new electoral system in which voting householders were to put forward three nominees and then a child was to draw the name of the winning candidate from a hat. To

---

[50] Robert A. Schneider, 'Crown and Capitoulat: Municipal Government in Toulouse 1500–1789', in *Cities and Social Change in Early Modern Europe*, ed. Philip Benedict (London: Unwin Hyman, 1989), 195–220. Schneider notes that the fate of the municipal government in Toulouse was 'inextricably bound up with the growing hegemony of the parlement' (199). The same could be said of the municipal government and the Parlement of Burgundy in Dijon. Philip Benedict agrees, 'The steady increase in the role of the court in local government characterized all cities which housed provincial parlements in this period.' Philip Benedict, *Rouen during the Wars of Religion* (Cambridge: Cambridge University Press, 1981), 34.

[51] Henri Drouot, *Flavigny contre Dijon, Un cas de Schisme Provincial* (Dijon, 1922), 99. About two fifths of the parlement favoured the League so that sixty-five officeholders, twenty-eight remained in Dijon either as Leaguers or tolerant of the League, while twenty-two espoused royalist convictions and established a royalist rump of the parlement in Flavigny. Fifteen others fled Dijon and tried to remain neutral. Many of the League parlementaires in Dijon abandoned the cause by 1591.

[52] The Parlement of Burgundy had been trying to control municipal elections since at least the middle of the sixteenth century. By 1560 the parlement was issuing orders against bribes, intrigues, coercion, threats and promises all associated with elections. The punishments for such crimes included capital punishment, but it is doubtful these regulations were well-enforced. Corrupt practices were 'regular routines' for sixteenth-century vote seekers and part of the normal election process in sixteenth-century Dijon. M. De La Cuisine, *Le Parlement de Bourgogne depuis son Origine jusqu'a sa Chute* (Dijon: J.E. Rabutot, 1864), vol. 1, 82, 119.

[53] See rosters of voters listed in the deliberations in the opening pages of *Archives Municipales*, Dijon (hereafter cited as AMD), B232, B233, B234, B235, B236, B237, B238, B239, B240, B241, B242, B243, B244, B245, B246, B247 (1594–1609).

[54] Holt, 'Popular Political Culture and Mayoral Elections', 98–116. See especially table 1 on pages 102–3.

[55] Gabriel Breunot, *Journal de Gabriel Breunot, Conseiller au Parlement de Dijon*, ed. Joseph Garner (Dijon: J. E. Rabutot, 1864), vol. 3, 153–85.

ensure compliance, a deputy was dispatched to court.[56] Enraged by the sovereign court's attempt to alter municipal tradition and override their municipal authority, the city council also sent a deputy to the king. They called on their governor, Charles de Gontaut, marshall Biron, to support their cause, and he willingly took the part of the town before the king. Biron kept many of his own clients on the town council, and the sovereign court's actions threatened his authority as well.[57]

The two deputies, Milletot, from the parlement, and Noblet, from the municipal government, met the king at Fontainebleau. Henry reportedly told Milletot that he wanted to maintain the parlement's authority. Likewise, he told Noblet that he wished to conserve Dijon's municipal privileges. Henry sought a compromise, and he wisely avoided favouring either side. He instructed his councillor in Paris, Pomponne de Bellièvre, to render an act in the *Conseil d'Etat* to resolve the quarrel. The king decided that he would select the next mayor of Dijon from a list of three candidates submitted by the town.[58]

This solution might have ended the quarrel, but the act was never formally issued so that in June 1599 the city government convoked the townspeople to elect a mayor under the traditional system. The parlement then tried to enforce their revised format.[59] Tempers boiled to the point that Dijon's governor, Biron, postponed the elections and forbade the revised format 'under pain of death'.[60] The governor's client and soon-to-be mayor, Jehan Jacquinot, announced that if an election were held, the governor would send in his troops, and the townspeople would 'curse the hour'.[61]

The next few months passed without any settlement or election. Emotions ran hot as the parlement worked to undercut the municipal government. It sent Henry a letter asking him to enact a regulation that prohibited any one man from serving as *vicomte-mayeur* for more than a one-year term. Finally, by letters patent of 5 September 1599 Henry ordered an election to be held on the 25th of the month. He ruled that the traditional format would be followed. Jean Jacquinot was elected mayor, and he was re-elected in 1600 and 1601. It appeared the *Chambre de Ville* had won.[62]

Henry IV used the excuse of electoral abuse to infiltrate urban politics. By exposing scandals he intervened in elections and reinforced the importance of royal participation in these events. His actions were shrewd because he could always deny that he was attacking municipal privileges and claim that he was ensuring peace and stability in the towns. He associated urban mismanagement with disorder caused by the religious wars and reinforced his obligation to preserve order.

---

[56] Joseph Garnier, *Correspondance de la Mairie de Dijon extraite des Archives de Cette Ville* (Dijon: J. E. Rabutot, 1870), vol. 3, 9.

[57] Breunot, *Journal*, vol. 3, 161. See also the numerous letters from Biron to the municipality in Garnier, ed., *Correspondance*, vol. 3.   [58] AMD, B235, fols. 233–45.

[59] Garnier, ed., *Correspondance*, vol. 3, 11.   [60] Ibid.

[61] AMD, B237, fols. 2–3; Breunot, *Journal*, vol. 3, 173.

[62] AMD, B237, fol. 36; B238, fol. 37v; B239, fol. 45v. Garnier, ed., *Correspondance*, vol. 3, 12–13, 25.

As king he believed he knew what was best for his subjects. Henry stated that he was aware of magistrates using their offices to advance their own private interests, and he obviously thought his own clients would do a better job. He could at least feel reassured that he and his clients shared common concerns.[63]

But Henry did not take advantage of every situation he encountered to supervise municipal elections. In 1599 Henry had used the quarrel between the Parlement in Dijon and the *Chambre de Ville* to demonstrate that he should select the mayor from a list of three candidates. This was the procedure Henry favoured. Even so, the king eventually enforced the traditional electoral format in Dijon and allowed the election to take place without innovation. In 1608–9 he raised the issue of mayoral appointment again and issued letters patent and a *lettre de jussion* in May 1609 ordering the city council to send him a list of the three highest vote-winners from which he would select the new mayor. He then chose the man who had earned the most votes in the 1609 election.[64] In his entire reign, therefore, Henry IV never imposed a single candidate on the former League town of Dijon, and he revised procedure only slightly.

LEAVING TOWNS ALONE

So far we have examined only towns in which Henry interfered in elections. There were, however, many former League towns that he left entirely alone or in which he made only slight alterations. Toulouse is a good example. During Henry's twenty-year reign, he never once appointed a *capitoul* to its municipal government. Elections did not take place without his knowledge, but he did not interfere in the process. In 1600, for example, Henry received a dispatch from one of his officers, Henry de Caumels, who had been sent to Languedoc to scrutinize events and report back to him. Writing to the king on 29 November De Caumels stated, 'We had a new election of *capitouls*. De Salluste, Du May, Du Faur, Grandelle, *avocats* Garroche, De Leigue, D'Agret, and D'Abauait were elected for the coming year. They are affectionate to the security of the town and to your service.'[65] Likewise in

---

[63] Henry IV, 'Lettres Missives de Henri IV conservées dans les Archives Municipales de la Ville de Troyes', ed. T. Boutiot, *Mémoires de la Société d'Agriculture, des Sciences Arts et Belles-Lettres du Département de l'Aube*, 21 (1857), 285–363. See esp. pages 343–6. Henry wrote, 'en ces dernières annees nous a esté faict plaincte en nostre conseil procede du peu de soing de ceulz qui ont esté admis depuis quelques annees aux charges de Maire et autre publicques dicelle ville negligeant le bien du peuple en la manutention des affaires communes de lad. ville sarrestant seulement a leurs interestz priuez pour la commodité desquelz neanmoings ils ne delaissent de sintroduire esd. charges par voyes ilicites et élections, praticques et brigues manifestes de la populace donnant communement sa voix à ceux desquels elle sattend de proffitter dune bonne chere ou autre utilité' (p. 343).

[64] AMD, B246, fols, 264v–66v; Holt, 'Popular Political Culture and Mayoral Elections', 112.

[65] BN, MSS fr. 23196, fols. 159rv. The eight elected *capitouls* were: Noble Marianne de Salluste, *docteur* and *avocat*, seigneur de Canet et Coubirac, Noble Antoine du May *docteur* and *avocat*, Noble Jacques du Faur, *docteur* and *avocat*, Noble Pierre Grandelle, *avocat*, Noble Anthoine Garroche, bourgeois, Noble Jean de Leigue, bourgeois, Noble Gerauld d'Agret, and Noble Pierre, d'Abauait, bourgeois. Anyone elected to the *capitoulat* was awarded nobility and so each *capitoul* was usually listed as

1603 the *juge mage* of the *sénéchausée*, a man named Clary, sent the king similar notification.[66] He called the election 'one of the greatest functions of my office'.[67] He went on to name the new *capitouls* and stated that he had exhorted them to perform their duties with care so that their actions would be testimonials of their faithfulness to the Crown.[68] Clary included a document for Henry to study revealing the results of the voting process. Thus, the king could see that for the parish of the Dalbade, Bertrand Fortis received twenty-two votes, to defeat Arnaud Rastel who earned six votes and Guillaume Fontrouge who got only two votes.[69] Henry may not have interfered directly in the elections in Toulouse, but his officials oversaw the events and kept him well informed.

In one instance Henry seemed to want to interfere in elections but then changed his mind. When the frontier town of Saint-Dizier in Champagne first surrendered to Henry in 1594, the king confirmed the inhabitants' ancient privileges and guaranteed their right to free elections. In the early 1600s royal officeholders from the *bailliage* courts at Vitry and Chaumont protested Saint Dizier's privileges and tried to usurp power from the *échevinage*. As an outgrowth of these quarrels, in 1608 Henry sent a mandate to Saint-Dizier calling for electoral modification. He instructed the town to go ahead with the upcoming election of twelve *échevins*, but ordered that the results be sent to him for final selection of the municipal government. Disturbed by the king's command, Saint-Dizier's magistrates called a general assembly of local elites. Afterwards they sent deputies to court to plead the rights of the town. Their arguments (or perhaps their bribes of influential patrons) must have been effective, for Henry complied with their wishes and restored their right to free elections without monarchical intervention.[70]

In cities like Meaux, Mâcon, Beauvais, and Reims Henry never intervened in municipal elections, and hundreds of towns throughout the country continued to elect magistrates as they had since the Middle Ages. The king actually strengthened the municipal government in Rouen after the city's capitulation by returning a few

---

'noble'. The men elected to the *capitoulat* were some of the wealthiest and most powerful in Toulouse. Many already possessed nobility before entering the municipal government through offices or family possession. *Archives Municipales*, Toulouse (hereafter AMT), BB21, fol. 1.

[66] *Juge mage* was the term given in the Midi to the king's leading officer in the *sénéchaussée*. These officers were often called *lieutenant-générals* in the *bailliages* in the north. *Bailliage* and *sénéchaussée* were equivalent terms in sixteenth-century France. See Gaston Zeller, *Les Institutions de la France au* XVIe *Siècle* (Paris: Presses Universitaires de France, 1948), 167.

[67] BN, MSS fr. 23197, fol. 519r. Clary called the election 'une des plus grandes actions de la fonction de mon office . . . '.

[68] Ibid., fol. 519v. The elected *capitouls* were: Noble Bertrand Fortis, *avocat*, Noble Pierre Gargas, *écuyer*, Noble Anthoine Celeri, *docteur* and *avocat*, Noble Philibert Fournerot, *avocat*, Noble Pierre Paucy, *marchand*, Noble Geraud Roque, bourgeois, and Noble Jean de Calvert, bourgeois. De Clary incorrectly listed Geraud La Roque as Jean La Roque. AMT, BB23, fol. 1.

[69] BN, MSS fr. 23197, fol. 520. *Capitouls* in Toulouse were elected by a thirty-member consular council made up of former *capitouls*.

[70] P. Guillemin, 'Saint-Dizier d'après les registres de l'échevinage 1573–1789', *Mémoires de la Société des Lettres des Sciences des Arts, de l'Agriculture et de l'Industrie de Saint-Dizier*, 4 (1890–91), 167.

minor privileges to the council and by reaffirming its control over finances.[71] The provincial Parlement of Rouen had usurped much authority from the municipal Council of Twenty-Four during the religious wars so that the latter body had been demoted to a weakened position. Henry tried to counterbalance the two institutions in Rouen by bolstering the authority of the city magistrates. It served his purposes to possess allies in both camps.[72]

At first glance it may seem confusing that Henry did not treat all former League towns alike in quashing municipal autonomy. This would more neatly fit his portrayal as an absolutist king. But Henry's interactions with former League towns were piecemeal and opportunistic. He intervened when invited or when real crises occurred. He ignored some towns at the expense of others, and exerted royal authority in situations where it was considered most necessary. Henry was well-briefed by town governors and royal commissioners, and genuinely interested in municipal politics. In 1594, Claude de la Châtre wrote to the magistrates in Bourges, and cautioned them that Henry IV had men throughout France who advised him on the towns.[73] Even so, sometimes the most attention Henry could devote to a town was a royal nod at local politics.

DECREASING THE SIZE OF URBAN GOVERNMENTS

Henry changed the size and form of a handful of municipal governments during his reign. He and his close advisors concluded that the roots of much urban turmoil stemmed from large, and by implication, unruly municipal governments. So he pursued a course of action after 1594 designed to decrease the size of town councils in a few League strongholds. He modified urban constitutions, and thus violated earlier capitulation promises to leave municipal privileges alone. Local opposition was always great, but the king expected to be obeyed. Reducing the size of urban governments was an important part of his attempt to control rebellious towns. Smaller numbers of magistrates were easier for Henry and his ministers to supervise.

Doullens was one of the first towns in which Henry decreased the size of the municipal government. In 1594 when the town surrendered, he immediately decreased the number of magistrates from twenty-four to seven, one mayor and six *échevins*. Four years later Doullens sent deputies to court to plead for the re-establishment of privileges that had not been granted at the town's submission, and in August 1598 Henry returned to Doullens's citizenry their right to all but one of

---

[71] Benedict, *Rouen during the Wars of Religion*, 231–2; Michel Mollat, *Histoire de Rouen* (Toulouse: Privat, 1979), 195.

[72] Benedict, *Rouen during the Wars of Religion*, 36, 231–2.

[73] Raynal, *Histoire de Berry*, vol. 4, 216. After warning the magistrates of Bourges to keep up their urban militia, La Châtre wrote, 'Le roy . . . a des hommes part toutes les provinces qui luy donnent advis de tout ce qui s'y fait.'

their former privileges. Henry ordered that the reformed number of seven be maintained.[74]

Other examples of reduction exist. During the War of the League in Troyes, the municipal government fluctuated in size from twenty-five members to around thirty-five. Two months after the town capitulated in March, 1594, Henry ordered the size of the city's council stabilized at twenty-five.[75] In 1595 Henry reduced the town council of Lyons from thirteen members to five. Henry seemed concerned with promoting efficiency in government, at least this was what he told the magistrates. In reality his actions in Lyons were related to a complicated municipal debt issue which is discussed in chapter eight.[76]

In Abbeville Henry reduced the size of the municipal government in 1596 from twenty-five members to nine, a mayor and eight *échevins*. Instead of electing an entirely new *échevinage* each year, the king ordered that only four *échevins* would be elected annually for two-year terms. He gave as his reason that he wished to make the deliberations of the town government less tumultuous and that he wanted to concentrate its affairs in more capable and loyal hands. In the letter Henry sent to Abbeville announcing his intent and in the act formally reducing the municipal council passed by the Parlement of Paris, large councils were acquainted with disorder. It was noted that when town councils were large, magistrates tended to shirk their duties because they believed the tasks would be done by others. Large councils also attracted *gens de métiers*, and the Crown wanted to create a more elite force in the city who enjoyed the respect of the people. Henry noted that he was following the example of Paris, which he labelled one of the best policed cities of the realm.[77]

Elections in Abbeville remained free, and Henry did not attempt to change their format because the bourgeois, merchants, and artisans in the city did not welcome his intervention. They argued that Henry had 'insulted' their privileges and took their complaint first to the *sénéchal* of Ponthieu and later to the Parlement of Paris. The parlement ruled against the town, however, handing down a judgement in 1598 ordering the execution of the king's orders.[78] The parlement also reminded the *Abbevillois* that 'privileges depend on the will of the prince and only have validity by his confirmation'.[79]

In January of 1598 when the parlementary councillors wrote the above words, they were reacting to a bitter lesson most recently learned. In March 1597, Abbeville's neighbour in Picardy, Amiens, had been captured by the Spanish, and

---

[74] Hippolyte Cocheris, *Notice et extraits des Documents et Manuscrits conservée dans les dépots de Paris relatifs à l'histoire de la Picardie* (Paris: Durand, 1858), vol. 2, nos. 15, 20.

[75] Théophile Boutiot, *Histoire de la Ville de Troyes et de la Champagne Méridionale* (Troyes: Dufey-Robert, 1873), vol. 4, 243–6.

[76] Jean-Baptiste Monfaulcon, *Histoire Monumentale de la Ville de Lyon* (Lyon: privately printed, 1851), 161. [77] Thierry, *Recueil des Monuments du Tiers-Etat*, vol. 4, 486–9. [78] Ibid., 485–6.

[79] Ibid., 489. The extract of the registers of the parlement states, 'les priviléges dépendent de la volonté du prince et n'ont de force qu'en la confirmation . . .'.

Henry had had to besiege the city to win it back. He also reduced the size of Amiens's *échevinage* in the aftermath of this ordeal underscoring his doubts about large municipal councils. He explained his decision to reduce Abbeville's *échevinage* as his way of assuring the safety of the realm from further Spanish invasion. Henry seems to have distrusted certain *Abbevillois*. Decreasing the size of the council was necessary to guarantee the surety of the town.[80]

THE EXTRAORDINARY CASE OF AMIENS

Henry's defeat of Amiens in 1597, and his subsequent punishment of the town government, represents one of his most thorough attacks on localized power.[81] Reference to Henry's treatment of Amiens is usually given in brief summaries of his 'drive to absolutism'. The king is shown overwhelming the town with his armies, imposing authority from above, and crushing opposition, resistance, and independence along the way. According to this assessment, the king retaliated for the Spanish capture and for Amiens's past treachery with the Catholic League. The implication is that he dealt with Amiens in the way he wanted to treat all former Catholic League towns if he could.[82] A fresh look at Henry's treatment of Amiens may shed light on his actions and resolve some of the contradictions in his relationship with the towns.

At daybreak on 11 March 1597 sixteen Spanish soldiers disguised as peasants penetrated one of Amiens's city gates, and with reinforcements they successfully took the city before 8:00 AM. The sneak attack had gone so smoothly that no one ever sounded the tocsin. Many *Amiénois* fought bravely, but the mayor, Pierre de Famechon, capitulated less than two hours after the first Spanish infiltration. Branded a traitor, Famechon escaped to Clermont while the *Amiénois* endured five days of pillaging by Spanish soldiers. Famechon had been negligent with Amiens's defences. Townspeople had warned him for weeks before the invasion about Spanish troop movement in the area, but he had done nothing to bolster the city's defences.[83]

Henry went dancing on the night of 11 March and learned about the loss of Amiens in the early morning hours of the next day. He left immediately for Picardy, having supposedly uttered the legendary, 'That's enough of being King of

---

[80] Ibid.
[81] Apaché, 'Images du siège d'Amiens de 1597', 32–40.
[82] Janine Garrisson, *Henry IV* (Paris: Seuil, 1984), 260–62.
[83] ADS, 1B 15, fols. 46–47; BN, MSS fr., Nouv. Acq., fols. 541–43rv; AMA, BB55, fols. 89–91; P. Daire, *Histoire de la Ville d'Amiens depuis son origine jusqu'à present* (Paris: Chez la Veuve de Laguette, 1757), 342–99. Many contemporary documents brand Famechon a traitor. To be fair, however, in 1596 Amiens had been severely hit by a bout of plague and many of the municipal officials had either died or left town. Famechon may have been doing all he could just to keep the municipal administration functioning. Many *Amiénois* did cooperate with the Spanish in the capture of their city. Claude Pécoul was a known traitor as was Adrien Rohault. See also, BN, MSS fr. Collection de Picardy, 121, fol. 254v.

France. It's time to be King of Navarre'.[84] He marshalled his forces, sending letters of recruitment to nobles throughout France and asking his towns to come to his financial aid. He called the event an 'inconvenience', but stated optimistically that he thought it would 'increase rather than diminish the courage and affection of those who are truly French and who want to render to their prince and country what they owe them.'[85] Eventually, the king gathered a royal army of approximately 23,000, but the process was slow. A large segment of his Protestant supporters turned their backs on him and failed to come to Amiens, while the Parlement of Paris refused to register the necessary acts required to raise funds for the siege. Many towns resisted sending any money at all to support the king.[86]

Despite these frustrations, Henry recaptured Amiens on 25 September. During his triumphal entry into the city, the inhabitants went wild with excitement. A choir sang a *Te Deum* in the cathedral, while the townspeople chanted 'Vive le roi'. Poems commemorated the event.

> If ever a prince on Earth
> Merited his people's adoration for his bravery
> It is this King
> so famous and so feared by his enemies
> Sent from heaven as Monarch to France'[87]

The *Amiénois* were less enchanted, however, two days later when the newly victorious king punished them for disloyalty. He replaced the municipal government installed by the Spanish with one appointed by himself. This 'reformed' government was significantly smaller in size than the *échevinage* associated with Amiens since the Middle Ages.

Losing Amiens had been devastating to Henry largely because of the huge costs involved in winning it back. In addition, when the Spanish captured Amiens they took over the munitions depot the king had built in preparation for a siege of Arras.[88] Throughout late 1596 and early 1597, Henry had repeatedly offered Swiss troops to the city to bolster its urban militia and to protect his munitions. But Amiens's magistrates rejected all of his offers and cited the city's privileged

---

[84] Pierre de L'Estoile, *Journal pour le règne de Henri IV*, ed. L.R. Lefèvre (Paris, Gallimare, 1948), 1, 497. 'C'est assez faict le roy de France, il est temps de faire le roi de Navarre'.
[85] Berger de Xivrey, *Recueil des Lettres Missives de Henri IV*, vol. 4, 697. Before leaving Paris Henry wrote to the city of Lyon on 12 March 1597 saying the recapture of Amiens 'doibt plus tost accroistre que diminuer le courage et l'affection de ceulx qui sont vrays François et veulent rendre a leur prince et à leur patrie la fidelité qu'ils leur doibvent, comme nous sommes asseurez que vous ferés.'
[86] Buisseret, *Henry IV*, 65–8.
[87] Calonne, *Histoire d'Amiens*, vol. 2, 230. The poem reads,
> Si jamais quelque prince habitant ici bas,
> Mérita que son peuple adorast sa vaillance,
> C'est ce Roy si fameux et si craint aux combas,
> Que les cieux ont donné pour monarque à la France.
[88] David Buisseret cites Sir Anthony Mildmay as saying that Henry lost 26 cannon, 40,000 shot, 8,000 *milliers* of powder, 8,000 *setiers* of wheat and 120,000 crowns in coin. Buisseret, *Henry IV*, 65.

exemption from billeting troops as the reason for their refusal.[89] When the Spanish took Amiens, Henry remembered bitterly the city leaders' refusal to accept his military aid. He believed exaggerated devotion to municipal privileges contributed to the Spanish capture of Amiens. He wrote, 'But the common fault of all the inhabitants here [Amiens] we ascribe to an obstinate attachment to the vanity of their privileges . . .'[90] Henry's hatred of privileges in this instance was so great that as part of his punitive legislation, he forbade the *Amiénois* from ever uttering the word 'privileges' again.[91]

In an edict issued 18 November 1597 the king curtailed magisterial authority by reducing Amiens's liberties and privileges. In the first article of the edict Henry reduced the size of the *échevinage* from twenty-five members to seven, and replaced the office of mayor with that of *premier échevin*. This article actually made official what the king had done to the *échevinage* immediately after the capitulation six weeks before. Several other articles dramatically altered the municipal government. Henry decreased the size of the electorate, and delegated responsibility for the surveillance of elections to four royally appointed officials. He specified that he would select the *premier échevin* each year, and stipulated that Amiens's governor would choose two of the remaining six *échevins*. The king also changed the day the municipal elections were held from the traditional date of 28 October, St Firmin's Day, to 25 September, the day commemorating Henry's reconquest of the city.[92] Even in the ritual celebration of future elections, the *Amiénois* would be forced to confront their past sins during the annual events. The election of the municipal government would never again be associated with the city's patron saint, but rather with the city's conqueror.

In total, twenty-eight articles severed the *échevinage* from its medieval heritage. One of the most serious blows to municipal authority annulled the right of the town council to dispense civil and criminal justice and transferred that power to the *bailliage*. As a result, the *échevins* were left with only the ability to oversee simple

[89] AMA, GG54, fols. 100–6rv; BB55, fols. 10–22rv. See also, Louis Boca and Armand Rendu, *Inventaire Sommaire des Archives Départementales Antérieures à 1790, Ville d'Amiens* (Amiens: Imprimerie Picarde, 1883), vol. 1, 103. Henry sent letters patent to the *bailliage* of Amiens sitting in Corbié on 4 June 1597 saying, 'Nous pouvons dire avec vérité avoir esté souvent très mal secourus, servis et obéys aux occasions qui se sont présentées, dont la perte de nostre ville d'Amiens peut, à nostre très grand regret, servir de tesmoignage: car continuans au soing que nous avons de veiller au salut de nos subjectz et recongnoisant que, par la rigueur de la maladie contagieuse qui avoit eu cours en ladite ville, pendant l'esté dernier, le peuple d'icelle estoit grandement diminué; craignans que nos ennemis se servissent de l'occasion pour y attenter, nous y avions expressément envoié six enseignes de Suisses, du régiment du colonel Galatty. Mais les habitans de ladite ville, au lieu de les recevoir et se fortifier de leur assistance, feirent difficulté de les loger, mesmes aux faulxbourgs de ladite ville, fondans leurs reffus sur la conservation de leur priviléges . . .'. During 1595–6 Henry did manage to place garrisons in Ham, Saint-Quentin, Péronne, Abbeville, Montreuil, and Boulogne. Charles Gomart, 'La Siège de La Fère par Henri IV', *La Picardie Revue Littéraire et Scientifique*, 13 (1867), 314.
[90] AMA AA39, pièce 7, fol. 2., 'Mais cette faute commune à tous les Habitans d'icelle, que nous ne voulons plus sinistrement imputer qu'a une opiniatreté de s'être trop attachés à la vanité de leurs privilèges . . .'.   [91] Ibid., fol. 8.   [92] Ibid., fols. 1–19.

police cases involving minor infractions. A major source of municipal patronage under magisterial direction was lost when Henry transferred authority over the local militia to the town governor. This included the right to name militia captains and gate officials. The magistrates were even prohibited from having anything to do with Amiens's gates, walls, moats, or other structures related to the city's defence. Similarly, the right to receive oaths of allegiance from the heads of the major guilds was taken from the municipal government and given to the lieutenant general of the *bailliage*. The magistrates were finally denied much of their former control over the municipal *octrois*, and a *receveur* named by the king was created to oversee the collection and use of these revenues. Henry denounced the municipal government and usurped its prestige. As a final symbolic gesture, he revoked the right of the magistrates to dress in robes of silk and damask representing the colours of the town. Henceforth, by order of the king, the *échevins* could wear only simple black robes.[93]

The most visible changes in Amiens's municipal government after 1597 were the decreased size of the *échevinage* and the urban electorate. Prior to 1597, those enjoying suffrage in Amiens included citizens in three categories, the bourgeois, members of the urban militia, and the militia captains.[94] Henry's legislation, however, restricted voting only to incumbent *échevins*, town notables, councillors, and militia captains.[95] This had the effect of reducing the number of voters in a city of around twenty thousand from well over one thousand to two hundred at best.[96] Only elections of the mayor had been free. *Échevins* had always been chosen through a system of cooptation in which incumbents nominated their successors. Under the new format, the king named the *premier échevin* from a list of seven. The *échevinage*, therefore, was closed to those unable to establish patronage ties with the king or high-ranking royal officials in Picardy.[97] In practical terms, this meant that the number of men in Amiens regularly associated with

93 Ibid.
94 Edouard Maugis, *Recherches sur les Transformations du Régime Politique et Social de la Ville d'Amiens* (Paris: Picard et Fils, 1906), 78–156; Pierre Deyon, *Amiens Capitale Provinciale, étude sur la société urbaine au 17e siècle* (Paris: Mouton and Co., 1967), 427, 430. A typical sixteenth-century election in Amiens generally functioned so that incumbent *échevins* nominated three notables for the office of mayor. Those three candidates were presented to the voters who cast their votes by placing ballots in one of three designated pots. The votes were counted by the lieutenant general of the *bailliage*, and the new mayor took his oath in front of the king's officer, the town governor, if possible, and other members of the *bailliage* and *échevinage*. *Échevins* essentially nominated each other in an elaborate system of cooptation.
95 AMA, AA39, piece 7. 'Town councillors' in the sixteenth and seventeenth centuries usually referred to men who had already served as *échevins* in the past or to wealthy bourgeois who acted in advisory capacities.
96 Population figures for Amiens during Henry's reign are indefinite because the city was often hard hit by plague during and after the years of the Catholic League and during the siege of 1597. Charles Engrand, 'Pesanteurs et dynamismes de l'économie et de la société amiénoises (1598–1789)', in *Histoire d'Amiens*, ed. Ronald Hubscher (Toulouse: Privat, 1986), 143–4.
97 In 1597 Henry's governor of Picardy was François d'Orléans, comte de Saint-Pol, and Louis Le Fèvre, sieur de Caumartin was the king's *intendant*.

municipal office holding decreased from seventy-eight individuals during the eleven year period 1587 to 1596 to twenty-three during the fourteen year period from 1597 to 1610.[98] Amiens's already small oligarchy became even more closed and tight-knit. In 1597, Henry selected the new seven member *échevinage*, reduced the size of the electorate, and ordered royal participation in the electoral process. As a result he guaranteed that a self-perpetuating, oligarchic elite would control Amiens's municipal government and that the vast majority of these men would be Bourbon clients.

The new municipal government of Amiens in 1597 consisted of Augustin de Louvencourt, Michel de Suyn, Jehan Cordelois, Jehan d'Aynval, Nicolas Piot, Antoine Dippre, and Antoine Pingré as *échevins* and Robert Correur as *premier échevin*. The men had been picked carefully and had long histories of royalist political convictions. Louvencourt, Correur, and Pingré, were the well-known royalists and loyal clients of Henry IV discussed in chapter two. Antoine Dippre had served Henry III until his death and then worked for Amiens's capitulation to Henry IV.[99] Less is known about Nicholas Piot and Jehan d'Aynval although both men had managed to win the 1594 magisterial election that returned many royalists to the municipal government in Amiens. It was this government that capitulated to Henry IV. Piot and d'Aynval also belonged to the small group of Huguenots in Amiens.[100] Michel de Suyn and Jehan Cordelois were both ennobled by Henry IV on 8 October 1594 for their participation in Amiens's capitulation.[101] Each of these seven men had served Henry faithfully in the past, and in time of municipal crisis he selected them for office.

In restructuring Amiens's municipal government, Henry demonstrated that privileges belonged first to him and then to a town. They existed through his royal authority and could be granted, augmented or revoked. In 1596 he had tried to change Amiens's municipal charter in order to station troops there, but the *Amiénois* proved too 'jealous of their privileges'.[102] They resisted change when change was necessary, and this must have influenced Henry's actions. Amiens had clearly overstepped its bounds as a corporate body, placing the realm at risk in 1597, and for many, the *Amiénois* got what they deserved. The experience may have even contributed to a nation-wide denigration of privileges in general. Under normal circumstances the French king and the municipal governments were not in opposite camps.[103] Henry depended on Amiens's elites to maintain royal authority

[98] See the election returns in AMA, BB45–BB58. A. Janvier, *Livre d'Or de la Municipalité Amiénois* (Paris: Picard, 1893), 227–42.
[99] BN, MSS fr., 8914, fols. 133–9; Janvier, *Livre d'Or*, 238–44.
[100] L. Rossier, *Histoire des Protestants de Picardie* (Paris: Res Universis, 1990), 112.
[101] F. Pouy, *La Chambre du Conseil des Etats de Picardie Pendant La Ligue* (Amiens: Delatte, 1882), 43–4.
[102] Berger de Xivrey, *Recueil des Lettres Missives*, 4, 696. Henry wrote that the *Amiénois* 'ont toujours esté jaloux de leurs privileges, qui leur donnoient exemption de garnison'.
[103] Schneider, 'Crown and capitoulat', 201–17; William Beik, 'Two Intendants Face a Popular Revolt: Social Unrest and the Structure of Absolutism in 1645', *Canadian Journal of History*, 9 (1974), 243–62.

in the Picard capital. But in 1597 he realized how dangerous town autonomy could be, and thus destroyed the medieval constitution of Amiens that had threatened national security.

CONCLUSION HENRY IV AND FORMER CATHOLIC LEAGUE TOWNS

Henry IV's actions show that he held concrete ideas about former Catholic League towns, and he understood the dangers rebellious towns could pose. When the towns jeopardized internal or external security, he responded quickly to settle unrest. There was nothing automatic about his actions because each town presented the king with different circumstances.[104] Henry's interaction with the towns was motivated by his need to preserve his kingship and defend his kingdom. In general he respected local custom and privilege. When a town's autonomy threatened the state, however, Henry protected the interests of the Crown. He aptly proved by his direct interventions that ancient rights and traditions only held validity when he sanctioned them. But he did not develop a municipal policy to attack the towns, nor did he think in terms of centralization. Henry reduced the size of several municipalities and manipulated elections in numerous towns. None of these actions were unusual for a Renaissance king.

Henry probably thought in terms of loyalty and boundaries. He was very concerned about frontier towns, and learned through the experience with Amiens that unfaithful town councillors and complacent inhabitants could harm France. Henry was interested in electoral reform largely because elections often set off urban turmoil, but he never developed a specific plan for electoral reform although he worried about corruption that made social unrest a possibility at election time. The king perceived a need to revise electoral formats, and he modified procedures when urban discontent and factional strife threatened internal peace.

In Paris and elsewhere, when Henry interfered in municipal elections it was not to destroy municipal privileges, or town autonomy, but rather to put his faithful subjects in municipal office. Drawing on his clientele network, Henry governed the towns by securing places of authority for the men he trusted. His survival as king depended on greater control of local situations than earlier rulers had achieved, and he scrutinized municipal politics to monitor discontent. If town leaders did not like his actions, they were threatened with loss of their privileges. Henry did not want to fight with municipal magistrates, and he was better known for his clemency. He preferred to encourage their trust. The king understood the dynamics of urban factions and tried to curtail disloyalty and augment his authority by building Crown clienteles in all key cities. By incorporating urban power relations into his rule, Henry strengthened his legitimacy as king. His austerity towards Amiens was

---

[104] Buisseret, *Henry IV*, 164–5.

justified and tempered by cooperation with most towns and by neglect of other towns. Only by comparing his relationship with former Protestant and royalist towns can Henry's governance of urban France be realized fully.

5

Henry IV and municipal franchises in royalist and Protestant towns

Henry IV's alliance with his royalist towns harkened back to the moment on 1 August 1589 when Jacques Clement drove his dagger into Henry III and brought the Valois succession issue to a head. Childless and dying, Henry III was forced to name a successor to the throne, and in his final moments he recognized his brother-in-law, Henry of Navarre, as the legitimate new king of France by hereditary right. This acknowledgement should have ensured Henry the throne. But the Catholic League was well-entrenched in the majority of French cities and towns, and zealous Catholics refused to accept a Protestant king. As the news of Henry III's assassination spread, few towns came forward to recognize the king. In 1589 Henry's power base thus consisted of about one-sixth of the country, and most of this support was from Huguenot towns and nobles in the southwest.[1] Only a handful of non-Protestant royalist towns accepted Henry as king.

Henry IV's relationship with Huguenot towns was far more complex than his affiliation with either League or royalist municipalities. League towns in 1589 perceived Henry as a heretic and a usurper; royalist towns viewed him as their king and ally. For the Protestant towns, Henry was the protector of the Huguenot movement. His relationship with the Protestant nobility and the towns stretched back to his boyhood. He became titular head of the Huguenot movement when he was only fourteen years old, and he spent most of his young manhood campaigning with the Huguenot armies. During the 1580s he consolidated his control over most of southwestern France.[2] But in 1593 he renounced his Calvinist faith and re-adopted Catholicism, a decision that strained his relationship with the Protestants who had done so much to support his kingship in the early years of his reign. Henry nevertheless promised his Huguenot allies that he would continue to protect them, and he rewarded them with the Edict of Nantes.[3]

This chapter examines Henry's relationship with the towns that supported him during the religious wars. These towns had recognized his legitimacy the instant he

---

[1] Jean-Pierre Babelon, *Henri IV* (Paris: Fayard, 1982), 465; David Buisseret, *Henry IV* (London: George Allen and Unwin), 29.   [2] Buisseret, *Henry IV*, 29.

[3] See for example the letter Henry sent to La Rochelle printed in L. Canet, *L'Aunis et La Saintonge, de la Guerre de Cent Ans à Henri IV* (La Rochelle: F. Pijollet, 1933), vol. 2, 272–3.

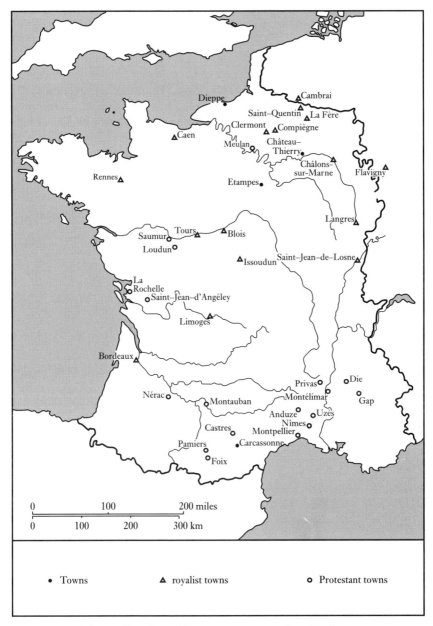

Map 2   Royalist and Protestant towns mentioned in the text

ascended the throne, and his relationship with them changed little after the wars. He rewarded them for their fidelity and generally left them alone. Protestant towns presented him with a more difficult situation because of the religious question. What will be argued below, however, is that in dealing with all French towns Henry IV pursued a stance of accommodation and conciliation. When he thought it necessary and possible, he intervened in royalist and Protestant towns just as he did in former League towns. Pressing practical problems caused royal intervention, and local politics involved the king in a complicated dialogue with local elites. Common sense dictated that, in the precarious years after 1593–4, he could ill afford to anger loyal supporters.

THE ROYALIST TOWNS

The important royalist towns giving immediate, unconditional support to Henry included Tours, Blois, Caen, Langres, Rennes, Châlons-sur-Marne, Clermont, and Saint-Quentin.[4] Smaller towns like Issoudun in Berry fought to remain loyal while surrounded by Catholic League towns, and certain towns like Flavigny and Saint-Jean-de-Losne in Burgundy became royalist strongholds after royalists arrived from Dijon following the League takeover. Henry would remember these towns throughout his reign with special affection. Saint-Quentin in Picardy swore to take no part in the League and devotedly acknowledged the Bourbon heir as king after Henry III's death. While visiting the town in 1590, Henry told the inhabitants: 'Despite my enemies, I am assured that I will always be king of Saint-Quentin.'[5] He ended a letter to the municipal government in 1594 with the statement that he needed no greater citadel in the town than the hearts of its people.[6]

Other royalist towns such as Limoges had populations divided in their loyalty between the king and the League. Influential citizens in Limoges belonged to the League during the early years of Henry's reign despite the fact that royalists controlled the municipal government. The town remained divided between royalists, Leaguers, and neutrals. Similarly, the Parlement of Bordeaux accepted Henry's kingship in 1589, but there was always a large League faction in the city. It took the troops of Jacques Goyon, marshall Matignon and the *lieutenant du roi* in Guyenne, to enforce royalist control over Bordeaux.

[4] August Poirson, *Histoire du Règne de Henri IV* (Paris: Didier, 1862), vol. 1, 47–8. Clermont and Montferrand were two towns during the sixteenth century that later united as Clermont-Ferrand. I refer only to Clermont here. Poirson's complete list of royalist towns also includes: Compiègne, Meulan, Etampes, Senlis, Pontoise, Dieppe, Coûtances, Saint-Lô, Château-Thierry, Metz, Flavigny, Saumur, Angers, Loudun, Niort, Fontenay, Carcassonne, Vitré, and Brest. Some of these towns, such as Pontoise, Angers, and Senlis, were unable to withstand League assault and eventually fell to the 'Holy Union'. In other cases such as Saumur, Château-Thierry or Fontenay, information regarding this period is scarce.
[5] Quoted in Georges Lecocq, *Histoire de la Ville de Saint-Quentin* (Marseille: Laffitte Reprints, 1977), 144. Henry stated, 'Malgré mes ennemis, je suis assuré que je serai toujours le roi de la ville de Saint-Quentin.' [6] Ibid., 145.

With so few non-Protestant towns willing to recognize Henry, the royalist towns became havens for exiled Crown supporters from League towns. Before his death, Henry III had transferred the *bailliage, siège présidial,* and *prévôté* in Vitry and the *monnaie* in Troyes to Châlons, as well as the *trésorerie* and *sénéchausée* in Riom to Clermont. Likewise the royalist rump of the parlement, *Cour des aides,* and *Chambre de comptes* in Rouen and Paris were re-established in Caen and Tours respectively. Most parlements, except for the one in Bordeaux, were divided during this period. The royalist towns acquired greater importance because of this influx of royal officials from League controlled towns, but they paled in comparison with the League strongholds. Although the port city of Bordeaux had a population of around 35,000, none of the other royalist towns possessed much wealth or large populations, especially in comparison with League cities. Rennes had a population of 17,500, Blois 16,500 and Tours 16,000.[7]

Royalist towns undoubtedly endeared themselves to the king as his many glowing letters to them so aptly reveal.[8] The previous chapter has shown that Henry intervened in League towns to promote stability and safeguard his place on the throne. He had little to fear, however, from his royalist towns and generally tried to please them when he could.

SWEARING ALLEGIANCE TO HENRY IV

Swearing loyalty to Henry IV was a dangerous action for royalist towns in 1589 because most of them were located in Leaguer provinces. All of the royalist towns, it should be noted, supported Henry III before his assassination and announced their acceptance of Henry IV within three weeks of the old king's death. Henry IV acted quickly to retain their allegiance. Almost immediately upon ascending the throne, he sent out circulars to the royalist towns imploring them to remain loyal. He promised that in exchange for their support he would uphold the Catholic faith. In his letter to Caen dated the first day of his reign, 2 August 1589, Henry declared that he would maintain the state 'without innovation to the Catholic, Apostolic, and Roman religion.'[9] He promised to preserve the Catholic church and do nothing detrimental to the public good.[10]

The loyalty of key provincial and town leaders was instrumental in the decision

---

[7] Philip Benedict, 'French Cities from the Sixteenth Century to the Revolution, An Overview', in *Cities and Social Change in Early Modern France,* ed. Philip Benedict (London: Unwin Hyman, 1989), 24–5. No figures exist for the size of Tours in 1600. Blois possessed about 16,500 around 1600. Châlons-sur-Marne was significantly smaller. The population figure for Châlons in 1500 was 9,000 and in 1700 12,500.

[8] For example, see the letters published in L. Barbat, *Histoire de la Ville de Châlons-sur-Marne* (Châlons-sur-Marne: L. Barbat 1860), vol. 2, appendix 1–38.

[9] Pierre Carel, *Histoire de la Ville de Caen sous Charles IX, Henri III, et Henri IV, documents inédits* (Paris: Champion Editeur, 1887), 220. Henry wrote he would conserve the state, 'sans rien innover au fait de la religion catholique, apostolique y romaine, mais la conserver de notre pouvoir, comme nous en ferons plus particulières et expresses déclarations . . .'.   [10] Ibid., 221.

to recognize Henry IV. Governor Rastignac of Basse Auvergne, for example, urged Clermont to recognize Henry, and all of the towns in Touraine including the capital, Tours, recognized him because of the insistence of the royalist governor, Gilles de Souvre. On 20 February 1589 town magistrates and notables in Saint-Quentin swore a *contre-ligue* oath under the leadership of their provincial governor, Henry d'Orléans, duke of Longueville, to oppose the schismatics and keep Picardy under royal authority.[11] Town governors were equally important. Thus, François de la Grange, seigneur of Montigny and governor of Blois, championed the royalist cause for his town; mayor and governor Marec de Montbarot did the same in Rennes.[12] Governor Philippe Thomassin likewise ordered the municipal leaders in Châlons-sur-Marne to join him in swearing an oath to, 'conserve the said town in obedience and devotion to the legitimate successor king of the Crown of France'.[13] The governor of Caen, Pelet de la Verune, was not quite so successful. He formally accepted Henry for his town ten days before the *échevins* of Caen drafted a letter to the king. They had spent the intervening time drawing up demands that they wanted met.[14] Nonetheless, Henry was glad to receive Caen's second formal declaration of allegiance on 10 October 1589. He wrote to the magistrates thanking them for their loyalty and acknowledging that their devotion 'confirms our good will towards you and augments the desire to gratify you'.[15]

In the case of Langres, the mayor, Jean Roussat, led the movement to recognize Henry. Langres was a frontier town and possessed a greater degree of autonomy than other royalist towns because of rights and concessions granted after the Hundred Years War. The office of mayor had more power than similar offices elsewhere.[16] A staunch defender of the Crown, Jean Roussat became a trusted client of Henry IV and a promoter of his legitimacy. When a messenger brought him the news of Henry III's death, he slapped the man and then cried bitterly when he realized the truth. Roussat then convoked a municipal assembly to swear loyalty to Henry IV.[17] 'The king is the king', he declared 'even if he is Protes-

---

[11] BN, MSS fr. 13071, 20 February 1589. The oath of allegiance was signed by Longueville along with the governor of Saint-Quentin, a host of nobles and royal officials, and Sebastien Diné, Saint-Quentin's mayor and city captain.   [12] Poirson, *Histoire du Règne de Henri IV*, vol. 2, 47–8.

[13] Edouard de Barthélemy, *Histoire de la Ville de Châlons-sur-Marne et de ses Institutions depuis son origine jusqu'en 1848* (Châlons-sur-Marne, E. Le Roy, Imprimeur-Libraire, 1883), 309. The document stated the signers would 'conserveront ladite ville en l'obéissance et dévotion du légitime successeur roy de la couronne de France'.   [14] Carel, *Histoire de la Ville de Caen*, 220–4.

[15] Henry IV, *Recueil des Lettres Missives de Henri IV*, ed. J. Berger de Xivrey (Paris: Imprimerie Nationale, 1846), vol. 3, 56. Henry wrote, 'Nous avons eu très agreable d'entendre par vostre lettre du dixiesme du passé et par vostre député, present porteur, la nouvelle asseurance que vous avés donnée de la louable resolution que vous tous, habitans de ceste ville de Caen, aves faicte de continuer envers nous la mesme fidelité et obeissance qu'aves tousjours portée aux feuz Roys nos predecesseurs: ce qui a d'autant plus confirmé nostre bonne volonté envers vous et augmenté le desir de vous gratifier.'

[16] E. Hugues, *Histoire de Langres au début du XVIIe siècle 1610–1660* (Langres: Chez-Dominique Gueniot Imprimeur, 1978), 29–32.

[17] Maurice Poinsignon, *Histoire générale de la Champagne et de la Brie depuis les temps les plus reculés jusqu'à la division de la province en département* (Châlons-sur-Marne: Martin Frères) vol. 2, 326.

tant'.[18] Under Roussat's leadership, the municipality signed an oath of allegiance to the Bourbon king.

[We pledge] to observe fully the fundamental laws and recognize Henry of Bourbon as our sovereign king and legitimate inheritor and successor of the Crown. We will render to him the same fidelity and obedience that we have shown to predecessor kings . . . [19]

Neither Roussat nor the inhabitants of Langres wavered from their commitment to Henry IV, and the king acknowledged their loyalty. He wrote to Roussat praising Langres's inhabitants, who 'have always been faithful to this Crown'.[20] He added, 'Because of your dexterity you know how to maintain them [the inhabitants] in their obedience.'[21]

ELECTION INTERFERENCE AND CROWN INTERVENTION

Had Henry been motivated to curtail town privileges, the evidence would appear in royalist election returns. Yet while he did attempt to manipulate elections in royalist towns, he did so only minimally. Of the towns under scrutiny here, there are only four cases of electoral manipulation, and then only for the highest municipal positions; the office of mayor in Langres, Saint-Quentin, and Bordeaux, and the post of *procureur syndic* in Rennes. In short, Henry IV never interfered in the election of *échevins* or other town councillors in royalist towns. Even his attempts to appoint the mayor in Langres, Bordeaux, and Saint-Quentin were more suggestions on his part than out-right orders.

Langres experienced the most direct electoral intervention. Since the municipal archives of Langres burned during the last century, the best surviving evidence of Henry's manipulation can be found in a letter that he wrote in 1592 to the sieur de Dinteville, lieutenant-general in Langres:

'I want you to oversee the selection process [in Langres] so that at the first election for the mayor's office, the sieur de Roussat will be appointed. I am been so very pleased by his past services which he performed with dignity that I will take it as a personal courtesy to see him

[18] Hugues, *Langres au début du* XVIIe *siècle*, 35. 'Le roi est le roi, même s'il est protestant', Roussat is purported to have said.
[19] M. Guyot de St Michel, *Correspondance Politique et Militaire de Henri le Grand, avec J. Roussat, Maire de Langres* (Paris: Petit, Library of M. and Mme le duc de Berry, 1816), 20–2. The oath stated, 'D'observer de point en poinct les loix fondamentalles d'icelle et particulièrement de recongnoistre comme nous recongnoissons Henry de Bourbon quatriesme du nom pour nostre Souverain Roy, comme légitime héritier et successeur de la dicte couronne. Lui rendre la mesme fidélité et obeissance qu'avons faites aux deffuncts Roys ses prédécesseurs, et encores de nous employer de nos vies et biens pour la juste vengeance du meurtre et assassinat commis à la personne au dict déffunct Henry troiesmet nostre très bon Roy . . .'
[20] Ibid., 26. Henry wrote, 'J'ay recu beaucoup de contentement ayant connu la résolution prise par les habitans de ma ville de Langres, de me rendre l'obeissance laquelle on est deve, c'est ce que je me suis tousjours promis d'eulx scachant qu'ils ont toujours esté très fidelles à ceste Kouronne et scachant que par vostre dextérité vous scaurez bien les contenir en ce debvoir.'   [21] Ibid.

elected again. It will reassure me to know that in your absence the business of the town will be handled smoothly and improved by his [Roussat's] command . . . [22]

Roussat held the office of mayor of Langres four times during Henry's reign. He maintained a regular correspondence with Henry after 1589, and advised the king on various matters concerning his town and province. He also received monies from the king as a client.[23] Henry frequently praised Roussat's loyalty.[24] During a dispute between Roussat and Dinteville, Henry wrote to the lieutenant-general of Champagne, the duke of Nivernois, and explained:

I pray of you, my cousin, to make it understood to each of them what is expected of them, especially the sieur de Dinteville. Tell him to conduct himself with prudence and aid the mayor and my other servants who are in Langres and facilitate what he can for the good of my service.[25]

In Bordeaux Henry was anxious to maintain Jacques Goyon, marshall Matignon, in the post of mayor. Matignon was a fervent royalist and a friend and client of the king. In March 1589 as a supporter of Henry III, Matignon had put down a disturbance raised by League adherents in the quarter of Saint-Michel. His loyalty did not waver once Henry IV ascended the throne. During debate in the parlement over the succession issue in August 1589, Matignon declared, 'There is no interregnum in this state, and when death comes the kings succeed by legitimate succession, not by election, and take the royal duty of their predecessor as has always been observed.'[26] Matignon had great influence in Bordeaux, and he promised Henry that he would devote his life to maintaining the city in royalist hands.[27] It is

<hr/>

[22] Berger de Xivrey, *Recueil des Lettres Missives de Henri IV*, vol. 3, 663. The king wrote, 'Monsieur de Dinteville, Suivant ce que je vous ay desjà escript, je vous prie tenir la main et faire tous les bons offices que vous pourrés, affin que, à la premiere eslection qui se doibt faire du maire de nostre ville de Langres, le sieur Roussat soit receu. Car j'ay tant de contentment de ses services passez, et il s'est sy bien et sy dignement acquitté de la dicte charge, que j'estimeray à beaucoup de service de le veoir de nouveau esleu en la charge, m'asseurant qu'en vostre absence les affaires de la dicte ville en iront mieux par son moyen: et n'estant ceste-cy pour aultre subject, je prie Dieu, Monsieur de Dinteville, vous avoir en sa saincte et digne garde. Du camp devant Provins, le 30ème jour d'aoust 1592.'

[23] See Guyot de St Michel, *Correspondance*; AN, 120 AP12, 'Dons du roi, 1589–1596', 160r. In June of 1595 Roussat received 1,000 *écus* from the king's coffers.

[24] Guyot de St Michel, *Correspondance*, 132. Henry wrote, 'Ce que nous avons et aurons toujours très agréable, sachant que personne ne peult entrer en ceste charge plus affectionné au bien et advancment de mes affaires, et au repos et conservation de tous vos concitoyens que vous'.

[25] Berger de Xivrey, *Recueil des Lettres de Henri IV*, vol. 3, 752–73. The king wrote, 'Quand à ce que vous m'escriviés touchant le maire de Langres, je vous ay prié avant vostre partement, que lorsque vous seriés sur les lieux, vous vous informeriés particulierement comme tout se passe en la dicte ville, pour me donner advis de ce que vous jugeriés y estre à faire pour mon service. Pour le particulier du dict maire, ses depportemens et actions passées ont faict congnoistre l'affection qu'il a à mon service, et combien il a servy pour contenir en debvoir le peuple de la dicte ville, avec lequel il a beaucoup de creance . . . .je vous prie, mon Cousin, de faire entendre et prescrire à chacun d'eulx ce qui est du debvoir de sa charge, speciallement au dict Sr. de Dinteville à se comporter tellement, par sa prudence, qu'il saiche s'ayder du dict maire et aultres mes serviteurs qui sont en la dicte ville, pour faciliter ce qui pourra ayder au bien de mon dict service.'

[26] Quoted in Camille Jullian, *Histoire de Bordeaux depuis les origines jusqu'en 1895* (Bordeaux: Feret et Fils, 1985), 385.

[27] François Gebelin, *Le gouvernement du Marechal de Matignon en Guyenne, pendant les premières années du règne de Henri IV 1589–1594* (Bordeaux: Mounastre-Picamil, 1912), 45.

no wonder then that Henry wrote to the *jurats* of Bordeaux in July of 1591 just before a mayoral election asking them to continue Matignon as mayor. Henry explained that his wish should not be interpreted as a threat to municipal privileges, but he found that 'no one in the office [of mayor] could bring more dignity and intelligence to [the office]'.[28]

Another case of election interference occurred in Rennes in 1603. The office of mayor did not exist in Rennes; the most important elected member of the town government was known as the *procureur syndic* or the *procureur des bourgeois*. A professional trained in law, the *procureur* was required to defend the liberties and privileges of the town before both secular and church courts. He also represented the bourgeois of Rennes before the Estates of Brittany.[29] Theoretically, the bourgeois of Rennes had the right to elect a new *procureur syndic* the first day of every third year. As part of a reorganization of the Rennes government in 1592, Henry made various changes in the electoral procedures that were, in fact, never carried out.[30] Henry seems to have left Rennes alone until 1603, when he chose the *procureur syndic* from a list of three candidates the town notables sent him. Charles de Cossé, *comte* de Brissac, lieutenant-general of Brittany, wrote to the bourgeois of Rennes in early February to inform them of Henry's decision. The king had opted for the traditional compromise and selected the candidate that had been the town's first choice.[31] Brissac's letter contained an interesting postscript indicating that the king's interference was not to be interpreted as a threat to the town's privileges. 'Gentlemen', he wrote, 'you will see that the king favours the future continuation of your entire liberty in the election of your *procureur des bourgeois*.'[32]

Henry's attempts at election manipulation were not always successful. Between 1587 and 1589, Sebastien Diné held the office of mayor in the town of Saint-Quentin. Henry was assured of his loyalty as a client of the duke of Longueville. In June 1590, when a new election for mayor was held, Henry sent word through Longueville that he wanted to continue Diné for another term; his second choice was a man named Jacques Ledosset. Saint-Quentin's town notables raised objections to the king's wish, however. They argued that it altered the traditional electoral format in which new *échevins* were elected on 20 June each year. The electoral assembly refused to heed the king's advice and elected Loys d'Origny as

---

[28] Berger de Xivrey, *Recueil des Lettres Missives*, vol. 3, 442. Henry explained, ' . . . n'y en pourvant avoir aucun en la dicte charge qui y puisse apporter plus de dignité et intelligence que luy, tant pour le bien de mon service que pour la conservation de la dicte ville, pour laquelle il seroit perilleux en ceste saison d'y admettre aucun aultre qui eust à commencer à s'instruire en la conduicte des affaires de la dicte ville . . . .'

[29] Henri Carré, *Recherches sur l'administration municipale de Rennes au temps de Henri IV* (Geneva: Megariotis Reprints, 1978), 25. In 1592 the office of mayor was created and awarded to the governor of Rennes. It was not an elected post.

[30] Jacques Brejon de Lavergnée, 'Rennes aux XVIᵉ et XVIIᵉ siècles', in *Histoire de Rennes*, ed. Jean Meyer (Toulouse: Privat, 1972), 142.　　[31] *Archives Municipales*, Rennes (hereafter AMR), Laisse 32.

[32] Ibid. Letter dated 12 February 1603. Brissac wrote, 'Messieurs, vous verrez comme le Roy a agreable a ladvenir la continuation de votre liberté entiere a lelection de votre procureur des bourgeois.'

mayor following the traditional procedures. A deputy was sent to the king, and Henry apparently agreed to the election of D'Origny with little comment.[33] D'Origny was not pro-League and had served the king faithfully. The town did not object to Diné because they wanted to disobey the king or because Diné's popularity had declined, but because they wanted to follow time-honoured routine.

Henry sometimes manipulated royalist town constitutions and altered the configuration of municipal assemblies. This occurred in Rennes and Blois. Rennes did not have a college of *échevins*. The municipal government was supervised by the governor of the town, the *procureur syndic*, a *contrôleur*, *miseurs* who performed financial duties, and an undetermined number of bourgeois. Henry II tried to create an *échevinage* in 1548, but the act remained a dead letter.[34] Finally, in 1592, Rennes petitioned Henry IV for the right to elect a council of *échevins*. The king granted the request, and a municipal government was devised consisting of six *échevins*, a *procureur*, one *contrôleur* two *miseurs*, and a *greffier*. Only the office of mayor was not made an elected post. The king awarded it instead to the governor of Rennes, Marec de Montbarot. Strangely enough, even though Rennes wanted to create an *échevinage*, Henry IV's edict received no more application than the previous one by Henry II, and the town continued to elect their traditional officers. *Miseurs* thereafter took the title of *échevin* when leaving office, but it was only an honorary tribute because no *échevinage* existed.[35]

Henry's attempts at municipal regulation amounted to very little in Rennes, but in Blois he was more successful. On many occasions during the sixteenth century, the municipal assembly in Blois had voiced objections to the growing number of royal officials who attended and dominated meetings of the council.[36] Criticizing this preponderance of royal officials, the *échevins* wrote to Henry IV asking for redress. They pointed out that at any given assembly of the municipality the president of the *siège présidial* attended along with the lieutenant-general, the lieutenant-particular, and the lieutenant-criminal from the *bailliage*, several *avocats*, *procureurs*, a *prévôt* and his lieutenant. Royal officials dominated the meetings because they possessed twelve votes against four from the *échevins*. To correct the imbalance, Henry issued an edict, dated 5 January 1610, stating that in the future eight notable bourgeois were to be elected as town councillors to participate in municipal deliberations.[37] The act was registered at a municipal

[33] *Archives Municipales*, Saint-Quentin, F6, assembly dated 20 June 1590. Charles Gomart, 'Saint-Quentin pendant la ligue et lors de la visite de Henri IV en 1590', *Mémoires de la Société Académique de Saint-Quentin*, 6, 2nd series (1847), 167.

[34] Jacques Brejon de Lavergnée, 'Justice et Pouvoir municipal à Rennes aux XVIe et XVIIe siècles', *Bulletin et Mémoires de la Société Archéologique du département D'Ile-et-Vilaine*, 86 (1984), 28.

[35] Ibid., AMR, (23 March 1592); Carré, *Recherches sur Rennes*, 18–23. Note that in 1596 the municipal government in Rennes commented that no *échevins* had been elected, and it was decided to elect eight. No election for the post of *échevin* was ever held, however.

[36] Alexandre Dupré, *Histoire de Blois* (Marseille: Laffitte Reprints, 1977), vol. 2, 191–2.

[37] BN, MSS fr. 18177, fols. 26rv; *Archives Municipales*, Blois (hereafter cited as AMB) BB17, fol. 111.

assembly dated after Henry IV's death on 28 December 1611.[38] The fact that Henry did not deny the request may seem strange, but Blois was regarded with special affection because of the town's history of loyalty to the Crown. The king's edict, moreover, did not deny access to the principal royal officials in Blois, and meetings of the assembly continued to be presided over by the lieutenant-general of the *bailliage*. Henry devised something of a compromise between the Crown and Blois's bourgeoisie. On paper things had changed, but the assemblies continued to meet without much innovation.

Occasionally Henry and a royalist town disagreed. The king decided to establish the Jesuits in Caen in 1608, and on 10 October he wrote to the *échevins* and announced their arrival. The *échevins* had already met and decided they did not want this religious order in their town.[39] In frustration they wrote to the marshall of Fervaques and asked for his help in persuading the king to change his mind. A few weeks later at a general meeting, the principal officers, nobles, and bourgeois of the town noted that Caen already had a university serving the needs of the inhabitants, and Jesuit instruction was not wanted.[40] Armed with a list of protestations, deputies left for the king's court. Henry refused to listen to their supplications, however, and on 6 December 1609, much to the town's chagrin, the king donated the college of Mont in Caen to the Jesuits.[41]

Even against these few examples of Henry's use of Crown authority to manipulate urban politics or override the will of the towns, the most obvious aspects of Henry's actions with his royalist towns were those associated with favour and praise. Caen was disappointed by the Jesuits, but the town magistrates had little to complain about since Henry generally tried to please them. Early in 1589, for example, the *échevins* in Caen petitioned the king to transfer the important fair of Guibray from outside the League town of Falaise to their own vicinity.[42] Henry complied and informed Caen that he would move the fair in recognition of 'the fidelity of the inhabitants of this town who have always served the defunct king and myself very faithfully'.[43] Unfortunately for Caen, once Falaise capitulated the next year and Henry needed to placate the ex-League town, the fair was reassigned to its original location.[44] Over the next few years Caen's municipality complained to the king about the loss of Guibray. He acquiesced after deputies went to court and promised monetary gifts from Caen's notables. To satisfy the town, in 1594 Henry established a new fair in Caen known as the *Foire Franche*.[45]

---

[38] AMB, BB 17, fol. 128v.   [39] Carel, *Histoire de la Ville de Caen*, 305.   [40] Ibid., 306–7.
[41] Ibid., 308; Hugues Neveux, 'Mutations Urbaines (xvie–xviiie siècles)', in *Histoire de Caen*, ed. Gabriel Desert (Toulouse: Privat, 1981), 157.
[42] Carel, *Histoire de la Ville de Caen*, 236–7. This occurred in October 1589.
[43] Ibid., 238. Henry wrote on 1 October 1589, 'Et laquelle foire avons transférons en notre ville de Caen, en reconnaissance de la fidélité des habitants d'icelle ville, qui se sont toujours très fidèlement comportés au service audit défunt roi et nous . . . '   [44] Ibid., 252.   [45] Ibid., 280.

THE REWARDS OF FIDELITY

Henry seemed to take special delight in praising and rewarding his royalist towns for their loyalty. In a letter to Caen written in the first year of his reign, he acknowledged that he wished to 'continue to be your good king, comfort you, and gratify you in all occasions that arrive . . . '.[46] These words sum up his attitude toward his royalist towns. He tried to repay the towns' fidelity in all situations that did not diminish his authority. The examples are numerous. In 1594 he awarded Tours the right to establish a university comparable to the one in Paris.[47] In 1592 he awarded Rennes with a *siège* of police that strengthened the municipal government's power by giving it full say in police matters over and above that of the *sénéschal*.[48] As a sign of affection for the town of Clermont in Auvergne, Henry granted the *échevins* in 1590 the right to wear councillor robes made of purple damask.[49] Only a king could sanction the right to wear purple since it was a regal colour.[50] The purple robes increased the prestige and visibility of Clermont's magistrates and elevated their status on the town's streets.

Henry IV reserved an exceptional affection for Châlons-sur-Marne. He confirmed the town's privileges in 1592, and discharged the inhabitants from contributions to a tax known as the *arrière-ban*.[51] Once in 1595 and again in 1610 Henry issued letters patents forbidding his officers to approach Châlons with their troops. Men at arms were told not to bother the town's inhabitants and that theft would be severely punished.[52] Finally, in 1592 as a symbolic token of his appreciation of Châlon's loyalty, Henry instructed that a medallion be minted in silver and bronze with his profile on the face of the coin and the words CATHALAVENESIS. FIDEI. MONVMENTHVM. or 'memorial to the fidelity of Châlons' on the reverse.[53] A short while later Henry wrote to the magistrates to thank them for their kindness and faithfulness. He ended the letter with the words, 'Ne m'oubliez mie'. Thereafter, the municipal militia took this expression as the device for their flag.[54]

---

[46] Ibid., 236–7. Henry wrote to Caen on 11 October 1589, '[E]t vous assurer qu'en continuant à nous estre bons et loyaux sujets, recongnaissant et vous tenant ungs avec le sieur de la Verune, votre gouverneur, et apportant l'affection que debvés ez occasions qui s'offriront pour le biens de notre service, ainsy que nous nous promettons que ferés, nous continuerons aussi de vous estre bon roy, vous soulaigner, et gratifier ez toutes occasions que s'en offriront et vous de livrerons bientsost, Dieu aydant, de l'oppression de noz ennemys . . . '

[47] L. Benoist de la Grandière, 'Abrége Chronologique et Historique de la Mairie de Tours', *Bulletin et Mémoires de la Société Archéologique de Touraine*, 47 (1908), 327. Lack of funds on the part of the town kept the university from becoming a reality during Henry's reign.

[48] Brejon de Lavergnée, 'Rennes aux XVIe et XVIIe siècles', 41.

[49] See act published in Ambroise Tardieu, *Histoire de la Ville de Clermont-Ferrand dépuis les temps les plus reculés jusqu'à nos jours* (Moulins: Imprimerie de C. Desrosiers, 1872), 412.

[50] E. Vial, *Costumes Consulaires* (Lyons: Librairie Ancienne de Louis Brun, 1904), 66–81.

[51] De Barthélemy, *Histoire de Châlons-sur-Marne*, 321.

[52] Ibid., 321–2, 330. See document 69 dated 29 April 1610 printed in Barbat, *Histoire de Châlons-sur-Marne*.

[53] Ibid., 313. The face of the coin read HENRICUS IV. DEI. GRATIA. FRANCIAE. ET. NAVARRAE. REX.

[54] Ibid.

Henry accommodated the municipal government in Châlons whenever he was able. By the specifications of the Edict of Nantes, for example, Châlons was established as a place of double faith, and by 1599 Protestants began to assemble there for worship. The arrival of the Protestants upset many, however, and deputies quickly left for the king's court to beg another solution. Two commissioners were sent to Châlons to oversee the execution of the Edict of Nantes along with a president of the Parlement of Paris. Henry agreed to forbid Protestant assemblies in Châlons and its *faubourgs*, but he refused to close the Protestant cemeteries. Members of the new faith could gather in Châlons for interments, and a Protestant church was established in nearby Compertrix.[55] Yet these concessions were not sufficient for the townspeople of Châlons, and again the municipality dispatched deputies to court. The matter was not completely settled until Henry agreed to move the sight of the Protestant church a greater distance from Châlons, to Vitry.[56]

A TRADITIONAL RENAISSANCE KING

The relationship Henry cultivated with his royalist towns was not altogether different from that he fostered with his former Catholic League towns. Unless they gave him cause for concern or sought his intervention he did not influence their daily affairs. There was certainly less opportunism on Henry's part in dealing with royalist towns to threaten municipal liberties. He did not attempt to deny royalist towns their traditional rights and privileges, and he seemed to want to reward their fidelity whenever possible. His relationship with the royalist towns was characterized by this thankfulness for their support during the religious wars.

Henry's leniency toward the royalist towns was also quite artificial given the nature of the municipalities under scrutiny. Only Langres and Clermont, in fact, enjoyed a certain autonomy. The others, Rennes, Caen, Tours, Blois, Bordeaux, and Châlons had already accepted the infiltration of royal officials into their administrative assemblies. Caen, for instance, was not a commune but rather a town of franchise supervised by the lieutenant-general of the bailiwick. Caen did not even have an elected mayor because, as far back as the fourteenth century, the Crown had replaced this officer with a royally appointed one.[57] In Rennes, Blois, Tours, and Châlons, the governors of these towns regularly sat in on municipal deliberations. The town governments of Rennes and Bordeaux were overshadowed by parlements that tried to direct their affairs. Henry II had reorganized Bordeaux's municipal government in 1550 along the lines of the *échevinage* in Paris, and from

---

[55] Ibid., 323–7.
[56] Ibid., document printed in Barbat, *Histoire de Châlons-sur-Marne*, 60; *Archives Municipales, Châlons-sur-Marne*, E. Supp. 4789, fols. 242–4. Noel Valois, ed. *Inventaire des Arrêts du Conseil d'Etat (Règne de Henri IV)* (Paris: Imprimerie Nationale, 1893), vol. 2, 5796.
[57] Neveux, 'Mutations Urbaines', 157.

that time, the king usually selected the mayor of the city himself. Most of the royalist towns, therefore, were already under greater Crown supervision by the reign of Henry IV than some of the more independent League towns, and because of the prevalence of royalist client-governors, Crown officials and their networks of allies, these towns remained loyal to the Crown. For example, Phillip Thomassin, governor of Châlons, was a faithful client of the king. Thomassin received at least 8,666 *écus* from Henry between 1589 and 1596 and did all within his power to keep Châlons loyal to the Crown.[58] Royalist clienteles undoubtedly held control over loyal towns and kept Catholic League influence at bay.

No fervent autonomy and return to medieval independence engulfed the royalist towns during the religious wars, and so they presented less of a threat to the king. Thus while in many ex-League frontier towns like Amiens and Abbeville, Henry reduced the size of the municipal governments after their capitulations, he left royalist frontier towns like Saint-Quentin alone.[59] Henry praised the fidelity of the inhabitants of Saint-Quentin in 1589 when he told them, 'you have never had a king who desires more to maintain you and your privileges'.[60] Henry reappointed the sieur de Roussat as mayor in the frontier town of Langres many times, but he never reorganized the municipal government there. In Clermont, a powerful urban centre in Auvergne, Henry did not tamper with the town's immediate liberties, although he did send several commissions into the province to verify municipal accounts and report back to him on justice, police, finance, and administrative matters.[61]

Henry IV's attitude toward his royalist towns can be summarized as follows: he rewarded the towns for their loyalty and concerned himself with more pressing matters. His greatest interest seems to have been in maintaining loyal clients in key posts in important cities like Langres on the frontier or in Bordeaux where pro–League forces continually stirred trouble. This was similar to his actions in dealing with Catholic League towns. Royal involvement in general with the municipalities was governed by the relative importance of each town. Because of their size and rebellious history, the king viewed the League towns as more dangerous, and he showed them more interest during his reign.

Given Henry's weak position in the early 1590s, he had no reason to threaten his client towns. Afterwards, once his reign was secure, he never risked irritating them by withdrawing municipal liberties. He rarely strengthened the royalist towns, but

[58] AN, 120AP 12, *Dons du Roi*, fols. 14, 34, 90, 154.
[59] Henri Martin, Henri Bouchot, Emmanuel Lemaire, eds., *Le Livre Rouge de L'Hotel de Ville de Saint-Quentin* (Saint-Quentin: Imprimerie Charles Poette, 1881), vol 3.
[60] Henry IV, *Recueil des Lettres Missives de Henri IV*, vol. 3, 75. Henry wrote on 8 November 1589, 'en consideration de la fidelité que vous nous aves conservée jusques icy, et que nous nous promettons que vous nous continueres toujours, vous cognoistrés par les effects, en ce qui s'offrira de vous gratifier, que nous vous avons en particuliere recommandation; que vous n'avés jamais eu Roy qui ayt desiré plus que nous de vous conserver en vous previleges, et sur tout de vous maintenir en la religion catholique, apostolique et romaine.'
[61] A. G. Manry, *Histoire de Clermont-Ferrand* (Clermont-Ferrand: Imprimerie Mont-Louis et de la Presse Reunies, 1975), 149.

he listened to them and rewarded them with unique distinctions. None of the rewards were meaningless since by granting special privileges or honours to the towns and magistrates, Henry strengthened his legitimacy and incorporated his subjects into his grandeur. On local issues royalist towns easily swayed the king to their positions.[62] As long as they remained loyal client towns Henry honoured them. He was not only confident in them but extremely aware of their fidelity which he wanted to maintain. In the royalist towns he made little effort to alter their constitutions or exert the authority of the Crown in their affairs. He worked with the towns and showed none of the absolutist determination so often associated with his reign.

HENRY IV AND PROTESTANT PRIVILEGE

During the first forty years of Henry IV's life his religious persona was deeply tied to the Protestant towns of France. Although he renounced Protestantism to save his life during the 1572 St Bartholomew's Day Massacre, his Protestant allies willingly accepted him as their leader after he abjured Catholicism in 1576 following his escape from Henry III's court. Between 1576 and 1593 Protestants took great comfort in the fact that their king shared their Calvinist beliefs. This made the shock of Henry's abjuration on 25 July 1593 all the more difficult to understand. Members of the reformed church had undoubtedly worried that the king might one day convert, but nothing prepared them for the defection of their powerful leader from the Calvinist church.[63]

To avert confusion surrounding his abjuration, Henry wrote many letters to his Protestant allies and towns shortly after the abjuration and promised to protect his Calvinist subjects. He guaranteed his Protestant towns that he would maintain their edicts of pacification, and he stressed that the abjuration had not changed the affection he felt for them.[64] The king wrote to the magistrates in La Rochelle only hours after converting and insisted he would continue to love his Huguenot brethren and shield them from oppression.[65] He emphasized the necessity of peace

---

[62] Limoges, a royalist town with a large League contingent, was an exception and is discussed in chapter 7.

[63] Michael Wolfe, *The Conversion of Henry IV Politics, Power, and Religious Belief in Early Modern France* (Cambridge, Massachusettes: Harvard University Press, 1993), 47–62, 136–41, 182–3.

[64] L. Canet, *L'Aunis et La Saintonge, de la Guerre de Cent Ans à Henri IV* (La Rochelle: F. Pijollet, 1933), vol. 2, 272–3.

[65] Berger de Xivrey, *Recueil des Lettres Missives de Henri IV*, vol. 3, 825. Henry wrote to La Rochelle, '[D]ont vous prions en demeurer trés asseurez et ne nous donner pas ce desplaisir qu'il en paroisse aucun indice de deffiance; ce qui nous seroit aussy moleste que nous sentons qu'il n'y a rien tant esloigné de nostre intention, laquelle, ainsy qu'elle ne changera point en ce qui sera de l'observation des dicts edicts, changera aussy peu en l'affection que nous vous avons tousjours portée, ayans toute occasion, pour les bons services et l'assistance que nous en avons tousjours eue, de vous aimer et gratifier, et preserver de toute oppression et injure . . . '

and encouraged his Protestant subjects to remain faithful to the Crown. Even so, shock, disbelief, and anger reverberated throughout the Protestant party.[66]

Paris may have been worth a mass, but it was also apparently worth losing longtime Huguenot allies. While the sieur La Force, the duke of Lesdiguières, and the baron of Rosny (Sully) continued to back the king after his conversion, Duplessis-Mornay, the duke of Bouillon, and the duke of La Trémoille withdrew their support from him.[67] The Protestant estrangement became particularly apparent in 1597 when many of the Huguenot nobles opted not to aid the king in battle at the siege of Amiens.[68] The Protestant leaders felt betrayed and wondered why the king did not immediately settle the toleration issue. As a recent convert to Catholicism, Henry had no intention of alienating his growing Catholic support by favouring the Huguenots soon after his abjuration.[69] He preferred to wait until his kingship was secure and then tackle the matter of Protestantism within a Catholic France.[70] In the meantime, to placate his Protestant towns, Henry sent letters reconfirming their municipal privileges, but these letters failed to quiet Huguenot fears.[71] Writing to a friend about the Protestant assembly at Loudun in 1596, for instance, the Huguenot leader Philippe Duplessis, sieur of Mornay, explained:

> Every one there desires peace, but every one is weary of the uncertainty of our condition . . . It is vain to preach patience to them. They reply that they have had patience, but to no purpose. The king has been reigning for seven years, and their condition daily grows worse. Everything is done for the League, and neither the court nor the tribunals refuse anything to its adherents. The story of the Prodigal Son does not compare with their treatment. At least, say the Huguenots, after having killed for them the fatted calf, let not the rope be left about their necks as the reward of our fidelity.[72]

In 1598 when the war with Spain ended and Henry decided to grant the Huguenots their edict of toleration, France contained some 1,250,000 Protestants. This figure represented only six per cent of the country's total population. Huguenots lived for

---

[66] It is interesting to note that on many occasions before his abjuration, Henry had promised his Huguenot supporters that he would never change his religion. Even after his reconversion, moreover, Henry was known to lapse now and then into Huguenot practices. He allegedly sang versions of Theodore Beza's psalms with his sister, Catherine of Bourbon, and her friends and questioned the eternal ramifications of his abjuration with Agrippa d'Aubigne. Henry M. Baird, *The Huguenots and Henry of Navarre* (New York: Charles Scribner's Sons, 1886), vol. 2, 260–1, 332.
[67] Buisseret, *Henry IV*, 46.   [68] Berger de Xivrey, *Recueil des Lettres Missives*, vol. 4, 826.
[69] Robin Briggs, *Early Modern France, 1560–1715* (Oxford: Oxford University Press, 1984), 73. Wolfe notes that facing an uncertain future, Protestants began to hold assemblies with increasing regularity after 1593 in which they discussed supporting other Protestant leaders such as Elizabeth I of England. Wolfe, *The Conversion of Henri IV*, 182.
[70] N. M. Sutherland, *The Huguenot Struggle for Recognition* (New Haven: Yale University Press, 1980), 328.
[71] See for example, letters sent by Henry IV to La Rochelle in April, August, and September of 1594. *Bibliothèque Municipale de La Rochelle* (hereafter cited as BMLR), MSS 82, 'Recueil des privileges', AA5, fols. 176–8, 181–3, 196–211.
[72] Quoted in Baird, *The Huguenots*, vol. II, 396; Philippe Duplessis-Mornay, *Mémoires et Correspondance de Duplessis-Mornay* (Paris: Chez Treuttel et Wurtz, 1824), vol. 6, 468.

the most part in five great regions and generally in towns. These areas were Guyenne (Aquitaine), Languedoc, Dauphiné, Saintonge, and Béarn and they included the important towns of La Rochelle, Saumur, Saint-Jean-d'Angély, Nérac, Loudun, Montauban, Castres, Montpellier, Nîmes, Anduze, Uzès, Die, Privas, Montélimar, and Gap.[73] The largest of these towns around 1600 were: La Rochelle (20,000), Montauban (17,000), Montpellier (15,500), Castres (15,500), and Nîmes (13,000).[74] Substantial Protestant enclaves also existed in Normandy. The towns were of fundamental importance to the Huguenots because they believed that the strong walls encircling their great municipalities gave them the protection they needed to prevent further slaughter by their enemies.[75] Along these lines, the Protestant noble François de La Noue wrote: 'we are determined not to relax our hold upon a single one of them, but to maintain them at any cost, until by some written edict such provision shall be made for our grievances that we shall no longer have occasion to fear.'[76]

Fitting the Huguenot component into Henry IV's regard for the towns brings the dimensions of his efforts at conciliation more clearly into focus. Henry intervened in Protestant towns to maintain order, restructure governments, and enforce the Edict of Nantes. Yet while the Edict complicated the dynamic between Henry and his Calvinist subjects, the Protestant towns were much less threatening to internal security as the wars ended than former-League towns that retained ultra-Catholic minorities, distraught over Henry's kingship. Henry even used the Edict to increase his legitimacy by obliging the Protestant towns to recognize that the enjoyment of their privileges was tied to his royal will. But Henry had neither the power nor the resources to force the Protestant towns to abjure, and as his relationship with Huguenot France deteriorated after 1593, accommodation proved the most logical course of action.[77]

THE EDICT OF NANTES

The Edict of Nantes, first signed in Nantes on 13 April 1598 resembled the documents Henry negotiated with the Catholic League towns upon their capitulations because the Edict granted specific rights and privileges to the king's Protestant subjects just as the capitulation treaties acknowledged the rights and privileges of the Catholic towns. Many of the Edict's provisions, in fact, reaffirmed the concessions awarded in earlier pacification treaties while the capitulation agree-

[73] Philip Benedict, *The Huguenot Population of France, 1600–1685: the Demographic Fate and Customs of a Religious Minority* (Philadelphia: Transactions of the American Philosophical Society, 1991), vol. 81; Janine Garrisson, *L'Edit de Nantes et sa revocation, Histoire d'une intolerance* (Paris: Editions du Seuil, 1985), 18, 46.
[74] Philip Benedict, 'French Cities from the Sixteenth Century to the Revolution: An Overview', in *Cities and Social Change in Early Modern Europe*, ed. Philip Benedict (London: Unwin Hyman, 1989), 25.   [75] Baird, *The Huguenots*, 397.   [76] Quoted in *ibid.*
[77] Mack P. Holt, *The French Wars of Religion, 1562–1629* (Cambridge: Cambridge University Press, 1995), 162–72. Holt notes that the Edict of Nantes was 'molded by his [Henry's] politics of appeasement' (p. 162).

ments worked out with the Catholic League towns reconfirmed ancient charters conceded by previous kings. Also, like capitulation treaties, the Edict ordered past wrongs and incidents of aggression forgotten 'as things that had never been'.[78] Of course the Edict of Nantes contained much more than any of the capitulation charters since it gave legal definition to the Protestant party and offered limited toleration for the practice of the reformed faith.[79] Its purpose was precisely stated in the preamble: to provide one general law, 'clear, pure, and absolute', regulating all differences between those of the two religions.[80] Michael Wolfe argues that while the Edict established peace it also institutionalized conflict by failing to resolve the dichotomy between Huguenot fidelity and religious non-conformity. Henry never pressed the issue since the faithfulness of his former Calvinist allies was vital to the establishment of stability between 1598 and 1610, but the conflict remained.[81]

The Edict of Nantes represented the end result of over two years of negotiations.[82] Its specifications were contained in four separate documents. The main body of the Edict consisted of ninety-two articles and was accompanied by fifty-six secret articles and two royal brevets. The secret articles clarified the main document, while the brevets dealt with sensitive issues that the king did not wish made public.[83] The Protestants wanted the document drafted in the form of an Edict thus forcing its registration by the parlements.[84] It was declared 'perpetual and irrevocable' by the king although the entire rationale for the document suggests that it was a temporary measure employed to bring peace until a time when confessional unity might be re-established.[85] Mack Holt argues that the Edict established a period of temporary religious co-existence and thus reflected Henry's commitment to Gallican France and the restoration of 'one king, one faith, one law'.[86] The royal brevets were set to expire in 1606 thus leaving the door open for a re-evaluation of peaceful co-existence at that time. The Edict can be interpreted as an exercise in power. Instead of coercing the Huguenots into reconversion, Henry offered them a period of grace in which they might follow his lead. In this way the Edict affected Huguenot thought and action by establishing recognized spaces for Calvinist worship while at the same time prolonging a sense of uncertainty in which gentle persuasion might be used to bring about a return to Catholicism.[87]

[78] Quoted in Roland Mousnier, *The Assassination of Henry IV*, trans. Joan Spencer (New York: Charles Scribner's Sons), 318.
[79] See Edict in BN, MSS fr. Nouv. Acq. 7191, fols. 242–336; A complete copy printed in French is found in Roland Mousnier, *L'assassinat d'Henri IV, 14 Mai 1610* (Paris: Editions Gallimard, 1964), 294–334. A copy in English is printed in Mousnier, *The Assassination*, 316–63.
[80] Quoted in Mousnier, *L'assassinat*, 296 and Mounsier, *The Assassination*, 318; see also, Sutherland, *The Huguenot Struggle*, 329.   [81] Wolfe, *The Conversion of Henri IV*, 183.
[82] Garrisson, *L'Edit de Nantes*, 15.
[83] Holt, *The French Wars of Religion*, 163–6; Buisseret, *Henry IV*, 70.
[84] Sutherland, *The Huguenot Struggle*, 329. The author notes: 'The Protestant demand for an edict was not so much an expression of their opinion on the relative juridical value of different forms of law, as a reflection, at best, of lack of confidence in the Crown and, at worst, of hostility to the king.'
[85] Mousnier, *L'assassinat*, 296.   [86] Holt, *The French Wars of Religion*, 163, 170.
[87] Richard Flathman, *The Practice of Political Authority, Authority and the Authoritative* (Chicago: University of Chicago Press, 1980), 150.

The provisions of the Edict of Nantes are well known. The main document granted liberty of conscience in matters of faith to French men and women in all parts of the realm. The liberty to exercise publicly the reformed religion was conceded to the Huguenots in the places where it had been practised in 1596 and up to August 1597. In all other areas of France two towns in each *bailliage* or *sénéchaussée* were to be designated as towns that permitted Protestant worship. Nobles could hold services in their homes, and at court they could practise their faith as long as they did so in private. Although it is not generally recognized, article 3 of the Edict re-established the Catholic religion in locations in which such worship had been prohibited by the Huguenots before article 9 permitted public exercise of the reformed faith.[88]

Other articles of the Edict of Nantes attempted to assimilate the Huguenots into the mainstream of French life by guaranteeing, for example, that all public offices would be open to them. Most conditions in the document, however, set the Huguenots apart and made them an exception. Thus to ensure the Huguenots proper non-suspect justice, Henry ordered that a special *Chambre de l'édict* associated with the parlements of Paris, Rouen, and Rennes be created to judge Protestant cases in those regions. Another *Chambre* previously established in Castres as part of the parlement of Toulouse was maintained, and two others were organized in connection with the parlements of Bordeaux and Grenoble. The Protestant church was also allowed to keep its ecclesiastical organization, but while the holding of consistories, colloquies, and provincial and national synods was authorized, all other political assemblies were prohibited.[89] The two secret brevets specified the payment of Protestant pastors from public funds and permitted the Protestants to retain all towns that they held in August 1597 for eight years following the publication of the edict. The king also agreed to pay the garrisons of the Protestant towns.[90]

Catholics and Protestants alike received the Edict of Nantes with overwhelming criticism. The parlements registered the Edict in their own time but under protest. Henry IV went to the Parlement of Paris in person and ordered the Edict's registration in 1599. Thereafter the parlements of Grenoble, Toulouse, Dijon, Bordeaux, and Rennes followed suit. Henry told deputies from the Parlement of Bordeaux, 'I have made an edict. I intend that it shall be obeyed. Whatever may happen, I mean to be obeyed. It will be well for you if you do so.'[91] Despite such strong language, the Parlement of Rouen held out and did not register the Edict until 1609.[92]

When the religious wars ended, many Catholics believed that the Edict of Nantes

---

[88] Mousnier, *L'assassinat*, 297–8; Sutherland, *The Huguenot Struggle*, 330; Ernest Lavisse, Jean Mariéjol, *Histoire de France Illustrée depuis les Origines Jusqu'à La Révolution 6: La Reforme et la Ligue, L'Edit de Nantes* (New York: A.M.S. Press, Inc., Reprints, 1969), 418–19.
[89] Sutherland, *The Huguenot Struggle*, 331.   [90] Ibid., 330–1.
[91] Quoted in Baird, *The Huguenots*, vol. 2, 437.
[92] Holt, *The French Wars of Religion*, 168; Buisseret, *Henry IV*, 72–3; Lavisse and Mariéjol, *Histoire de la France*, vol. 6, part 1, 421–2.

transformed the Huguenot community into a privileged elite. The Protestants emerged from the wars as a separate political entity that controlled large areas of France. At least two-hundred Protestant towns dotted the French landscape, and many of them were fortified and garrisoned under the sanctions of the Edict. But in creating the 'state within a state' and giving it a temporary life of eight years, Henry also established a precedent for greater Crown interaction with the Protestant towns. Royal agents were sent out from Paris to enforce the Edict, and the privileged status was set to be re-evaluated when the royal brevets expired.

THE EDICT OF NANTES IN THE PROTESTANT TOWNS

Even if the Edict of Nantes offered privileged status to the French Protestants, they did not receive it with rejoicing, and protests occurred in many towns. The bone of contention that aggravated the Huguenots was that the Edict re-established Catholicism in Protestant towns. Henry sent commissioners out to the localities to publish the Edict of Nantes, but these royal agents confronted difficulties in convincing town councils to go along peacefully with the religious settlement. The Protestant magistrates objected to re-introducing the Mass within their town walls. Thus, while the Edict of Nantes appeared to favour French Protestants within the realm, it also incited friction between the king and the Huguenot municipal leaders over the Catholic issue.

This situation was nowhere more apparent than in the Huguenot fortress of La Rochelle. In July 1599 the king's commissioners, Messieurs de Parabère and Langlois, arrived in the town to publish the Edict and oversee its enactment.[93] The two men immediately called a meeting of the town magistrates and notables and explained the conditions in the documents. Parabère emphasized that the Edict of Nantes was designed for Protestants and Catholics alike. This meant that he expected the town leaders to designate a church where the Catholics could worship and hold Mass. After leaving the town council, the king's agents met with La Rochelle's Huguenot pastors and members of the consistory. Parabère warned the ministers that the king counted on the obedience of La Rochelle and intended to punish anyone who refused to accept the Edict of Nantes.[94]

Despite the forcefulness of the king's agents, publishing the Edict proved no easy matter in La Rochelle. The town contained roughly 16,000 to 18,000 Protestants and 2,000 to 4,000 Catholics.[95] The day after their initial meeting with the town's leaders, Parabère and Langlois began arguing with the mayor and his councillors. The magistrates agreed to the publication of the Edict, but they wanted

---

[93] David Parker, *La Rochelle and the French Monarchy: Conflict and Order in Seventeenth-Century France* (London: Royal Historical Society, 1980), 127. Parker explains that 'Parabère was the Protestant governor of Niort, and Langlois, sieur de Beaupaire, was a *maître de requêtes*.'

[94] Jacques Merlin, *Diaire de Jacques Merlin ou Recueil des choses les plus mémorables qui se sont passés en ceste ville de La Rochelle*, ed. Charles Dangibeaud (La Rochelle: Archives Historiques de la Saintonge et de L'Aunis, 1878), vol. 5, 87–8.   [95] Parker, *La Rochelle*, 126.

to modify it with certain conditions. They agreed to allow limited Catholic worship in the church of Saint Marguerite but refused to permit the Catholics to engage in public religious spectacles and condemned the observation of Catholic holy days in the Protestant stronghold.[96] La Rochelle's mayor, Alexandre de Haraneder, sieur de Roulraux, explained that Parabère and Langlois could publish the Edict and enforce its execution, but he insisted that the *corps de ville* would not make any specific agreements with the Catholics. The municipal authorities thus refused to accept responsibility for establishing the provisions of the Edict.[97]

Parabère understood that La Rochelle's leaders were trying to establish a dangerous precedent. If he allowed the Protestants to revise the Edict, the Catholics might do the same and the entire process of publishing the important document and registering it in the parlements would be impeded.[98] Henry needed the compliance of La Rochelle to the Edict of Nantes in order to have it registered by the parlements. Parabère wrote immediately to the king and informed him of his difficulties stating that he would try to solve the problems by holding a conference with the Protestants and the Catholics.[99]

Days of turmoil and discussion followed. La Rochelle's religious and secular leaders wanted to publish the Edict of Nantes with a letter of protestation attached, but Parabère rejected the idea. Next, the Protestant ministers in the town slipped a copy of their complaints to members of La Rochelle's *siège présidial* to guard until such time as they might be made public. The mayor spoiled the plot, however, by informing the king's commissioners. Learning of the indignation, Parabère exploded in anger and argued:

When the Council of His Majesty finds out that the Edict has been received here, but with protests attached, what will he say? . . . Have you no regard for the affairs of the king? Have you no respect for him? Doesn't the affection that he has for you and the care that he has shown you move you to consent to something that is of urgent necessity?[100]

The trickery of La Rochelle's leadership, moreover, was not Parabère's only problem. He soon learned that the townspeople were equally disturbed by the Edict and ready to act on their rage. Violence broke out on 4 August when a mob of

[96] Ibid., 127. The *corps de ville* wanted to limit Catholic processions, forbid Catholic rites at burials, and prohibit the public display of holy bread before Catholic communion.
[97] Merlin, *Diaire*, 90; Louis-Etienne Arcère, *Histoire de la Ville de La Rochelle et du Pays d'Aulnis* (La Rochelle: Chez Rene-Jacob Desbordes, 1757 and Marseille: Lafitte Reprints, 1975), vol. 2, 77.
[98] Merlin, *Diaire*, 91; Canet, *L'Aunis et La Saintonge*, vol. 2, 278–80.
[99] BN, MSS fr. 23195, fol. 432.
[100] Merlin, *Diaire*, 96. Parabère stated, 'Quand le conseil de Sa Majesté entendra que l'édit a esté receu ici, mais avec protestation à l'encontre, que dira-t-il? Avec quelle hardiesse osera-t-il enjoindre aux autres cours de parlement, de la part du roy, qu'elles procèdent à la vérification de l'édit? Ne voulez-vous point avoir égard aux affaires de votre roy? Ne voulez-vous point avoir quelque respect pour lui? L'affection qu'il vous porte, le soin qu'il a de vous ne vous émouveront point pour accorder quelque chose à la nécessité urgente d'icelle?'

artisans and labourers vandalized the church of Saint Marguerite. They smashed windows, destroyed the lectern, tore up the sanctuary's floorboards, and desisted only after the mayor threatened them with punishment.[101]

The controversy finally ended on 5 August when the Edict of Nantes was published without restrictions or grievances. Parabère agreed in his capacity as commissioner of the king to hear the letter of protestation read in private, but he refused to have it made public.[102] At the sound of the trumpet royal officials announced the specifications of the Edict in all quarters of the city, and the mayor turned the key to the church of Saint Marguerite over to Parabère.[103] Times were not quiet, however. The Catholics began practising their faith in La Rochelle, but not without enduring abuse from Huguenot protestors.[104] An uneasy peace existed between the two groups that often dissolved into confrontation, and members of the Catholic community regularly wrote to the king or his ministers complaining of their treatment.[105] Catholics found it hard to repair their church because Protestant gangs assaulted Catholic carpenters during the day and sabotaged renovation work at night.[106]

La Rochelle was not unique in questioning the Edict of Nantes. Henry's agent in Languedoc, Henry de Caumels, warned the king, 'many are not happy with their duty'.[107] Montpellier and Nimes both sent deputies to court with *cahiers des grievances* denouncing sections of the Edict.[108] The Catholic issue was particularly disturbing in Montauban. There the bishop who came to lead the Catholic followers in the town encountered an angry mob of artisans and students when he tried to claim the church of Saint Louis. Eventually, with the aid of an *arrêt* from the king, the Catholics returned to Saint Louis, but the church was in a shambles and had been burned.[109]

Anti-Catholic sentiment inspired by the Edict of Nantes's publication stirred resentment in large and small towns alike. In 1600 in the little municipality of Fiac in Languedoc, for example, eighty to one hundred Protestant residents and soldiers roused by news of the Edict stormed the town's chateau, pillaged the Catholic

[101] Ibid., 99; Arcère, *Histoire de la Ville de La Rochelle*, vol. 2, 80.
[102] Arcère, *Histoire de la Ville de La Rochelle*, vol. 2, 80.
[103] Joseph Guillaudeau, *Diaire de Joseph Guillaudeau, sieur de Beaupreau (1584–1643)*, ed. Louis Meschinet de Richemond (La Rochelle: Imprimerie Nouvelle Noël Texier et Fils, 1908), 24–5.
[104] Merlin, *Diaire*, 99, 107; Guillaudeau, *Diaire*, 26. Over five hundred Catholics attended Mass in La Rochelle on 6 August 1599.   [105] For example, BN, MSS fr. 15900, vol. 2, fol. 469.
[106] Parker, *La Rochelle*, 128.
[107] BN, MSS fr. 23196, fol. 159. Letter dated 29 November 1600 from De Caumels to Henry IV.
[108] Leon Ménard, *Histoire Civile Ecclésiastique et Litteraire de la Ville de Nismes* (Nismes: Chez-Hugues-Daniel Chaubert, 1754 and Marseille: Laffitte Reprints, 1976), vol. 5, 313.
[109] Janine Garrisson, 'La reconquête catholique (17e siècle)', *Histoire de Montauban*, ed. Daniel Ligou (Toulouse: Editions Privat, 1984), 136. The Catholics also won the right to worship in the church of Saint-Jacques, although the town's Protestant administrators, who had turned the church into an arsenal, were permitted to continue to use the clock in the church's tower for calling out the city militia. Noël Valois, *Inventaire des Arrêts du Conseil d'Etat (Règne de Henri IV)* (Paris: Imprimerie Nationale, 1893), vol. 2, 10635. For more anti-Catholic sentiment, see 15621.

church, and chased all of the Catholics out into the countryside, wounding and killing many of them in the process. The mob directed their anger at the municipal officials as well and assaulted the town hall. In their fury, they destroyed precious documents, specifically the registers of the town's municipal deliberations. They even killed their *premier consul*, Jean Bordouche, during the tumult when he tried to prevent their entry into the chateau by blocking the main gate. The portcullis was cut, and the unfortunate man was split in half.[110]

Urban upheavals quickly drew the attention of the king and his agents in the provinces. Henry de Caumels wrote to Henry from Languedoc and called the Fiac fiasco, 'the beginning of disorder that merits exemplary punishment'.[111] He asked that the duke of Ventadour be dispatched with his troops to re-establish order.[112] The incident reveals the level of urban disturbance roused by the Edict of Nantes. Church burnings were also common and represented collective Protestant anxiety over the Edict. In Pamiers in Henry's Comté de Foix, a violent reaction to the Edict caused the inhabitants to burn the designated Catholic church of St Heleine.[113]

If re-instituting Catholic mass in Protestant towns posed numerous difficulties for the king and his royal agents, re-integrating Catholics into Huguenot municipal governments also presented problems. Soon after the Edict was registered by the parlements at Toulouse and Grenoble, Henry sent orders to the towns of lower Languedoc and Dauphiné to allow Catholics to participate in their municipal governments by serving as magistrates. These administrations were known as governments *mi-partie*. The regulation reinforced clauses within the Edict that awarded Catholics living in Protestant towns the right to their own churches and cemeteries and the right to participate in municipal self-government through membership on town councils. When the commissioners overseeing the implementation of the Edict of Nantes in Dauphiné arrived in the town of Gap in 1601, for example, they altered the composition of the town consulate. Henceforth, instead of three Protestants, the municipal government was to consist of one Protestant, one Catholic, and a third drawn from either group. A sixteen-member municipal council was ordered divided equally between eight Protestants and eight Catholics.[114]

Gap accepted the change without protest, but this was not the case in every municipality. When the Protestant consuls in the garrisoned town of Montélimar in Dauphiné first heard about Catholics joining their government, one member

---

[110] BN, MSS fr. 23196, fols. 173, 178, 180, 181, 184.
[111] Ibid., fol. 180. The commissioner wrote, 'C'est ung commencement de desordre qui merite une punition exemplaire.'
[112] Ibid. It isn't clear whether Ventadour went to Fiac or not, but this is what Henry de Caumels called for.
[113] BN, MSS fr. 23196, fol. 57. Henry's kingdom of Navarre became part of the French Crown in 1607.
[114] Joseph Roman, *Histoire de la Ville de Gap* (Gap: Imprimerie J-C. Richaud Librairie-Editeur, 1892), 181.

suggested avoiding the annoyance altogether by massacring all the town's Catholics.[115] Henry IV's commissioners in the province, however, forced the issue, and Catholics did earn places on Montélimar's consulate. Thus on 27 December 1599 two Protestants and one Catholic were elected to the office of consul, and six Protestants and three Catholics were elected to the office of councillor. Other Protestant town governments in Dauphiné experienced the same fate as Montélimar.[116]

Henry IV's mandate regarding the complexion of municipal governments additionally troubled Huguenot inhabitants in Nîmes, and Uzès. Immediately these towns sent deputies to court to argue their case against including Catholics on their town consulates. The magistrates in Nîmes were so shocked by Henry's action that they did not believe his order. They suspected that the Catholics had misinterpreted the Edict of Nantes or had willfully re-interpreted the king's words in order to infiltrate the urban consulates. Once the truth was learned, days of discussion ensued over how to convince the king that he had been misguided. Nîmes's elites felt that no good could come from including Catholics on the consulate.[117] Their deputations to court failed, however, and in 1601 the citizens in the towns of lower Languedoc held their first elections under the new provisions. Catholics won places by the king's command enforced by his royal agents in the provinces.[118]

Henry had attempted to re-assimilate the Catholics into public offices in the Protestant towns as quickly as possible after the publication of the Edict of Nantes. This was done out of fairness to the Catholics, and as a means of returning stability to the towns after the Wars of Religion. It was a bold measure because the king gambled with alienating the Huguenots and rousing trouble in the towns. But Catholics lived in the Protestant towns, and they stood a better chance of decent treatment in their daily lives with Catholic magistrates on the municipal councils. Henry might have also been preparing the way for a return to Catholic orthodoxy throughout France. If he did envision a Catholic France, he needed to lay the groundwork by incorporating Catholics in Protestant town governments as quickly as possible. Even so, Henry never ordered the integration of Catholics into Protestant municipal governments in parts of southwestern France, in lower Poitou, Aunis, and Saintonge. La Rochelle was located in the *pays d'Aunis*, but there is no evidence that the king ever tried to force the city's government to include Catholics in their ranks.

Henry may have treated La Rochelle with kid gloves, but the structure of the municipal governments in the south-west might have influenced his actions as well. In the Midi the consulates were small, usually consisting of four to eight men. In Poitou, Aunis, and Saintonge, the local governments were quite large, often

---

[115] Baron de Coston, *Histoire de Montélimar et des Familles Principales qui ont habité cette ville* (Paris: Editions du Palais Royal, 1973), vol. 2, 536.　　[116] Ibid., 540.
[117] *Archives Municipales*, Nîmes, LL15, fols. 154–70; see letter from king on fol. 169.
[118] Ménard, *Histoire Civile*, vol. 5, 315.

including one hundred or more members. La Rochelle's municipality had been modelled on the *Etablissements de Rouen*, and the city was governed by one *maire*, twelve *échevins*, twelve *conseillers*, and seventy-five *pairs*.[119] Moreover, while the consulates often included a member from each of the various sectors of the society so that one lawyer, one bourgeois, one merchant, and one labourer were elected to each of four positions in the governments, town councils conforming to the *Etablissements* were strongly oligarchic. *Pairs* held their offices for life and passed their positions on to family members. *Echevins*, *conseillers*, and *pairs* chose their mayors every year from among themselves. Forcing Catholics into La Rochelle's municipal government, therefore, would probably have been a formidable task because the system was totally controlled by oligarchic families and not as easily manipulated from outside. The body of magistrates was so numerous that Henry would have had to create a large Catholic oligarchy to balance the Protestant one. Splitting the *corps de ville* in half and forcing fifty Catholics into the municipal government would have been impractical, and it would have undoubtedly upset La Rochelle's Huguenots and incited trouble for the king. Preserving the goodwill of the strongest Protestant fortresses was probably utmost in Henry's mind since he did not order the consulate in the second most powerful Protestant town of Montauban to include Catholics in its administration either. Whether for the sake of friendship or prudence, Henry appeared unwilling to take the risk, and La Rochelle and Montauban remained Protestant towns administered uniquely by Huguenot officials.[120]

MONITORING THE PROTESTANT TOWNS

Henry kept a keen eye on the Protestant towns although he rarely manipulated elections. The king's abjuration had strained his relations with his Huguenot subjects, and problems with the Edict of Nantes did nothing to endear him. On most matters concerning royal authority, therefore, Henry presumably decided not to push issues too far. He seemed content to leave his Protestant towns quietly alone.

Even so, one instance in which Henry influenced the structure of a Protestant town government occurred in Montauban. Montauban possessed a consulate consisting of six members elected to represent six categories within the town. The first consul was a noble or lawyer, the second a royal official, the third a merchant, the fourth a notary, the fifth an artisan, and the sixth a peasant. They were elected each year by a council of twenty-four who were appointed by an assembly of the

[119] A. Giry, *Les Etablissements de Rouen, Etudes sur l'Histoire des Institutions Municipales* (Paris: F. Vieweg, 1883), 33.

[120] Catholics began to sit permanently on Montauban's consulate after 1632, and La Rochelle reaccepted Catholics after the siege of 1628. H. Le Bret, *Histoire de Montauban* (Marseille: Laffitte Reprints, 1976), vol. 2, 398; Kevin Robbins, 'The Families and Politics of La Rochelle, 1550–1650', (Ph.D. thesis, Johns Hopkins University, 1990), 262–324.

town's leading notables.[121] The consulate and the Protestant consistory worked together to administer the town. A royal official known as the *sénéchal du Quercy* represented the king's authority in Montauban, but he rarely visited the town and resided in Toulouse.[122] In 1600 the *syndic* of Montauban and the parlement in Toulouse called upon Henry IV to settle an election dispute and to issue revised election procedures for the town to follow.[123]

The king's intervention was necessitated by a matter that went back to 1598 when Montauban's incumbent consuls decided to discard the town's normal election rules and designate their own successors. Scandalized by the disregard of traditional procedures, the electorate and the leaders of the town designed new voting regulations in 1599 and sought the king's ratification of their work. Henry issued letters patent confirming the new procedures on 25 February 1600, and the parlement in Toulouse registered the letters on 7 March.[124] Preceding the annual 1 January election under the new regulations, representatives from the town's five quarters or *gaches* named a council of forty made up of town notables.[125] These forty in turn chose another council of twenty from among themselves. The incumbent consuls and the council of twenty then elected six consuls for the new term. Peasants did not participate in this election as they had in the past, and the notables involved in the election selected the peasant who would serve as the sixth consul. The reform thus promoted a tightening of the municipal oligarchy.[126] Henry sanctioned Montauban's new regulations. He had acted on the invitation of the municipal government and not out of intent to infringe on the town's liberties.[127]

Henry maintained an interest in elections in his Protestant towns and in conserving loyal leadership. The Crown's concerns for stability and the towns' perception of their privileges, however, often set them at loggerheads. In Saint-Jean d'Angély in Saintonge, the municipal leaders raised an uproar in 1601 when Henry decided

---

[121] Janine Garrisson, 'La Genève Française, 16eme siècle', in *Histoire de Montauban* (Montauban: Editions Privat, 1984), 100.

[122] Ibid. Disputes between the *sénéchal* and the consulate were frequent. Maurice Langevin, 'Le Consulat de Montauban', *Bulletin Archéologique, Historique, et Artistique de la Société Archéologique*, 114 (1979), 39–47; E. Forestie, *La Vie municipale au XVIeme siècle d'après les comptes consulaires de Montauban pour 1518* (Montauban: E. Forestie, 1887). Henri Lebret, *Histoire de Montauban, Revue et Annotée d'Après les Documents Originaux* (Montauban: Chez-Rethone, 1841), vol. 2, 99–100.

[123] *Archives Communales*, Montauban (hereafter cited as ACM) 6BB2 (1508–1600), letter dated 8 July 1599.   [124] Ibid., letters dated 12 and 16 July 1599, 25 February 1600 and 7 March 1600.

[125] Ibid., *Procès verbal* of Jean de Vicoze, *conseiller du roi, Lieutenant général en la sénéchausée de Quercy*, dated 31 January 1600.

[126] ACM, 6BB2 (1508–1600), *Procès verbal* of Jean de Vicose dated 31 January 1600. Redefining the standards by which the sixth 'peasant' consul was measured was not unique to Montauban. During the last half of the sixteenth century and the first part of the seventeenth century, consulates throughout the south of France became increasingly more oligarchic and elite. As Pierre Goubert believes, status and wealth went hand in hand. In some instances, property qualifications were raised during the period so that peasants and laborers were no longer eligible for places on the consulates. This was the case in Narbonne. See, L. Favatier, 'La Vie municipale à Narbonne au XVIIe siècle', *Bulletin de la Commission Archéologique de Narbonne*, 2 (1892–3), 241–72, 355–72.

[127] ACM, 6BB2 (1508–1600), letters patent of Henry IV dated 25 February 1600.

to appoint his client, the sieur of Beaulieu, as lieutenant in the town to command in the absence of its governor, Hercule de Rohan, duke of Montbazon. Previously, a militia captain named the sieur de Desajos held the post, but the man was ill and the mayor of the town, Jean Dabillon, was acting in his place. Saint-Jean's leaders called Beaulieu a 'lieutenant of a lieutenant', and they sent letters to the court asking Henry to rescind his order. Henry rejected their plea. The town then decided to dispatch deputies to court to try and dissuade the king from appointing Beaulieu. In the eyes of the municipal leaders, the installation of the king's lieutenant jeopardized their town privileges. Under the medieval charter, it was the mayor's place to command in absence of the governor, and the municipal magistrates felt threatened by Beaulieu.[128] The magistrates asked Henry to leave the town in the mayor's hands, but the king refused. It was important to him to control the leadership of key towns. He told Sully that he would continue to appoint a lieutenant in Saint-Jean because he could not be sure that the duke of Montbazon, a trusted noble and client, would always be governor of the town.[129]

The question of leadership was an important issue in all the towns, but local politics and familial rivalries often obstructed the Crown's directives. For instance, Henry's decision concerning the governorship of Montélimar spurred a small revolt in 1601. Trouble began in 1599 when Henry named René de la Tour, sieur de Governet to the position of governor of the town, but the inhabitants vehemently opposed this move. Governet was hated in Montélimar because in 1598 he had killed the town's governor, Louis de Marcel, baron Du Poët, in a duel. Although it was said Governet deeply regretted this act, he went unforgiven by the townspeople who preferred that Louis de Blain de Marcel du Poët, the nephew of the slain governor, receive his uncle's post.[130]

The young Du Poët believed likewise, and trouble ensued when Governet arrived in Montélimar in 1601 to take possession of his governorship. Du Poët and a troop of soldiers captured the town's citadel and tormented the inhabitants with cannon fire.[131] Henry sent an agent, Arthur Prunier, sieur de Saint-André, to investigate. He reported to the king on 15 June, 'The inhabitants of the town have their hearts with you Sire, but their lives and their possessions depend today on the discretion of the sieur Du Poët.'[132] To settle the matter Henry sent in troops, and Du Poët immediately turned over the citadel to the king's captain.[133] Governet took

---

[128] BN, MSS fr. 23196, fol. 530, 532; Louis-Claude Saudau, *Saint-Jean d'Angély d'après les Archives de L'Echevinage et les Sources Directes de son Histoire* (Marseille: Laffitte Reprints, 1976), 236–7. Martin Ruzé, sieur de Beaulieu, was one of Henry IV's secretaries of state. Saint-Jean d'Angély sent a letter to Henry that reads, 'Votstre Maieste Sire est d'huement informee quelz sont les privilleges et statutz que les roys voz devanciers nous ont octroyes pour services grandz et signalles randus a vostre Couronne et quil vous a pleu despuis vostre advenement a Icelle confermer . . . '

[129] BN, MSS fr. 13665 'Recueil des lettres de Henry le Grand', fol. 15.

[130] De Coston, *Histoire de Montélimar*, 532–63.   [131] BN, MSS fr. 23196, fols. 385–9.

[132] Ibid., fol. 385. The letter read, 'les habitans de la ville ont le coeur à vous, Sire, leur corps et biens dependent aujourdhuy de la discretion dud. Sieur du Pouet.'

[133] Ibid., fol. 417.

up his post, and astonishingly Du Poët was forgiven. It was said he had not intentionally disobeyed the king for his quarrel had been with Governet on a personal level.[134] Both men were clients of the duke of Lesdiguières and allied with the king. Ironically, the feud formally ended in 1609 when the young Du Poët married Governet's daughter at the urging of Henry IV.[135]

In none of the three examples given here did Henry IV directly intervene in town politics to usurp municipal liberties. In Montauban the town leaders called him in to give legal sanction to their reforms. He did not go beyond the town's recommendations either and insist on his direct involvement in the annual elections. Similarly, despite what the magistrates of Saint-Jean d'Angély thought about Henry's appointment of Beaulieu, the king did not revoke any of the town's privileges. Beaulieu's presence threatened the mayor, but he also strengthened Henry's authority in the town. That was exactly the king's intention. Lastly, Du Poët's revolt necessitated the king's intervention in Montélimar. Swift action always accompanied urban strife when tense situations threatened to get out of control. Henry was quick to increase his authority in localities where he felt it was important, and to advise reconciliation and negotiation as much as possible. On these issues whether a town was Protestant, royalist, or Leaguer did not really matter. There seems to be little indication, therefore, that Henry's policy towards the towns was meant to usurp their urban authority. Henry's actions promoted peace and order, and created places for his clients in key positions.

This is not to say that Henry was not keenly interested in and observant of his Protestant towns. As in all towns throughout the realm governors, commissioners and/or other royal officials in the localities reported to the king regularly on the status of his urban centres. These men took messages from the king out into the provinces and reported back to him on the state of his towns. During the sensitive period when Henry was working to force the registration of the Edict of Nantes in the parlements, for example, J. J. de Mesmes, an agent in Provence, informed his king, 'I will write to the principal magistrates of the towns and tell them to thwart all seditious conduct.'[136] In Languedoc around the same time, Henry de Caumels called the province 'the most divided with the most violent spirit'[137] Fearing a Protestant uprising, the agent asked Henry to 'send us commissioners of such quality and capability that they will be able to maintain your subjects in their obedience to your commandments'.[138]

Similarly, during the wake of the Biron conspiracy, Henry sent officials to

---

[134] De Coston, *Histoire de Montélimar*, 560–1. [135] Ibid., 533.
[136] BN, MSS fr. 23196 fol. 134v. Letter dated 1 September 1600 from J. J. de Mesmes to Henry IV. The agent wrote, '[J'] escriray aux principaux magistras des villles pour empescher touttes occasions de sedition'.
[137] Ibid., fol. 57 letter dated 16 May 1600 from Henry de Caumels to Henry IV. Caumels used the words, 'les plus divisees et les esprits plus remuens et violents'.
[138] Ibid. Caumels wrote, 'donner des commissaires de telle qualite et capabilité quils puisent ramener et contenir vox subiectz en leurs devoir et faire obeir a voz commandemens . . .'.

troubleshoot in the towns. After Biron's execution, Henry wanted to round up the marshall's co-conspirators. In late 1602 he invited to court the malcontent Henri de La Tour d'Auvergne, duke of Bouillon, to explain himself. Instead the duke went into Languedoc and tried to stir up trouble before he fled France altogether. Raymond de Vicose was then on assignment for Henry in the Midi, and in early 1603 he reported on Bouillon's arrival in the Protestant town of Castres. Henry's man went immediately to Castres and extended the goodwill of the king to the town's inhabitants and beseeched them to remain faithful to the Crown. Vicose wrote to Henry and informed him that his subjects in Castres expressed a fervent loyalty for their king, and the municipal government had dispatched deputies to court to testify to their devotion.[139] These words undoubtedly pleased the king who was always interested in municipal loyalty.

THE PRIVILEGES OF LA ROCHELLE

If Henry preferred an individual Protestant town, it was probably La Rochelle since the king and the town had a long history of shared experience and knew each other well. Henry spent at least twelve sojourns there between 1557 and 1589, arriving on the first occasion when he was only five years old. As a young man Henry was received in the city with love and respect, and as leader of the Protestant party he established his base of operations there in 1586. In 1587–8 he celebrated his victory at the battle of Coutras in La Rochelle, and the next year he returned there to recover from an illness. The townspeople prayed for their protector's health, and they rejoiced with him when he recovered. Henry enjoyed immensely his stays in La Rochelle. He took a *Rochelais* mistress, Ester Imbert, and produced an illegitimate son, Gédéon, who died in childhood.[140]

While Henry probably savoured good memories of La Rochelle, it was one of the towns he needed to watch carefully. Tarnished relations following his abjuration was one problem, but Henry also had to be wary of the town's extensive privileges. La Rochelle was one of the few cities of the realm that professed direct allegiance to the Crown and recognized no intermediary authority between its *corps de ville* and the king.[141] La Rochelle's independence was so strong that even within the Protes-

---

[139] BN, MSS fr. 23197, fol. 564. Letter dated 16 January 1603 from Raymond de Vicose to Henry IV. See also fol. 507 and BN, MSS Dupuy 61, fol. 294. For a similar kind of letter see one written by the duke of Lesdiguières to the town of Gap. He warned the consuls to take precautions and protect their town so that no trouble arrived that would endanger their own security or the service they owed the king. In M. Charronet, *Guerres de religion et la Société Protestante dans les Alpes* (Gap: M. Charronet, 1861), 262, letter dated 6 July 1603 from Lesdiguières to Messieurs les Consuls de Gap.

[140] Canet, *L'Aunis et la Saintonge*, vol. 2, 267–72; Buisseret, *Henry IV*, 6; Arcère, *Histoire de la Ville de La Rochelle*, vol. 2, 69–70; M. Jourdan, *Les Amours de Henri de Navarre à La Rochelle* (Paris: Imprimerie Imperiale, 1868). There is some confusion regarding Ester Imbert. She may also have been known as Ester de Boyslambert.

[141] Parker, *La Rochelle*, 19. Marseilles is another example of an independent town that recognized no intermediary between its government and the Crown.

tant community, the city was regarded as a province unto itself at meetings of the general assemblies of the Huguenot party.[142]

The *Rochelais* espoused republican ideologies by taking pride in their right of urban self-government that dated back to the foundation of the city's *droit de commune* during the mid-twelfth century.[143] The *corps de ville*, consisted of approximately one-hundred members headed by a mayor who was elected annually by cooptation. The city government held controlling power over municipal administration, finance, and justice. The Crown's representatives, the town's governor and his lieutenant, were denied any right to act in these spheres. Francis I briefly curtailed the town's growing autonomy in 1530, but Henry II reinstated the old constitution and its right of self-government in 1548. The Crown bolstered its authority in La Rochelle by naming a *sénéchal-gouvernor* to the town in 1550 and by placing a royal garrison in the city.[144] A revolt in 1568, however, forced the departure of the king's troops, and when they marched away, the *sénéchal-gouvernor* took flight as well. In 1573 and 1576 Henry III respectively exempted the town from all garrisons and governors. Thus, by the reign of Henry IV, the Crown's authority in La Rochelle resided with a *sénéchal* who had very little power. His only influence over the town was the right to select a mayor from a list of three candidates submitted to him every year by the *corps de ville*. Even so, the process proved to be an empty formality because the *sénéchal* rarely attended.[145]

La Rochelle had substantial financial as well as political privileges. One of the most important was the exemption from *all* customs taxes on incoming merchandise. During the last half of the sixteenth century, the town managed to resist the Crown's attempts to bypass the privileges and collect new impositions on commodities. The bourgeois even held special exemptions to taxation on drugs and spices entering La Rochelle.[146]

How did Henry feel about La Rochelle's privileges? He certainly was well advised. Jean de Sponde, his client and lieutenant general in the *sénéchaussée* of La Rochelle between 1591 and 1594, kept him well informed. Sponde recognized that the Crown was losing substantial tax monies by allowing La Rochelle its exemptions. He denounced the town's special standing, and fought with the *corps de ville* on numerous issues. In a letter to Henry, Sponde argued that the townspeople

[142] Etienne Trocmé, 'La Rochelle de 1560–1628. Tableau d'une société reformée du temps de guerres de religion.' (Thesis, Bachelor of Theology, Faculté libre de théologie protestante, Paris: 1950), 198. This was true after 1596.
[143] A. Giry, *Les Etablissements de Rouen*, (Geneva: Slatkine Reprints, 1975), vol. 1, 55–84. Giry believes Henry II or Richard I conferred La Rochelle's first charter. Louis-Etienne Arcère says it was given by Eleanor of Aquitaine. Arcère, *Histoire de la Ville de La Rochelle*, vol. 1, 179–81. For more on La Rochelle's organization see, Robbins, 'The Families', 57–95.
[144] Etienne Trocmé, 'Réflexions sur le séparatisme rochelais (1568–1628)', *Bulletin de la Société de L'Histoire du Protestantism Français*, 122nd year, July–September (1976), 205.
[145] Trocmé, 'La Rochelle', 170–80; E. Trocmé, 'Du Gouverneur à L'Intendant, l'Autonomié Rochelaise de Charles IX à Louis XIII', *Recueil de Traveaux Offerts à M. Brunel*, 2 (1955), 616–32; Robbins, 'The Families', 57–69. [146] Trocmé, 'La Rochelle', 204.

pocketed substantial profits from their '*prétendues exemptions*', that could be more wisely spent if they reached the king's coffers.[147] He urged, 'I humbly implore Your Majesty not to favour the *Rochelais* . . . it is not reasonable that they have more gratifications than your other subjects.'[148] Sponde's disdain for the municipality brought about his downfall. La Rochelle's notables expelled him in May 1592, and although he connived on the outside to subvert their authority, he died three years later without ever having returned to the town.[149] Thereafter, two other men filled the office of *sénéchal* in La Rochelle during Henry's reign, but they were powerless and rarely spent time there.[150]

Henry did not act on Sponde's advice and never diminished La Rochelle's privileges. On the contrary, he reconfirmed them on numerous occasions. In April 1592 during the siege of Rouen he sent letters patent to La Rochelle stating that because of the town's great loyalty to the Crown, he was re-sanctioning their privileges, franchises, and liberties.[151] Henry issued similar letters to the municipality in 1593, and in 1594 he again promised not to raise customs duties, impositions, or salt taxes in La Rochelle.[152] Henry never reneged on these agreements. When news of a tax on incoming merchandise called the *sol pour livre* reached the town in 1602, the municipality immediately sent deputies to Henry to label the tax 'a complete subversion of all the privileges it has pleased Your Majesty to confirm for us'.[153] The king responded by saying that he had no intention of raising the new tax in their town.[154] On another occasion in 1609 Henry recognized the privileges and exemptions of La Rochelle again, including the right to forego taxes on drugs and spices without any restrictions.[155]

Henry acted cautiously with La Rochelle. He forced the issue concerning the Edict of Nantes and re-established Catholicism in the town, but in all other cases in which he might have extended his influence, Henry left the town alone. By the end of his reign, the city was stronger than it had ever been. David Parker notes, 'Henry IV, who in general did not shrink from undermining municipal independence,

---

[147] BN, MSS Dupuy, 61, fol. 300. Also printed in 'Lettres Diverses', *Archives historiques de la Saintonge et de l'Aunis*, 12 (1884), 405–7.

[148] Ibid. Sponde wrote, '[J]e vous supplie très humblement que pour le regard des Rochelois vous ne les veuillés gratifier que de l'exemption des vins de leur cru seulement, à quoy le seigneur de Saint-Luc et le reste de vostre armée se soubsmectront, quelque incommodité que cela leur apporte, moyennant que vostre majesté pour le moins en tire quelque advantage, qui pourra estre tel qu'en accordant aux Rochelois l'exemption du payement du convoy pour leur vins, ils fassent un présent de vingt mille escus à vostre majesté ou bien au pis aller de la moytié . . . Mais pour les autres marchandises, sire, il n'est nullement raisonnable qu'ils ayent plus de gratifications que vos autres subjects.'

[149] Arcère, *L'Histoire de la Ville de La Rochelle*, vol. 2, 95–6. Jean de Sponde was from lower Navarre, the son of a councillor who served Henry's mother, Jeanne d'Albret. A Protestant, Sponde re-adopted Catholicism in 1593, the same year as the king.

[150] Trocmé, 'Du Gouverneur à L'Intendant', 618. Sponde's successors were Robert Artus de la Roque in 1592 and René de Tallansac, sieur of Loudrières in 1607.

[151] AMLR. MSS 82, AA5, fols. 162–5.   [152] Ibid., fols. 176–8, 181–3.

[153] BN, MSS fr. 23197, fol. 12. The *Rochelais* used the words 'une subversion entiere des privileges quil vous a plus nous confirmer . . .'   [154] Arcère, *La Histoire de la Ville de La Rochelle*, vol. 2, 113–14.

[155] AMLR., MS 82 AA5, fols. 183, 184–7.

Henry IV and the Towns

handled the *Rochelais* with great care.'[156] Henry's reluctance to press issues that might have weakened municipal autonomy may have stemmed from a desire to placate his long term friends and not sabotage his relations with former wartime allies.[157] Henry also knew that his minister Sully was well known in La Rochelle and enjoyed a large clientele there. He sent Sully to the Protestant stronghold in 1604, and the inhabitants received him like a governor, complete with a ceremonial entry.[158] Since Henry had spent so much time in the town before 1589, moreover, he knew many of the municipal magistrates personally and certainly understood the *Rochelais* attachment to their faith and privileges.[159] Considering Henry's personal history, he may have even held the *Rochelais* with special affection and rewarded them by leaving them alone. Perhaps this was why Henry expressed great emotion when deputies from La Rochelle arrived before him in Poitou in 1605. They came to pledge their devotion and reassure him after the exposure of a conspiracy involving the marquise of Verneuil. Before they left they offered him the key to La Rochelle as proof of their devotion. Overcome by the gesture, Henry hugged the deputies three times.[160]

Henry's political manoeuvres were always tempered with concern for security. He never attacked La Rochelle's urban independence. As the leading Protestant stronghold, the city undoubtedly influenced other Huguenot towns. As a major Atlantic coast port poised on France's western frontier, the city was accessible to the Spanish and the English. Henry needed La Rochelle's loyalty. Thus during a period when he was expanding his authority in other parts of the realm, Henry allowed La Rochelle to rebuild its fortifications and construct some of the most expensive and imposing ramparts of the day. Sections of the wall were even put up with monies from the Crown. Ironically, Henry's administration had helped to pay for one of the most immense symbols of municipal independence of the era, the nearly impregnable fortress of La Rochelle.[161]

---

[156] Parker, *La Rochelle*, 35.
[157] Henry did force certain issues regarding the treatment and privileges of Catholics in La Rochelle between 1604 and 1607. See ibid., 128–9.   [158] Canet, *L'Aunis et La Saintonge*, vol. 2, 283.
[159] Ibid., 267–8. Henry made twelve trips to La Rochelle during his life in 1558, 1565, 1568, 1569, 1570, 1570–71, 1573, 1576, 1582, 1586, 1588, and 1589.
[160] Arcère, *La Histoire de la Ville de La Rochelle*, vol. 2, 116.
[161] Trocmé, 'La Rochelle', 202–3. Major improvements were made on La Rochelle's ramparts between 1596 and 1604 and 1608 and 1611. Most of the money needed for the repair work was raised by the *corps de ville*, but under the specifications of the Edict of Nantes, La Rochelle was to receive 6,000 *livres* every year for construction and maintenance of the fortress. Trocmé says (p. 203) that these funds were slow to arrive, and the town raised 18,000 to 24,000 *livres* on its own each year to cover the expense. Kevin Robbins records that by 1612 the town wall was eight to twelve feet thick and covered a boundary of over 3,100 metres. Robbins, 'The Families', 39. Agrippa d'Aubigne called La Rochelle one of the best fortified towns in Europe. Agrippa d'Aubigne, *Histoire Universelle* (Paris: Librarie Renouard, 1900), vol. 3, 382.

CONCLUSION HENRY IV AND HIS MUNICIPAL ALLIES

The king's relationship with his Protestant towns demonstrates his policy of accommodation and his willingness to treat each town separately. During the same years that Henry undermined municipal rights and franchises in former Catholic League towns, he confirmed and enhanced the privileges of his Huguenot towns. At the same time that he reduced the size of municipal governments of former League towns, he increased the size of town councils in the Protestant towns in order to give places to Catholics. The Huguenots represented only a fraction of the country, but they emerged from the Wars of Religion with their municipal charters intact and their independence largely unchallenged. The Edict of Nantes forced them to accept Catholics within their gates, but it also gave them special ranking within the country and established the 'state within a state'. Even so, Henry's reign was the twilight of their municipal independence, for his treatment of them, both in enforcing the Edict and refusing to diminish their privileges, created a contradiction in French political society that not only marginalized the Huguenots but further alienated them from the rest of France. The quest for Henry's legitimacy caused him to address Calvinist France and solve temporarily the problem of religious diversity by granting the Huguenots the right to worship in specified sites. Yet the Edict of Nantes only perpetuated the duality of sixteenth-century existence between what many saw as good and evil, Catholic and Protestant.[162] Once the king was Catholic, the ramifications of this duality proved more significant and generated internal pressures on Huguenots to convert. Louis XIII and Richelieu never had to legitimize their authority in the same way as Henry IV. Thus, in the 1620s and 1630s they destroyed the Huguenot urban autonomy that Henry IV had outwardly respected.[163]

Under the watchful eyes of the king and his agents Protestant privilege for the Huguenots most often meant that Henry stayed close enough to command their allegiances yet far enough away to ensure their loyalties. Any Crown objective conceived to curtail municipal independence went unexecuted on the Protestant towns, particularly with regard to the greatest strongholds. If anything, Huguenot municipalities became even more removed from Crown control during Henry's reign with the fortification of cities and the maintenance of garrisons allowed under the 'brevets' attached to the Edict of Nantes. Philip Benedict believes that such boundary demarcation also weakened the natural links that bound Catholics and

---

[162] If Calvinists represented an 'Other' in French society, the Edict assimilated their existence into the established duality of good and evil. This ultimately had an impact on Protestant political conduct and laid the groundwork for their eventual conquest. William Connolly, 'The Dilemma of Legitimacy', in *Legitimacy and the State*, ed. William Connolly (New York: New York University Press, 1984), 222–45, esp., 242–4.

[163] For an account of the siege of La Rochelle see, P. S. Callot, *Jean Guiton Maire de La Rochelle et le siège de 1628* (La Rochelle: Quartier Latin, 1967). Vezio Melegari, *Great Military Sieges* (New York: Exeter Books, 1972), 146–9; Wolfe, *The Conversion of Henri IV*, 182–3.

Huguenots together across the religious divide. 'Mutual suspicion, continued skirmishing over the precise extent of the legal privileges granted the Reformed, and intermittent violence continued to mark relations between the groups.'[164] After Henry ceased being the Huguenot 'protector', therefore, he remained the source of their legitimacy by enforcing the Edict of Nantes. Throughout the reign his position remained far too tenuous for him to implement measures that might have severed the vital links in his command over the Huguenots, and he probably never wanted to anyway. Instead, he granted them an Edict that offered protection by allowing Crown supported Protestant strongholds. In this way he made the Protestant towns institutional clients by rewarding them with special liberties in exchange for their loyalty. Municipal policy for the Protestant towns meant that their corporate rights and privileges would be respected by the Crown since to do otherwise would endanger the exclusiveness of their status, the very situation that provided the basis for their security within the Catholic realm. As Michael Wolfe has noted, dependence on the Crown was the price the Huguenots paid for their protection from Catholic hostility.[165]

If Henry had possessed the power to bring the Protestant towns to heel, he probably would have. Yet since he lacked the ability to create 'one king, one faith, one law' in 1598, he opted to permit Protestant privilege under his authority. He gave *de jure* recognition to a *de facto* situation. This had the advantage of making Henry the legitimating agent and placed even angry Protestants into a situation in which they had to recognize that their freedom was dependent on the king's goodwill. Although Henry specified that the Edict of Nantes was irrevocable, all Protestants knew that royal edicts could be cancelled almost as easily as they could be granted. Henry had few options. If he had attacked Protestant France militarily, he risked the humiliation of having the whole country witness his inability to coerce the towns to obey him. Instead he quarantined the Calvinists and gave them time to convert. In the meantime he could regain the legitimacy he lost with them at his abjuration, and they could prove their loyalty to the rest of France.[166]

Henry intervened on occasion in Protestant towns just as he did in former League towns. From the king's point of view the Protestant towns were less dangerous than former Catholic League towns, but they were also less stable than the royalist towns. In a sense, Protestant hands were tied. The Huguenots had failed to win the civil war without their leader abjuring their religion, and in 1598 there were no alternative candidates for the throne who would have helped them. Facing this reality, Henry might have believed that in time they would abjure themselves. So he mollified them with political concessions and gave himself the

[164] Philip Benedict. '*Un roi, une loi, deux fois*: Parameters for the History of Catholic-Reformed Co-existence in France, 1555–1685', in *Tolerance and Intolerance in the European Reformation*, ed. Ole Peter Grell and Bob Scribner (Cambridge: Cambridge University Press, 1996), 93.
[165] Michael Wolfe, 'Protestant Reactions to the Conversion of Henry IV', in *Changing Identities in Early Modern France*, ed. Michael Wolfe (Durham: Duke University Press, 1997), 384.
[166] Wolfe, *The Conversion of Henry IV*, 183.

option of evaluating the Protestant position later on in his reign. In 1606 little had changed, and Henry renewed the royal brevets attached to the Edict of Nantes. If Henry had lived and enjoyed a long reign, however, it might have been he rather than his son and Richelieu besieging La Rochelle in 1627–28.[167]

[167] I came to this conclusion in 1992. See also, Holt, *The French Wars of Religion*, 171–2; Wolfe, *The Conversion of Henri IV*, 182. Wolfe states, 'Some observers thought it likely that the converted king, after he had dealt with the Spanish menace, would turn his attention to the internal threat posed by the Huguenot "state within a state"' (p. 182).

6

Clientage and clemency: the making of municipal officials

As we have seen, Henry wanted loyal clients in municipal office throughout France. Focusing his attention on border towns and on former Catholic League towns, he exercised royal authority in municipal affairs by intervening in elections and by ordering that elections be held in the presence of his representatives. This raises questions about the long-term impact of Henry's interventions. Social historians have shown that during this period, municipal governments were oligarchic and controlled by self-perpetuating elites.[1] The nomination of candidates by incumbents and the restriction of candidates to kin caused most town governments to be dominated by a handful of elite families. As demonstrated in earlier chapters, Henry initially put royalists in municipal office in League towns after their capitulation. But what happened to the ousted officials? Were they banned forever from municipal politics? This chapter will explore the social composition of municipal governments and investigate trends in sixteenth-century municipal officeholding that influenced the configuration of town councils during Henry's reign. The ways Henry gathered information about electoral candidates and chose appointees will be examined.

THE SOCIAL BACKGROUND OF MUNICIPAL OFFICIALS

A profile of the men who held municipal offices during Henry's reign is not hard to compile. Municipal officials were usually either merchants, lawyers, officeholders, or bourgeois elites who lived off their *rentes*. They were citizens who possessed authority, had married well, and could loan the town or its governor money if necessary. They came from families with a tradition of municipal officeholding, and they used the prestige associated with municipal service to advance their careers. A sketch of the life of Jacques de Puget offers a glimpse at a typical magistrate who held municipal office during Henry's reign.

Jacques de Puget lived in Toulouse. He was the son of a merchant who traded in

---

[1] Marcel Couturier, *Recherches sur les structures sociales de Châteaudun 1525–1789* (Paris: SEVPEN, 1969); Pierre Goubert, *Beauvais et le Beauvaisis de 1600 à 1730, Contribution à l'histoire sociale de la France au XVIIe siècle* (Paris: SEVPEN, 1960).

salt, dry goods, dyes, and medicinal supplies. The Puget familymen traditionally sought municipal office, and Jacques's father was made a *capitoul* in 1573.[2] As a young man, Jacques de Puget had enjoyed an impressive start. In 1573 when he married Françoise de Barthès, he received from his father 4,000 *livres*, a hotel, and another house. His mother, Germaine de Corail, turned over half of all her wealth to him, and Françoise's dowry brought him another 2,000 *livres*. Jacques de Puget became a lawyer, but he was often listed in contemporary documents as a notable bourgeois because he maintained some interest in his father's spice and drug business. Puget took his father's lead and served in the city government. He was elected to the *capitoulat* in 1591, 1599, and 1606. Puget also bought a small estate in 1603 for 3,375 *livres* and became the sieur de Gaffelaze. It was said he loved books and had a head for mathematics. He additionally held the office of treasurer in charge of collecting taxes in Toulouse for the construction of a bridge over the Garonne known as the *Pont-Neuf*.[3]

In 1591 Puget had been a zealous Leaguer, but after Toulouse's capitulation he enjoyed Henry's clemency and became a loyal subject. Puget even acted as master of ceremonies for the memorial service held after Henry's assassination in 1610. Puget loaned the *capitoulat* 7,500 *livres* in 1606 for the ceremonial entry of the duke of Montmorency, and in 1611 he loaned the diocese of Toulouse 6,000 *livres*. He made solid marriages for his daughters and bought offices for his sons. His nephew, Jacques de Puget, became a president in the parlement of Toulouse.

Through marriage alliances made for themselves and their children, Jacques de Puget and his brother, François, were related to six other families connected to the *capitoulat*. Still, none of Jacques's nor François's children donned the red and black robes of the *capitouls*. They all held royal offices instead, especially in the parlement. The *capitoulat* in Toulouse was one of the most respected municipal governments in France. The office came with ennoblement, and the prestige of the position long outlasted the zenith of the city's municipal autonomy. It was very common, however, for families like the Puget to rise to a certain stature and leave municipal officeholding behind for the more distinguished status of robe officialdom.[4]

Many historians have noted that as a general trend merchant oligarchies controlled town governments during the first half of the sixteenth century. But by the

[2] Baron de Puget, 'Le Capitoul Jacques de Puget (1544–1626)', *Revue Historique de Toulouse*, 22 (1935), 192–96. Other Puget sat on the *capitoulat* in 1547, 1550, 1554, and 1563.
[3] This paragraph and the next are based on Puget, '*Le Capitoul*' and *Archives Départementales*, Haute Garonne, *Repertoire des Insinuations*, Registre 14, fols. 355–8. *Archives Municipales*, Toulouse (hereafter AMT), BB22, fol. 322.
[4] The same was true of magisterial families in other towns. In Amiens, for example, the merchant, Jehan Thierry, held the office of *échevin* in 1594–5, 1597, and 1610. He was also *premier échevin* in 1605, 1606, and 1608. Thierry bought his son, also Jehan, three fiefs, a seigneury, and the office of lieutenant general in the *bailliage* of Amiens. The younger Thierry never served in the *échevinage*. A. Janvier, *Le Livre D'Or de la Municipalité Amiènoise* (Paris: Picard, 1893), 290–315; Pierre Deyon, *Amiens, capitale provinciale, étude sur la société urbaine au 17e siècle* (Paris: Mouton, 1967), 273, 326, 262, 277.

latter part of the century lawyers and minor officeholders competed with the merchant-bourgeois for inclusion on the town councils. Henri Drouot attributed this change to opportunities taken by ambitious lawyers during the Wars of Religion. In his classic study of Burgundy, Drouot argued that towards the end of the sixteenth century lawyers, eager to acquire offices in the sovereign courts and municipal administrations, found their aspirations blocked on the one hand by patrimonial practices of passing offices from father to son and on the other by rigid merchant oligarchies. Social anxieties thus bred revolutionary zeal that caused the lawyers to use League allegiances to seize municipal power.[5] Drouot's thesis works for Burgundy, and the history of Paris seems to validate his argument as Denis Richet and J. H. M. Salmon have both shown the social differences that existed between the Catholic League's 'Sixteen' and the parlement of Paris.[6] Philip Benedict, however, has questioned Drouot's thesis regarding the rest of urban France by arguing that in Rouen, League municipal officials did not differ from their predecessors in either wealth or social background. Benedict contends that the League victory revealed the triumph of one faction of 'ins' over another.[7]

Undoubtedly, the social composition of any municipal government reflected the political and economic environment of the town. Thus, a major port city like La Rochelle was dominated by a merchant oligarchy while a large trading and banking centre like Lyons maintained a high percentage of businessmen involved in municipal politics. Lyons operated as a commercial hub but also included a large number of officeholders in the town government. The most influential members of the municipality in Lyons, for example, were often presidents in the *siège présidial* or treasurers in the *bureau des finances* in the city. Others were listed as 'the greatest bourgeois'. The existence of a parlement in Toulouse presupposed the inclusion of large numbers of lawyers in urban affairs. Toulouse, Agen, and Mantes, moreover, all had large populations of lawyers and officeholders staffing local courts as well as the parlements of Toulouse, Bordeaux, and Paris respectively.

During Henry's reign, men are generally listed in election returns as either *avocat* or bourgeois with those specified as bourgeois usually having a slight majority in numbers over those cited as *avocat*. Listing a magistrate as 'bourgeois', however, poses problems for the historian because the word had many different

[5] Henri Drouot, *Mayenne et la Bourgogne, Etude sur la Ligue (1587–1596)* (Paris: August Picard, 1937), vol. 1, 43–55, 334–343.

[6] Denis Richet, 'Sociocultural Aspects of Religious Conflicts in Paris during the Second Half of the Sixteenth Century', trans. Patricia Ranum in *Ritual, Religion, and the Sacred: Selections from the Annales*, eds. Robert Forster and Orest Ranum (Baltimore: The Johns Hopkins University Press, 1982), 182–212; J. H. M. Salmon, *Society in Crisis, France in the Sixteenth Century* (New York: St Martin's Press, 1975), 234–75.

[7] Philip Benedict, *Rouen During the Wars of Religion* (Cambridge: Cambridge University Press, 1981), 182; Peter Ascoli, 'French Provincial Cities and the Catholic League', *Occasional Papers of the American Society for Reformation Research*, 1 (December 1977), 20, 39; See also, Anne H. Guggenheim, 'The Protestant Notables of Nîmes During the Era of Religious Wars', *The Sixteenth Century Journal*, 3 (1972), 80–96.

meanings. Roland Mousnier notes that in some documents bourgeois signified all of the citizens of a town, while in others it represented members of the third estate as distinguished from robe nobles and clergymen.[8] In most towns bourgeois was a judicial title denoting natives of the municipality who contributed to the town's tax assessments and met certain property qualifications.[9] This means that in a majority of towns, merchants actively trading in one or more commodities and wealthy nobles living off their *rentes* might both be listed as bourgeois in contemporary documents. As a general trend, lesser merchants without great wealth were squeezed out of municipal office by the end of the sixteenth century, and wealthier ones were buying offices for themselves and their sons.[10] Lawyers and officeholders were usually cited as either *avocat, docteur en loi*, or by the title of their office. These offices ran the gamut from more substantial ones such as president in a *Chambre des comptes*, to less important ones such as *élu* in an *élection*. Municipal magistrates generally held lesser royal offices that did not come with ennoblement. They were often magistrates in the *présidial* courts, lieutenant generals and councillors in the *bailliages* and *sénéchaussées*, and *avocats* and *procureurs du roi* in the royal courts. Important robe officials like the presidents and councillors of the sovereign courts often sat in on council meetings in supervisory positions, but they did not normally hold elected posts in the municipal administrations although members of their clienteles frequently did.[11] Finally, in some documents, magistrates are listed as '*écuyer*'. These were nobles who owned seigneuries and lived nobly off their *rentes*. In most instances, they had recent merchant backgrounds. The social stigma associated with the incompatibility of nobility and commerce was not as prevalent among the municipal magistrates as it was with their social superiors. In many towns ennoblement came with municipal office and so wealthy bourgeois with vital commercial interests and substantial merchants earned nobility through public service. Men ennobled in this way were referred to as *noblesse de la cloche* because they answered the bells that chimed over town halls. This nobility was considered inferior, however, to ennoblement by birth or high office.

While municipal governments were thus composed of men of means, the consulates in the south generally had a greater diversity of membership than the *échevinages* in the north because magistrates were sometimes elected to *échelles* so that these governments were more representative of diverse professions.[12] This was not true of the very distinguished *capitoulat* of Toulouse, the most influential of all

---

[8] Roland Mousnier, *The Institutions of France under the Absolute Monarchy 1589–1789, Society and the State*, trans. Brian Pearce (Chicago: University of Chicago Press, 1974), 236.   [9] Ibid.

[10] Gayle Brunelle, *The New World Merchants of Rouen* (Kirksville, Missouri: Sixteenth Century Journal Publications, 1991), 16, 121–46.   [11] Ibid., 221–4.

[12] Consulates in the south often consisted of four to eight *échelles*. The first *échelle* might be designated for nobles and bourgeois only, the second for lawyers, the third for merchants, and the fourth for peasants. A member from each of these groups would be elected to each *échelle*. L. Favatier, 'La vie municipal à Narbonne au XVII siècle', *Bulletin de la Commission Archèologique de Narbonne*, 2 (1892), 243–5.

the consulates in the Midi. *Echevinages* rarely gave access to artisans and peasants and became the exclusive domain of the 'bourgeois' and lawyers as the seventeenth century progressed.

Accessibility to municipal office varied from town to town. In municipalities like La Rochelle and Poitiers, magisterial offices were sold outright or passed from father to son. In Amiens, a very small, tightly knit group made the *échevinage* their exclusive reserve. Yet in many towns, while the socio-economic background of the magistrates may not have been very dissimilar, the availability of office within the ranks of the elite was not always limited to just a few select families. Consequently, Drouot's thesis and the more recent argument by Henry Heller that the Wars of Religion were class wars fought by an urban proletariat resentful of the social and economic hegemony seems questionable.[13]

Calculations reflecting the availability of office in eight select towns are given in table 1. Percentages are derived by comparing the number of different family names on the municipal councils with the maximum number of magisterial positions open within the towns during Henry's reign. Consideration is made for positions that were renewed every two years such as the office of *prévôt des marchands* in Lyons. The table reflects individual participation only and does not calculate families related by marriage. It shows that while historians are correct in saying that access to municipal posts was limited to a handful of families, the turnover in some towns between individuals was quite fluid. Variations between the towns expose a fluctuation in turnover rates based on persons with different last names between the narrowly inscribed oligarchy in Amiens, and the more accessible town governments in Blois, Toulouse, and Lyons. Since individual family names are counted only once in this table, the turnover rate was slightly higher than the percentages reveal, because brothers, cousins, or even unrelated persons sharing the same last name were credited with having held only a single municipal office, when in fact, different persons with the same last name may have served several times.

HENRY IV AND THE MAGISTERIAL ELITE

What status of man Henry preferred for municipal office is hard to discern. In some instances he favoured royal officeholders and in other cases he endorsed merchants. One can search for patterns in his selections, but they seem to indicate simply that he favoured men for municipal office who were loyal to him.

Of the men Henry appointed as mayor in the city of Nantes, all six held royal offices.[14] Henry's preference, however, may have only confirmed the fact that in

---

[13] Henry Heller, *Iron and Blood Civil Wars in Sixteenth-Century France* (Montreal: McGill-Queen's University Press, 1991), 105–36.

[14] Alexandre Perthuis, Stéphan de la Nicollière-Teijeiro, *Le Livre D'Oré de L Hôtel de Ville de Nantes* (Nantes: Jules Grinsard, 1873), 177–213; Guy Saupin, 'La Vie Municipale à Nantes sous l'Ancien Régime, 1565–1789', (Thèse, University of Nantes), 1981, 316, 330; Guy Saupin, 'Les elections municipales à Nantes sous l'Ancien Régime', *Centre Généalogique de l'Ouest*, 35 (1983), 87–93.

Table 1 *Degree of turnover in municipal officeholding by family, 1589–1610*

Town	No. of places	No. of different names	Per cent
Blois	38	37	97%
Montauban	126	114	90%
Lyons	40	36	90%
Nîmes	76	66	87%
Rouen	36	30	83%
Toulouse	181	143	79%
Mantes	44	29	66%
Agen	132	76	58%
Amiens	72	24	33%

Source: AM, Blois, BB13–17; AM, Montauban, 1BB28–37; AM, Lyons, BB132–146; AM, Nîmes, LL13–17; AM, Rouen, AA20–1; Charles Picard, *Catalogue des maires et échevins de la Ville de Rouen* (Louviers: Izambert, 1895); AM, Toulouse, BB16–23; AM, Mantes-la-Jolie, BB22; Jules Sarret, *Préfets et Magistrats Municipaux d'Agen* (Agen: Vonnet et Fils, 1886); AM, Amiens, BB54–7.

Nantes, municipal posts had already become the reserve of officeholders. In choosing *échevins*, he showed greater diversity. Of the twelve *échevins* he appointed in Nantes between 1598 to 1610, six held royal offices, five were merchants, and one practised law.[15] During Henry's reign merchants and bourgeois continued to be well-represented in most towns on the municipal councils although officeholders often dominated the mayors' seats. In certain key towns Henry appeared to bow to Henry II's 1547 legislation that declared royal offices incompatible with municipal ones. In 1597 in Amiens when Henry reorganized the *échevinage* he barred simple merchants and artisans from the municipal government, and he specified that only two robe nobles would be allowed on the town council each year.[16] The latter may be interpreted as a pro-bourgeois stance, but the regulation went unheeded so that between 1600 and 1625 twenty-three robe nobles and eleven merchants won positions in the *échevinage*. After 1615 and until past the middle of the seventeenth century, all of Amiens's *premier échevins* held prestigious offices that granted ennoblement.[17] As a general trend royal officeholders took control of the municipal governments from the merchant-bourgeois during the seventeenth century. This in part reflected the increasing number of offices that were sold during the religious

[15] Saupin, 'La Vie', 2, 383–4; *Archives Municipales*, Nantes, BB24, 25, 26, 27. Elections were held on 25 April in 1598, and on 1 May every year thereafter.

[16] Augustin Thierry, *Recueil des monuments, inédits de l'histoire du Tiers-Etat* (Paris: Firmin-Aidot Frères, 1867), vol. 3, 1097, clause 5.

[17] Yves Barel, *La Ville médieval, système social, système urbaine* (Grenoble: Presses Universitaires de Grenoble, 1975), 464; Janvier, *Le Livre D'Or*, 300ff.

wars by both Henry III and Henry IV.[18] Royal officeholders did not always make the most loyal subjects, but because they depended on the king for the confirmation of their charges and salaries, they potentially represented the Crown's strongest allies in the towns.[19]

Henry's choice of municipal personnel also exposes a tendency to contain the municipality within a small oligarchy. In Limoges he decreased the size of the electorate from all heads of households to one-hundred bourgeois, strengthening the oligarchy in the process. In Montauban the consulate itself voted to do away with the peasant voice in the election process. Whether coming from above or emanating from within, the oligarchic nature of municipal government became more apparent as the seventeenth century progressed.[20] Henry's main preoccupation was to ensure calm in the towns and on occasion he had to widen the electorate so that persons clamouring for office might be given the opportunity to serve. In Lyons around 1600, the governor, Philibert de La Guiche, informed Henry that a growing numbers of non-natives, or men who had lived in Lyons for less than ten years, were distraught over their inability to acquire municipal posts. These were notable bourgeois but as newcomers to Lyons, residency requirements barred them from magisterial office. La Guiche explained that the *échevinage* had become the domain of established families.[21] Henry decided in 1603 to allow non-natives in municipal office in Lyons, and he subsequently opened the *Hôtel de Ville* to greater participation in urban politics.[22]

Statistics showing the social background of the men who held the office of mayor or its equivalent in six select towns are provided in table two. These figures reveal that royal officials already monopolized the highest municipal offices in the towns during Henry's reign. Only in Amiens were wealthy bourgeois able to maintain a greater presence over officeholders in the position of *premier échevin*, and this situation changed during the next reign in favour of the royal officials. Yet Henry's decision to choose a certain individual probably had more to do with the election itself or his own personal interest than with the person's title or status, since he seemed to choose candidates who had received the greatest number of votes, or individuals he knew personally.

[18] Roland Mousnier, *La Vénalité des offices sous Henry IV et Louis XIII* (Paris: Presses Universitaires de France), chapters 1 and 2.
[19] Roger Charter, Guy Chaussinand-Nogaret, Emmanual Le Roy Ladurie, eds., *Histoire de la France Urbaine*, vol. 3, *La Ville Classique de la Renaissance aux Révolutions* (Paris: Editions du Seuil), 179.
[20] Annette Finley-Croswhite, 'Absolutism and Municipal Autonomy: Henry IV and the 1602 Pancarte Revolt in Limoges', in *Society and Institutions in Early Modern France*, ed. Mack P. Holt (Athens: University of Georgia Press, 1991), 80–97; Daniel Ligou, *Histoire de Montauban* (Toulouse: Privat, 1984), 131–3.
[21] BN, MSS fr. 23197, fol. 173rv.
[22] In the final decision made in February 1603 Henry ordered that all *prévôts des marchands* had to be natives of Lyons, but *échevins* could be non-natives as long as they had resided in the town for ten years or more. BN, MSS fr. 15900, vol. 2, fol. 536; A. Kleinclauz, *Histoire de Lyon* (Lyon: Librairie Pierre Masson, 1939), vol. 2, 6.

Table 2 Town configuration defined by social status for offices of prévôt des marchands, maire, vicomte-maieur, and Premier échevin

TOWN	Sword noble	Officeholder	Bourgeois	Merchant	Lawyer	Unknown	Total
Dijon 1594–1610	4/25%	7/44%	2/12%	0/0%	3/19%	0/0%	16/100%
Amiens 1597–1610	1/10%	2/20%	7/70%	0/0%	0/0%	0/0%	10/100%
Lyons 1598–1610	0/0%	7/87.5%	1/12.5%	0/0%	0/0%	0/0%	8/100%
Poitiers 1594–1607	0/0%	14/82%	3/18%	0/0%	0/0%	0/0%	17/100%
Abbeville 1594–1610	0/0%	12/54%	10/46%	0/0%	0/0%	0/0%	22/100%
Nantes 1598–1610	0/0%	7/100%	0/0%	0/0%	0/0%	0/0%	7/100%

Source: F. Amanton, 'Precis Historique et Chronologique sur L'établissement de la commune et des vicomtes mayeurs ou maires de Dijon', *Mémoires de la Commission des Antiquités du Departement de la Cote-D'Or*, 3 (1869–73), 61–74; A. Janvier, *Livre D'Or de la Municipalité Amiénoise* (Paris: Alphonse Picard, 1893), 290–315; *Archives Municipales*, Amiens, BB 54–57; Jean Baptiste Chaussonet, *Armorial consulaire de la ville de Lyon avec les noms, Surnoms, Qualitez et Conditiones de Messieurs les Prévôts des Marchands, échevins de la ville de Lyon depuis l'année 1595* (Lyon, n.p. 1741); *Archives Municipales*, Lyon, BB132–146; Charles Babinet, 'Les maires de Poitiers', *Bulletin et Mémoires de la Société des Antiquaires de l'Ouest*, vol. 20 (1897), 725–750; F. C. Louandre, *Les Mayeurs et les Maires d'Abbeville* (Abbeville: Imprimerie T. Jeunet, 1851), 40–4; Alexandre Perthuis, Stephan de la Nicolliere-Teijeiro, *Le Livre D'Ore de L'Hôtel de Ville de Nantes* (Nantes: Imprimerie Jules Grinsard, 1873), vol. I, 177–213.

Henry IV's relationship with Jehan Roussat, mayor of Langres, underscores the personal nature of his kingship and the importance he perceived in establishing faithful clients in key positions. Their relationship characterized what Roland Mousnier described as a *maître-fidèle* alliance that included total devotion on Roussat's part to the king.[23] Henry referred to Roussat using the language of clientage and called him his *amé* and *féal*, his 'bon et fidèl serviteur', and 'l'un de mes plus fydelles'.[24] The history of this two-person relationship rarely involved Henry exerting power over Roussat. But Roussat's support extended Henry's power base in Langres in numerous ways. The patron–client tie proved productive and beneficial for both parties. One might even speculate that the bond between kings and urban elites held the potential to be more durable ties than the bonds between kings and nobles. Sharon Kettering has observed that the closer a client was in rank and power to his patron, the less likely the relationship would be an enduring one.[25] A man like Roussat was far removed from Henry in terms of social status and was thus perhaps a more reliable client than higher ranking nobility.

Jehan Roussat was descended from a family from Moulins who had served the counts of Berry. He won the office of mayor in Langres in 1584, 1590, 1592, and 1601 and also held the title of lieutenant-general in Langres during his lifetime. Roussat established himself as a loyal royalist by serving Henry III and by giving his allegiance to Henry IV.[26] Roussat served the king in numerous ways. He sent the king money on many occasions and supplied Louis de Gonzague, the duke of Nevers, with loans as well. The loyal mayor furnished the king's army with provisions and munitions and supported him with troops. In March of 1591, Henry sent Roussat a letter and asked for his military support. 'Mount your horse and join my other followers with your company to give assistance to the sieur of Dinteville or to my cousin the marshall Aumont . . .'[27] The mayor gave the king advice and sent him encoded letters detailing enemy troop movements and plans. Henry responded with appreciation. 'Monsieur Roussat', the king wrote in 1595, 'I received your letters and the advice you gave me concerning the movements of my

[23] Roland Mousnier, 'Les Concepts d'"Orders', d'"états', de 'fidélité' et de 'monarchie absolue' en France de la fin du XVe siècle à la fin du XVIIIe', *Revue Historique*, 247 (1972), 289–312; 'Les fidélités et les clientèles en France aux XVIe, XVIIe, et XVIIIe siècles', *Histoire sociale, Social History*, 15 (1982), 35–46.
[24] M. Guyot de St Michel, ed. *Correspondance Politique et Militaire de Henri le Grand, avec J. Roussat, Maire de Langres* (Paris: Petit Libraire de M. et Mme. le duke de Berry), 1816, 133 and throughout. This volume is particularly important because Langres's archives were destroyed by fire in the eighteenth century. No letters from Roussat to Henry have survived.
[25] Sharon Kettering, *Patrons, Brokers, and Clients in Seventeenth-Century France* (New York: Oxford University Press, 1986), 30.   [26] Guyot de St-Michel, *Correspondance*, viii-x.
[27] Ibid., 83–4. Henry wrote, 'Je vous prie monter à cheval avec vostre compagnie et vous joindre avec mes aultres serviteurs pour assister le sieur de Dinteville, ou mon cousin le maréchal Daumont, lequel doibt estre bientost entre la Bourgongne et la Champaigne avec les forces . . .'

enemies. [I] owe much to the care with which you write me so often.'[28] Henry asked Roussat 'to do all things possible to advance my plans'.[29]

For Henry IV, Roussat's service helped to ensure the loyalty of Langres. 'I was put at ease to learn that you will continue in your office as mayor of my town of Langres', Henry wrote to Roussat in 1590.[30] Henry's letters stress that Roussat must do all he can to keep the inhabitants of Langres loyal. When Henry heard of a conspiracy involving Langres's Catholic League bishop, Charles Descars, he told Roussat to expel all troublemakers from the town. 'Tell the inhabitants', Henry wrote, 'that I will keep them in my protection against all those who would do otherwise'.[31] Learning of another conspiracy the king told Roussat to watch closely the 'étrangers' in Langres as they often stirred up trouble.[32] Henry also emphasized that it was important to scrutinize the *échevins* to make sure they did not fall prey to Catholic League patronage.[33] Dissension in the *Hôtel de Ville* meant instability in Langres that the king could ill afford. Henry recognized that as mayor, Roussat had his own clientele network in Langres and that network assured Henry of much support. He encouraged Roussat to use his money to 'gaigner des hommes' and to fortify those who Roussat knew to be true royalists.[34] Roussat served as Henry's mouthpiece and publicized his legitimacy. In 1590 Henry sent Roussat a detailed memoir of the battle of Ivry and instructed the mayor to share it with the royalists in and around Langres.[35]

Roussat's clientage obviously helped to avert treason in Langres and to strengthen Henry's kingship, but the mayor's extreme devotion is telling because in the early 1590s Henry was in no position to hand out marvellous rewards to his servant. While Roussat opened his purse readily for the king, he did so knowing that justly deserved prizes might be far off in the future.[36] Henry proved his good patronage to

---

[28] Ibid., 121; See also, 56, 65, 146. Henry wrote, 'Monsieur Roussat, j'ay receu vos lettres et les advis que vous m'avez donné des mouvemens de mes ennemys, et loue beaucoup le soing que vous avez de m'en escrire si souvent.'

[29] Ibid., 155. Henry used the words 'ayder à tout ce qui pourra servir à l'advancement de mes affaires'. From the letters it is obvious that Roussat was in frequent contact with Nevers, the governor of Champagne, and Dinteville, the governvor of Langres. In Nevers's letters to Roussat, however, included in the volume cited here, it does not appear the mayor was a client of the provincial governor. Nevers referred to Roussat using the word *amé* and he spoke of their *amityé*, but he never used the word *féal*. Perhaps Roussat was on an outer circle of loose affiliation with the governor's clientele.

[30] Ibid., 75, Henry's letter begins, 'Mons. Roussat, J'ay esté fort aise d'entendre que vous ayez esté continué en la charge de maire de ma ville de Langres. Vous m'avez si fidellement et dignement servie en la dicte charge par le passé, que j'en ay contentement et me promets que ne ferez moings bien à l'advenir.'

[31] Ibid., 67, see also 33. Henry wrote, 'Assurez les que je les tiendray en ma protection contre tous ceulx qui vouldroient entreprendre quelque chose au contre.'   [32] Ibid., 33-4.

[33] Ibid., 37. His letter reads, 'Je vous ay bien voullu escripre la présente pour vous prier de tenir la main que les eschevins de ma dicte ville effectuent ce que leur direz estre nécessaire de faire pour ce regard comme je leur escript qu'ils facent.'   [34] Ibid., 146, 33.   [35] Ibid., 57.

[36] Ibid., 34. Henry wrote, 'Quant aux frais et advances que vous avez faictes pour mon service, ma volonté est que vous soyez remboursé sur les premiers et plus clairs deniers qui se trouveront en ma dicte ville de Langres.'

his client after Roussat's brother was assassinated by the Catholic League. Henry promised to avenge the murder with swift justice in 1592.[37] In 1601, moreover, the king commanded his *Chambre des comptes* to reimburse Roussat for the great sums he had borrowed in France, Germany, and Switzerland during the religious wars. He ordered the *receveurs* not to give Roussat any trouble or even ask for justifications since the money had been spent on 'choses secrettes' to besiege towns, chateaux, and fortresses, and to raise armies for the war.[38] Roussat served the Crown from around 1584 to 1610 at great expense. But only praise was immediately forthcoming from Henry IV. The reciprocal nature of clientage often worked that way, and in Roussat's case patience paid off.[39]

SELECTING MUNICIPAL OFFICIALS

How did Henry decide whom to select for municipal posts? He probably knew many individuals personally. During the religious wars the king spent years fighting in the provinces and developed an unrivalled knowledge of his kingdom and its people.[40] But he did not know men in every town. The institution of the Crown in the sixteenth and seventeenth centuries exercised its authority through personal ties and relationships. Henry thus relied on the system of clientage and was well informed by his advisors, ministers, *intendants*, mayors, and town and provincial governors in the localities who had their own clienteles.[41]

In towns far from Paris Henry depended heavily on royal agents to monitor events in the provinces. Among other things these men supervised elections. As *intendant général de la justice* in Marseilles, for instance, Guillaume du Vair kept Henry minutely aware of the urban turbulence that rocked municipal elections in the city. Henry wrote to Du Vair in 1598 and commented on his service: 'We had already learned about the new election of town officers from our nephew, the duke of Guise, before your letter arrived. We understand that it went well and are pleased with the good persons elected. We approve, like we always do, all that you

[37] Ibid., 88.   [38] Ibid., 146–7.

[39] Robert R. Harding, *Anatomy of a Power Elite: The Provincial Governors of Early Modern France* (New Haven: Yale University Press, 1978), 36–7.

[40] David Buisseret, *Henry IV* (London: George Allen & Unwin, 1984), 88.

[41] William Beik, *Absolutism and Society in Seventeenth-Century France, State Power and Provincial Aristocracy in Languedoc* (Cambridge: Cambridge University Press, 1985), 15; Sharon Kettering lists Henry's important clients in the provinces in *Patrons, Brokers, and Clients*, 232–3. These clients included Claude Groulard, Henri de Bourbon-Montpensier, Georges de Brancas, Aymar de Chaste, and Charles Timoléon de Beauxoncles in Normandy; René de Rieux, sieur de Sourdéac in Brittany, Guillaume Fouquet, sieur de La Varenne, Duplessis-Mornay, and Claude de La Châtre in the Loire valley, Sully and the sieurs de Lussan and Saint Luc in the West, Alphonse d'Ornano in Guyenne, Jacques Nompar de Caumont de La Force in Béarn and Navarre; Montmorency-Damville in Languedoc; Du Vair and the duke of Guise in Province; Lesdiguières in Dauphiné; the duke of Nevers in Champagne; and Dominique de Vic, Charles de Rambures, and Eustache de Conflans in Picardy. See also Buisseret, *Henry IV*, 88–94.

will do and secure for the good and the benefit of the town'.[42] Far away in Marseilles
Henry understood that the city could not fall under leadership disadvantageous to
him, and Du Vair served as his source of information and control.[43] Through Du
Vair's advice, Henry knew when urban unrest reached levels in which it was
necessary for him as king to postpone, cancel or manipulate the events to ensure
peace and calm in the provinces.[44]

Other nobles and agents performed similar duties for Henry in other parts of the
realm. The duke of Lesdiguières sent letters regarding elections in Provence and
Dauphiné to the king just as Alphonse d'Ornano did for Guyenne.[45] In 1594
Lesdiguières acknowledged that the king had ordered him to do all he could under his
commission 'to fortify the affection of the nobility and the towns' for the king's
service.[46] Henry relied on the nobility to carry out his orders and to advise him on the
towns. Lesdiguières sent Henry lists of men from Aix considered loyal to the king so
that the Crown could support them for municipal office.[47] In 1597 Henry wrote to the
town governor of Lyons, Philibert La Guiche, and told him to oversee the upcoming
election so that only loyal subjects were elected to municipal office. This does not
mean that the governor's task was easy. In 1601, for example, when La Guiche read
out the king's list of three choices for the office of *prévôt des marchands*, the crowd
greeted his pronouncement with anger, and a scuffle broke out between the governor
and the town's *procureur général*. The electorate rejected the king's instructions, and
La Guiche refused to participate in the election because, as he told the magistrates, 'It
is the custom for the governor to make the *échevins*'.[48] Henry settled the matter two
years later by ordering that henceforth he would appoint the *prévôt* himself from a list
of three candidates submitted to him by the town.[49]

Although Henry was not prone to intervene in Huguenot towns as frequently
as he did in former Catholic League towns, he customarily acknowledged their
election results and received reports from royal officials regarding electoral problems.[50] In 1600, for example, Henry de Caumels wrote to the king from Saintes to

[42] Gustave Fagniez, 'Douze lettres Inédites de Henri IV Concernant les Affaires de Marseille 1597–
1607', *Revue Henri IV*, 3 (1912), 4–5. Henry wrote, 'Nous avons à la vérité esté advertiz par nostre
neveu le duc de Guise, au paravant la reception de vostre lettre, de la nouvelle ellection faicte des
officiers de la ville que nous entendons estre fort bonne et de personnes de bonne qualité et qui ont les
autres parties requisés pour ceste occasion. Nous la louons et approuvons, comme nous ferons
tousiours tout ce qui sera pour vous faict et procuré pour le bien et commodité de la ville'.
[43] BN, MSS fr. 16656, fols. 15–21, 55–6.
[44] Guillaume du Vair, *Lettres Inédites de Guillaume du Vair*, ed. Philippe Tamizey de Larroque (Paris:
Auguste Aubry, 1873).
[45] François de Bonne, le duc de Lesdiguières, *Actes et correspondance du Connêtable de Lesdiguières*, ed.
Cte. Douglas and J. Roman (Grenoble, Edouard Allier, Imprimeur, 1878). See for example, vol. 1,
244 regarding elections in Lyons.
[46] Ibid., 222. The noble wrote, 'le Roy m'avoit commandé d'entrer [Provence] pour fortiffier l'affection
de la noblesse et des villes qui s'estoyent depuis peu recogneuz et embrassé son service.'
[47] Ibid., 244.
[48] Quoted in A. Kleinclauz, *Histoire de Lyon* (Paris: Masson, 1939), vol. 2, 6. La Guiche's protestation
reads, 'que c'était la coutume du gouverneur de la ville d'en faire les *échevins*'. For more, see *Archives
Municipales*, Lyons (hereafter cited as AML), BB138, fols. 178–87.   [49] AML, AA24, fol. 55.
[50] *Archives Municipales*, La Rochelle, MS 82 AA5, fols. 272–6.

Saintonge about an election he had nullified after learning that a man had schemed to win the mayor's seat with the collusion of a few *échevins*.[51] The king also relied on incumbent municipal magistrates who had served him faithfully in office. This explains why during the early years of his reign he often continued the officers of a town government for a second term instead of holding a new election. He also counted on the influence of incumbents. In 1602 he wrote to the former *capitouls* in Toulouse after an election for the coming year expressing his approval of the election results and gratitude for the influence they had had over the election.[52]

The great nobles and the royal commissioners established clienteles in the provinces and looked after the towns' interests, especially at court. Patron–client relationships often existed between the governors of the towns or provinces and the municipalities themselves. Thus if the king wanted to intervene in elections, but a town was against the action, the governor might argue the town's case to the king. This occurred, for instance, with Henry, Aix, and the duke of Lesdiguières in 1594.[53] The towns solicited patrons at court and paid them for their services.[54] The king acknowledged the practice and wrote to the municipality at Blois, 'It is a well-served custom to give little presents and honours to governors, chiefs, and captains, especially in time of war, just as other towns do in order to be better treated.'[55] Blois's magistrates sent a silver clock to an unnamed noble at court to advance the town's interests.[56] Even so, not all towns enjoyed good relations with their governors. Lyons and La Guiche are a case in point. Eustache de Réfuge, the king's *intendant* in Lyons called their relationship a 'mauvais ménage'.[57] La Guiche's authority had to be reinforced in Lyons with a steady stream of royal *intendants*.

The king's secretaries of state also influenced elections. The chancellor, Bellièvre, took a great interest in town government, and after he left office, Villeroy took over for him. In 1602, for example, when Henry intended to appoint one hundred bourgeois in Limoges to act as electors in the upcoming magisterial elections, the town government wrote to Bellièvre and asked him to use his influence with the king in the selection process.[58] Bellièvre took special interest in his native town, Lyons, and the magistrates relied on his support. Thus after sending a list of three candidates for the office of *prévôt des marchands* to the king for final selection, the municipal government wrote to Bellièvre in 1603 and asked him to please support the candidate with the majority vote, Antoine Henry, the sieur de

[51] BN, MSS fr. 23196, fols. 10–11. Later dated 28 February 1600 from Henry de Caumels to Henry IV.
[52] AMT, BB277, fol. 22.   [53] De Bonne, *Actes et Correspondance*, vol. 1, 244.
[54] *Archives Municipales*, Blois, BB17, entry dated 6 October 1609. The municipal government in Blois sent deputies to court to solicit patronage in order to obtain *octrois* for repairs needed on bridges in the town.
[55] Alexandre Dupré, *Analyse des procès verbaux des assemblées municipales de la ville de Blois du 17 Janvier 1566 au 28 Decembre 1661* (Blois: n.p.), 183. The notation reads, 'C'est une coutume bien servant de faire tel petits présents et honneurs aux gouverneurs, chefs, et capitaines des garrisons, même surtout en ce temps de guerre comme font les autres villes pour en être mieux et plus doucement traitéer.'
[56] Ibid.   [57] BN, MSS fr. 15899, fol. 219.   [58] Ibid., fol. 644.

la Salle. 'The sieur de la Salle is not only desired by all', the magistrates told Bellièvre, 'but he is needed in this charge.'[59] Not surprisingly, Henry IV appointed Antoine Henry as Bellièvre's choice and as the highest vote getter in the election. In Poitiers, moreover, Henry promoted Sully's control of patronage in 1609 by withdrawing the right of the municipal government to name the town's militia officers and giving that privilege to his favourite minister.[60]

In Paris Henry had a more immediate presence over elections. Every August after the event was held and the results had been tabulated, a cortege of councillors, notables, and members of the electoral panel called *scrutateurs*, set out to find the king, wherever he might be in or around the city. In 1605, for example, they went to him at the hotel of his friend, Sebastien Zamet.[61] The *scrutateurs* presented balloting information to the king which he reviewed and then chose for the office of *échevin* the men who had received the most votes, 'la pluralité des voix'. The new officers immediately took their oath of office on bended knee, one hand between the king's hands, and the other on a 'tableau juratoire' revered by the town.[62] The election only became official when approved by the king.

Henry depended on his advisors, but he also selected men for municipal office because he believed in their loyalty. In 1607, for example, Jehan d'Aultry was in Paris as a deputy to court from the town of Troyes to report the death of the town's mayor, Jacques Le Be. As fortune would have it, Henry decided to make d'Aultry the new mayor, on the advice of Champagne's governor, the duke of Dinteville, and his royal secretary, the seigneur of Gèvres. The deputy explained to his colleagues in Troyes:

[W]hen the king saw me, he came to me and took my hand. Then in the presence of all the great nobles, he said these very words: 'The mayor of Troyes is dead, I want you to serve me in his place assuring me that you will fulfill this charge with the same good service you have shown me in the past.[63]

---

[59] BN MSS fr. 15900, vol. 1, fol. 536, letter dated 13 December 1603. The magistrates wrote, 'Ladicte sieur de la Salle est non seulement desere de tous mais aussi très necessaire à ceste charge.'

[60] *Archives Communales*, Poitiers, registre 64, fols. 151–3. Sully was governor of Poitou and enjoyed a large clientele in Poitiers.

[61] In 1605 he was at Zamet's, but in 1604 the cortege went to Fontainebleau, and in 1602 they were forced to ride out to Mantes. Paul Guerin, ed., *Registres des Délibérations du Bureau de la Ville de Paris 3: 1602–1605* (Paris: Imprimerie Nationale, 1905), 156, 345, 476.   [62] Ibid.

[63] Quoted in Théophile Boutiot, *Histoire de la ville de Troyes et de la Champagne Meridionale* (Marseille: Laffite Reprints, 1977), vol. 4, 307. Louis Potier, sieur de Gevres was one of Henry's secretaries of state. D'Aultry stated, 'Il y a environ trois semaines, j'étais à Paris, M. de Gèvres me fit savoir que j'aie à me trouver le lendemain au lever du Roi. Voulant me défendre d'un tel honneur, je priai M. M. de Grèvres et Dinteville de m'en excuser près de S. M. Mais je fus contraint d'obeir. A son lever, le Roi, m'ayant aperçu, il vint à moit et me prit la main. En présence de plusieurs princes et grands seigneurs, il usa de ces mêmes mots, "je veulx que vous me serviez en sal place m'asseurant que vous vous acquitterez de ceste charge aussy bien que vous avez faict du passé et que vous me ferez aussi bon service". A quoy prenant la parolle pour supplier Sa Majesté de m'en excuser, le Roi me répliqua: "Je le veulx, ne m'en parly plus, je m'asseure que vous ferez bien." Et à l'instant, S.M. donna l'ordre à M. de Gèvres de m'expédier la dépêche contenant ma nomination.'

Whether d'Aultry remembered the event exactly as it happened is a matter of speculation, but he was made mayor by the will of the king shortly after leaving Paris.[64]

Finally the queen, Marie de Medici, also had her clients and exerted influence over elections in Paris. In July and August of 1603, for example, the king wrote to the *échevinage* in Paris saying that it was the queen's wish that Léon Dollet be elected *échevin* for the upcoming term.[65] When the election took place, however, Dollet only received eight votes, while two opponents, Louis Le Liepvre and Gabriel Flexelles, received fifty-three and forty-nine votes respectively. But Flexelles did not win the election. When Henry reviewed the ballots he named Le Liepvre and Dollet to the posts.[66]

Emphasis is most often placed on things Henry changed, on elections he manipulated and administrations he infiltrated. The question should also be asked: what impact did the king's manipulations have on the municipal governments? When Henry made a direct appointment he overwhelmingly chose the status quo. He made his selections from the circle of wealthy elite who had made municipal officeholding their domain. He made no radical changes by placing an artisan in office or by bringing in an outsider. Henry's interests as we have seen were related to Crown loyalty. He viewed politics on a personal level, and whether a man had been Leaguer, royalist, or neutral during the wars seemed far more important to him than whether a man was a lawyer or a merchant. The political distinction was significant when League towns capitulated, and Henry injected royalists into municipal governments and banished the most notorious Leaguers. Former Leaguers were not kept out forever, however. Over the whole 1589–1610 period, therefore, very little changed in most French towns in terms of the social composition and familial make-up of the municipal governments. In most former League towns it also appears that many men who were at first ousted from municipal power after the wars ended returned to their places in the oligarchies by the end of Henry's reign. Amable Thierry, a notorious Leaguer in Lyons, for example, was expelled in 1594 but returned to the municipal government as an *échevin* in 1606. Henry's policy of reconciliation meant his clemency eventually won him almost the whole of France.[67]

The history of Amiens offers a good example of this point. Between 1588 and 1594 two of the most notorious Leaguers in the city were Adrien de Maroeuil and Antoine de Berny. Maroeuil was a *conseiller* at the *siège présidial* in Amiens while

[64] Ibid.
[65] *Registres de Délibérations du Bureau de la Ville de Paris*, vol. 13, 132, 145–6; Jules Berger de Xivrey, ed., *Recueil des Lettres Missives de Henri IV*, (Paris: Imprimerie Nationale, 1850) vol. 5, 671.
[66] *Registres des Délibérations de Paris*, vol. 13, 156–7.
[67] See for example a letter from 1600 in which Henry forgave the notorious League magistrate from Lyons, Claude de Rubys. Henry extended to Rubys his 'grace speciale'. Antoine Pericaud, ed. *Notes et Documents pour servir à L'Histoire de Lyon sous le Règne d'Henri IV, 1594–1610* (Lyon: Imprimerie de Mougin-Rusand, 1845), 155–6.

Berny held the offices of *conseiller du roi* and *receveur général du taillon*. Both men were very powerful in the city and served in the municipal government throughout the period of the League. Maroeuil was mayor in 1590 and *échevin* in 1589, 1591, and 1594. As the duke of Aumale's client, Berny was mayor in 1593 and *échevin* in 1589, 1592, and 1594.[68] Both Berny and Maroeuil were councillors in the Leaguer *Chambre des Etats de Picardie*.[69] During the League these two men wielded immense municipal power. Maroeuil read the changing political climate better than Berny, however, and joined the royalist cause in 1594. He helped chase the duke of Aumale from the city after the Catholic League collapsed and was elected in 1595 to the municipal government. But Berny fled with Aumale and was banished from Amiens by Henry IV for several years after the town's capitulation. Maroeuil's transformation into a loyal royalist occurred rapidly. Henry selected him as *premier échevin* in September 1598, and he served as *échevin* in 1600 and 1602, and was re-elected as *premier échevin* in 1603. Berny's name is absent for a decade from the lists of municipal officials. He reappeared in 1608, however, and then held the office of *échevin* for three consecutive years between 1608 and 1610.[70]

The only person Henry and most of the town officials seemed unwilling to forgive in Amiens was Pierre de Famechon, mayor of the city during the humiliating capture of the town by the Spanish in 1597. Famechon was banished for years from Amiens after its recapture, and even though he tried to regain his influence within the municipal oligarchy after his return around 1600, he never succeeded during Henry's reign.[71] Famechon's grandson, nonetheless, served in the municipal government in 1663, and his great grandson bought the office of mayor in 1696 after the position was made venal.[72] This fact alone underscores the importance of family service in local government that the French Crown under the Old Regime never weakened or thought to destroy.

CONCLUSION: HENRY IV AND MUNICIPAL OLIGARCHIES

With few exceptions League allegiances do not appear to have tainted a man's career permanently. In Toulouse, for example, everyone holding the position of *capitoul* more than once during Henry's reign served under the Catholic League administration and again in the early 1600s.[73] This indicates that there was a continuity to municipal officeholding that Henry never altered and probably never

[68] Janvier, *Le Livre D'Or*, 290–315.
[69] *Archives Municipales*, Amiens (hereafter cited as AMA), BB49, fol. 57v.
[70] Janvier, *Le Livre D'Or*, 290–315; Albéric Calonne, *Histoire de la Ville d'Amiens* (Marseilles: Laffitte Reprints, 1976), vol 2, 82–132; AMA BB53, fols. 165–70.
[71] AMA, BB56, fols. 56v., 67–8, 85, 102.   [72] Janvier, *Le Livre D'or*, 257, 265.
[73] These men were Thomas Barrassi, *capitoul* in 1592 and 1600; Vidal Confort, *capitoul* in 1593 and 1602; Thomas Foucaud, *capitoul* in 1592 and 1605; Jacques Puget, *capitoul* in 1592 and 1606; Marianne de Salluste, *capitoul* in 1592 and 1601; Pierre Rahou, *capitoul* in 1593, 1600, and 1608; and Jean Thomas, *capitoul* in 1592, and 1602. AMT, BB 276–277, elections listed the beginning of each year.

considered changing. Henry did not have the bureaucratic manpower to infiltrate the towns with outside Crown officials. He could not even place an *intendant* in every town to supervise elections. Moreover, the towns possessed long standing institutions, and Henry never indicated by his letters or his actions that he knew of a workable alternative to the system in place. That system belonged to certain families. Once Henry's reign was secure he seemed content to allow former Leaguers to return to their magisterial venues proving that his post-League clemency was not a temporary expedient but a permanent characteristic of his reign. Henry's reign stands out because at the end of the religious wars specific problems caused him to intervene in several town governments. He was most successful in this initiative when he reduced the size of municipal governments and oversaw elections. Yet even though Bellièvre's letters indicate that reducing many town governments to the size of the Paris *échevinage* was discussed, no steps were ever taken to carry out the plan on a large scale.[74] By and large Henry ruled the towns by the traditional methods of clientage, and he depended upon established families to fill municipal posts and support his legitimacy. As his reign grew more secure, former League affiliations no longer seemed important as long as the Crown was assured of a man's loyalty and a town's allegiance. What Henry did best was inspire the confidence of municipal officials who in turn gave him their support. The king's clemency with regard to former Leaguers will be proven again in the next chapter, particularly in relation to Limoges.

[74] BN, MSS fr. 15911, fol. 18.

7

Urban protest in Poitiers and Limoges: the *pancarte* riots

Even after the peace settlement of 1598, the internal dynamics of urban life were turbulent. Small, localized riots occurred frequently in the late sixteenth and early seventeenth centuries and reflected the collective way townspeople expressed their anger.[1] Popular defiance challenged local and Crown authority, and the repercussions of its use were often costly. During Henry's reign, urban riots in Poitiers and Limoges broke out in response to a new tax on towns the Crown briefly collected. In repressing the riots, Henry disciplined the rebellious towns by revoking their privileges. This chapter continues a major theme of the book in emphasizing that Henry's relationship with his towns incorporated a detailed understanding of local affairs which he used in problem solving. When Henry disciplined his towns, he also tried to ease anxieties that resulted from the Wars of Religion and still occasionally erupted into violence. In Limoges, in particular, Henry's settlement of a local crisis reiterated his post-League policy of reconciliation by permitting ex-Leaguers to return to the *Hôtel de Ville* as a way of stabilizing a town still troubled by religious unrest. In addition, tax riots were sometimes a last step in fiscal negotiations in which the king asked for a specific amount of money in a tax or loan and then accepted a reduced amount as a compromise. The riots were meant to reduce the amount that the king was willing to accept. Urban tumult in Poitiers and Limoges thus caused the Crown to repress opposition predictably while simultaneously drawing the king and his agents into the complex webs of human interactions and histories that characterized these early modern towns.

THE SOL POUR LIVRE OR 'PANCARTE'

When Henry conceived the idea of the *sol pour livre* he hoped to use the tax to ease the Crown's chronic budget deficits. Between 1589 and 1596 Henry's finances were as precarious as his political position. The Crown possessed vast fiscal resources.

---

[1] For example, see Henry Heller's list in, Henry Heller, *Iron and Blood Civil Wars in Sixteenth-Century France* (Montreal: McGill-Queen's University Press, 1991), 42–4; William Beik, *Urban protest in Seventeenth-Century France, The Culture of Retribution* (Cambridge: Cambridge University Press, 1997), 254.

The three great taxes, the *taille*, a hearth tax based on a given contribution of a jurisdictional unit; the *gabelle*, a sales tax on salt; and the *aides*, indirect taxes on wine and foodstuffs, represented enormous sums available to the Crown, but much of the king's tax monies never reached his coffers. The direct tax system imposed in sixteenth- and seventeenth-century France had been instituted by 1379, but the French Renaissance monarchs never developed effective controls over their administrative personnel.[2] Hence, much of what technically belonged to the king ended up in the purses of great nobles, royal officials, special agents, and municipal elites.[3] Privileged status presented other difficulties for the Crown since many towns were exempt from the *taille*, and in the towns notable citizens were exempted from various urban levies.

Before 1594, Henry had actually controlled very little of France and thus had to struggle with a reduced tax base. Before the capitulations, he was unable to collect taxes in Brittany, Normandy, or Languedoc, or to use the resources of important financial centres like Paris or Lyons. From 1589 to 1596, he was forced to implement a series of short-term expedients to fund his wars with the Catholic League and Spain.[4] He created offices, alienated the royal domain, raised taxes in areas under his control, issued letters of nobility, and borrowed heavily in order to pay his troops and creditors and continue the war effort.[5]

After 1594, more money became available through the settlements made with Catholic League magnates, provinces, and towns. But the cost of the pacification treaties posed a heavy burden on the Crown and offset any immediate gains made from tax monies redirected to the royal treasury. In fact, the large sums demanded by League magnates forced Henry to create new taxes in order to pay them. Sully inflated the figure but estimated the price of peace at 32 million *livres*. The true amount was probably closer to 24 million *livres*.[6]

At the same time that the king was ending the civil wars in France, he was preparing for a war with Spain, which began in 1595 and proved disastrous. By the next year the Spanish had occupied Ardres, Calais, Cambrai, Doullens, and La Fère, and threatened most of Picardy. Henry laid siege to La Fère and eventually recaptured the town on 16 May 1596. But the seven month military operation was expensive and set the king behind in repaying his Swiss creditors.[7] He was forced to

---

[2] James B. Collins, *Fiscal Limits of Absolutism, Direct Taxation in Early 17th-Century France* (Berkeley: University of California Press, 1988), 27.

[3] J. Russell Major, *Representative Government in Early Modern France* (New Haven: Yale University Press, 1980), 260.

[4] James B. Collins, 'Un problème toujours mal connu: les finances d'Henri IV', in *Henri IV, le Roi et la Reconstruction du Royaume* (Pau: Association Henri IV 1989 et J. & D. Editions, 1990), 148.

[5] Ibid.; Major, *Representative Government*, 260.

[6] Martin Wolfe, *The Fiscal System of Renaissance France* (New Haven: Yale University Press, 1872), 221; David Parker, *The Making of French Absolutism* (London: Edward Arnold, 1983), 47; Auguste Poirson, *Histoire du Règne de Henri IV* (Paris: Didier, 1862), vol. 1, 660–9.

[7] Richard Bonney, *The King's Debts, Finance and Politics in France 1589–1661* (Oxford: Clarendon Press, 1981), 47; David Buisseret, *Henri IV* (London: Unwin Hyman, 1984), 60–1.

stop campaigning and call an Assembly of Notables at Rouen to help with his financial problems.[8] Henry sought to convince the Assembly that he had an insufficient tax base, and he invited ninety-four dignitaries to the Assembly including envoys from key towns.[9] He included them because he needed to rally support for increased urban taxes. After great opposition the Assembly grudgingly accepted the idea of a five per cent tax on commodities entering the towns.[10]

The *sol pour livre* or *'pancarte'* was designed to reduce pressure on peasants in the countryside by taxing merchants and artisans in the towns. The king established the tax by royal edict on 10 March 1597, and the *Cour des aides* registered it under protest on 30 March.[11] The edict levied a five per cent sales tax on important commodities sold in towns throughout France. The tax was to be collected wherever fairs and markets were held. Designed to tax goods sold in bulk, the *pancarte* was levied on merchants, who passed the added cost on to consumers. Items sold singularly in boutiques were exempt from the five per cent tax.[12] The *Conseil du roi* devised a schedule of duties pertaining to taxable goods, and royal officials posted placards on town gates listing these specifications. The *sol pour livre* drew its popular name from these placards or *'pancartes'*.[13] Taxable commodities included wine, cider, beef, veal, lamb, goat, pork, bacon, tallow, herring, cod, salmon, mackerel, wax, drugs, spices, linens, draperies, wool, silk, leather, woad, tapestries, pelts, iron, steel, copper, carbon, and many other items.[14] Tax exempt

[8] Mark Greengrass, *France in the Age of Henri IV, the Struggle for Stability* (London: Longman Group Ltd., 1984), 95.

[9] Jules Berger de Xivrey, *Receuil des Lettres Missives de Henri IV* (Paris: Imprimerie Nationale, 1848), vol. 4, 657. Henry could have called an Estates-General but chose an Assembly instead. In 1596 he dared not risk the further controversy that an Estates-General might rouse. Wolfe, *The Fiscal System*, 222–3.

[10] J. Russell Major, *Bellièvre, Sully and the Assembly of Notables of 1596* (Philadelphia: The American Philosophical Society, 1974), 64, 13–14, 16, 21, 24; Major, *Representative Government*, 263. The towns called to the assembly were Paris, Rouen, Bourges, Bordeaux, Orléans, Moulins, Amiens, Troyes, Tours, Châlons-sur-Marne, Lyons, Dijon, Marseilles, and Aix. Most of the reforms outlined by the Assembly of Notables, moreover, were doomed to failure. See also, Bonney, *The King's Debts*, 49–50; Wolfe, *The Fiscal System*, 222–4; Collins, *Fiscal Limits*, 76–7; J. J. Clamageran, *Histoire de L'Impôt en France* (Paris: Librairie de Guillaumin et Cie., 1868), vol. 2, 335–50.

[11] A. Fontanon, ed., *Les Edicts et Ordonnances des Rois de France* (Paris: J. du Puy, 1611), vol. 2, 532–3; Major, *Bellièvre, Sully, and the Assembly of Notables*, 24; Albert Chamberland, 'Jean Chandon et le Conflit entre La Cour des Aides et le Conseil du Roi', *Revue Henri IV*, 2 (1907–8), 113–25.

[12] Clamageran, *Histoire de L'Impôt*, vol. 2, 364; Noël Valois, *Inventaire des arrêts du Conseil d'Etat, règne de Henri IV* (Paris: Imprimerie Nationale, 1886–1893), vol. 2, 6231. 'Arrêt ordonnant que toutes les villes sans exception payeront l'impôt du sol pour livre reconnu juste par les Notables.' Although acts were promulgated before 1601 ordering the establishment of the *sol pour livre* (especially in 1599) it does not appear that serious efforts were made by the Crown to collect the tax before 1601. See for instance an *arrêt* dated 13 February 1599, in Valois, vol. 1, 5237. 'A esté resolu au Conseil de Sa Majesté de faire les depesches qui ensuivent, pour l'establissement du sol pour livre ès généralitez de Champaigne, Poictiers, Bourges, Limoges, Moulins, Auvergne, et Lyon . . .'

[13] Wolfe, *The Fiscal System*, 224.

[14] Clamageran, *Histoire de L'Impôt*, vol. 2, 365. Other items were often added to this list of taxable goods. See for example, Valois, *Inventaire des arrêts*, vol. 2, £6,000. 'Arrêt autorisant Antoine Hervé, fermier du sol pour livre en la ville de Paris, à percevoir le droit de pancarte sur certaines sortes de

goods consisted mainly of staple foodstuffs such as, flour, seeds, grains, vegetables, poultry, eggs, fruit, herbs, butter, milk, hay, and live lambs and pigs brought to town by peasants from the countryside.[15]

The main function of the *pancarte* was a broadening of the tax base that would allow greater funds to flow into the royal treasury. It was not a new tax. The *pancarte* dated back to medieval sales taxes levied by nobles and eventually by kings. Known as *impositions sur les ventes*, these taxes had always been unpopular with townspeople.[16] In fact, the Crown was imposing the *pancarte* in certain towns before the Assembly of Notables met in 1596–7. Between February 1593 and September 1594, municipal deliberations from the royalist town of Blois refer frequently to grievances stemming from a sales tax on merchandise called the *pancarte*. A deputy from the municipal government of Blois went to court in 1594 to complain of hardships resulting from this tax.[17]

People condemned the *pancarte* all over France. Henry's government tried to lessen this discontent by abolishing the tolls created since 1585 on some roads, and promising a diminution of *tailles*, mostly in the countryside. Total Crown revenues began decreasing after 1598 with the return of peace, and Henry and Sully hoped to lower other taxes as well. Sully was also auditing the towns' financial accounts in an effort to lessen the exploitation of poor inhabitants by elites. By decreasing what townspeople paid in corrupt levies, Sully thus made the collection of the *pancarte* potentially more feasible. The towns cried poverty, however, saying the bulk of their population could not support additional taxes on commodities. Parisian officials went further and argued that the *pancarte* would actually destroy the city's commercial base by causing foreign merchants to take their business elsewhere.[18] Growing discontent caused Henry to allow favoured towns to pay lump-sum subventions to avoid the tax.[19]

In 1601, the Crown began seriously to try to collect the *sol pour livre*, and Poitiers and Limoges exploded in tax riots. As a result the *pancarte* was suppressed on 10 November 1602, although it was raised for several years to come in many towns in order to pay the subventions promised to the Crown. In a number of instances towns simply borrowed monies from rich creditors to pay the subventions that replaced the tax. The Assembly of Notables estimated the *pancarte* would net around 7 million *livres* for the Crown. The tax actually brought in 1,563,594 *livres*.[20]

---

denrées ou de marchandises non mentionées en l'édit de 1597, telles que le vin d'Espagne, la vache, le marsouin, la baleine, le thon, l'anchois et tout autre poisson de mer sale, la teinture d'Inde, les meules de moulin, les cordages, la parchemin, les cendres, les plumes d'autruche, l'acier, les verres, le vieux linge.' [15] Clamageran, *Histoire de L'Impôt*, vol. 2, 365. [16] Ibid., 366.
[17] *Archives Municipales*, Blois, BB14. Deliberations dated 10 and 12 February, 1593, 22 February 1593 and 9 September 1594. [18] BN, MSS fr., 11088, fol. 351.
[19] Clamageran, *Histoire de L'Impôt*, vol. 2, 363, 367–8; Roland Mousnier, *L'assassinat d'Henri IV 14 Mai 1610* (Paris: Editions Gallimand, 1964), 172; Jean-Pierre Babelon, *Henri IV* (Paris: Fayard, 1982), 775; Yves-Marie Bercé, *The Birth of Absolutism: A History of France, 1598–1661*, trans. Richard Rex (New York: St Martin's Press, 1992), 21–2.
[20] Roland Mousnier, *The Assassination of Henry IV*, trans. Joan Spencer (New York: Charles Scribner's

THE *PANCARTE* RIOT IN POITIERS

Poitiers was the first town to protest the *pancarte* by rioting. Rumblings of trouble began in 1599 when the town magistrates sent a delegation to court to oppose the tax.[21] Thereafter, outrageous rumours circulated that Henry wanted to force the *gabelle* on Poitiers and planned to impose a tax on conjugal relations.[22] Rebellion finally broke out in May of 1601 when the king's commissioner, Pierre d'Amours, arrived in Poitiers with the intention of publishing the tax and overseeing its collection. D'Amours was a member of the king's *Conseil d'Etat*, and was named *commissaire des finances* in 1601. He left for Poitiers on 30 April under orders to establish the *sol pour livre* in towns throughout Poitou.[23]

Immediately d'Amours faced trouble. He arrived in Poitiers on 2 May 1601 and convoked an assembly to secure support for the new tax without success. D'Amours wrote to Chancellor Bellièvre, ten days after his arrival that he had been unable to do anything towards establishing the *pancarte*. He stated that none of Poitiers's leaders would help him and that they opposed the tax vehemently. D'Amours feared urban unrest.[24] He reported to Bellièvre that Poitiers was populated by people of 'little quality'. 'It is dangerous', he commented, 'to live among people who behave in such fashion.'[25] D'Amours held four assemblies at the *Maison de Ville*, but could not convince the town's leadership to accept the tax.[26]

D'Amours misgivings soon proved true. Determined to carry out his instructions, he assembled the town leaders early on the morning of Tuesday 15 May to discuss at length his intention of publishing the *pancarte*. Placards were nailed around town at all intersections, on church doors, and the town gates. To the sound of a trumpet, the royal commissioner read aloud the king's edict establishing the tax. Crowds gathered, hurled insults at d'Amours and impeded his return to his hotel. Then violence exploded. With d'Amours safely in his lodgings, troubled townspeople took their anger out on each other, and street fighting ensued. It was

Sons, 1973), 188–9; Clamageran, *Histoire de L'Impôt*, vol. 2, 363, 367–8; Valois, *Inventaire des arrêts*, vol. 2, 7155. 'Arrêt autorisant les villes de marches des généralites de Bourges, Poitiers, Limoges et Riom à remplacer par une subvention le nouvel impôt du sol pour livre.' For other subventions see 5928, 6025, 6026, 6093, 6096, 6097, 6320, 6368. 6603, 6631, 6696, 6700, 6744, 6830, 6902, 7076, 7078, 7255, 7306, 7347, 7361, 7409, 7416, 7429, 7431, 7460, 7503, 7538, 7587, 7935, 7940, 7997, 8374, 8479, 8562, 8974, 9005, 9234, 9400, 9440, 9683, 9996, 10453, 10905, 10928, 10932, 11225, 11748, 11858, 11862, 11891, 11899, 12465, 12871, 13349, 15058.

[21] *Archives Communales*, Poitiers (hereafter ACP), Registre 58, fol. 72.

[22] Henri Ouvré, *Essai sur l'histoire de Poitiers depuis la fin de la Ligue jusqu'à la prise de La Rochelle (1595–1628)* (Poitiers: A. Dupré, 1856), 10–12. Other rumours specified that people would be taxed for childbirth and death. See, Yves-Marie Bercé, *Revolt and revolution in early modern Europe, An essay on the history of political violence*, trans. Joseph Bergin, (New York: St Martin's Press, 1987), 111.

[23] Alfred Barbier, *Pierre d'Amours, Commissaire des Finances à Poitiers sous Henri IV (1601)* (Poitiers: Imprimerie générale de l'Ouest, 1880), 7–15; Alfred Barbier, 'Les Intendants du Poitou', *Mémoires de la Société des Antiquaires de l'Ouest*, 7 (1884), 3.

[24] BN, MSS fr. 15899, fol. 866.

[25] Ibid., fol. 869. D'Amours wrote, 'Il est dangereuse de vivre parmi une peuple conduise de telle facon.'

[26] Ibid.

reported that no one could walk through the town that evening without being threatened by angry mobs.[27]

D'Amours reported to Bellièvre that he had spent most of the day in the *Maison de Ville*, hiding from several hundred people who planned to kill him. He claimed to have narrowly escaped an attempt on his life the next day while returning to his lodgings in the company of the mayor, several *échevins*, and Scévole de Saint-Marthe, a royal official and client of Henry IV. D'Amours reported to Bellièvre that when he and a small band of municipal officials left the *Maison de Ville*, a crowd of rock-throwing troublemakers pursued them. One of them grabbed d'Amours and accused him of wanting to ruin Poitiers. When he arrived at his lodgings, he was met by rude men and women brandishing 'grands couteaux' and carrying 'grosses pierres'. 'Without Sainte-Marthe', the commissioner wrote, 'I would have been killed.'[28] That night armed guards stood at the entrance to his lodgings, and the following morning he once again tried to publish the *pancarte*. An angry mob assembled, and d'Amours feared for his life. At this point he lost his nerve and fled Poitiers. 'I gave in to their fury', he told Bellièvre, 'and the little respect that they hold for the king.'[29] He left for nearby Châtelleraud and sought help from the Crown.

News of the *pancarte* riot in Poitiers reached Henry within a few days. The king feared that it might develop into a massive wave of rebellion that would sweep urban France.[30] In a letter to the duke of Montmorency, Henry compared the uprising in Poitiers to the protest against the *gabelle* that had occurred in Bordeaux in 1548 during the reign of Henry II.[31] He told Montmorency that he intended to punish the inhabitants of Poitiers.[32] He decided to treat Poitiers with the same severity that had been used to quash the revolt in Bordeaux. He revoked the privileges of the town and sent the governor of Poitiers, Charles de Lorraine, duke of Elbeuf, and his troops to put down the revolt.[33]

Henry and his ministers worried about the urban unrest in Poitiers because of an incident in their collective memory of the town's history. Poitiers had been a Catholic League stronghold for five years between 1589 and 1594. When the

[27] Ibid., fol. 298.
[28] Ibid. D'Amours explained, 'Et certes sans ledicte sieur de Ste.-Marthe, je seray mort.'
[29] Ibid. D'Amours explained he left 'pour ceder a leur fureur et le peu de respect qu'ils portent a Sa Majesté.' This entire account of the riot is taken from the series of letters located in BN MSS fr. 15899 that D'Amours wrote to Bellièvre after the *pancarte* riot. See fols. 294, 296, 298, 300, 302, 306, 307, 647, 866–69.
[30] Claude Groulart, 'Mémoires de Claude Groulart, Premier Président du Parlement de Normandie, où Voyages par lui faits en Cour', M. M. Michaud and J. Poujoulat, eds., *Nouvelle Collections des Mémoires pour servir a L'Histoire de France depuis le XIIIe siècle jusqu'à la fin du XVIIIe* (Paris: Chez L'Editeur du Commentaire analytique du Code Civil, 1838), 586–7.
[31] Berger de Xivrey, *Recueil des Lettres Missives*, vol. 5, 417–18. In the letter Henry refers to the siege of Bordeaux by the constable Montmorency whom Henry II sent to the city in 1548 to put down an insurrection over the *gabelle*. See Robert Boutruche, *Bordeaux de 1453 à 1715* (Bordeaux: Federation historique du Sud-Ouest, 1966), 302–4.   [32] Ibid.
[33] Groulart, 'Mémoires', 586–7.

insurrection in favour of the League had occurred, the inhabitants of Poitiers chased their royalist governor from the town, making him jump the ramparts in the process. A few days later Henry III arrived outside Poitiers, but he was refused entry, an act not easily forgotten.[34] D'Amours made reference to this event repeatedly in the letters he sent to Bellièvre during the *pancarte* riot. Henry wrote to Montmorency, 'The town is governed by worthless magistrates who abuse their charges and commit wrongs. It is the only town of the realm, as you well know, to have ever refused entry to its own king, Henry III.'[35] Henry IV believed that the riot was an event God allowed to happen so that Poitiers could be punished for its past as well as its present transgressions.[36] 'It is a weak and hostile town', the king wrote to Montmorency, 'that must be bridled in a fashion to ensure that it will never be able to kick its Prince again and cause injury.'[37]

That D'Amours had exaggerated the seriousness of the disturbance became apparent when Elbeuf arrived at the gates with his troops. The duke, expecting to encounter strong resistance, found only anxious townspeople frightened over how the king intended to punish them. Elbeuf immediately sent two town notables to D'Amours in Châtelleraud to beg his forgiveness and invite him back to Poitiers. The commissioner returned on 12 June and wrote Bellièvre that his peril had ended.[38]

D'Amours's relief proved short-lived. Town councillors now wrote to the king alleging that D'Amours had dramatized the events of 15 and 16 May. They stated he had overreacted and had been chased out of town by a group of old women. By blaming the unrest on women, the town councillors dismissed the seriousness of the event and portrayed the king's official as a laughing stock.[39] In response D'Amours wrote letter after letter to Bellièvre, Villeroy, and Sully stressing the truthfulness of his version of the event and swearing his dedication to the king.[40]

To return calm to Poitiers, Elbeuf replaced the tax with a subvention of 10,000 *écus*. This figure included 4,000 *écus* in place of the *pancarte* and 6,000 *écus* levied on the town for Henry's marriage to Marie de Medici that Poitiers had yet to pay. Because the money had to be raised, the *pancarte* was levied until 1605. Elites tried to claim exemptions, but the king ordered the tax levied on the entire population. Scévole de Sainte-Marthe was appointed mayor of Poitiers by Henry in 1601 and oversaw the collection of the *sol pour livre*. He used militia officers to collect the tax when no receivers could be found. The subvention was never paid in full, however,

---

[34] Belisaire Ledain, *Histoire sommaire de la ville de Poitiers* (Fontenay: Auguste Baud, 1889), 158.
[35] Berger de Xivrey, *Recueil des Lettres Missives*, vol. 5, 422. Henry wrote, 'Elle [Poitiers] est gouvernée aussy par des magistrats de petite estoffe, lesquels sont en possession d'abuser de l'auctorité de leurs charges et de mal faire. C'est la seule ville de ce Royaume qui a refusé l'entrée à la propre personne de son Roy, comme vous sçavés qu'elle fit au feu Roy . . . '   [36] Ibid.
[37] Ibid. The king declared, 'Cest une ville foible et hargneuse, que il faut brider de façon qu'elle ne puisse jamais plus regimber contre son prince et faire mal.'
[38] BN, MSS fr. 15899, fols. 294–6.
[39] ACP, registre 59, fol. 101, 106; Bercé, *Revolt and revolution*, 110–12.
[40] BN, MSS fr., 15899, fols. 296, 300, 302, 304, 306, 307.

even after it was decreased to only 5,000 *livres*. Poitiers paid 3,433 *livres* to the Crown as a subvention in 1608.[41]

Finally, Elbeuf ordered the town council of Poitiers to send deputies to court to apologize to the king and ask his forgiveness. Marc Jarno, an *échevin*, undertook this task with trepidation. He arrived in Paris in September, and his timing was fortunate because the queen, Marie de Medici, was in labour with her first child. Anticipating the birth of a possible heir, Henry was light-hearted and accepted the contrition of Poitiers's deputy. 'If I can count on the love and devotion of your citizens', Henry told Jarno, 'I will not only be a good king but also a good father.'[42] Before drafting a letter to Poitiers's town councillors exhorting them to love their king and pray that God would give him a son, Henry spoke these words to Jarno:

My repentant children always find me full of indulgence; but when they are disobedient and don't love me, they deserve all of my severity. Prove your regret by ending the calamities that plague your government and putting a stop to troublemakers.[43]

The next year on 19 May 1602, the king entered Poitiers and formally re-established the town's privileges.[44]

The *pancarte* incident was in many ways a typical tax riot of the early modern period. Towns regularly rioted in objection to royal financial measures they found oppressive, but these were not full scale rebellions. Characteristically, fiscal griev-ances stirred emotions while rumours heightened tensions until some event, like the publication of a new tax or the arrival of a royal official, sparked hours or days of violence. The crowd generally consisted of urban plebeians; artisans, day labourers, shopkeepers, journeymen and servants, as well as the poor and the homeless. Typically women were present and instigated fracas.[45] The mobs directed their violence not at the king, but his royal agent who brought the bad news to town. D'Amours wrote to Bellièvre and explained that the mobs in Poitiers consisted largely of people of low status, but he noted some men of prominence in the crowds. Since Poitiers's leadership did not prevent the tumult, d'Amours implied they supported it.[46] D'Amours's words should not be taken at face value, however.

---

[41] Ouvré, *Essai sur l'histoire de Poitiers*, 15–20, 24–5; ACP Casier 23, 138, act dated 14 August 1608; ACP, reg. 60, fols. 31–7, 45–51, 63. The *pancarte* was raised in Poitiers until 1605, and surplus monies were used to finance the municipal debt and repair the town ramparts. Poitiers did not pay the Crown until 14 August 1608 when 3,433 *livres*, 11 *sous*, 2 *derniers* were turned over as a subvention in lieu of the *pancarte*.

[42] Quoted in Ouvré, *Essai sur l'histoire de Poitiers*, 18. Henry stated, 'Si je puis compter sur l'amour et le dévoûment de vos concitoyens, je serai pour eux non-seulement un bon roi, mais un bon pere.'

[43] Ibid. The quote reads, 'Le repentir de mes enfants me trouve toujours plein d'indulgence; mais quand ils sont désobéissants et n'aiment pas leur roi, ils doivent s'attenndre à toute ma rigueur. Prouvez vos sentiments en dissipant les calomnies qui courent sur mon gouvernement, et en faissant arrêter les calomniateurs.'   [44] BN, MSS fr. 15899, fol. 657; Ledain, *Histoire de Poitiers*, 159.

[45] Perez Zagorin, *Rebels and Rulers, 1500–1660*, vol. 1, *Society, States, and Early Modern Revolution Agrarian and Urban Rebellions* (Cambridge: Cambridge University Press, 1982), 237–45.

[46] BN, MSS fr., 15899, fol. 869; William Beik, *Absolutism and Society in Seventeenth Century France: State Power and Provincial Aristocracy in Languedoc* (New York: Cambridge University Press, 1985),

As William Beik has noted, 'it would be a serious error to picture *échevins* and protesters united against the agents of external forces because the "community" was more complex than that'.[47] Municipal magistrates' failure to act quickly to repress rioters does not mean they promoted disturbances. They had to manage the cities and collect their own taxes, and any kind of disorder proved to be dangerous.[48] Poitiers's town councillors seemed unable to control the populace after D'Amours's arrival, which became as troubling for them as for the king's commissioner.

The riot in Poitiers was caused by more than concern about taxes since confessional strife lingering from the religious wars came to the surface. Fiscal complaints had led the people to riot, but once their anger exploded, hatred between Protestants and Catholics energized their passions as well. Jean Calvin was a native of Poitiers, and as a result of his missionary efforts there was a strong Protestant faction in the town.[49] D'Amours himself was a Protestant, which may have deepened the suspicions of Poitiers's Catholic inhabitants. In his letters to Bellièvre, D'Amours mentioned the presence of those belonging to the *religion prétendu réformée*, and he attributed some of the violence that occurred during the revolt to religious tensions.[50] Four months before the *pancarte* riot occurred, several masked men had murdered one of Poitiers's leading Catholic nobleman. A witness to the murder, wounded in the attack, identified one of the assassins as a Protestant nobleman who was a citizen of the town. The man was hunted down, tried, and executed in the town's main square.[51] If D'Amours was right, anxiety and hatred stemming from this event fuelled the dynamic of the *pancarte* disturbance, turning it into a far more complex urban conflict than previously believed.

Henry's handling of the riot was typical of a Renaissance monarch. When settling crises, French kings tended to operate between the poles of paternalistic forgiveness and vengeful chastisement. Henry went to both extremes.[52] Originally, the king took the hard line and revoked the defiant town's privileges and sent in

189–92; 'The Culture of Protest in Seventeenth-Century French Towns', *Social History*, 15 (1990), 1–23; John Bohstedt, 'Riots and Community Politics in England and Wales 1790–1810' (Cambridge: Harvard University Press, 1983); Zagorin, *Rebels and Rulers*, vol. 1 237–45. For the best works on provincial rebellion to date see: René Pillorget, *Les Mouvements Insurrectionnels de Provence entre 1596 et 1715* (Paris: Editions A. Pedone, 1975); Yves-Marie Bercé, *Histoire des Croquants* (Paris: Editions du Seuil, 1986); Yves-Marie Bercé, *Revolt and Revolution*; Boris Porshnev, *Les Soulevements populaires en France de 1623–1648* (Paris: SEVPEN., 1963); Emmanuel Le Roy Ladurie, *Carnival in Romans*, trans. Mary Feeney (New York: George Braziller, Inc., 1979); David Warren Sabean, *Power in the Blood. Popular Culture and Village Discourse in Early Modern Germany* (Cambridge: Cambridge University Press, 1984); Sharon Kettering, *Judicial Politics and Urban Revolt in Sseventeenth-Century France: The Parlement of Six, 1629–1659* (Princeton: Princeton University Press, 1978); Peter Burke, 'Insult and Blasphemy in Early Modern Italy', *The Historical Anthropology of Early Modern Italy: Essays on Perception and Communication* (Cambridge: Cambridge University Press, 1987), 95–109.
[47] Beik, *Urban Protest in Seventeenth-Century France*, 114.   [48] Ibid., 95.
[49] Jacques Peret, 'De la Renaissance à Louis XIV: vitalité, violence et misère', in *Histoire de Poitiers*, ed. Robert Favreau (Toulouse: Privat, 1985), 193.   [50] BN, MSS fr. 15899, fol. 866.
[51] B. Ledain, 'Les Maires de Poitiers', *Bulletin et Mémoires de la Société des Antiquaires de L'Ouest*, 20 (1897), 747–8.   [52] Zagorin, *Rebels and Rulers*, vol. 1, 239.

troops to put down the revolt. In 1602, however, the king had to deal with the Biron conspiracy, which changed his approach to Poitiers. Charles de Gontaut, marshall Biron, conspired with the Spanish to assassinate Henry IV, and the conspiracy included the collusion of several French nobles and high officials. Henry learned of the plot in March 1602, which may have influenced his decision to restore Poitiers's privileges during his visit to the town two months later.[53] He also decided to forego a plan to reorganize the *échevinage* that had been discussed in 1601.[54] Had there been no Biron conspiracy, perhaps Henry would have revised election procedures directly after the riot. He did so, anyway, in 1609.

In 1609 Henry reduced the size of the town council in Poitiers from ninety-three to seventy-five, and established new election procedures forbidding persons to canvas votes for the mayor's office by dishonest means. He outlawed elections by *vive voix* and introduced the secret ballot. Most importantly, he ordered that municipal offices could no longer be sold outright or passed from uncle to nephew, godfather to godson, or brother to brother, and could only be transferred from father to son if the son was over twenty-five years of age.[55] Of course Henry did not have the administrative personnel to enforce these regulations, but their promulgation marks a step in the development of more orderly election procedures.

Henry thus enacted reforms to curtail the social unrest that accompanied elections and perhaps to make it easier for his own trusted men to win municipal seats. In Poitiers a tightly knit oligarchy exchanged offices among themselves and kept all but a very few families from attaining municipal power. This situation made Poitiers liable for trouble every election day and angered those who felt denied a fair chance to run for office. A similar problem caused La Rochelle to explode in open revolt against the municipal government in 1618.[56] Henry told the municipal magistrates in Poitiers to accept these changes without complaint, otherwise he warned he would abolish their privileges.[57] Obviously the *pancarte* riot provided Henry with a good deal of information about the town's municipal government and probably influenced his decision to change its election procedures in 1609.

---

[53] Ouvré, 'Essai sur Poitiers', 19; Buisseret, *Henry IV*, 112–15. Charles de Gontaut, *maréchal* de Biron began conspiring with the Spanish in 1598 to assassinate the king. By 1601 he was planning with the Spanish to lead an uprising of nobles to include the comte de Soissons, the comte d'Auvergne and the prince de Joinville. One of Biron's agents, Jacques de La Fin, informed Henry IV about the conspiracy in March 1602. Biron was eventually brought to court, exposed and tried. He was decapitated at the Bastille on 31 July 1602.

[54] BN, MSS fr., 15899, fol. 296. D'Amours wrote to Bellièvre: 'It is necessary to change the *cour de ville* and the *conseil de ville*. The number of councillors must also be reduced, otherwise, the king will never be obeyed.' See also Berger de Xivrey, *Recueil des Lettres Missives*, vol. 5, 524, 587.

[55] AN E21, fol. 40r dated 9 April 1609 and fol. 349 dated 16 May 1609. ACP, Reg. 64, fols. 83–4.

[56] Kevin C. Robbins, 'The Families and Politics of La Rochelle, 1550–1650', (Ph.D. thesis., The Johns Hopkins University, 1990). See chapter 3, 135–92.

[57] Ouvré, 'Essai sur Poitiers', 33.

THE 'PANCARTE' RIOT IN LIMOGES

If Henry thought his troubles with the *pancarte* issue were over in September of 1601, when he accepted the apology of Marc Jarno for Poitiers, he soon found himself mistaken. The king had been threatened by the Poitiers riot and had moved cautiously to dispel the tumult, but he had not yet been persuaded to abolish the hated tax. Controversy surrounding Pierre d'Amours reaction to the discontent in Poitiers may have led the king to discount the riot to some extent after he and the town came to terms over the issue. The incident, after all, had only included a few hundred townspeople. Efforts were still being made by the Crown in late 1601 and early 1602 to collect the tax. Yet outcries against the *pancarte* from numerous urban centres continued to plague Henry until another riot occurred against the tax in the Spring of 1602. Popular effervescence engulfed Limoges between 20 and 22 April 1602, upsetting the peace during the wake of the Biron conspiracy and causing the king to reconsider the plausibility of increasing the tax assessment on urban France.

The tumult set off in Limoges on 20 April 1602 began when a *chevalier* of the *guet* from Orléans named Lambert, under orders to publish the *pancarte* and announce its collection in all public squares, arrived in the town with a company of archers. Trouble brewed as Lambert began his mission. Murmurs and cries denouncing the *pancarte* arose from an anxious crowd until Lambert could no longer hear his own voice over the noise. When a group of angry women sparked an attack from the agitators and wounded two of the archers with rocks, the officer and his men retreated to their hotel, bolting the doors behind them.[58] For the rest of the day 'a deafening ferment' hung in the air.'[59] Instead of dwindling during the night, moreover, the number of protesters grew so that by the next day they occupied all the main avenues in Limoges. In the morning they assaulted the house of a *trésorier de France*, Jehan du Verdier d'Orfeuille, who had signed the *pancarte* and was blamed for it. The windows of his house were broken, but no attempt was made to penetrate the interior. Before noon, the crowd dispersed and d'Orfeuille was able to leave his dwelling to go and dine with the town's bishop, Henri de la Martonie. He was spotted, however, passing by the town's fish market and the riot recommenced. A group of rock-throwing women chased him to the bishop's residence. Severely shaken, the treasurer remained there for several days.[60]

The following morning, all the boutiques in Limoges were closed. Troops of agitators formed and marched on the *Maison de Ville* where they called for the consuls to chase Lambert and his archers from the town. At this point, for the first time since the trouble began, the municipal magistrates took the initiative. They

---

[58] Bonaventure de Saint-Amable, *Histoire de Saint Martial apôtre des Gaules, et Notamment de L'Aquitaine et du Limosin, Ecclésiastiques ou Civils, des Saints et Hommes Illustres et Autres choses depuis Saint Martial jusques à Nous* (Limoges: Anthoine Voisin, 1685), vol. 3, 812; M.P. Laforest, *Etudes sur les Anciennes Provinces de France, Limoges au* XVIIe *Siècle* (Limoges: Librairie de J. B. LeBlanc, 1862), 33–4.   [59] Laforest, *Etudes*, 35.
[60] Bonaventure de Saint-Amable, *Histoire de Saint Martial*, vol. 3, 812.

spoke to the people and attempted to quiet them. The rioters left the *Maison de Ville* in an excited state, however, and proceeded to the Place Saint-Michael of the Lions before the hotel 'Breuil', where Lambert was in conference with the governor of Limoges, the baron of Châteauneuf. Four to five thousand protesters were said to have gathered in the place and began hurling insults at Lambert. They attacked the hotel, but were repelled by a strong defence from within. The town magistrates, thinking their warning sufficient, had failed to follow the crowd to the hotel 'Breuil'. They arrived at the 'Breuil' much later, after the riot had long since gotten out of control. One of them, Jacques Martin a president at the *siège présidial* of Limoges and former consul, persuaded the people that he would negotiate with the king to suppress the hated tax. His influence calmed the rioters, and they allowed the consuls to enter the hotel. That evening Lambert was given safe-conduct from Limoges, and peace was restored.[61]

To punish the town for its disobedience, Henry dispatched Antoine Le Camus, sieur de Jambeville, the president of his *Grand Conseil*, with a special commission to restore order and render justice there. Jambeville arrived on 19 May and immediately held a session with the municipal government. He informed them that the king considered the riot 'a pure rebellion' and that all disobedience went against the authority of the Crown.[62] The king understood that not all of the townspeople had participated in the disturbance, and he decreed that only the guilty would be punished. Jambeville then addressed the town magistrates directly. The individuals the king perceived as most responsible for the sedition, he announced, were the consuls who had failed to act properly to prevent and/or dispel the riot. For this reason the king called for the resignation of all twelve ruling consuls, and Jambeville asked them to take off their consular capes and put them on a table before him. In their place the king chose directly, with no recommendation from the townspeople, six new consuls to serve out the rest of the term. These six were: Jean de Mauple, *trésorier général de France*; Jean Bonin, *procureur du roi au siège présidial*; Gaspard Benoist, *élu de l'élection*; Joseph de Petiot, *juge de la ville*; Thomas Durand-Brugière, bourgeois; and Pierre DuBois, bourgeois-merchant. All six protested, but in the end they had no choice but to follow the king's command, take the consular oath, and be inducted into office.[63] Henry's punishment did not stop here. His reduction in the size of the consular government in Limoges from twelve

---

[61] Information on the revolt is slight. The deliberations of the municipality give no detail whatsoever on the incident itself. See Bonaventure de Saint-Amable, *Histoire de Saint-Martial*, vol. 3, 812; Laforest, *Etudes*, 33–8; Jean Levet, *Histoire de Limoges 1: Des Origines à la fin de l'Ancien Régime* (Limoges: René Desagne, 1974), 251. A few letters found in the *Bibliothèque Nationale* and quoted below also shed some light on the aftermath of the riot.

[62] *Archives Municipales*, Limoges (hereafter, AML), BB2, fol. 41r. Dates vary as to when Jambeville actually arrived in Limoges.

[63] Louis Guibert, ed., *Registres Consulaires de la Ville de Limoges, Second Registre (1592–1662)* (Limoges: Imprimerie de Chapoulaud Frères, 1884), 60; E. Ruben, 'Changements Introduits en 1602, par Henri IV dans le mode d'élection et le nombre des consuls de Limoges', *Bulletin de la Société Archéologique et Historique du Limousin*, 3 (1857), 147–8.

to six was made permanent, and he diminished the size of the electorate from an indeterminate number of citizens, who held suffrage rights, to only one-hundred bourgeois, who were to be elected in groups of ten from each of the ten *quartiers* of Limoges before the consular elections each year. In this way the incumbent consuls would choose the one-hundred bourgeois the day before the actual consular elections, and these one-hundred would in turn elect the six new consuls. In addition, for the first election held under this new system in December 1602, Henry declared that he would himself choose the one-hundred bourgeois.[64]

Jambeville remained in Limoges throughout June dispensing justice in the name of the king. Most of the people connected with the riot were among the poorer inhabitants of the town, and in a letter to the chancellor, Bellièvre, he wrote that he was 'losing his mind' trying to separate the truth from the lies in all of the conflicting stories he had heard.[65] Many of the protesters had fled the town after Jambeville's arrival, but two were caught in Bergerac and returned to Limoges. They were broken on the wheel on 10 June in the Place Saint-Michael of the Lions, the scene of much of the riot. One of the men, Jean Farne, was considered particularly abhorrent because during the tax riot he not only robbed and murdered a merchant but also absconded with the host from Saint-Michael's Church. Jambeville told Bellièvre that when 'Christ's body' was found, a joyful procession of 7,000 returned the sacred host to the church.[66] The incident discloses once again that the tax riot also incorporated other societal strains connected with the religious wars into its potent dynamic.

It might appear that Henry's decision to revise election procedures in Limoges was the direct result of the *pancarte* riot and his wish to punish individual errant magistrates. In this sense the riot has always been viewed as the sole stimulus for his interaction with Limoges, and the conclusion is often drawn that he only responded to municipal situations when civil strife forced his attention.[67] But the riot in Limoges was more serious than the one in Poitiers and included a greater dimension of ongoing urban religious/political unrest. No doubt Henry used the opportunity of the riot to strengthen the Crown's authority in the town, but closer examination of the local history reveals that Limoges was a troubled place during his reign and inclined to minor disturbances and riots.[68] Municipal elections before 1602 often brought on problems between former Leaguers, Protestants, and royalists, to the extent that Henry was forced to intervene frequently in the municipal

---

[64] Act printed in Guibert, *Registres Consulaires*, 62–5, and in Ruben, 'Changements', 149–51.

[65] BN, MSS fr., 15899, fol. 849v.

[66] Ibid., fols. 849–50; Laforest, *Etudes*, 41–2; F. Marvaud, *Histoire des Vîcomtes et de La Vîcomté de Limoges* (Paris: Chez J.B. Dumoulin, 1873), vol. 2, 347; Bonaventue de Saint-Amable, *Histoire de Saint Martial*, vol. 3, 812.   [67] David Buisseret, *Henry IV*, 165.

[68] The observation is discussed below. For a good town history of Limoges see Paul Ducourtieux, *Histoire de Limoges* (Limoges: Imprimerie Librairie Limousine Ducourtieux, 1925). For a short summary of civil disorder in Limoges during Henry's reign see: Marvaud, *Histoire des Vîcomtes*, vol. 2, 312–54.

government. In this light, the *pancarte* riot seems not to have been the catalyst that sparked the king's action, but rather the climax of many years of urban conflict that he decided to settle once and for all. Henry condemned the twelve consuls of 1602 for failing to suppress the riot, but in reality he was blaming the institution of the consulate itself, which had caused him too many problems and no longer functioned to maintain peace.

More than just the riot, therefore, influenced Henry's design for Limoges. His anxieties were revealed in a speech Jambeville delivered to the consulate during his stay in the town. He told the town government that in Henry's judgement the traditional election procedure (before 1602) brought about nothing more than 'intrigues, seditions, and tumults'.[69] The king believed, furthermore, that the riot in Limoges was preceded by a takeover of magisterial posts by people of low quality. Jambeville warned the consuls that such an insolent government awaited some terrible accident that would bring about the town's destruction.[70] For this reason Henry interceded and altered the process of the consular elections. He claimed he was acting in the best interest of the town, but he also told the duke of Montmorency that he wanted to make an example of Limoges.[71]

Limoges had a complicated history of election tumults which Henry had tired of confronting by 1602. Part of the problem stemmed from a rift within the community between various interest groups, who periodically tried to gain control of the municipal consulate. Old hostilities generated by the Catholic League lingered for most of Henry's reign, even though the townspeople were by and large loyal to the king.

Tensions were high between Catholics and Protestants in Limoges as well as between former zealous Leaguers and Catholic 'politiques', and this fact contributed greatly to the election disputes that occurred frequently in the town. The viscountcy of Limoges belonged to the Albret family, until it was finally united with the kingdom of France in 1606 by the last king-viscount, Henry IV.[72] Before Henry's reign, however, his mother, Jeanne d'Albret as viscountess of Limoges had encouraged the spread of Protestantism in the region. To counteract the Huguenot strength, Catholic confraternities employed vigilante tactics and used murder and pillage to forestall the spread of the new religion.[73] The Huguenots were far from idle victims, nonetheless, for in Limoges the clergy regularly paid companies of armed guards to keep their churches from being pilfered.[74] Evidence that some of

---

[69] Guibert, *Registres Consulaires*, 61.   [70] Ibid.

[71] Berger de Xivrey, *Recueils des Lettres Missives*, vol. 5, 597. Henry wrote to the duke of Montmorency, 'Je prendray resolution avec mon conseil, de l'ordre que je dois establir en la dicte ville de Limoges pour rompre les partialitez qui sont en icelle, ensemble de l'exemple qui se doibt faire pour la punition des mauvais et contenir les bons en l'affection qu'ils ont au bien de mon service.' For a similar observation of the kind of partisanship that existed in Limoges see Jambeville's letter to Bellièvre in BN, MSS fr., 15899, fols. 849rv–50r.   [72] Marvaud, *Histoire des Vicomtes*, vol. 2, 384–85.

[73] Louis Guibert, *La Ligue à Limoges* (Limoges: Imprimerie-Libraire Ducourtieux, 1884), 2–4.

[74] Mauvaud, *Histoire des Vicomtes*, vol. 2, 202.

the more influential bourgeois had become Protestants exists for the 1563 elections. In that year Charles IX made an unprecedented move and manipulated the elections so that only Catholics won places on the consulate.[75]

The history of the Catholic League in Limoges is also of particular interest. The League was never completely successful in taking over the town, although throughout the period 1589 to 1594 many important citizens openly belonged to the League, and conflict always existed between this group and the consulate that was controlled by an alliance of royalists and Protestants. In 1589, after the death of Henry III, the bishop Henry de la Martonie, leader of the League in Limoges, attempted to overthrow the municipal government in the city.[76] Yet the events that occurred between 15 and 17 October 1589 reveal a complex situation in which Leaguers, royalists, and Protestants were all forced to defend themselves in an environment in which anarchy reigned for several days.[77]

No one was safe as the various factions vented their hostilities on their enemies. The danger is aptly illustrated by a skirmish that occurred between a group of Leaguers and members of the consulate on the first day of the coup. When four royalist consuls and the king's *intendant*, Meric de Vic, tried to persuade a group of League guards to release several recently captured Huguenot hostages, they were met by rock-throwing street fighters who yelled: 'Death to the Huguenots, Kill, Kill, Long live the Cross!'[78] The consuls attempted to calm their assailants, but eventually began to retreat when a leader of the League movement, the judge and fellow consul, Martial de Petiot, arrived with his troops and fighting broke out. The situation was quite hopeless, however, because most of the consuls were unarmed. They held their consular capes over their heads and waved them wildly as a sign to the mob to remember their distinguished places in the society. The leader of the aggressors, moreover, was their zealous peer and colleague in the municipal government, meaning the consulate itself was engaged in civil war. Gunfire erupted and when the smoke cleared the consul, Etienne Pinchaud, lay dead in the street, his ineffective cape draped uselessly across his chest. Another consul, Thomas Durand-Brugière, was wounded in the attack.[79]

By the second day of the coup most of the consuls had locked themselves in the

[75] Ibid., 221–2. Charles IX asked for the names of twenty-four candidates from which he chose the twelve consuls. He named only Catholics who were inducted into office on 17 January 1564.
[76] Henry de la Martonie became bishop of Limoges in 1585. In 1589 he adopted the cause of the League, but became a loyal servant to Henry IV after the king's reconversion to Catholicism in 1594. Martonie's oath of loyalty to Henry IV is published in *Archives Historique de la Gironde* (Bordeaux: Imprimerie G. Gounouilhou, 1879), vol. 14, 318.
[77] See Guibert's excellent account in *La Ligue à Limoges*, 15–57. No document exists in Limoges relative to the League. Guibert used a remarkable document drawn up by the *siège présidial* after the coup failed and now found at the Archives Nationales. See *Archives Nationales*, KK1212, 'Informations et procedures faites contre ceux de la Ligue, de la trahison et conspiration faite contre la ville de Limoges, pour tirer hors de l'obeissance de Sa Majesté, le 15 Octobre 1589.' An excellent account of this 998 page manuscript is found in Guibert's *La Ligue à Limoges*.
[78] Quoted in Guibert, *La Ligue à Limoges*, 21. The crowd cried, 'Mort aux Huguenots! Tue! Tue! Vive le Croix!.' [79] Ibid., 22–4.

château and the town was riddled with barricades. The Leaguers occupied the churches of the town, and from a central command in the church of Saint-Michael, they organized forays to murder Huguenots and pillage the houses of both Protestants and Catholic 'politiques'. The League movement had no cohesion, however, and after two days of terrible violence the participants began to abandon the cause. Control was regained by the royalists on the third day, and four leaders of the coup were executed on the sight of Pinchaud's murder. The viscount of Pompadour had originally given aid to the League in Limoges, but he left the city when he heard that the duke of Epernon was on his way to relieve the royalists. Epernon arrived on the 19 October with two thousand men in arms and five-hundred cavalry. His troops pillaged the town the following day. The homes of the compromised were ransacked, and the Leaguers themselves were either fined or exiled.[80]

This kind of violence and destruction produced bitterness on the part of the consulate and the townspeople, and since nothing was really resolved by the coup of 1589, Limoges remained divided between Leaguers and royalists for years to come. Problems began to arise in earnest when exiled Leaguers returned and settled in Limoges with the king's sanction in February of 1596. Their reinstatement was met with great rejoicing by the townspeople, and a *Te Deum* was sung to celebrate the reconciliation.[81] Thereafter factions quickly reformed. Disturbances and tumults between the groups became common.[82] Le Camus de Jambeville even expressed frustration over this problem in a letter he wrote to Bellièvre during his investigation of the *pancarte* riot. Lamenting over the difficulties he faced in settling the affair, Henry's officer stated, 'it will take a more able man than myself' to put an end to this confusion.[83]

Political and religious passions, moreover, seemed to erupt each year around election time. In December 1591, for example, the *Maison de Ville* was mobbed during the consular elections by a group of royalists who demanded that neither a Leaguer nor a Huguenot be allowed in the municipal government. Although the agitators were mostly labourers and merchants, the instigators of the disturbance were actually two very influential persons in Limoges, Jacques Martin, a president at the *siège présidial*, and his brother the lieutenant criminal. The consuls quickly

---

[80] Ibid., 22–8; Marvaud, *Histoire des Vîcomtes*, vol. 2, 314–19; Emile Ruben, Félix Achard, Paul Ducourtieux, eds., *Annales Manuscrites de Limoges dites Manuscrit de 1638* (Limoges: Ducourtieux Editeur, 1867), 364–70.
[81] Bonaventure de Saint-Amable, *Histoire de Saint Martial*, vol. 3, 809; Mauvaud, *Histoire des Vîcomtes*, vol. 2, 342. Michel Cassan, 'Les Lendemains des Guerres de Religion', *Croyances, Pouvoirs, et Société des Limousins aux Francais*, ed. Michel Cassan, (Le Louvanel: Les Editions Cles Monedières, 1988), 267.
[82] See example of social tension provided by Michel Cassan in his article, 'Mobilité Sociale et Conflits Religieux: L'Exemple Limousin (1550–1630)', in *La Dynamique Sociale dans L'Europe du Nord-Ouest (XVIe-XVIIe Siècles), Acts du Colloque de L'Association des Historiens Modernistes des Universités*, 12 (1987), 80–3.
[83] BN, MSS fr., 15899, fol. 849v. Jambeville used the words, 'qu'il y faillor un plus habille homme que moi.'

fled from the scene of the incident and the town militia dispelled the tumult. Subsequently, Martin and his brother were exiled along with other participants for their involvement.[84]

The election of 1593 took place in the presence of the governor of Limoges, and in 1594 a member of the king's *Conseil Privé* observed the event. In 1596 (after the return of exiled Leaguers) and for the succeeding three years, however, tensions were so high that Henry was forced to intervene each year and select directly ten of the twelve municipal magistrates. Fraud was revealed in the election process in 1600 when it became known that the Huguenots had brought a number of artisans to the *Maison de Ville* and paid them each ten *sous* to vote for Huguenot candidates. The governor of the province, the duke of Epernon, informed the king of the circumstances, and Henry decided to choose the twelve consuls from a list of thirty notables.[85] In 1601 Henry sent a list of thirty names to Limoges from which he allowed a regular election of ten consuls. The newly elected ten in turn chose the final two consuls to make up the normal, pre-1602 twelve member municipal government.[86] Finally, in May 1602 following the *pancarte* riot, Henry established his six appointees in municipal office. In December of that same year when new elections were to be held, and the king had decided that for the first election observed under the new system he would choose the one-hundred bourgeois himself, he wrote instead to the town saying that he did not have the time to select the electorate and so maintained the six consuls from 1602 in office for the year 1603.[87] The first time incumbent consuls were allowed to name one-hundred bourgeois did not occur until December 1604 because the king made the selection in December 1603. Except for the 1601 election, therefore, Henry controlled most of the appointments to consular offices in Limoges between 1596 and 1603.[88]

Annual elections in Limoges clearly provided the setting in which popular violence was not necessarily inevitable, but at least probable. The crowding together of people from all strata of the city produced a volatile situation. Often the municipal authorities could not maintain control, and hostilities frequently exploded. Whether consuls were Catholic or Protestant, ex-Leaguer or royalist, was a matter of sufficient concern to the voting populace to engender the threat of suspicion, fraud, bribery, and/or riot in every election from 1591 to 1600. These disturbances subsequently forced Henry to intervene to maintain order. His action following the *pancarte* riot was thus made as a bold attempt to quell recurring trouble in Limoges, trouble that too often caused unruly elections. He did not make strictly retaliatory responses to punish the town. In the king's edict announcing the

[84] Marvard, *Histoire des Vîcomtes*, vol. 2, 332; Ruben, *Annales*, 373.

[85] A. Coissac, *Le Consulat à Limoges au XVIe Siècle* (Limoges: Imprimerie F. Plagnes, 1937), 34–6; Ducourtieux, *Histoire de Limoges*, 181.

[86] AML, BB2, fols. 46–7; Ducourtieux, *Histoire de Limoges*, 181.

[87] Henry's letter is dated 7 December 1602 and printed in: Guibert, *Registres Consulaires*, 66; Coissac, *Le Consulat à Limoges*, 37.

[88] Regarding the December election of 1602 see letters in BN, MSS fr., 23197, fols. 143, 187, 192, 195.

restructuring of the municipal government in Limoges, he pointed not to the *pancarte* riot as the reason behind his decision but to the divisions within the society that existed and provoked disorder. Henry stated:

> The long duration of civil wars and troubles of our realm have greatly debased the morals so that good regulations that were instituted in our towns to prevent disagreements among the inhabitants have served to separate and divide them as so often occurs to our very great regret in our town of Limoges, the capital of Limousin . . . [89]

Henry did use the opportunity of the *pancarte* riot to exert greater Crown control over the municipal government, and his actions were in part punitive. Undeniably, however, his decisions were aimed at resolving more enduring issues than the riot itself. In terms of the tax issue Limoges got off with paying a one time subvention of 500 *livres*, but the changes made to Limoges's municipal government were far more significant.[90]

This point is made clear by examining the transformation Henry IV's legislation wrought on the composition of Limoges's consulate. On the one hand, reducing the number of consuls elected each year from twelve to six made the town government smaller and more easily observable by the Crown. On the other hand, the king's decision to decrease the size of the electorate from all heads of households considered citizens to only one-hundred bourgeois, who were themselves chosen by incumbent consuls, recast a loosely oligarchical town government into a tighter oligarchical structure that was commanded by a handful of the city's most influential robe and bourgeois families. The post-1602 electoral system thus functioned to guarantee that the same elite families would dominate the town council. For example, between 1592 and 1602 (excluding the year 1599) elections were held for 112 consular positions, and, of this number, ninety-two individuals filled the offices (several persons were elected more than once). Within the group of ninety-two, there are eighty different family names. These eighty family names represent seventy-one per cent of the total 112 revealing a twenty-nine per cent rate of repetition of family names in the consulate. In contrast, during the latter period, 1602 to 1610, although the number of available offices shrank to only forty-eight filled by forty-one individuals, a disproportionately smaller number of family names are represented. The dramatic change is revealed by a drop in family names to only twenty-six names or fifty-four per cent of the total forty-eight. This exposes a forty-six per cent rate of repetition and proves an

---

[89] Printed in Ruben, 'Changements,' 149. 'Mais la longeur des troubles et guerres civilles de notre royaulme a tellement deprave les meurs que, quelques bons reglementz qui ussent estes institues en nosd. villes, au lieu questans observees ilz debvoyent servir de rampart contre la discorde des habitans dicelles, ilz ont servy de subject a les partialiser et diviser, dont a notre tres grand regret notre ville de Lymoges, capitalle de notre pais de Lymousin cest souvent resantie.'

[90] The *pancarte* issue in Limoges was resolved seven months after the riot when the tax was officially removed. Levet, *Histoire de Limoges* vol. 1, 251–2.

Table 3.   *Number of consular positions, family names, and percentage of recurring family names in Limoges's municipal government, 1592–1610*

Years	1592–1602 (excluding 1599)	1602–1610
Total consular positions	112	48
Family names appearing in consulate	80 (71%)	26 (54%)
Rate of repetition of family names in consulate	29%	46%

Source: AM Limoges, BB2 (elections held 7 December each year), fols. 3–138. Louis Guibert, ed., *Registres Consulaires de la Ville de Limoges, Second Registre (1592 -1662)* (Limoges: Imprimerie de Chapoulaud Frères, 1884), 1–2 20–1, 21–2, 31–4, 39–40, 41–2, 43, 44–5, 46–7, 57–8, 59, 73, 79, 113, 115, 117, 129, 133.

increase over the first rate of repetition of more than one third. These findings are shown in table 3.[91]

It is also interesting to note that of Henry IV's original six consuls from 1602–3, four were royal officeholders, one was listed as a bourgeois, and the last as a bourgeois merchant. Theoretically, by the act of 1602, the six consuls chosen each year were to be selected from citizens on the *taille* roles.[92] This charge should have barred from municipal office royal officeholders who were exempt from the tax.[93] But Henry ignored the stipulation when he named four royal officeholders in 1602–3. Not surprisingly, royal officeholders continued to share importance with the commercial bourgeois (as they had done in the late sixteenth century) in Limoges's municipal government well into the mid-1650s.[94] Tables 4 and 5 reveal the social position of the forty-one different consuls who held municipal office

[91] All statistical information for this and the following paragraphs is drawn from: AML, BB2 (elections held 7 December each year), fols. 3–138; Guibert, *Registres Consulaires*, 1–2, 20–1, 21–2, 31–2, 32–4, 39–47, 57–9, 73, 79, 113, 115, 117, 129, 133.
[92] See act printed in Guibert, *Registres Consulaires*, 63. It reads, 'the said six consuls taken from the number of inhabitants contributing to our *taille* . . .'   [93] Laforest, *Etudes*, 44.
[94] During the Middle Ages municipal governments were made up almost exclusively of merchants. By the sixteenth century regulations were devised to prohibit royal officeholders from municipal posts, but these were increasingly overridden and annulled as robe elite forced their way into the urban oligarchies and confiscated municipal offices. This transformation may not have been as dramatic as it sounds, however, since in many towns numerous powerful fifteenth-century families continued to control urban politics through their descendants in the sixteenth and seventeenth centuries. But while the oligarchic families of the fifteenth century were solidly merchant-bourgeois, after the mid-sixteenth century they increasingly bought royal offices while maintaining interests in local municipal affairs. See Jacques Paton, *Le Corps de Ville de Troyes, 1470–1790* (Troyes: J-L Paton Imprimeur-Editeur, 1939), 76–92; Richard Gasçon, *Grand commerce et Vie Urbaine au XVIe siècle, Lyon et ses marchands* (Paris: SEVPEN, 1971), vol. 1, 409–13; Pierre Deyon, *Amiens, capitale provinciale, étude sur la société urbaine au 17e siècle* (Paris: Mouton and Co., 1967), 270–7; Philip Benedict, 'French Cities from the Sixteenth Century to the Revolution: An Overview', in *Cities and Social Change in Early Modern France*, ed. Philip Benedict (London: Unwin Hyman, 1989), 35–6; Roger Chartier, Guy Chaussinand-Nogaret, Emmanuel Le Roy Ladurie, *et al.* eds., *Histoire de la France Urbaine*, vol. 3, *La Ville Classique de la Renaissance aux Révolutions* (Paris: Editions du Seuil, 1981), 178–9.

Table 4. *Social composition of municipal officeholders in Limoges, 1602–10*

Category	Number	Percentage
Royal Officials	19	47%
Listed only as *Sieur de*	4	10 %
Bourgeois	17	41%
Merchant	1	2%
Total	41	100%

Source: see table 3.

between 1602 and 1610. Although six consuls were elected each year, seven persons held the office on two occasions between 1603 and 1610. Unfortunately, it is not known if the magistrates listed on the election returns as 'bourgeois' were practising commerce or simply drawing income from their investments. Since many of the well-known wealthiest merchants in Limoges were listed only as 'bourgeois', however, it is assumed that a strong link was maintained between the consular magistrates and commerce, although clearly less prestigious merchants were no longer finding places in the municipal government, and the artisan presence was lost.[95]

The most dramatic impact Henry IV's 1602 reform of the Limoges town government had on the municipality had to do with the reintegration of formally ostracized ex-Leaguers. Evidence shows that ex-Leaguers regained their economic viability quite rapidly following their return in 1596. Yet they were almost completely denied participation in the municipal government until 1602.[96] Of ninety-two individuals who served as municipal consuls from 1592 to 1602, only three managed to hold office in the 1602 to 1610 period.[97] This decrease in representation would not be especially significant if their sons and/or nephews figured in the latter period. But, in the case of Limoges, there is a virtual changeover of personnel, so that of the 106 different family names drawn from the overall 1592 to 1610 period, only eleven names are common to both the pre- and post-1602 categories.[98] Even

[95] This was the case in Amiens and Rouen. See Deyon, *Amiens, capitale provinciale*, 273–91; Gayle Brunelle, *The New World Merchants of Rouen 1559–1630* (Kirksville, Missouri: Sixteenth Century Journal Publishers, 1991), vol. 16. Sources listed for all three tables are given after table 3. Archival documents dating from the sixteenth and seventeenth centuries in Limoges are quite scarce. Parish records are very incomplete, but for more information see Cassan, 'Mobilité Sociale et Conflits', 71–92; Michel Cassan, *Le Temps des Guerres de Religion, Le Cas du Limousin (vers 1530–vers 1630* (Paris: Publisud, 1996), 301.

[96] For the economic reintegration of the Leaguers see Michel Cassan's two articles, 'Les Lendemains', 266–82, and 'Mobilité Sociale et Conflits', 71–92.

[97] Guibert, *Registres Consulaires*, 21–22, 59, 115. The three consuls who held municipal office in both the pre- and post-1602 periods were: Durand-Brugière, in 1595 and 1602–3, Joseph Croisier, in 1597 and 1604, and Jehan Guerin, in 1597 and 1607.

[98] All statistical information is developed from the sources listed in note 91. The eleven family names were: Brugière, Benoist, Croisier, Douhet, Descoutures, Guerin, Martin, Petiot, Saleys, Vidaud, and Vertamond.

Table 5. *Breakdown of positions listed in election returns for forty-six consuls*
1602–1610

Position	Number	Percentage
Trésorier Général	4	10%
Lieutenant-Général	1	2%
Conseiller Siège Présidial	2	5%
Procureur du roi	3	8%
Avocat du roi	2	5%
Médecin du roi	1	2%
Receveur general	1	2%
Juge	3	8%
Élu	2	5%
Sieur de	4	10%
Bourgeois	17	41%
Marchand	1	2%
Total	41	100%

Source: AM, Limoges, BB2 (elections held 7 December each year). Louis Guibert, ed., *Registres Consulaires de la Ville de Limoges Second Registre (1592–1662)* (Limoges, Imprimerie de Chapoulaud Frères, 1884).

more striking is that while only a handful of ex-Leaguers managed to hold municipal office between 1592 and 1602, twenty-eight out of forty-one individuals, or sixty-eight per cent of those who served as consuls between 1602 and 1610, were either ex-Leaguers themselves or related to the greatest League families.[99]

Each year between 1602 and 1610 at least three of the six consuls were former Leaguers, and in 1608 and 1610 all six consuls had either supported the League coup in 1589 or belonged to families that had done so. Finally, of the seven persons who held the consular office more than once between 1602 to 1610, all seven were ex-Leaguers.[100]

The *pancarte* riot of 1602 was far from a one-time crisis that provoked Henry IV into action in Limoges, and his reorganization of the town's municipal government had an enormous impact on the complexion of its personnel. The ex-Leaguers in Limoges unquestionably owed their political reinstatement into municipal power to Henry and the legislation promulgated after the *pancarte* riot. Michel Cassan, the most recent historian of the town's administrative and religious history, calls Henry's decision to favour the ex-Leaguers the 'triumph of Catholicism'.[101] Cassan

[99] Information on League families is drawn from AN, KK1212, and published in Guibert, *La Ligue à Limoges*, 2–58. The list of exiled Leaguers is printed on pages 47–8. Michel Cassan, 'Laics, Ligue et Reforme Catholique à Limoges', *Histoire Economie et Société*, 10 (1991), 159–75.
[100] These observations were achieved by comparing Guibert, *Registres Consulaires*, 59, 73, 79, 113, 115, 117, 129, and 133 with Guibert, *La Ligue à Limoges*, 2–58.
[101] Cassan, 'Les Lendemains', 278.

notes that after recovering political power, the ex-Leaguers went on to herald Catholic reform in the town.[102] This may have been the case, but Henry's decision to reintegrate ex-Leaguers into the town's consulate came only in 1602. The king had been observing and manipulating elections in Limoges throughout the entire course of his reign, and during the 1596 to 1600 period he clearly selected faithful royalists for municipal office. What was the reason behind this delay in the reintegration of former Leaguers? One can only speculate, but perhaps a period of time was necessary for Leaguers to prove their fidelity to Henry IV before they could be trusted in municipal office. As discussed in chapter six, in League towns in the 1590s Henry tended to promote men in municipal office who joined the royalist movement before a town's capitulation. But, by the end of Henry's reign in most of the largest former League towns, ex-Leaguers, particularly those connected with families that had traditionally held municipal office, were reintegrated into city government. Henry's actions in Limoges certainly adds validity, moreover, to the idea that after the Edict of Nantes the king hoped eventually to re-establish 'one king, one faith, one law' in France. A new commitment to a Gallican monarchy may well have influenced Henry's decision in 1602 to allow the ex-Leaguers to return in force to the *Maison de Ville*.[103]

The great significance of 1602 in Limoges, therefore, is that of the six consuls Henry IV chose for municipal office, two were former Leaguers and two came from families that solidly supported the Catholic League.[104] Since these six consuls eventually selected the one-hundred bourgeois, who in turn elected the succeeding six consuls, the enduring presence of ex-Leaguers in municipal government was virtually guaranteed.[105] In one sense this restructuring of the municipal government was simply a return to the natural order of things, since many of the men who served as consuls between 1602 and 1610 came from families that had traditionally monopolized municipal offices since the fifteenth century.[106] More importantly, the 1602 restructuring of Limoges's municipal government was a conscious effort on Henry's part to end the electoral turmoil that plagued the town throughout his reign, and it promoted a new integration of the town's elites. The consuls Henry appointed represented the various confessional and political constituencies in Limoges. He even selected a Protestant, Thomas Durand-Brugière, to serve as one of the six in 1602.[107] Such effort proves the king was a serious and reform-minded ruler who deliberately devised municipal reforms based on his detailed under-

---

[102] Ibid., 278–82.
[103] Mack P. Holt, *The French Wars of Religion, 1562–1629* (Cambridge: Cambridge University Press, 1995), 163.
[104] Guibert, *Registres Consularies*, 53. Gaspard Benoist and Joseph de Petiot had belonged to the Catholic League. Jehan Bonin and Pierre du Bois came from League families.
[105] See the very interesting letter the consuls of 1602 wrote to the chancellor Bellièvre regarding the king's selection of 100 bourgeois in: BN, MSS fr. 15899, fol. 644.
[106] Cassan, 'Les Lendemains', 277–8. The Petiot, Saxon, and Saleis, families, for example, were three of these families who traditionally sought consular office.
[107] Cassan, *Le Temps des Guerres de Religion*, 300.

standing of town issues. Henry did not need the *pancarte* riot to rouse his interest in municipal matters in Limoges, but he used the event to his advantage and augmented his royal control of municipal affairs. While re-establishing order and stability in Limoges, Henry conditioned the town to greater intervention from the Crown. That Henry seems to have been so strict on Limoges may have stemmed from the fact that in a real sense the *pancarte* issue had exposed a major weakness on the part of the Crown to tax urban France. Limoges undoubtedly presented a lesson to other towns of the realm about the ramifications of disobeying the king, but the real significance of the king's intervention is revealed in the way he used the riot to settle more enduring problems stemming from the religious wars. In the long span of early modern French history the *pancarte* riots are fairly insignificant, yet they represent microcosms of the multifaceted religious issues that divided France during the religious wars.

HENRY IV AND THE 'PANCARTE'

The towns' angry reaction to the *pancarte* helped convince the king and his ministers to revoke the tax. The riots were successful in the towns in the sense that their outcomes secured from the Crown the right to pay subventions instead of the *pancarte*, and then the tax was eliminated altogether meaning it did not become a permanent urban tax during Henry's reign. For the Crown, moreover, the *pancarte* was not necessarily a failure. True, the Crown never realized the estimated 7 million *livres*, but it probably never expected to. Tax collections in early modern Europe rarely filled estimated potential. In fact, the over 1.5 million *livres* the *pancarte* delivered was not an insignificant sum. After the *sol pour livre* was revoked, moreover, Sully immediately raised the salt tax and levied the *taille* in many towns that held exemptions to the tax.[108] In the meantime, Henry used the excuse of the riots first in Limoges in 1602 and then in Poitiers in 1609 to reorganize two unruly municipalities, and in the process sent warnings to all of urban France that the Crown's authority was great and disobedience would not be tolerated. Examined from this point of view, one can speculate that the *pancarte* was a great success for the Crown and even augmented Henry's legitimacy. Above all else, what he proved in the riots and their suppression was that his political authority and his reign were grounded in effectiveness.[109] The next chapter will investigate how Henry worked to decrease urban indebtedness after the religious wars.

[108] Mousnier, *The Assassination of Henry IV*, 189.
[109] Margherita, Ciacci, 'Legitimacy and the Problems of Governance', in *Legitimacy/Légitimité Proceedings of the Conference held in Florence June 3 and 4 1982* (New York: Walter De Gruyter, 1985), 24.

8

Municipal finance and debt: the case of Lyons

In 1609 a deputy from Bayonne, M. de Lèspes de Hureaux, intruded on Henry IV in the gardens at Fontainbleau and begged him to revoke an edict establishing royal control over customs taxes in the city. The king had been peacefully feeding some ducks, and he bluntly told the man to go away.[1] Lèspes de Hureaux persisted, however, explaining that his town was too poor to pay more taxes. Henry rebuked the man by saying that at least thirty bourgeois in Bayonne were wealthier than its governor. Turning towards a secretary, the king declared, 'They are rich . . . and three-hundred of their bourgeois wear silk.' He then chided the deputy, 'You are glorious and employ your time dancing and making merry.'[2] The king ended the conversation by adding, 'Imagine, former kings granted *octrois* to the towns to be used for upkeep, but over the ages they have converted these taxes into their own personal profit.'[3]

Henry and his finance minister, the duke of Sully, firmly believed that town councillors misappropriated funds from municipal *octrois* and overburdened those who paid city taxes with too many demands. Both men accused the towns of financial corruption.[4] To ensure that royal tax monies ended up in the king's coffers and not in magisterial pockets, the minister used his power to inspect municipal budgets and exert tighter control over municipal finances. The Wars of Religion had created debt and taxation problems that caused the king and his minister to investigate the municipal use of tax monies. After the wars ended, the Crown involved itself closely in municipal financial affairs in order to encourage greater financial efficiency and liquidate war debts. In these instances Henry revealed himself to be extremely authoritative, less paternal and more absolute. After a brief

[1] Quoted in R. Cuzacq and B. Detacjepare (eds.), *Bayonne sous l'Ancien Régime, lettres missives des rois et reines de France à la ville de Bayonne* (Bayonne: Saint-Sever-Sur-Adour: J. Glize, 1934), vol. 2, 408–10.

[2] Ibid., 409. The king stated, 'Et pour les biens ils sont riches, car 30 bourgeois de Bayonne ont à présent plus de moyens que, cydevant [les guerres] . . . ! Et y a 300 bourgeois à Bayonne qui vont habillés en soye . . . ' Some moments later the king asserted, 'mais vous estes glorieux et emploiés le temps d'aller braves à festins et danser.'

[3] Ibid., 410. Henry said, 'Que pensez-vous, les roys mes prédécesseurs ont donné aux villes des deniers par octroy pour les emploier aux réparations d'ycelles, et par succession de temps les ont converti à leur profit particulier.'

[4] Although Maximilien de Béthune spent most of Henry's reign as the baron of Rosny, I have referred to him throughout the chapter by his more popular title earned in 1606, the duke of Sully.

survey of municipal taxes and the Crown's efforts to audit town financial accounts, this chapter will explore the municipal debt liquidation issue in the city of Lyons.

TAXING THE TOWNS

Towns represented a substantial reserve of wealth for the French monarchy. Through direct and indirect taxes, forced loans, and gifts, the towns offered great sources of capital to their kings. But channelling that income into the hands of a king was not an easy task. Many towns possessed privileges that exempted them from the *taille*, excluded the wealthiest elites from municipal levies, and made gifts and forced loans hard to collect. Negotiation was common in Old Regime France as kings asked for enormous sums but encountered cries of poverty from the towns, thus necessitating compromise. Few kings expected to raise the full amount they demanded from the towns. In 1597 while trying to recapture Amiens from the Spanish, for example, Henry requested 30,000 *écus* from the city fathers of Toulouse. The *capitouls* offered 15,000 *écus* but then paid only 7,480 *écus*.[5] In 1599, Henry ordered Toulouse to pay him the remaining 7,520 *écus*.[6] Protracted bargaining followed between Toulouse's deputies at court and the king's ministers. Eventually, in 1601 an agreement was reached. Toulouse consented to give up 5,800 *écus* in order to be discharged from the debt still owed; 5,000 *écus* were slated for the king's coffers and 800 *écus* for the agent who negotiated the transfer of funds.[7]

As *surintendant des finances*, Sully devised strategies to raise royal revenues from the towns. He increased both direct and indirect taxes, levied new taxes, and forced privileged, traditionally tax-exempt citizens to pay taxes. In 1605, five years after Henry acquired Bourg-en-Bresse from Savoy, the inhabitants were told to contribute three-hundred more *livres* to the *taille* than they had paid the year before.[8] Municipal officials found the large increase 'bien étrange', and complained that Henry had granted them barely enough *octrois* to keep the town functioning.[9] At one point, the town government had become so short of funds that they sent a deputy to the king to plead poverty. The town could not afford the cost of a carriage, so the deputy walked to Lyons to meet with royal officials.[10] Henry and Sully also tried to levy new taxes on towns. If this strategy failed they attempted to coerce towns into buying exemptions from new taxes or buying reconfirmations of tax exemptions. Privileges were granted by the king only to be denied and then repurchased.

Exemptions and reconfirmations or repurchases proved profitable. In 1604 in

---

[5] *Archives Municipales*, Toulouse (hereafter AMT), BB20, fols. 93–4, 105–9, 227–8, 250–4, 260–4.
[6] AMT, EE21, letter dated 16 May 1599.   [7] AMT, BB21, fols. xxii–xix.
[8] Jules Baux (ed.), *Mémoires Historiques de la Ville de Bourg Extraits des Registres Municipaux de l'Hôtel-de-Ville de 1536–1789*, vol. 3, *1594 à 1605* (Bourg-en-Bress: Imprimerie Milliet-Bottier, 1870), 305.   [9] Ibid., 307.   [10] Ibid., 162–3.

Toulouse, the Crown tried to raise the *taillon*, a tax associated with the *taille* and usually destined for military purposes. Henry had exempted the city from this tax as recently as 1601. Protracted bargaining with Sully and Brûlart de Sillery resulted in Toulouse buying a reconfirmation of the exemption for 20,000 *écus*.[11] These kinds of practices often increased urban indebtedness and forced town councillors to have to negotiate loans in order to purchase reconfirmations. Additional costs were incurred because of the need to pay individuals at court who would use their influence to the city's advantage. Thus, Toulouse paid the queen 2,000 *pistoles*, a valet involved in securing the queen's patronage 1,500 *livres*, and another great lady at court 3,000 *livres*. A few years later Toulouse spent another 18,500 *livres* to buy an exemption from the *taille*.[12]

Negotiations were not considered corrupt by contemporaries, and merely reveal the overlap in public and private interests in early modern France. Towns had to maintain patrons at court on a constant basis.[13] The *échevins* of Blois bought a silver clock in 1593 to send to one of their patrons at court to ensure the continuation of his services.[14] In 1606 when Amiens's patron, the sieur de Caumartin, left France on a diplomatic mission to Sweden, the *échevinage* sent deputies to court with money to solicit the aid of another patron.[15] A deputy to court from Agen wrote back to his town in 1605 asking for a 'well-filled purse' in order to secure patrons.[16]

In the long-term, Sully wanted to replace municipal tax collectors with royal tax officials to gain control of the tax system that was normally managed by town magistrates or local dignitaries. When Sully reviewed the tax records for the city of Paris in 1600, for example, he asked to see documents relating to collection of the *aides*. The Parisian magistrates denied his request because such taxes fell under the jurisdiction of the city. Sully got the accounts, but only after a bitter struggle.[17]

Royal intervention in municipal financial affairs caused a flare-up at Nantes in 1608–9. The problem centred around a tax known as the *liart pour livre* which before 1608 had been a levy of three *deniers per livre* paid on imported goods by foreign, mostly Portuguese, merchants. In an effort to help Nantes balance its municipal budget, Henry and Sully tried to impose the tax on all merchants of Nantes.[18] Outrage over the *liart* issue caused the *Nantais* to meet with town leaders

[11] Nicolas Brûlart, sieur de Sillery was a member of the king's council and eventually succeeded Bellièvre as chancellor in 1607. David Buisseret, *Henry IV* (London: George Allen and Unwin, 1984), 97.   [12] AMT, BB22, fols. 89–100; BB23, fols. 250–60.

[13] Robert Harding, 'Corruption and the Moral Boundaries of Patronage in the Renaissance', in *Patronage in the Renaissance*, ed. Guy Fitch Lytle and Stephen Orgel (Princeton: Princeton University Press, 47–64.

[14] Alexandre Dupré, *Analyse des procès verbaux des assemblées municipales de la ville de Blois du 17 janvier 1566 au 28 decembre 1611* (Blois: n.p., 1842), 183.

[15] *Archives Municipales*, Amiens (hereafter AMA), BB58, fol. 34.

[16] J. Russell Major, 'Henry IV and Guyenne: A Study Concerning the Origins of Absolutism', *French Historical Studies* 4 (1966), 379.

[17] Paul Guerin, ed., *Registres des Déliberations du Bureau de la Ville de Paris*, vol. 12, *1598–1602* (Paris: Imprimerie Nationale, 1909), 238–9.

[18] *Archives Municipales*, Nantes (hereafter AMN), AA7, 4. *Arrêt*, dated 1 March 1608.

in two general assemblies in April 1608. The majority did not want to contribute to the tax, and they vehemently opposed the Crown's fiscal intervention.[19] Claiming that extension of the tax to all merchants was against the city's privileges, the municipal government dispatched deputies to court to ask the king to levy the tax only on foreign merchants.[20]

In May a small riot occurred over the *liart*. Three hundred townspeople stormed the *Hôtel de Ville* to stop the execution of the king's act establishing the tax.[21] The incident enraged Henry who retaliated in June by suspending all of the city's *octrois*.[22] Demanding an explanation, Henry ordered the city's mayor to court. The mayor denied that a riot had taken place. While the mayor was at court, he received a letter from his vice-mayor saying that the inhabitants were again at each other's throats.[23] The disturbance ended in August 1608 when the king suppressed the *liart* and restored the city's *octrois*.[24] Furious, Sully accused the townspeople of Nantes of 'making a lot of noise over a little thing'.[25] In his letter to Gilles Maupeou, his *intendant* in Brittany, Sully instructed the man to revoke the tax. Sully quipped, 'If afterwards, they [the councillors] lack the funds for their expenses, it will be up to them to find the means.'[26] Because the *liart* was revoked for all inhabitants including foreigners, the municipal government of Nantes lost an important source of revenue.

AUDITING MUNICIPAL FINANCIAL ACCOUNTS

The Crown sought to audit the books of municipal tax officials, in an effort to check for mismanagement of funds and to investigate how local levies were spent. The office of *grand voyer* was created for Sully in 1599. Through this office Sully exerted influence in municipal affairs all over France.[27] On 2 August 1605, for example, Henry issued a general ordinance, ordering all French towns to send their *octrois* records to the *grand voyer* every three years for auditing.[28] Sully intended to impose a regularized system of *octrois* once he digested these tax records. After 1605 Sully appears to have exercised extensive control over the *octrois* through auditing

[19] Ibid., BB26, fols. 167–70, 182–5, 213–15.
[20] Ibid., AA7, 19; BB26, fols. 163–4.
[21] Ibid., AA7, 20. Letter from Henry IV to the *sénéchal* asking for information concerning the rebellion. For general assemblies of inhabitants, see 11.
[22] Ibid., AA7, 27, 28, 29. Letters dated 17 June 1608; BB26, fols. 206–7.   [23] Ibid., AA7, 30.
[24] Ibid., BB26, fols. 224–6; Noël Valois, *Inventaire des Arrêts du Conseil d'Etat Règne de Henri IV* (Paris: Imprimerie Nationale, 1893), vol. 2, 12034.
[25] AMN, AA7, 27. Sully wrote, '[Les] Messieurs de Nantes font tant de bruit pour si peu de chose . . .'
[26] Ibid. 'Si par après ils manquent des fonds pour les dépenses de leurs affaires, ce sera à eux d'en chercher . . .'
[27] In effect, with the office of *grand voyer* Sully was in charge of all roads, bridges and canals in France. With the office he was able to appoint a number of subordinate officers to monitor events in the provinces and towns. David Buisseret, *Sully and the Growth of Centralized Government in France, (1598–1610)* (London: Eyre and Spottiswoode, 1968), 106–7.
[28] *Archives Nationales*, 120, AP1, *Les papiers de Sully*, fols. 136–7, fol. 210.

municipal tax records.[29] The inventory of acts passed by the king's council between 1605 and 1610 is full of edicts ordering the verification of accounts and debts.[30] In 1606, for instance, Sully sent commissioners to Toulouse to audit the financial registers of the *capitoulat*.[31] The *capitouls* fought the measure from 1606 to 1609, but were forced at last to send their accounts to the *Chambre des comptes*. In 1609 Henry forbade the *capitoulat* to increase municipal taxes without his permission.[32] In 1607 a special commission was created to go into the towns to examine how municipal taxes were spent and investigate alleged fraud and incompetence.[33] Although the commission was later suspended, Sully had established a greatly improved, more organized structure by 1610 for the control and regulation of municipal finance.[34]

Sully's work to gain access to municipal ledgers was thorough. While trying to establish *élections* in Guyenne in 1605, for example, he called for the towns' tax records to prove they were imposing levies without the king's approval.[35] The town of Agen, after a rigorous examination, was accused of financial misconduct. Agen's deputy at court, Julien de Camberfore, sieur de Selves, wrote his fellow councillors that they must send, 'good documents to justify our debts, because here, it is necessary to see everything!'[36] Selves believed Agen was being made a scapegoat for the misconduct of other towns.[37]

After Sully completed the review of Agen's books, Selves received a list of problems the *Chambres des comptes* had found in the records. Citing the lack of conformity of style in accounting practices, the document stated that receipts were regularly put in expense columns and vice versa. Notations for receipts were often illegible, and justifications of expenditure were frequently missing. In some places, officials of the *Chambre des comptes* thought inscriptions had been 'refait'.[38]

Deputies like Selves did not feel welcome at court and resented Sully's determination and inflexibility. Selves noted that it was difficult to see the minister because he was always surrounded by his *créatures* and frequently stormed out of meetings

[29] Robert S. Trullinger, 'The Royal Administration of Bretagne under Henry IV (1598–1610)' (Ph.D. thesis Vanderbilt University, 1972), 311.

[30] Valois, *Inventaire des arrêts*, vol. 2. For verification of accounts see: 9493, 9608, 9872, 10092,10271, 10850, 11199, 11372, 11611, 12034, 12055, 12266, 12536, 12778, 12807, and 12862. For verification of debts see: 9389, 9390, 9459, 9637, 9650, 9651, 9775, 9786, 9817, 9855, 9967, 9981, 9989, 10114, 10157, 10187, 10238, 10325, 10496, 10377, 10465, 10482, 10687, 10766, 10782, 10860, 10869, 10959, 11051, 11076, 11088, 11163, 11177, 11250, 11268, 11289, 11296, 11324, 11353, 11418, 11559, 11564, 11570, 11739, 11888, 11993, 12027, 12034, 12069, 12108, 12230, 12233, 12266, 12281, 12291, 12379, 12435, 12461, 12583, 12623, 12628, 12824, 12985, 13009, 12808, 12433, 12745, 12769, 12799, 12808.

[31] AMT, BB23, fols. 290–2; CC26, fols. 123–7.

[32] Ibid., BB23, fols., 83–4, 152, 173–81, 183–91, 252, AA22, deputy to court papers of Antoine Ambelot.   [33] Valois, *Inventaire des Arrêts*, vol. 2, 11199.

[34] Robert S. Trullinger, 'The *Grand Voyer* as an Instrument of Royal Centralization in Brittany under Henry IV', *Proceedings of the Western Society for French History*, 3 (1975), 31.

[35] Major, 'Henry IV and Guyenne', 363–83.

[36] *Archives Communales*, Agen (hereafter ACA), CC123, fol. 1. Selves wrote on 16 March 1605 and asked for 'de bonnes pieces pour justifiés les debtes car on veut icy voir tout!'   [37] Ibid.

[38] Ibid., CC123. Letter dated 14 February 1605.

when the auditing of accounts was discussed. Selves saw little advantage to acting in conjunction with the deputies from other towns.[39] Believing Sully wanted to usurp municipal liberties he wrote, 'Adieu liberties and privileges! Consular charges will no longer have their lustre or power.'[40]

In some instances the Crown's intervention in fiscal matters worked to the towns' advantage. As *grand maître de l'artillerie* and *surintendant des fortifications et bâtiments*, Sully made notable progress in extending and repairing roads and canals, and in restoring and improving town ramparts and buildings throughout France.[41] Sometimes Sully advised the king to raise municipal taxes when investigations demonstrated the need. In other cases, the Crown supported municipal increases over the objections of the provincial estates who felt threatened by royal intervention and worried about regional price rises.[42] Henry IV's assassination cut Sully's tenure in office short, but research indicates that his intervention in municipal financial affairs was far reaching.[43] In Saint-Malo, Nantes, Rouen, Amiens, Limoges, Toulouse, Paris, and many other towns, he supervised the inspection of municipal accounts.[44] He realized probably more than Henry the advantages to be gained from an aggressive monarchy and efficient administration that ignored municipal custom and privilege.

THE DEBT ISSUE IN LYONS: THE EDICT OF CHAUNY

French towns during the Wars of Religion had accrued enormous debts, and as part of Henry's effort to return prosperity to France, he promised to find ways to amortize these burdens. Debt liquidation furnished royal officials with an excuse to investigate almost every aspect of municipal government. Lyons is a case in point and provides an interesting backdrop for considering the Crown's interest in municipal finance.

Lyons was the perfect arena for the expansion of monarchical power. With neither a parlement nor provincial estates to champion autonomy, Lyons had less recourse than other important towns to institutions that might have defended its interests. Lyons was the only city in which Henry maintained a special agent or *intendant* throughout his reign. The king also had a close personal relationship with the royal governor of the city, Philibert de La Guiche.

To restore royal authority and civil order in newly won Lyons, Henry IV

---

[39] Georges Tholin, 'Des Tailles et des Impositions au Pays d'Agenais durant le XVIe siècle jusqu'aux réformes de Sully', *Recueil des travaux de la société d'agriculture, sciences et arts d'Agen*, 23 (1875), 131.

[40] Cited in ibid. Selves wrote, 'Après cela vous verres bien des choses plus dommageables. Adieu libertés, privilèges! Charges consulaires ne seront plus en leur lustre ny pouvoir.' Also cited in Major, 'Henry IV and Guyenne', 378.   [41] Buisseret, *Sully*, 120–69.

[42] Trullinger, 'The *Grand Voyer*', 26–34.

[43] James B. Collins, *The State in Early Modern France* (Cambridge: Cambridge University Press, 1995), 22–7. Collins notes that Sully centralized government 'in very old-fashioned ways' (26).

[44] Valois, *Inventaire des arrêts*, vol. 2, 9872, 10316, 11664, 11951, 12034, 12055, 12291, 12596.

dispatched his chancellor, Bellièvre, to the town in 1594 shortly after the League town capitulated.[45] Bellièvre, served Henry on this mission much like a precursor of Richelieu's *intendants*. As a native of Lyons, the chancellor faced a difficult task. Viewed as the city's greatest patron, he was expected to stabilize his hometown. Catholic League sentiment remained strong among the clergy, and Henry's decision to maintain a Swiss garrison in Lyons did not endear him to the population.[46] Throughout 1594, Bellièvre tried to persuade the king to visit Lyons to dispel the bewilderment surrounding the League's defeat.[47] By December, when Henry still had not come, Bellièvre decided to postpone the upcoming elections of new municipal magistrates because he feared civil strife.[48]

Henry finally arrived in Lyons in September 1595 and Bellièvre returned to Paris. Before the minister left, however, he submitted a plan to the king for the reorganization of the *échevinage*, adopted in the Edict of Chauny on 14 December 1595.[49] By the terms of the edict, Henry imposed a prevotal system of government on the town similar to the one in Paris. He replaced the mayor with a *prévôt des marchands* and reduced the number of *échevins* from twelve to four. He also directly named Lyons's first *prévôt* and two of the four *échevins*.[50]

The Edict of Chauny provides interesting insight into Henry IV's restructuring of the municipal government. Mixing flattery and intimidation, the king stated that he hoped to make Lyons more like Paris. Paris, he argued, was a greater city than Lyons, but was administered effectively with only one *prévôt des marchands* and four *échevins*. Henry stated that a small municipal government would greatly enhance the '*répos*, *seureté*, and *tranquilité*' of Lyons.[51]

Henry IV's reasoning behind the Edict of Chauny is stated clearly in the document. He wanted to re-establish order in this formerly rebellious League town. Reducing the size of large municipal governments was an understandable

---

[45] For Lyons's troubled history during the Catholic League see: A. Kleinclauz, *Histoire de Lyon* (Librairie Pierre Masson, 1939), I 441–58; Rayond F. Kierstead, *Pomponne de Bellièvre, A Study of the King's Men in the Age of Henry IV* (Evanston, Illinois: Northwestern University Press, 1968), 77–9; M. Sudan, *Recherches sur Le Rétour de la Ville de Lyon à La Monarchié sous Henry IV* (Lyon: Imprimerie de Ballande, 1814), 17–32; Jean Canault, ed., *Vie du Maréchal Alphonse D'Ornano, Lieutenant General en Dauphine, Languedoc et Guyenne et Maire de Bordeaux (1548–1610)* (Aubenas-en-Vivarais: Imprimerie Lienhart, 1975), 119–22; Jules Berger de Xivrey, ed., *Recueil des Lettres Missives* (Paris: Imprimerie Nationale 1848), vol. 4, 95–100.

[46] Kierstead, *Bellièvre*, 76–7; Jean Mariéjol, *Charles-Emmanuel de Savoie, duc de Nemours, Gouverneur du Lyonnais, Beaujolais et Forez (1567–1595)* (Paris: Hachette, 1935), 225–40; Sébastien Charléty, *Histoire de Lyon* (Lyon: A. Rey, 1903), 113–14.

[47] Kierstead, *Bellièvre*, 83.

[48] BN, MSS. fr. 23195, fols. 147–8; MSS fr. 16661, fols. 422–5.

[49] E. Halphern, (ed.), *Lettres inédites du Roi Henri IV au Chancelier de Bellièvre* (Paris: Chez-Auguste Abbey, 1872), vol. 1, 198.

[50] Kierstead, *Bellièvre*, 88–9; Jean Baptiste Monfalcon, *Histoire Monumentale de la Ville de Lyon* (Paris: privately printed, 1851), 161; Marc Guyaz, *Histoire des Institutions Municipales de Lyon* (Paris: E. Dentu, 1884), 245.

[51] *Archives Municipales*, Lyons (hereafter AML), BB134, fols. 7–9; see edict printed in Monfaulcon, *Histoire de Lyon*, 161.

tactic aimed at stemming social unrest.[52] The policy also gave the king the opportunity to select loyal officials for key municipal posts. Thus, by reducing the size of the municipality at Lyons, Henry also appointed three of the five town magistrates and naturally placed formerly exiled royalists in the posts. The man he chose as *prévôt* in 1595, Rene Thomassin, sieur de Montmartin was a well-known faithful servant of the Crown.[53]

Henry also gave another reason in the Edict of Chauny for his decision to reduce Lyons's municipality. It is the first justification listed in the document. Hoping to improve the city of Lyons, the king stated that it was his intent 'to put business here [Lyons] in such an ordered state that it will flourish for a long time and the town will grow in grandeur and prosperity.'[54] Henry directly linked financial improvement with decreasing the size of the city's *échevinage*. More precisely, in the Edict he took his first steps towards liquidating Lyons's huge municipal debt amassed during the Wars of Religion and before.

Lyons's capitulation treaty worked out with the Crown contained financial clauses guaranteeing that Henry would liquidate the city's debts, even those incurred during the War of the Catholic League.[55] This was not unusual. Other former League towns made similar agreements with the king either at their capitulations or shortly thereafter. Lyons's municipal debt was one of the largest in France. At around 600,000 *écus* in 1595, this reflected in large part the Crown's debt as it consisted of loans contracted by the town for the French kings during the Wars of Religion. The debt of the *échevinage* represented half of that figure, 300,000 *écus* or 900,000 *livres*.[56] This portion of the debt had been accumulated largely as a result of shortsighted budgetary tactics practised by town councillors. Published figures of municipal debt during Henry's reign are not easily found, but the ones available indicate that Lyons's state of indebtedness was exceptionally great. In 1595 Arles owed approximately 700,000 *livres*, Tours, 440,000 *livres*, Aix, 360,000 *livres*, Dijon 240,000 *livres*, Nantes, 150,000 *livres*, and Amiens, 150,000 *livres*.[57] Only Paris and

---

[52] BN, MSS fr. 16661, fols. 422–5; Augustin Thierry, *Recueil des monuments inédits de l'histoire du Tiers-Etat, Première série, Chartes, coutumes, acts municipaux, statutes des corporations d'arts et métier des villes et communes de France, Région du Nord*, (Paris: Typographie de Firmin Didot Frères, 1856), vol. 4, 486–9.

[53] Jean Baptiste Chaussonat, *Armorial Consularie de la Ville de Lyon* (Lyon: Bibliothèque de Lyon, s.d.) These three royal appointees were, René Thomassin, sieur de Montmartin, Antoine Henry, sieur de la Salle, *Conseiller du roi et trésorier général des finances*, and André Laures, sieur de la Sarra, *juge conservateur des privilèges des foires de Lyon*. All three men were exiled royalists during the period of the Catholic League. Montfalcon, *Histoire de Lyon*, 160; Sudan, *Recherches*, 23.

[54] Monfaulcon, *Histoire de Lyon*, 160. The document reads, 'et mettre les affaires d'icelle en tel estat qu'elle pût longuement subsister, et s'accroistre en toute sorte de grandeur et prospérité.'

[55] Richard Bonney, *The King's Debts, Finance and Politics in France 1589–1661* (Oxford: Clarendon Press, 1981), 43.

[56] AML, BB136, fol. 150.

[57] James B. Collins, 'Un problème toujours mal connu: Les finances de Henri IV', in *Henri IV et La Reconstruction du Royaume* (Pau: L'Association Henri IV, 1989 and D. Editions, 1990), 159–60.

Marseilles amassed larger debts than Lyons with obligations of 4 million *livres* and 1.5 million *livres* respectively.[58]

Lyons's importance as a banking centre had much to do with the city's debt. Lyons had become a hub of international finance in the late fifteenth century when several great Italian banking families established agencies there.[59] The city's international prominence naturally drew the attention of the French monarchy, so that by the mid-sixteenth century, the city's municipal government was loaning money to the Crown in much the same fashion as the *Hôtel de Ville* in Paris. Town magistrates borrowed funds on their own personal credit, and then relinquished the sums to the Crown in return for higher municipal taxes. The revenues generated from these taxes were in theory then applied to the repayment of the city's debt.[60] Creating new taxes only worked for so long, however, and in 1555 the Crown tried to consolidate its loans with an experiment known as the *Grand Parti*. The *Grand Parti* operated much like a sinking fund. Henry II enticed merchant-bankers to invest in the plan by guaranteeing a specific amortization rate paid quarterly on the loans at Lyons's four fairs. Initially the *Grand Parti* was a success, but the French defeat at Saint-Quentin in 1557, the bankruptcy of Spain's Philip II, and the untimely death of Henry II caused financiers to grow cautious. The French monarchy then reneged on its repayment commitment.[61]

While the failure of the *Grand Parti* represented one important element in Lyons's municipal debt, loans contracted during the Catholic League wars posed a far greater burden on the city. Maintaining armies to protect Lyons and guard the Saône and the Rhône rivers and paying the cost of fortifications and civil defence all weighed heavily on the city's treasury. To meet rising expenses, Lyons's municipal magistrates had been forced to go to the *marché des change* and borrow on their own credit in the name of the town.[62]

A spiralling municipal debt caused problems for the city government. Until 1589 persons entering the municipal government at election time were expected to discharge outgoing councillors of their part in the city debt. In this way the debt was passed on each year from one group of magistrates to another. After 1589, however, the debt had grown so large that only a few persons in the city were financially able and willing to shoulder the burden on their personal credit. Many wealthy royalist and neutral families left Lyons after the League takeover. Thus, the number of persons capable of floating the city's debt grew even smaller after 1589. As a result incumbent councillors from the 1589 elections remained in office until 1592 when mock elections were held. The pool of men qualified to fulfil the

[58] Ibid., 160. Françoise Bayard, 'La Méthode Sully en Matière de Finances: Les Traités de Rachats', xviie *Siècle*, 44 (1992), 53.
[59] Wolfe, *The Fiscal System*, 106.   [60] Ibid., 108.
[61] Ibid., 110–13; Roger Doucet, 'Le Grand Parti de Lyon au XVIe Siècle', *Revue Historique*, 171 (1933), 473–513; 172 (1934), 1–41.
[62] Roger Doucet, *Finances Municipales et Crédit Public à Lyon au XVIe Siècle* (Paris: Librairie des Sciences Politiques et Sociales, 1937), 114–18.

political and financial needs of Lyons had evolved into a small and elite Catholic League oligarchy.[63]

Henry's knowledge of Lyons's financial situation makes his action in 1595 more understandable. His restructuring of the municipal government abolished the practice of *échevins* reimbursing each other at every election by making such repayment impossible. Henry's action was shrewd. It gave him leverage against a closed caste of financial elites in the urban government. If the king had not prohibited borrowing by *échevins* and the transfer of debt from one group of councillors to another, it would have been impossible for him to have ejected wealthy League sympathizers from the municipal government after Lyons's capitulation. The huge debt and the system devised to manage that liability would have demanded their presence even though Henry's political survival called for the replacement of ex-Leaguers with loyal royalists. The re-organization of Lyons's *échevinage*, therefore, represented not only a first step towards debt liquidation, but also a political move to ensure the city's loyalty by breaking up the remnants of Catholic League clienteles. When the Edict of Chauny was first publicized in Lyons, the town notables rushed to the *Hôtel de Ville* to discuss its ramifications. They were terrified that a decreased number of *échevins* could not support a large debt. They did not immediately comprehend that this was exactly the king's intent.[64] Henry had created a small *échevinage* incapable of assuming responsibility for floating gross sums and no longer dependent on the former Catholic League financial elite.[65] Most importantly, he knew the re-created *échevinage* was loyal to him.

LIQUIDATING LYONS'S DEBT

During Bellièvre's tenure in Lyons, one of his assignments was to verify the municipal debt and ascertain what was due each creditor or group of creditors. His report to the king specified that the town's obligation was great and supported by twelve *échevins* who, in leaving their charges, were replaced by persons chosen more for their financial resources than their probity.[66] In 1595 in order to liquidate the debt, Henry granted Lyons two specific *octrois* for six years, the *tiers surtaux de la douane*, a customs tax on commodities and foodstuffs, and the levy of 4 *livres* on each *pièce de vin* entering the town. These *octrois* were renewed in 1600 and 1606. The Crown also designated a tax farmer to collect the sums and turn over to the *échevinage* 60,000 *livres* allocated to the amortization.[67] The king strictly forbade

---

[63] Ibid., 113, 118–20.

[64] AML, AA140, n.p. This document is dated only 1595, but its contents indicate that it was written shortly after the Edict of Chauny was published in Lyons. [65] Ibid., BB133, fol. 70.

[66] Ibid., fol. 25.

[67] Ibid., fols. 25, 69; Jacques Permezel, *La Politique Financière de Sully dans la Généralité de Lyon* (Lyon: Imprimerie Audin, 1935), 83.

newly elected *prévôts des marchands* and/or *échevins* from reimbursing their predecessors in office or from contracting more debts for the town in their names. All creditors were to be paid only with revenue coming from the municipal *octrois*. Persons who had loaned money to the king for Lyons's capitulation were promised compensation before all other creditors.[68] This last measure not only incorporated some of the king's royal debt with that of Lyons, but placed ex-Leaguers at an economic disadvantage and possibly frustrated the attempts of some to recover their pre-League prestige.

The *Conseil d'Etat* led by Sully, and Henry IV's *commissaires* gradually took control of the city's liquidation operation. As the king's *surintendant des finances*, Sully directed the fate of Lyons's *octrois*, Meric de Vic, one of the king's *conseillers d'Etat* and a special agent in Lyons between 1597 and 1600, noted in a letter to the municipality that without Sully, Henry IV would neither 'discuss nor resolve anything related to finances or *octrois*'.[69] Since Henry and Sully both believed that municipal officials lined their pockets with money raised from taxes owed to the Crown, they were eager to check Lyons's financial accounts and ready to use the debt liquidation problem as a means of gaining access to the city's tax ledgers. Sully also believed that much of France's urban debt had been negotiated fraudulently. The experience with Lyons did nothing to dispel their belief in municipal corruption.[70]

On 12 July 1601 the *Conseil d'Etat* issued an edict ordering Lyons's city government to turn over its municipal debt records along with its receipt and expenditure accounts for the repayment of the debts to the king's officials in Paris.[71] This verification included the accounts of money obtained from municipal *octrois*. Sully wanted a general audit of the town's financial documents to check for both fraud and poor accounting procedures. Therein began a long process alienating the town from the Crown. At first the *Lyonnais* refused to comply, and later the material sent to Paris was considered insufficient.[72] In 1602 Sully told Lyons's deputy at court, Jean Sève, the sieur de Froment, that the account books were in such bad shape that the *Conseil* did not know how to proceed. The minister explained there were no records for an infinite number of expenditures.[73] In February 1602, another edict was issued telling Lyons's municipal government to send more detailed records relating to their debt.[74] In a meeting of the *Conseil d'Etat* held one month later, a scribe noted that any verification of Lyons's debt was impossible because too many receipts and expenditures were listed in gross sums and others were justified with

[68] AML, BB135, fol. 68.
[69] Ibid., AA45, fol. 132. Meric de Vic was *maître des Requêtes, conseiller d'Etat, président à la Chambre des comptes, trésorier de France* at Blois, and *président au parlement de Toulouse*. He served Henry in Lyons as *intendant* between 1597 and 1600, leaving the city to serve as ambassador to Switzerland. See Permezel, *Politique Financière*, 16. 'Sans ladite Rosne', De Vic wrote, 'nous parle ny resoult aucune chose en matiere finances ou octrois'.   [70] Bayard, 'La Méthode Sully', 54.
[71] Valois, *Inventaire des arrêts*, vol. 2, 6338.   [72] AML, BB139, 74–5.   [73] Ibid., fols. 7rv.
[74] Valois, *Inventaire des arrêts*, vol. 2, 6904.

obscure citations.[75] Similar *arrêts* calling for the clarification of the city's financial registers and the remission of accounts to royal officials were promulgated in 1606, 1608 and 1609.[76]

The liquidation of Lyons's debt was a wearisome process that spanned the whole of Henry's reign, and will only be summarized here. Meric de Vic originally inspected the town's records to verify all just titles contracted since 1570 and to revoke those entailing fraud. He also reduced the interest on some loans in which the rate was thought to be excessive. Repaying the debt was an onerous task since interest due continued to inflate the sum. For this reason, in 1596 the Crown divided the debt into two parts consisting of the principal and the interest. Interest was paid on the principal amount at $8\frac{1}{3}$ per cent, while interest was paid on the interest portion of the debt at 5 per cent. These rates were retroactive to 1 September 1595. The system worked well, and by 1605 the total debt of Lyons had fallen from 1,635,306 *livres* to 527,183 *livres* representing a decrease in the original amount by two thirds.[77]

Even though substantial progress had been made in liquidating Lyons's debt, complications relating to the debt repayment plan became apparent by 1604 when the original rate of interest on the capital sum proved too heavy for the town inhabitants to support. The tax burden of the municipal *octrois* was such that any increase in impositions would have put too great a strain on the city's taxpayers. The Crown responded with a new edict issued on 23 December 1604 which reduced the rate of interest. Retroactive to 1594 and valid until 18 February 1602 the $8\frac{1}{3}$ per cent rate was decreased to $6\frac{2}{3}$ per cent. Only 5 per cent was to be paid on the principal portion of existing *rentes* after 18 February 1602. All superior interest previously reimbursed to creditors was applied to their principals further reducing the town's debt.[78]

While the liquidation of Lyons's debt was going well from the Crown's point of view, it seemed like a nightmare to the municipal magistrates who were caught between the designs of the Crown and the demands of their creditors. Town leaders wrote frequently to the king, his advisors, and their own patrons at court describing the town's poverty and depopulation.[79] Although the Crown viewed Lyons as an important commercial centre with many foreign bankers, locals complained that all commerce and industry had been destroyed during the wars. Forced loans on the generality to which Lyons was required to contribute increased the tax burden on the town. The city contributed to the siege of La Fère, and three times in 1597 its wealthy citizens had been asked to contribute to the king's military expenses.[80] In 1602 the Crown tried abortively to impose a tax called the *sol pour livre* on the town. Opposition eventually forced the Crown to accept a subvention of 18,000 *écus* in its place. New taxes were additionally imposed on taverns, cabarets, wine sold in bulk,

[75] BN, MSS fr. 16661, fol. 452.
[76] Valois, *Inventaire des arrêts*, vol. 2, 10642, 12055, 13332.
[77] BN, MSS fr. 16661, fols. 438–42.   [78] Ibid.; Permezel, *La Politique Financière*, 86–9.
[79] For example, BN, MSS fr. 15900, vol. 1, fol. 353.   [80] Kleinclauz, *Histoire de Lyon*, vol. 2, 11.

playing cards, and tarot cards. In 1607 the king succeeded in forcing all persons, including those previously exempt from taxation to contribute to the portion of the municipal *octrois* on wine that normally went to the king.[81] These taxes were over and above the *octrois* the city government collected from the townspeople to repay the debt of the *échevinage* as well as support the city's daily operation.

By 1601 the municipal leaders in Lyons expressed discontent over taxes. Pierre de Baillon, the *prévôt des marchands* journeyed to Paris to try and gain an audience with the king and beg him to settle Lyons's troubled affairs.[82] Baillon explained that too many foreign merchants and bankers had left Lyons during the wars, and high taxes were hurting mercantile interests and destroying commerce in the city.[83] Baillon enjoyed the support of Bellièvre at court, but with Sully the deputy found only anger and mistrust.[84] Upset with Baillon's requests Sully told him that 'the town of Lyons is worth nothing to the king, in fact, it costs him 100,000 *écus* per year; the inhabitants are mutinous and seditious.'[85] Sully's fury stirred him further. 'The king', he said, 'will no longer stand by his accord with you since you do not want to obey his commandments . . .'[86] Enraged, Sully accused the town magistrates of lining their pockets with municipal tax monies.[87]

Sully knew how to hold a grudge. When Jean Sève, the sieur de Fromente, went to court in November 1601 taking the city's financial records for the *Conseil* to verify, Sully gave him the cold shoulder.[88] Sève also carried a *cahier* of grievances composed by the city officials referring to the town's debt and tax issues that he hoped to present to the king. Nearly a year later, Sève was still at court and making no apparent progress in convincing Henry or his ministers of Lyons's poverty.[89] Another deputy, Jean Goujon, told the city notables that Sully harboured a special hatred for Lyons.[90] The *échevinage* feared that the *Conseil d'Etat* was planning to 'abolish' their *octrois*, 'annul' concessions granted at the town's capitulation, and re-establish the 'terror' that had existed in 1595.[91] The state of Lyons's indebtedness in 1604 is given in table 6 and a list of the city's creditors is provided at the end of the chapter.

After 1602 tension concerning Lyons's municipal debt grew worse. Henry wrote that he deplored the terrible state of the city's fortifications, and urged the town notables to repair the walls using money from a wine tax.[92] Antoine Rougier, the

---

[81] Ibid.

[82] Antoine Pericaud, ed., *Notes et Documents pour servir à L'Histoire de Lyon sous le Règne d'Henri IV, 1594–1610* (Lyon: Imprimerie de Mougin-Rusand, 1845), 174.

[83] BN, MSS fr. 15900, vol. 1, fol. 353.

[84] See often used quote from Ibid. in which a municipal councillor says that Bellièvre, 'n'ose au Conseil dire mot, tant M. de Rosny [Sully] a pris d'autority.' 174.

[85] Ibid. The deputy wrote that Sully said, '[L]a ville de Lyon ne vault rien au Roy, au contraire luy couste par an cent mille escua; que les habitans sont des mutins et seditieux . . .'

[86] Ibid. '[L]e roy n'est pas plus tenu de maintenir ce qu'il a accordé, que l'on ne veult obeyr à ses commandemens et resolutions . . .'   [87] Ibid.   [88] AML, BB138, fol. 154.

[89] Ibid., BB140, fols. 54–62.   [90] Pericaud, *Notes*, 174.

[91] AML, AA24, letter dated 17 October 1602.

[92] Ibid., AA68, letter dated 8 May 1601. A similar letter is found in Pericaud, *Notes*, 175.

city's *receveur des deniers communs dons et octrois*, conceded with melancholy that the town was too poor to meet all of its obligations for the normal operation of the municipality.[93] To add to the financial burden, Henry IV often dipped into the city's funds earmarked for amortization further inhibiting the liquidation process.[94] The *échevinage* tried to persuade the king that some relief could be found if he would re-establish a town government with twelve members and allow them once again to procure loans using their own credit.[95]

Increasing the size of the *échevinage* was the only way the town magistrates could see to end their plight, and they petitioned Henry with this request in 1605.[96] Lyons's creditors were furious with the king's 1604 decision to decrease the rate of interest on their loans. Although not a creditor himself, Bellièvre's son echoed the anxiety of the group when he wrote to his father saying, 'I pray of you to advise me so that I can understand the justice of this affair which goes against the public faith and the law.'[97] The creditors sent their own deputies to court as well. Believing the *échevinage* conspired with the king to reduce the interest on their loans, they demanded that Henry pay interest at the rate promised in 1595.[98] By 1607 the creditors were still arguing with the king. They said that his decision to pay first the claims of those individuals or groups who made favoured deals with the Crown put other, less wealthy creditors, at a disadvantage. Thus, the creditors claimed, some persons had not received any repayment in over five years and had been ruined financially.[99] In 1607 Henry and Sully grew tired of hearing the sorrows of town deputies, and they decided to end the municipal debt problem once and for all. In that year, Sully began to negotiate with financiers called *partisans* to collect taxes and make payments on *rentes* or *domaine*.[100] The *partisans*, independent business-men who contracted with the Crown to perform some duty such as collecting taxes, bought the right to a *parti* for a substantial sum of money. This arrangement brought additional revenue to the king. In return, a *partisan* was allowed to collect certain taxes and then reimburse creditors, keeping all surplus revenue for himself. *Partisans* were known to make as much as ten to twenty-five per cent profit on the sums they collected. Between 1607 and 1609, the Crown issued at least 173 of these agreements.[101]

All of the contracts negotiated in this fashion were approved by the king in his *Conseil d'Etat* as *arrêts*, and the documents listed the exact specifications of the

[93] AML, BB139, fol. 27v.
[94] Permezel, *La Politique Financière*, 89.
[95] AML, BB140, fol. 59v.
[96] Ibid., BB142, fols. 19–20.
[97] BN, MSS fr. 15900, vol. 2, fol. 588. The letter reads, 'Je vous supplieray tres humblement Monsieur de considerer la justice de c'est affair et ne le conserver, me favorisant de vos bons avis pour parer a un si grand coup et ruyneur, contre la foy publique et les loix.'
[98] Ibid.
[99] AML, BB143, 72v–75r; Bayard, 'La Méthode Sully', 55.
[100] Buisseret, *Sully*, 90.
[101] Bayard, 'La Méthode Sully', 56.

Table 6. *General state of indebtedness for the town and community of Lyons,*
23 December 1604

Origin of Loan	Amount		
	livres	*sous*	*deniers*
Capital known as '1st Principal' earning $8\frac{1}{3}$%	13,186	11	6
Interest amassed on principal before edict of 1596			
regulating interest earning 5%	244,993	4	10
'2nd principal' or interest on interest earning 5%	48,998	8	8
Heirs of Emmond de Reynauld de Saint-Marcelin	0	0	0
Heirs of Pierre Garbot	0	0	0
Marquis de Final	15,750	0	0
Loan made for capitulation in 1594	7,147	0	0
Loan remaining from 1589	127,057	8	6
Captain Sinsseu, Henri Pheiffer, Jehan Georges de			
Castania, Nicholas Sizoniacre, Nicolas Varoche,			
Guillaume Balthazad, Captain Burquy	16,454	0	0
Loan for demolition of Citadelle	13,500	0	0
Arrières of *rentes* on Gabelles from the reduction of			
Lyons to Edict of Chauny	24,000	0	0
Sieur de Champier	16,086	9	0
Total	527,171	40	30
Equals	527,173	2	6
Total given in document	527,183	2	6

Source: *Bibliothèque Nationale*, MSS fr. 16661, fols. 438–42.

financial agreements.[102] To liquidate Lyons's debt, the king's council issued contracts to two financiers, Jean de Moulceau and Antoine Douelles.[103]

News of the contracts made with these two *partisans* devastated the leaders in
Lyons. While Moulceau's *parti* failed to grant him possession of all municipal
octrois, Douelles's *parti* left the *échevinage* with little control over the financial
affairs of the town. Douelles's contract specified that for six years he could collect
the *octrois* the king had originally granted to Lyons in 1595 for the amortization of
the debt. During that time he was expected to oversee personally the repayment of

[102] J. F. Bosher, *French Finances, 1770–1795 From Business to Bureaucracy* (Cambridge: Cambridge
University Press, 1970), 9, 12. For information on other *partis* established during the reign of Henry
IV see, Albert Chamberland, 'Recherches Critiques sur les Réformes Financières en Champagne à
L'Epoque de Henri IV et Sully', *Travaux de l'Academie de Reims*, 111 (1902), 15–29. For contracts,
see Valois, *Inventaire des arrêts*, vol. 2, 12098, 12762, 12782, 12785, 13063, 13064, 13069, 13070,
15343, etc.
[103] Valois, *Inventaire des arrêts*, 12098, 12762, 15343. Françoise Bayard identified Moulceau's contract in
AN E16 B, fol. 91, dated 15 March 1608. Bayard, 'La Méthode Sully', 67. For more on *partisans* see
Françoise Bayard, *Le Monde des financiers au XVIIe siècle* (Paris: Flammarion, 1988); Daniel
Dessert, *Argent, pouvoir et société au Grand Siècle* (Paris: Fayard, 1984).

creditors thus denying the municipal government any part in the liquidation process.[104] Douelles also had the option of repurchasing *rentes* and/or *domaine* in the name of the king for up to 600,000 *livres*.[105]

It seemed to Lyons's notables, that the problems in repaying creditors stemmed from Henry's decision to forbid further borrowing by municipal officials. In the letter of grievance presented to the king and his ministers by a deputy to court, François Clapisson, Lyons's town magistrates defended their administration in a bold statement, 'If the creditors are not paid, it is because of the king and no one else.'[106] The *échevinage* proposed that instead of contracting with *partisans*, Henry would do better to grant Lyons's municipal government greater *octrois* with which to finish the reimbursement process.[107] One of Clapisson's greatest fears was that at the end of Douelles's six year *parti*, the municipal *octrois* levied for the repayment of Lyons's debt would become a permanent tax collected yearly for the benefit of the king.[108] In the minds of Clapisson and his fellow councillors, imposing such a 'taille annuel' not only violated Lyons's privileges and franchises but created a dangerous threat to the inhabitants of the town that would surely bring about their 'isolation and ruin'.[109]

Clapisson succeeded in cancelling Douelles's *parti*. Yet Moulceau's was re-negotiated and re-established by an *arrêt* on 30 June 1609. Beginning in January 1610 and continuing for nine years, Moulceau was awarded the collection right to the wine and customs taxes Henry had previously established for debt liquidation. The contract stated, however, that in 1619 these taxes would be definitively abolished. Granted the right to direct the reimbursement of creditors, Moulceau was instructed to turn over 72,000 *livres* each year to the *échevinage* for their municipal budget, 50,000 *livres* of which was specified for maintenance and repairs. Moulceau's contract also instructed him to repurchase *rentes* and *domaine* up to 600,000 *livres* during the first six years of his tenure. At the end of the six years, the repurchase contracts would be inspected by the king and his *Conseil*.[110]

Clapisson reported on his mission at court at a general assembly held by the *échevinage* on 20 August 1609. Having first spoken against *partisans*, Clapisson had since come to accept the town's fate, albeit with consternation, once he recognized that Lyons's opposition fell on deaf ears at court. 'Unfortunately, we now join the Estates of Brittany and Burgundy and many of the best towns of the realm', he said, 'who were also forced to accept *partisans* regardless of their privileges . . .'[111] He harangued his fellow citizens about the merits of the *parti*. Stressing that creditors

---

[104] BN, MSS fr. 16661, fols. 444–5.   [105] Permezel, *La Politique Financière*, 93.

[106] AML, BB145 fol. 77v. 'Sy que sy lesdictes creanciers ne sont payer c'est par le faict du Roy et non aultre.   [107] Ibid., 78.

[108] Ibid., 68; Permezel, *La Politique Financière*, 93. Clapisson's commission as deputy to court is dated 19 June 1608. AML, BB144, fols. 70–1; BB145, fol. 107.   [109] AML, BB145, fol. 68r.

[110] Ibid., CC4099, Printed loose document entitled, 'Extraict des Registres du Conseil d'Etat'.

[111] Ibid., BB145, fol. 106. Clapisson stated, 'Nous avons este contraincts de recourir a la second a l'exemple des Estats de Bretaigne, de Bourgougne, et des meilleures villes du Royaulme. L'esquelles ont este forcees nonobstant de leurs privilleges de subir le joug des partisans . . .'

would be assured of payment, he noted that the good families who had loaned money for the benefit of the town would not fall into ruin. The fact that the *échevinage* still maintained control over the municipal administration without rendering account to the court was another important point the deputy mentioned. Clapisson did not pretend, however, that he had achieved a major victory for Lyons. Competition for the *parti* had been steep, and Lyons probably had little chance of outbidding wealthy financiers. The deputy thus urged his fellow magistrates to accept their position. By confronting the Crown with the town's opposition, Clapisson learned the limits of royal compromise. In a long speech, he lamented:

> It is sweeter and more tolerable to observe the king's law, which to obey means life but to disobey means death. This law [the establishment of Moulceau's *parti*] seems rude, but it is his law, and although we have opposed it, he [Henry] simply told us that it is his will. The laws and wishes of the king rendered both justly and unjustly make good, fair, holy, and sacred what was previously malicious and perverse. The town of Bordeaux did not understand this secret and saw her walls razed, her houses and town burned, her privileges revoked, her parlement prohibited, and her best men broken. So we conclude that a good law was not made when the tyrannical *partisans* were irrevocably established during the absolute empire of this great king.[112]

Henry was by no means apologetic for the decision to use the *parti* in Lyons. If anything, the king seemed annoyed with the constant stream of deputies the city sent to court. He informed the municipal government in July 1609 just after the *partisan* issue was settled, 'We always recall your fidelity and good service even though you seldom merit this grace . . . '[113] In a similar tone Nicolas de Villeroy, the king's secretary of state, also wrote to Lyons's town council and called Clapisson's duties at court 'pénibles poursuites'.[114] He warned the *échevinage* to accept the king's decision concerning Moulceau. 'By my interest in your well-being', Villeroy stated, 'I exhort you to atone for errors you committed in the past by exercising a good and faithful administration in the future. This is the true means of assuring the king's satisfaction with your actions.'[115] Moulceau appears to have performed

---

[112] Ibid., BB145, fols. 108rv. Clapisson stated, '[C]e qui nous a faict et doibt faire trouver desormais non conditions plus doulcer et supportables en observant la Loy du Prince a quelle obeir est vivre, desobeir est mourir. Ces loix semblent rudes mais ce sont ses loix, nous avons opposé la force de nos raisons. Il nous a simplement dict que c'est son vouloir. Les loix et le vouloir du prince rendrent juste l'injuste, equitable l'Inicque, sainct et sacre ce qui estoit au paravant vicieux et prophane. La ville de Bourdaux aux pour n'avoir entendre ce secret a veu ses murailles razees, sa maison de ville brusler, ses privilleges revocquez, ses parlements interdict et ses premiers hommes au tombeau, doncq a vos droict n'y avait aucune apparance que nous peussions compatir soubz la tirannie des partisans. Lesquels se fussent establir Infailliblement durant lempire absolu dece grand prince.'

[113] Ibid., BB145, fols. 109v–10r; J. Berger de Xivrey and J. Guadet (eds.), *Recueil des Lettres Missives de Henri IV*, (Paris: Imprimerie Nationale, 1854), vol. 7, 737.

[114] AML, AA53, fol. 110, letter dated 8 July 1609.

[115] Ibid. Villeroy wrote, 'Mais je vous prie et exhorte comme interesse en votre prosperite de recompenser par votre fidelle et loyalle administration au future les defaulx pretendues en celle du passé, car c'est le vray moien d'asseurer vos affaires, rendre le Roy contant de vos actions, fermer la bouche a vos ennemis et courrir a vos amys.'

his duties admirably. Despite Henry's death and the fall from power of the duke of Sully, Lyons's debt was completely liquidated in 1615, and Moulceau was thereafter discharged from his contract.[116] Table 7 lists Lyons's creditors in 1598.

CONCLUSION: HENRY IV, SULLY, AND MUNICIPAL FINANCE

A municipal historian once commented, 'Henry IV was not well-liked in Lyons, and Sully was detested.'[117] The reasons for this assessment are not hard to understand. Henry IV and Sully intervened in both the political and the financial spheres of Lyons's local government with unmistakable calculation. Their actions undermined the traditional workings of the *échevinage* and expanded royal involvement in urban government. Neither king nor minister showed much reverence toward municipal privileges and franchises, which both men believed hampered royal administration and protected corrupt town councillors. Sully's understanding of state finances was crucial in training teams of financial administrators and developing a more efficient administration.[118] He clearly understood the level of financial abuse perpetrated by town councils and devised means to monitor their administration of municipal tax monies while exposing their abuses.[119] Indeed, he may well have redefined for the king and the French public what constituted a financial abuse as he criticized and corrected what had long been normal operating procedures for tax collection and debt financing in the towns of early modern France. Defining abuses also lent legitimacy to Henry's authority to correct problems related to municipal debt and finances. Instead of imposing his monarchical will on the towns, Henry had invented reasons to exert his authority for the perceived common good. Substantial success had been achieved by 1610 in auditing the tax records of the towns either under the direction of the *Chambre des comptes*, the *Cour des aides* and/or by Sully himself.

The debt liquidation issue in Lyons raises more questions than it answers. Historians most often interpret reduction in the size of municipal governments as a political move calculated to extend tighter control by royal authorities over town councils. But in Lyons the decision to reduce the size of the city government was an important component of the Crown's financial policy. Henry decreased the number of Lyons's administrators so that the local government would never again be large enough to support a huge debt. Henry was adamant on this issue and refused to revoke the Edict of Chauny. Lyons's history is somewhat unique, however. While

---

[116] Permezel, *La Politique Financière*, 95; AN E54 B, fol. 261 dated 29 November 1616.
[117] Charlèty, *Histoire de Lyon*, 116.
[118] J. H. M. Salmon, 'Justice, Finance and Administrative Revolution: Comments on Bernard Barbiche's "Henri IV, Sully et la Première Monarchie Administrative"', *Proceedings of the Annual Meeting of the Western Society for French History*, 17 (1990), 24–9; Buisseret, *Sully*, 119; Bayard, 'La Méthode Sully', 62.
[119] Maximilien de Béthune, *The Memoires of the duke of Sully, Prime Minister to Henry the Great*, trans. Charlotte Lennox (Philadelphia: Edward Earle, 1817), vol. 5, 406–12; Pericaud, *Notes*, 174.

Table 7. *List of creditors cited in 1598 in the municipal deliberations of Lyons's échevinage*

Name	Amount		
	écus	sous	deniers
M. Francois de Guerrier, sieur de Combellard, one of most notable bourgeois	476	45	3
Noble Antoine Grollier, sieur de Servières, Maitre d'hôtel ordinaire du roi (Royalist)	262	43	6
Noble Antoine Henry, sieur de la Salle, Conseiller du roi, trésorier général des finances en la généralité d'Auvergne, Prévôt des marchands in 1604–5 (Royalist)	562	4	0
Noble Antoine Laurens, sieur de la Sarra, Juge conservateur des privileges des foires de Lyon, Echevin in 1596 (Royalist)	483	48	0
Noble Jacques Jacquet, sieur de la Verrière, secretaire du roi, Echevin in 1598–9 (Royalist)	1062	38	3
Noble Alexandre Pollaillon (other titles unknown)	485	37	0
Noble Gaspard Mormeux (other titles unknown)	483	43	3
Heirs of Noble Jehn Pelletier (other titles unknown)	538	45	3
Heirs of Noble Hugues Valentin (other titles unknown)	592	17	13
Noble Durand Colhabaud, marchand, Echevin in 1605–6	615	30	9
Noble Claude Vizé, one of most notable bourgeois	598	58	0
Noble Martin Cornet, baron de Moutribloud (other titles unknown)	1687	47	6
Heirs of Noble Jean-Baptiste Regnauld (other titles unknown)	866	12	3
Noble Guyot de Masso, sieur de Saint Andre holding right to loan of M. Claude de Rubis (Rubys was a Leaguer)	95	0	0
Noble Charles Noirat, bourgeois-marchand, Echevin in 1604	326	14	10
Noble Richard de Sarrazin holding right to loan of Charles Noirat	232	14	3
Noble Louis de Berny (other titles unknown) (Leaguer)	585	11	9
Noble Anthoine Teste (other titles unknown) (Leaguer)	328	37	9
Noble Amable Thierry, bourgeois, Echevin in 1606–7 (Leaguer)	620	32	9
Noble Louis Prost (other titles unknown)	329	24	9
Noble Ponson Bernard, Echevin (other titles unknown) (Leaguer)	377	13	4
Noble Gaspard Mormeu holding right to loan by Ponson Bernard, Echevin (Leaguer)	472	49	3
Noble Guillaume Charrier, bourgeois-marchand, Echevin in 1596–7 holding right to loan by brother Noble Antoine Charrier	313	31	0

Table 7 (*cont.*)

Name	Amount		
	écus	*sous*	*deniers*
Richard de Sarrazin holding right to loan by Noble Guillaume Gella	41	41	9
Noble Rene de Thomassin, sieur de Montmartin, Prévôt des Marchands in 1596–7 (Royalist)	381	16	3
Damoiselle Catherine Bruyer widow of Noble Jehan Charbonnier (other titles un-known)	72	16	3
Noble Richard de Sarrazin, holding right to loan by heirs of Charbonnier	25	35	6
Sieur Gondz Jaconni (other titles unknown) holding right to loan by heirs of Charbonnier	94	8	6
M. Antoine Capponi (other title unknown) holding right to loan by heirs of Charbonnier	70	34	0
Sieur Alexandre Orlandin, bourgeois holding right to loan by heirs of Charbonnier	95	50	3
To heirs of Xpostle Fiot, bourgeois holding right to loan by heirs of Charbonnier	19	5	0
Total	13183	897	135

Source: AM, Lyons, BB 135 fols. 67v-71r; AML, BB381, 'Rolle des natifs de la Ville de Lyons', fols. 13–19.

most magistrates throughout France loaned money to their town governments and took out *rentes* in the name of their towns, the floating of a city debt as practiced in Lyons required banking skills and techniques unknown in urban centres without large populations of Italian and Spanish merchants, bankers, and negotiators.

The Crown's financial policy with regard to municipal debt as managed by Sully substantiates observations other historians have made of his administration.[120] There was nothing innovative in the measures he used, but the fact that they were carried out with such rigour and determination caused the impressive success of the amortization of debts throughout urban France. Henry was in no position to impose sanctions with force if the towns in France resisted the debt liquidation scheme. But since the debt crisis was very real, the Crown's blueprint for amortization, while unpopular, proved effective. The accomplishment increased Henry's power and prestige and enhanced his reputation as a problem-solver. Further examination of the debt liquidation issue in other towns during Henry's reign, should demonstrate more completely Sully's enormous influence over municipal finance and what appears to have been a conscious attempt to bring the municipal tax structure under greater Crown control.

[120] Collins, 'Un problème toujours mal connu', 145–64.

Henry IV, urban autonomy, and French absolutism

This study of Henry IV and the towns adds another dimension to the growing body of revisionary literature questioning the meaning of the term 'absolutism' in the early modern historical context. It has been shown that the king's most overt attacks on a few towns did not mean that he harboured designs to emasculate urban governments. Henry sometimes intervened in elections and reduced the size of town councils. He overrode medieval exemptions and taxed the towns. He forced discontent town-dwellers to accept the Edict of Nantes as well as his post-war debt amortization plan. But these actions must be weighed against his attempts to work with the towns, reward them, and bring their elites into his royal clientele. The French Wars of Religion were in large part a major urban conflict, and the end of the wars brought about a resolution in the Crown's struggle with the towns, if only temporarily. Even so, Henry's relationship with the towns was complex and contradictory. The towns may have resisted any blatant movement towards more authoritative rule on his part while still depending on him to act as a problem-solver in matters related to debt, riot, factional politics, and national security, the very issues that necessitated the king's interference in town politics.

If the wars stimulated a revival of urban autonomy, they also prevented towns from being able to establish permanent security for their inhabitants. The Catholic League, in particular, had promised harmony and neighbourliness reinforcing a sixteenth-century ideal of urban solidarity. But instability resulted as League promises failed to materialize and Guisard largess declined causing town populations to grow divided. Religious sentiment could not insulate France from its own centrifugal forces. By 1594 the Catholic League ironically seemed to threaten urban autonomy, and at that point, town populations looked to Henry IV to restore an administrative, authoritative, and religious unity to the kingdom never realized by the Catholic League.[1]

No systematic plan to destroy the privileges and franchises of France's urban centres can be found in the papers of Henry and his ministers. Indeed, in the sixteenth century such an idea would have been misguided. Privileges functioned

---

[1] This paragraph is based on my 'Confederates and Rivals: Picard Urban Alliances during the Catholic League, 1588–1594', *Canadian Journal of History/Annales canadiennes d'histoire*, 31 (1996), 376.

as important incentives to townspeople to remain loyal to the king since he could augment, diminish, or revoke them, and they provided the Crown with lucrative payments when they were reconfirmed and reissued. The granting of privileges also served to legitimate Henry's kingship when he issued the charters in his name. They were his very tangible peace offerings to former enemy towns at the end of the religious wars as well as rewards for fidelity to his loyal towns. In exchange for peace, Henry extended Crown patronage to the towns and renewed their privileges. By reissuing town privileges to former Catholic League towns, moreover, the king presented himself as the giver of public liberties. Thus, the act of renewing the charters underscored his policy of conciliation and offered proof of his clemency. Henry used charters of privileges and franchises after the civil wars to re-establish communion between the Crown and the towns.[2] Afterwards when he seriously tampered with municipal liberties he did so not out of a simplistic desire to crush municipal autonomy but in reaction to major problems that threatened the Crown: Lyons and municipal debt in 1595; the Spanish capture of Amiens in 1597; Limoges and the *pancarte* riot in 1602. These acts meant Henry was an astute politician but hardly an absolute monarch. He had to rule, as Yves-Marie Bercé has said, 'from day to day'.[3] In reconstructing France, he confronted problems in piecemeal fashion, but the accumulated success of his involvement with the towns strengthened the power of the Crown.

Recently many scholars have announced the death throes of 'absolutism' by suggesting the word is a meaningless anachronism. For example, Nicholas Henshall argues that in unearthing the complex and subtle ways early modern government worked without the autocrats and bureaucrats envisioned by an earlier generation of scholars, the continued use of the word 'absolutism' is 'a hopelessly confusing half-measure'.[4] Along the same lines Roger Mettam states, 'Absolutism should have no place in a discussion of the power of the Crown in early modern France.'[5] Discontinuing its use entirely, however, seems too extreme since seventeenth-century legal jurists referred to the power contained in the idea of an 'absolute' king so often in their political rhetoric, and certainly all kings, Henry IV included, wanted absolute power. The 1609 quote of the *Lyonnais* deputy cited in chapter eight calling Henry's reign an 'absolute empire' proves that even town deputies were exposed to such ideas at court.[6] As a concept, the idea of the 'absolute' king was an important part of the early modern *mentalité*. It may be

---

[2] Louis Olga Fradenburg, *City Marriage Tournament Arts of Rule in Late Medieval Scotland* (Madison: University of Wisconsin Press, 1991), 43–4. Fradenburg argues that the re-establishment of communion between a king and his subjects was a major function of town charters.

[3] Yves-Marie Bercé, *The Birth of Absolutism, A History of France, 1598–1661*, trans. Richard Rex (New York: St Martin's Press, 1992), 11.

[4] Nicholas Henshall, *The Myth of Absolutism: Change & Continuity in Early Modern European Monarchy* (New York: Longman, 1992), 212.

[5] Roger Mettam, *Power and Faction in Louis XIV's France.* (Oxford: Basil Blackwell, 1988), 34.

[6] *Archives Municipales*, Lyons, BB145, fol. 108v.

proven a myth, but myths have meaning. Roland Mousnier argued many years ago that the ideas the French monarchy and society generated after 1610 had much to do with the myth of Henry IV created by his untimely death.[7]

This assessment of Henry IV and the towns also underscores the importance that the system of clientelism played in expanding the king's power base and reiterates the importance Sharon Kettering attaches to his reign.[8] If Henry had a 'municipal policy' it involved placing men he could trust in key magisterial posts around the country. And this tactic holds true for all the towns, whether identified as Leaguer, royalist or Protestant. When Henry surveyed his country's urban landscape he saw loyal towns and disloyal towns. Remaking unfaithful urban centres into trusted 'institutional' clients proved a main priority. There was no failure of clientage during and after the Wars of Religion, moreover, for Henry conquered his towns through the effective employment of key urban clients. In fact, he used clients to mobilize power and give legitimacy to his rule. Thereafter, he continued to expand his royal clientele network during the course of his reign to enhance stability. Nobles and royal commissioners understood the king's need to capture town loyalty by placing trusted clients in municipal posts, and many of them worked for the king in that direction. French monarchs had long manipulated clientage to administer France, but the Wars of Religion forced Henry to make better use of a system already in place. His clients brokered the peace he offered to urban France and gave Henry access to networks of urban power inside the towns. His effective control of the patron–client system thus laid the groundwork for Richelieu's later creation of royal clientele networks throughout France.[9] Henry's success should not be exaggerated, however. As Stuart Carroll observes, 'Clients and agents did not ensure 'control' of popular forces. Rather, they facilitated channels of communication . . .'[10] Henry's directives and mandates to the towns often entailed complicated negotiation processes that involved both the Crown and the towns in give and take.[11] This was how the traditional French Renaissance monarchy and the emerging absolute state operated at the end of the sixteenth century.

Henry's attempts to create urban clients also exposes his comprehension of the internal dynamics of towns and emphasizes the fact that it would have done him little good to destroy privileges throughout France. Such a move would have only

[7] Roland Mousnier, *L'assassinat d'Henri IV Le problème du tyrannicide et l'affermissement de la monarchie absolue* (Paris: Gallimard, 1964); for a more recent discussion of this argument, see, Denis Crouzet, *Les Guerriers de Dieu La Violence au Temps des Troubles de Religion Vers 1525 - Vers 1610* (Paris: Champ Vallon, 1990), vol. 2, 585–603.

[8] Sharon Kettering, *Patrons, Brokers, and Clients in Seventeenth-Century France* (New York: Oxford University Press, 1986), 222–3.

[9] Ibid., 233.

[10] Stuart Carroll, 'The Guise Affinity and Popular Protest During the Wars of Religion', *French History*, 9 (1995), 129.

[11] J. Russell Major, *From Renaissance Monarchy to Absolute Monarchy French Kings, Nobles, and Estates* (Baltimore: The Johns Hopkins University Press, 1994), 164.

antagonized the very men he wanted to win over.[12] Instead Henry collaborated with key individuals in the towns who supported his rule and were rewarded by him after the wars for their devotion. Understanding clientelism as a system of power, therefore, instead of simply a system of social organization means acknowledging that Henry accumulated power as he acquired urban clients and ensured their places of power among their fellow town-dwellers in the provinces. This form of reciprocity between the king and his elite subjects was part of the political legitimation process. Henry's grasp of the patron-client system divulges one of the reasons he successfully ended the religious wars and explains why his rule proved so effective. His ability to create urban clients was an integral part of his political achievement and a key facet of his 'art of rule'.[13]

In 1984 Mark Greengrass argued that Henry's reign involved a protracted 'struggle for stability', and his thesis remains an important backdrop to any discussion of Henry IV's success as a ruler.[14] What Greengrass defines as a 'struggle for stability' after the religious wars has been further explored here as a quest for legitimacy covering Henry's entire reign. Only by being accepted throughout the country as the legitimate king of France could Henry restore peace to the body politic. Since Henry's kingship was disputed in 1589, he pursued legitimacy through political strategies, ceremonial acts, and demonstrative displays of greatness to gain political acceptance throughout the realm. Political events like his abjuration, his absolution by Clement VIII, his coronation at Chartres, and his entry into Paris and other Catholic League towns forged a new image of kingship whose legitimacy had been won in the hearts and minds of the people. Gradually success bred success as opponents lost their patrons and turned to the king instead.[15] The new image of Henry as the clement conqueror was then generated throughout French society. Henry's strength resided in part in his knowledge of personalities and his ability to turn former enemies into clients. As his legitimacy became sound, stability returned, and Henry's power and authority achieved their greatest potential to create change.[16] Stronger monarchy was the result, emerging out of the chaos of the Wars of Religion.[17] Henry's pursuit of legitimacy laid the

[12] Robert Descimon, 'L'Echevinage Parisien sous Henri IV (1594–1609)', in *La ville la bourgeoisie et la genèse de l'etat moderne (XIIe–XVIIIe siècles* (Paris: Centre Nationale de la Recherche Scientifique), 113–50.

[13] Fradenburg, *City, Marriage, Tournament*; Alex Weingrod, 'Patronage and Power', in *Patrons and Clients in Mediterranean Societies*, ed. Ernest Gellner and John Waterbury (London: Gerald Duckworth and Co., 1977), 41, 47.

[14] Mark Greengrass, *France in the Age of Henri IV The Struggle for Stability* (London: Longman, 1984, 1995). See also, Richard Bonney, 'Was there a Bourbon style of government?', in *From Valois to Bourbon, Dynasty, State and Society in Early Modern France*, ed. Keith Cameron (Exeter: University of Exeter, 1989), 160–77.

[15] Barry Barnes, *The Nature of Power* (Chicago: University of Illinois Press, 1988), 123.   [16] Ibid.

[17] Mack P. Holt, *The French Wars of Religion, 1562–1629* (Cambridge: Cambridge University Press, 1995), 210–11.

groundwork for that change as he refashioned the image and practice of kingship in heralding the transition from Valois to Bourbon rule. His relationship with the towns reveals a key aspect of this political transformation. He formulated a more authoritative response to municipal affairs for reasons of political expediency. As a result he brought the towns closer in line with the ideals of the French state. The beginnings of absolutism can be seen in Henry's pursuit of political legitimacy as he won his people's consent to rule and rebuild France. Reforging a solid alliance between ruler and ruled, Henry reopened the dialogue between the Crown and the towns, enhancing his authority and the power of the Crown in the process.

Bibliography

MANUSCRIPT SOURCES
Paris
Archives Nationales

90, AP 32 'Documents relatifs aux règnes de Henri IV et Louis XIII'
120, AP 1–50, 'Papiers de Sully'
1 'Règlements fait au Conseil du roi (1598–1610)'
2 'Etats-généraux de l'Epargne'
3 12 *Dons du Roi*
4 38–43 – 'Ponts et chaussées'
E 1a–26a,'Papiers des Conseils du Roi'
KK 1013, 'Recueil de lettres et d'arrêts relatifs à la ville de Paris'
KK 1212, 'Information sur la Ligue à Limoges'
V6 1221, 'Conseil privé, Minutes de résultat (1579–1602),'

Bibliothèque Nationale

Fonds français:
   15483, 'Recueil de plans de villes'
   15575–80, 'Lettres de Henri IV'
   15890–912 'Papiers de Bellièvre'
   16660–2, 'Recueil de pièces concernant Dauphiné, Lyonnais et d'Auvergne'
   16833, 'Lettres originaux de Henri IV'
   20427–82, 'Recueil de lettres . . . à l'histoire de France'
   23194–8, 'Recueil de pièces relatives aux affaires intérieures de la France, règne de Henri
      IV'
   23295–6, 'Histoire de la ligue'
Pièces Originales, 56, 886, 1098, 1762, 2284
Cabinet d'Hozier, 3, 218, 134, 497
Dossiers bleus 48, 260, 408
Miscellaneous documents: 2149, 2196, 2945, 3411, 3542, 3852, 3946, 3960, 4037, 4102,
   4719,5010, 5078, 8419, 13071, 18158, 20649, 21722, 28117, 32869
Fonds nouvelles acquisitions français:
   3375–429, 3432–77, 22225–33, 'Papiers relatifs à l'histoire du Tiers – Etat provenant

d'Augustin Thierry'
7237, 'Entrées des rois et reines dans les villes du royaume'
7284, 'Privilèges accordés à diverses villes'
22290–307, 'Mélanges historique'
Collection Picardie:
  58, 'Lettres patentes d'Henri IV relative à la Picardie'
  90, 'Extraits relatifs à Amiens'
  91, 'Notes et documents sur Abbeville'
  96, 'Extraits des déliberations d'Amiens'
  112 bis, 'Extraits pour l'histoire d'Amiens'
Collection Dupuy:
  62, 'Délibérations de plusieurs villes'
  89, 'Discours de voyage d'Henri IV'

Bibliothèque de l'Arsenal

4031 'Mémoires historiques de la ville de Mantes'
4094 'Mémoire concernant la ville de Mantes par J. de Chèvremont'

Abbeville
Archives Municipales (housed in *Hôtel de Ville*)

MSS 310
MSS 20.088, 'Manuscrit de Waignart'

Agen
Archives Municipales (housed in Archives Départementales du Lot et Garonne)

AA18–19, 'Lettres patentes des rois'
CC110, 131 'Comptes'
CC123–4, 'Minutes et lettres des députés à la cour pour la ville'

Albi
Archives Municipales (housed in Archives Départementales du Tarn)

AA2, 'Constitutifs et politiques de la commune'
BB28–29, 'Délibérations de la ville, 1589–1610'

Amiens
Archives Départementales de la Somme

1B12–14, 1B72, 1B1720, 1B2078, 'Registres aux chartes'
E28825, 29713, 30576, 30644, 'Etudes des Notaires'

Bibliography

Archives Municipales (housed in Bibliothèque Municipale)

AA19, 'Chartes, privilèges, statuts, lettres'
AA120–21, 'Documents de la Ligue'
BB54–57, 'Délibérations de la ville, 1594–1610'
CC 807–818, 'Comptabilité'
EE 330, 'Artillerie et munitions'
FF 485–665, 'Inventaires après déces'
FF1249–52, 'Tutelles'

Musée de Picardie

CB6 Archives de la Société des Antiquaires de la Picardie, 'Manuscrits originaux des échevins d'Amiens'

Blois
Archives Municipales (housed in *Hôtel de Ville*)

BB13–17, 'Délibérations de la ville, 1588–1611'

Châlons-sur-Marne
Archives Municipales (housed in Archives Départementales de la Marne)

E Supplement 4758, 'Lettres missives'
E Supplement 4789–92 'Délibérations de la ville'

Dijon
Archives Municipales (housed in *Hôtel de Ville*)

B73–9, 'Voyages en cour'
B103 'Repas'
B232–47, 'Déliberations de la ville, 1594–1610'
Miscellaneous documents:
   B13,14, 15, 20, 30, 31

Foix
Archives Municipales (housed in Archives Départementales de l'Ariège)

1E Supplement Foix BB6, 'Délibérations de la ville, 1582–1605'
1E Supplement Foix CC102, 'Comptes'

La Rochelle
Archives Municipales (housed in Bibliothèque Municipale)

MS 40, 'Manuscrit de Jean Merichon 'Livre de la Poterne'
MS 82, 'Recueil des privilèges'

Bibliography

MS 90, 'Statuts de Corps de Ville'
MS 95, 'Manuscrit de Pierre Mervault'
MS 153, 'Annales de La Rochelle'
MS 164, 'Recueil de pièces concernant les catholiques rochelais à la fin du XVIe siècle'

Limoges
Archives Municipales (housed in Bibliothèque Municipale)

BB2 'Registres Consulaires 1592–1662'

Lyons
Archives Municipales (housed in Archives Municipales, avenue Adolphe Max)

AA21, 24, 45, 54, 68, 77, 78, 86, 112, 140, 'Chartes, privilèges, statuts, lettres'
BB132–46, 'Délibérations de la Ville 1595–1610'
CC1454, 1486, 1550, 1468, 'Comptes'

Bibliothèque Municipale de Lyons
MS 1477, 'Livre de partie des Harangues prononcées par M. Balthasar de Villars'

Mantes-la-jolie
Archives Municipales (housed in Bibliothèque Municipale)

BB22, 'Délibérations de la ville 1592–1606'
CC51–58, 'Comptes'

Montauban
Archives Municipales (housed in Archives Départementales du Tarn et Garonne)

AA5, 'Livre Noir du consulat'
AA16–19, 'Privilèges'
1BB28–37, 'Délibérations de la ville, 1589–1610'
6BB2 (1508–1600) 'Elections'
CC25, 'Comptes'

Nantes
Archives Municipales (housed in Archives Municipales)

AA6–7, 'Chartes, privilèges, lettres'
BB21–27, 'Délibérations de la ville 1588–1610'

Narbonne
Archives Communales (housed in Bibliothèque Municipale)

BB5–7, 'Délibérations 1585–1610'

Bibliography

Nîmes
Archives Municipales (housed in Archives Départementales du Gard)

AA1, 'Lettres des rois'
AA3, 'Ordonnances des commissaires'
DD4, 'Lettres de cachet des rois'
LL13–17, 'Délibérations de la ville 1586–1612'

Poitiers
Archives Communales (housed in Bibliothèque Municipale)

Registers 59–64 'Registres des délibérations 1600–1609'
Casiers 23, 51, 37, 38, 'Lettres, statuts'
K33–34, 'Comptes'

Rennes
Archives Municipales (housed in Bibliothèque Municipale)

Laisse 9, 32, 'Lettres'
Registers 471–9, 'Délibérations de la ville 1591–1610'

Rouen
Archives Municipales (housed in Bibliothèque Municipale)

A20, 'Elections'
A21, 'Délibérations, 1591–1602'

Saint-Quentin
Archives Municipales (housed in *Hôtel de Ville*)

F6, 'Délibérations, 1589–95'
Laisse 151, 'Lettres Diverses'
A22, 'Délibérations, 1603–1615'

Toulouse
Archives Municipales (housed in Bibliothèque Municipale)

AA16–21, 'Chartes, privilèges, statuts, lettres'
AA67, 'Livre des serments'
AA69, 'Noblesse Capitulaire'
AA77, 'Titres intéressants'
BB16–23, 'Délibérations de la ville 1587–1610'
BB182, 'Lettres envoyées par les Capitouls'
BB188, 'Elections Capitulaires'
BB194, 'Liste alphabétiques des Capitouls'
BB200, 'Listes pour la composition des conseils'

Bibliography

BB225, 'Enreigistrement par les Capitouls de lettres de maîtres concédées par le roi et la reine'

BB276–277, 'Annales Manuscrits de la ville de Toulouse' Livre 4 (1587–1601), Livre 5 (1602–1617)

CC982, 'Exemptions des Capitouls de la Taille'

CC1520, 'Debts de la ville'

CC185, 'Impôts'

GG 1–10, 26, 28, 29, 30, 85, 86, 92, 195–6, 198, 222, 224, 225, 'Registres des mariages, et batêmes'

Archives Départémentales de l'Haute Garonne

Miscellaneous Documents:
C2292, 3E11787, 3E11877, 3E11807

Tours
Archives Municipales (housed in Hôtel de Ville)

AA2, 4, 5, 10, 'Chartes, privilèges, statuts, lettres'

BB3, 'Elections'

BB34–6, 'Délibérations de la ville 1584–1633'

United States
Archives of the Church of Jesus Christ of the Latter Day Saints, (accessed at the Virginia Beach, Virginia Reading Room)

1348781, 1552846, 1552621, 1552622, 1552723, 1551726, 1551729, 1552846, 1569163, 1874025, 1873668, 'Registres paroissiaux, Amiens'

PRINTED SOURCES

Aubigne, Agrippa d', *Histoire Universelle*, Geneva, Droz, 1981, 3 vols.

Barthélemy, Edouard de, 'Lettres inédites du maire et des échevins de la ville de Troyes aux habitants de Châlons-sur-Marne à l'occasion de la mort de Henri III', *Mémoires de la Société d'Agriculture des Sciences, Arts et Belles Lettres du département de l'Aube*, 34 (1870), 103.

Baux, Jules, ed., *Mémoires historiques de la ville de Bourg, Extraits des registres municipaux de l'Hôtel-de-Ville de 1536–1789*, Bourg-en-Bress, Milliet-Bottier, 1868–88, 5 vols.

Benoist de la Grandière, L., *Abrège Chronologique et Historique de la Mairie de Tours*, Tours: Péricat, 1908.

Bernard, Ponson, 'Journal de Ponson Bernard', ed. F. Rolle, *Revue du Lyonnais*, 30 (1865), 440–8.

Bonaventure de Saint-Amable, *Histoire de Saint-Martial, apôtre des Gaules, et Notamment de l'Aquitaine et du Limousin, ecclèsiastique ou civils, des saints et hommes illustrés et autres*

Bibliography

choses depuis Saint-Martial jusques à nous, Limoges: Anthoine Voisin, 1685, 3 vols.

Breunot, Gabriel, *Journal de Gabriel Breunot, conseiller au Parlement de Dijon*, ed. Joseph Garnier: Dijon, Rabutot, 1864.

'Brief Traité des Misères de la Ville de Paris', *Archives curieurses de l'histoire de France depuis Louis XI jusqu'à Louis XVIII*, ed. M. L. Cimber and F. Danjou, Paris: Members de L'Institute Historique, 1837, 271–85.

Carel Pierre, ed. *Histoire de Caen sous Charles IX, Henri III, et Henri IV, documents inédites*, Paris: Champion, 1887.

Coderis, Hippolyte, ed., *Notices et extraits des documents manuscrits conservés dans les dépôts de Paris relatit à l'histoire de la Picardie*, Paris: Durand, 1858.

Cuzacq, R. and Detchepare, J., eds., *Bayonne sous l'ancien régime, lettres missives des rois et reines de France à la ville de Bayonne*, Bayonne: J. Glize, 1934, 3 vols.

Dare, Nicholas, ed., 'Collection de Documents inédits relatifs à la Ville de Troyes et à la Champagne méridionale', *Société Acadèmique de l'Aube*, 3 (1886), 5–162.

Drouot, Henri, ed., 'Relation inédité de la reddition de la ville et du château de Dijon à Henri IV', *Mémoires de la Société Bourguignonne de Géographie et d'Histoire*, 27 (1911), 203–51.

DuBois, A., *La Ligue: Documents relatifs à la Picardie d'après les registres de l'échevinage d'Amiens*, Amiens, Yvert, 1859.

Dumont, Francois, Bertheau, Solange, and Kustner, Elisabeth, eds., *Inventaire des Arrêts du Conseil Privé Règne de Henri III et Henri IV*, Paris: Centre Nationale de la Recherche Scientifique, 1971–78, 4 vols.

Duplessis-Mornay, Philippe, *Mémoires et Correspondance pour servir à l'histoire de la réformation et des guerres civiles et religieuses en France*, Paris: Chez-Treuttel et Wurtz, 1824–5, 12 vols.

Dupré, Alexandre, *Analyse des procès verbaux des assemblées de la ville de Blois du 17 janvier 1566 au 28 decembre 1611*, Blois: n.p., 1842, 2 vols.

DuVair, Guillaume, *Lettres inédites de Guillaume du Vair* ed. Philippe Tamizey de Larroque, Paris: Auguste Aubry, 1873.

Espinas, G., *Recueil des documents relatifs à l'histoire municipale en France, des origines à la révolution*, Artois: Espinas, 1934–43, 3 vols.

Félix, J. ed., *Entrée à Rouen de Roi Henri IV en 1596*, Rouen: Imprimerie de l'Esperance Cagniard, 1887.

Fontanon, Antoine, ed., *Les edits et ordonnances des rois de France dépuis Saint Louis jusques à présent avec les vérifications, modifications, et déclarations sur icelles*, Paris: J. du Puys, 1611, 4 vols.

Garnier, Joseph, ed., *Correspondance de la Mairie de Dijon, extraite des Archives de Cette Ville*, Dijon: Rabutot, 1870. 3 vols.

Godefroy, Théodore, *Le Cérémonial François contenant les Cérémonies Observées en France aux sacres et couronnements du roys et reynes de quelques anciens ducs de Normandie, Aquitaine, et de Bretagne*, Paris: S. Cramoisy, 1649.

Guillaudeau, Joseph, *Diaire de Joseph Guillaudeau, sieur de Beaupreau (1584–1643)*, ed. Louis Meschinet de Richemond: La Rochelle, Noël Texier et Fils, 1908.

Henry IV, 'Cinq lettres de Henri IV sur la fin de la Ligue en Bourgogne (1594–1595)', *Mémoires de l'Académie de Dijon* (1924), section 2, 257–68.

Copie de deux lettres du roy l'une envoyée à messieurs les Maire, échevins, et habitans de la ville de Dijon, l'autre au sieur de Franchèse, commandant au Chasteau de ladite ville, Lyon: Iullieron and Ancelin, 1594.

Correspondance Politique et Militaire de Henri le Grand, avec J. Roussat, Marie de Langres, ed. M. Guyot de Saint Michel, Paris: Mme le duke de Berry, 1816.

'Douze lettres inédites de Henri IV concernant les Affaires de Marseille', ed. Gustave Fagniez, *Revue Henri IV*, 3 (1909), 1–16.

Henri IV en Gascogne, sa correspondance avec Denis de Mauléon de Savaillan pièces inédites, ed. B. A. Pocquet du Haut-Jussé, Auch: Cocharaux, 1931.

Henri IV peint par lui-même dans deux discours de ce Prince: L'un à l'assemblée de Rouen en 1596, l'autre aux Députés de la ville de Beauvais en 1594, Paris: Imprimerie de Monsieur sous la direction de P. T. Didot, 1787.

'Lettres de Henri IV aux Archives Municipales de Bergerac', ed. André Jouanel, *Bulletin de la Société Historique et archéologique de Périgord*, 81 (1954), 53–6.

Lettres inédites de Henri IV, ed. Prince Augustin Galitzin, Paris: Techener, 1860.

Lettres inédites de Henri IV à M. de Pailhès, gouverneur du comté de Foix, et aux consuls de la ville de Foix, 1576–1602, Paris: Champion, 1886.

Lettres inédites du Roi Henri IV au Chancelier de Bellièvre du 8 fevrier 1581 au 23 septembre 1601, ed. E. Halphern, Paris: Chez Auguste Abbey, 1872.

'Lettres Missives de Henri IV Conservées dans les Archives Municipales de la Ville de Troyes', ed. T. Boutiot, *Mémoires de la Société d'Agriculture, des Sciences Arts et Belles-Lettres du département de l'Aube*, 21 (1857), 285–363.

Quelques lettres inédites relatives à la Touraine, ed. Prince A. Galitzin, Tours: Société des Bibliophiles de Touraine, 1860.

Recueil des lettres missives de Henri IV, ed. J. Berger de Xivrey and J. Guadet, Paris: Imprimerie Nationale, 1843–56, 9 vols.

'Une lettre inédite de Henri IV aux habitants d'Orléans, le 6 janvier 1598', ed. J. Soyer, *Bulletin de la Société archèologique et historique de l'Orléanais*, 19 (1921), 198–9.

Inventaire-sommaire des Archives communales antérieures à 1790, Ville d'Agen, ed. M. M. Bosvieux and G. Tholin, Paris: Paul Dupont, 1884.

Inventaire-sommaire des Archives communales antérieures à 1790, Ville d'Amiens, ed. Georges Durand, Amiens: Imprimerie Piteux Frères, 1897.

Inventaire-sommaire des Archives communales antérieures à 1790, Ville de Beauvais, ed. Renaud Rose, Beauvais: Imprimerie Centrale Admistrative, 1887.

Inventaire-sommaire des Archives communales antérieures à 1790, Ville de Clermont-Ferrand, ed. Teilhard de Chardier, Clermont-Ferrand: Imprimerie et Lithographie, 1902.

Inventaire-sommaire des Archives communales antérieures à 1790, Ville de Dijon, ed. M. De Gouvenais, Paris: Paul Dupont, 1867.

Inventaire-sommaire des Archives communales de Langres antérieures à 1790, Ville de Troyes, ed. Julien de la Boullaye, Troyes: Finé, 1882.

Inventaire-sommaire des Archives communales antérieures à 1790, Ville d'Orléans, ed. M. Vevrier du Maraud, Orléans: Imprimerie E. Chenu, 1866.

Inventaire-sommaire des Archives communales antérieures à 1790, Ville de Narbonne, ed. Germain Mouynès, Narbonne: Gaillard, 1877.

Inventaire-sommaire des Archives communales antérieures à 1790, Ville de Nîmes, ed. Bessot de Lamoht: Avignon, Seguin Frères.

Bibliography

La Faille, Germain de, *Annales de la Ville de Toulouse depuis la réunion de la comté de Toulouse à la couronne de 1271 à 1514*, Toulouse: Colomiez, 1687.

Traité de la Noblesse des Capitouls de Toulouse avec des additions et remarques de l'auteur sur ce traité, Toulouse: Colomiez, 1707.

Lemaire, Emmanuel, ed., *Procès vervaux des séances de la chambre du conseil des maires, échevins, et jurés de Saint-Quentin*, Saint Quentin: Société Académique de Saint-Quentin, 1912.

Leroux, Alfred, ed. *Documents Limousins des Archives de Bordeaux et autres villes*, Tulle: Corrézien Républicain, 1912.

Lesdigières, Duc de, *Actes et Correspondance de Connetable de Lesdigières*, ed. Cte Douglas and J. Roman, Grenoble: Allier, 1878, 2 vols.

L'Estoile, Pierre de, *Mémoires-Journaux de Pierre de L'Estoile*, ed. P. Bonnefon, Paris: Alphonse Lemerre, 1875–96, 12 vols.

The Paris of Henry of Navarre as seen by Pierre de l'Estoile, Selections from his Mémoires-Journaux, trans. and ed. Nancy Lyman Roelker, Cambridge, Massachusetts: Harvard University Press, 1958.

Mallet, Ernest, ed., *Registres des délibérations municipales de la Ville de Pontoise (1608–1683), règne d'Henri IV et Louis XIII*, Pontoise: Bureaux de la Société Historique, 1899.

Matthieu, Pierre, *L'Entrée de très grand Prince Henri IIII en sa bonne ville de Lyon*, Lyon, s.d.

Merlin, Jacques, 'Diaire de Jacques Merlin ou Recueil des choses les plus mémorables qui se sont passés en ceste ville de La Rochelle', ed. Charles Dangibeaud, *Archives de la Saintonge et de L'Aunis*, 5 (1878), 63–380.

Nevers, Duc de, *Copie de certaines lettres escripts par M. le duc de Nevers, duke of Mantoue . . . .avec deux autres lettres de MM. les Maire et Echevins de la ville de Troyes à MM. de la ville de Reims pour les engager à ouvrir leur portes aux troupes royales*, n.p., 1594.

Les Mémoires de M. le duc de Nevers, Prince de Mantoue, ed. sieur de Gomberville, Paris: Jolly, 1665, 2 vols.

Pagès, J., *Manuscrits de Pagès, marchand d'Amiens écrits à la fin du 17e siècle et au commencement du 18e siècle sur Amiens*, Amiens: Douchetez, 1857, 5 vols.

Palma-Cayet, Pierre-Victoir, *Chronologie novenaire contenant l'histoire de la guerre sous le règne du très chrèstien roy de France et de Navarre Henry IIII*, Paris: Richer, 1603, 3 vols.

Patte, Jehan, *Journal Historique de Jehan Patte, Bourgeois d'Amiens (1597–1617)*, ed. J. Garnier, Amiens: Lemer Ainé, 1863.

Pericaud, Antoine, ed., *Notes et documents pour servir à l'histoire de Lyon sous le règne d' Henri IV (1594–1610)*, Lyon: Mougin-Rusand, 1845.

Pussot, Jehan, 'Journalier ou Mémoires de Jehan Pussot, Notices biographique et bibliographique', ed. Edouard Henry, *Travaux de l'Académie Impériale de Reims*, 23,(1855–56), 106–79.

'Mémoires ou Journalier de Jean Pussot', ed. Edouard Henry, *Travaux de L'Académie Impériale de Reims*, 25 (1856–7), 1–263.

Recueil d'Actes de Chroniques et de Documents Historiques ou inédites 1: Privilèges de la Ville de Nantes, Nantes: Société des Bibliophiles Breton et de l'Histoire de Bretagne, 1883.

Recueil des chartes, lettres-patentes, édits, declarations, réglements et arrêts donne par nos rois depuis 1271 jusque et compris le règne de Louis XV, le Bien-Aimé, par lequels les bourgeois et habitants de Lyon, eux et leur posterité one été maintenues dans leurs anciennes coutumes,

Bibliography

libertés, franchises, privilèges, et immunités, Lyon, Imprimerie d'Ainé de la Roche, 1771.

Recueil général des anciennes lois françaises depuis l'an 420 jusqu'à la Révolution de 1789, ed. François A. Isambert, Paris: 1822–33, 29 vols.

Registres consulaires de la ville de Limoges, Second Registre (1592–1662), ed. Louis Guibert, Limoges: Chapoulaud Frères,1884, 3 vols.

Registres des délibérations du Bureau de la Ville de Paris, ed. Paul Guérin, Francois Bonnardot, and Louis Le Grand, Paris: Imprimerie Nationale, 1902–1921, vols. 9–15.

Rousseau, Jean-Jacques, *The Social Contract*. ed. Charles Frankel, New York: Hafner Publishing Company, 1947.

Sully, duke of, 'Lettres inédites de Sully', ed. David Buisseret and Bernard Barbiche, *Annuaire-Bulletin de la Société de l'Histoire de France* (1974–75), 81–117.

Mémoires des Sages et Royales Oeconomies d' Estat Domestiques, Politiques, et Militaires de Henry Le Grand, ed. M. Michaud and J. Poujoulat, Paris: Didot-Frères, 1837, vols. 2 and 3.

The Memoires of the duke of Sully Prime-Minister to Henry the Great, trans. C. Lennox, Philadelphia: E. Earle, 1817, 5 vols.

Les Oeconomies Royales de Sully, ed. David Buisseret and Bernard Barbiche, Paris: Klincksieck, 1970–88, 2 vols.

Thou, Jacques-Auguste de, *Histoire universelle depuis 1543 jusqu'en 1607*, Basle: Brandmuller, 1742, 12 vols.

Valois, Noël, *Inventaire des arrêts du Conseil d'Etat, régne de Henri IV*, Paris: Imprimerie Nationale, 1886–93, 2 vols.

SECONDARY SOURCES

Abord, Hippolyte, *Histoire de la Réforme et de la Ligue dans la Ville d'Autun*, Paris: Dumoulin, 1855–86, 3 vols.

Aldeguier, Auguste d', *Histoire de la ville de Toulouse depuis la conquête des Romains jusqu'à nos jours*, Toulouse: Degalier and J. B. Paya, 1830–5, 4 vols.

Amalric, Jean-Pierre, 'L'épreuve de force entre Montauban et le pouvoir royal vue par la diplomatie espagnole', *Bulletin de la Société de Tarn-et-Garonne*, 108 (1983), 25–40.

Amantan, Ferdinand, 'Prècis Historique et Chronologique sur l'Établissement de la Commune et des Vîcomtes-Mayeurs de Dijon', *Mémoires de la commission des antiquités du département de la Côte-D'Or*, 8 (1873), 61–74.

Anglo, Sydney, *Spectacle, Pageantry, and Early Tudor Policy*, Oxford: Clarendon Press, 1969.

Apaché, Roger, 'Images du siège d'Amiens de 1597 ou l'émphemère célébrité du malheur', *Terre Picardie*, 9 (1985), 32–40.

Appleby, Andrew B., 'Grain Prices and Subsistence Crises in England and France, 1590–1740', *The Journal of Economic History*, 39 (1979), 865–87.

Apostolides Jean-Marie, *Le Roi-Machine, Spectacle et Politique au Temps de Louis XIV*, Paris: Editions de Minuit, 1981.

Arcère, Louis-Etienne, *Histoire de la Ville de La Rochelle et du Pays d'Aulnis*, La Rochelle, René-Jacob Desbordes, 1757; Marseille: Laffitte Reprints, 1975, 2 vols.

Bibliography

Archer, Ian, *The Pursuit of Stability, Social Relations in Elizabethan London*, Cambridge: Cambridge University Press, 1991.

Arendt, Hannah, *On Violence*, London: Allen Lane, 1970.

Ascoli, Peter, 'French Provincial Cities and the Catholic League', *Occasional Papers of the American Society for Reformation Research*, 1 (1977), 15–37.

'The Sixteen and the Paris League, 1585–1591', Ph.D. diss., University of California, Berkeley, 1971.

Auber, L'Abbé, *Histoire de la Cathédrale de Poitiers*, Paris: Derache, 1899, 2 vols.

Babeau, Albert, *Henri IV à Troyes*, Troyes: Dufour-Bouquot, 1879.

La Ville sous l'ancien régime, Paris: Didier, 1880.

Babelon, Jean-Pierre, *Henri IV*, Paris: Fayard, 1982.

Baird, Henry Martin, *History of the Rise of the Huguenots of France*, New York: Scribner, 1879, 2 vols.

The Huguenots and Henry of Navarre, New York: Scribner: 1886, 2 vols.

Baratier, Edouard, ed., *Histoire de Marseille*, Toulouse: Privat, 1973.

Barbiche, Bernard, 'Henri IV, Sully et la première monarchie administrative', *Proceedings of the Western Society for French History*, 17 (1990), 10–23.

Sully, Paris: Michel, 1978.

Barbiche, Bernard and David Buisseret, 'Sully et la surintendance des finances', *Bibliothèque de l'Ecole des Chartes*, 123 (1965), 538–43.

Barbier, Alfred, *Pierre d'Amours, Commissaire des Finances à Poitiers sous Henri IV (1601)*, Poitiers: Imprimerie générale de l'Ouest, 1880.

Barnavi, Elie, 'Fidéles et partisans dans la Ligue parisienne (1585–1594)', *Hommage à Roland Mousnier clientèles et fidélités en Europe à l'époque moderne*, ed. Yves Durand, Paris: Presses universitaires de France, 1981, 139–52.

Le parti de Dieu. Etude sociale et politique des chefs de la Ligue parisienne, 1585–1594, Louvain: Nauwelaerts, 1980.

Barnes, Barry, *The Nature of Power*, Chicago: University of Illinois Press, 1988.

Barnes, Sandra T., *Patrons and Power Creating a Political Community in Metropolitan Lagos*, Bloomington: Indiana University Press, 1986.

Barthélemey, Edouard, de, *Histoire de la ville de Châlons-sur-Marne et de ses Institutions depuis son origine jusqu'en 1848*, Châlons-sur-Marne: E. Le Roy, 1883.

Barthes, Roland, *Mythologies*, trans. Annette Lavers, New York: Hill and Wang, 1972.

Baudouin-Lalondre, M, *Le Maréchal Claude de la Chastre*, Bourges: Sire, 1895.

Baumgartner, Frederic J, *France in the sixteenth century*, New York: St Martin's Press, 1995.

Radical Reactionaries; the Political Thought of the French Catholic League, Geneva: Droz, 1976.

Bayard, François, 'La Méthode Sully en Matière de Finances: Les Traités de Rachats' xviie siècle, 44 (1992), 53–76.

L'économie française aux XVIe, XVIIe et XVIIIe siècles, Gap: Ophrys, 1991.

Le Monde des financiers au xviie siècle, Paris: Flammarion, 1988.

Beik, William, *Absolutism and Society in Seventeenth-Century France, State Power and Provincial Aristocracy in Languedoc*, Cambridge: Cambridge University Press, 1985.

'The culture of protest in seventeenth-century France', *Social History*, (1990), 1–23.

'The Parlement of Toulouse and the Fronde', in *Society and Institutions in Early Modern*

Bibliography

France, ed. Mack P. Holt, Athens: University of Georgia Press, 1991, 132–52.

Urban Protest in Seventeenth-Century France, The Culture of Retribution, New York: Cambridge University Press, 1997.

Bendix, Reinhard, *Kings or People: Power and the Mandate to Rule*, Berkeley: University of California Press, 1978.

Benedict, Philip, 'Catholics and Huguenots in Sixteenth-Century Rouen: The Demographic Effects of the Religious Wars', *French Historical Studies*, 9 (1975), 209–34.

ed., *Cities and Social Change in Early Modern France*, London: Unwin Hyman, 1989.

'French Cities from the Sixteenth Century to the Revolution: An Overview', in *Cities and Social Change in Early Modern France*, ed. Philip Benedict, London Unwin Hyman,1989, 7–68.

The Huguenot Population of France, 1600–1685: The Demographic Fate and Customs of a Religious Minority, Transacations of the American Philosophical Society, vol. 81, Philadelphia: The American Philosophical Society, 1990.

Rouen during the Wars of Religion, Cambridge: Cambridge University Press, 1981.

Benedictow, O. J., 'Morbidity in Historical Plague Epidemics', *Population Studies*, 41 (1987), 401–31.

Bercé, Yves-Marie, *The Birth of Absolutism A History of France, 1598–1661*, trans. Richard Res, New York: St Martin's Press, 1992.

Histoire des Croquants, Paris: Editions du Seuil, 1986.

'Limoges au début du xviie siècle', *Transactions du colloque pluridisciplinaires: Le Limousin au XVIIe siècle, 9–10 Octobre, 1976*, Limoges: La Société Pluridisciplinaires de Limoges, 1976, 131–8.

Revolt and revolution in Early Modern Europe, An Essay on the History of Political Violence, trans. Joseph Bergin, New York: Saint Martin's Press, 1987.

Bergin, Joseph, *Cardinal Richelieu Power and the Pursuit of Wealth*, New Haven: Yale University Press, 1985.

'Henri IV and the Problem of the French Episcopate', in *From Valois to Bourbon, Dynasty, State, and Society in Early Modern France*, ed. Keith Cameron, Exeter: Exeter University Press, 1989, 127–443.

Bertucat, Charles, *La Juridiction Municipale de Dijon*, Dijon, J. Nouvry, 1911.

Bimbenet, Eugene, *Histoire de la Ville d'Orléans*, Orléans: Herluison, 1881, 2 vols.

Bloch, Jean-Richard, *L'Anoblissement en France au temps de François 1er, Essai d'une définition de la condition juridique et social de la noblesse au début du XVIe siècle*, Paris: Félix Alca, 1934.

Bohstedt, John, *Riots and Community Politics in England and Wales 1790–1810*, Cambridge, Massachusetts: Harvard University Press, 1983.

Boissevain, Jeremy, *Friends of Friends Networks, Manipulators and Coalitions*, Oxford: Basil Blackwell, 1974.

Boissonnade, Paul, *Les Voies de communication en Poitou sous le règne de Henri IV et l'oeuvre du gouvernement royal*, La Flèche: E. Besnier, 1909.

Bohanan, Donna, *Old and New Nobility in Aix-en-Provence, 1600–1695: Portrait of an Urban Elite*, Baton Rouge, Louisiana: University of Louisiana Press, 1992.

Bon, Henri, *Essai historique sur les Epidémies en Bourgogne depuis l'établissement des Bourgondes en Gaule jusqu'à la Révolution*, Dijon: Paul Berthier, n.d.

Bibliography

Bonnardot, François, 'Essai historique sur le régime municipal à Orléans', *Mémoires de la Société Archèologique et Historique de l'Orléanais*, 18 (1884), 133–59.

Bonney, Richard, 'Absolutism: What's in a Name?', *French History*, 1, (1987), 93–117.

'The Failure of French Revenue Farms, 1600–60', *Economic History Review*, 2nd series, 32 (1979), 11–32.

The King's Debts, Finance and Politics in France, 1589–1661, Oxford: Clarendon Press, 1981.

'Was there a Bourbon Style of Government?' in *From Valois to Bourbon, Dynasty, State, and Society in Early Modern France*, ed. Keith Cameron, Exeter: Exeter University Press, 160–77.

Bordes, Maurice, *L'administration provincial et municipale en France au XVIIIe siècle*, Paris: Société d'Edition d'Enseignement Supérieur, 1972.

Bosher, J. F., *French Finances, 1770–1795, From Business to Bureaucracy*, Cambridge: Cambridge University Press, 1970.

Boulding, Kenneth, *Three Faces of Power*, Newbury Park, California: Sage Publications, 1989.

Bourçier, François, 'Le régime municipal à Dijon sous Henri IV', *Revue d'Histoire Moderne*, 8 (1935), 85–117.

Bourquin, Laurent, 'Pratiques politiques et image de la noblesse ligueuse: L'exemple d'Antoine de Saint-Paul', *Histoire, economie, et société* (1990), 185–95.

Boussinesq, G., 'Sommes promises aux chefs de la Ligue', *Revue Henri IV*, 1 (1905–6), 164.

Boutier, Jean, Dewerpe, Alain, Nordman, Daniel, *Un tour de France royal, le voyage de Charles IX (1565–1566)*, Paris: Aubier Montaigne, 1984.

Boutiot, Théophile, 'Décentralization administrative: Des maires, des échevinages et des conseils de ville depuis le XIIe siècle jusqu'en 1789', *Mémoires de la Société Academique*, 24 (1870), 5–29.

Histoire de la Ville de Troyes et de la Champagne Méridionale, Troyes: Dufey-Robert, 1873, 4 vols.

Querelles entre le Baillage et l'Echevinage de Troyes à l'occasion de la Preséance, Troyes: T. Boutiot, 1864.

Boutruch, Robert, *Bordeaux de 1453 à 1715*, Bordeaux: Fédération Historique du Sud-Ouest, 1966.

Breuil, A., *La Confrérié du Notre-Dame du Puy d'Amiens*, Amiens: Duval et Herment, 1854.

Braudel, Fernand, *Civilization and Capitalism, 15th–18th Centuries 1: The Structures of Everyday Life, The Limits of the Possible*, trans. Sian Reynolds, New York: Harper and Row, 1981.

The Mediterranean and the Mediterranean World in the Age of Philip II, trans. Sian Reynolds, New York: Harper and Row, 1972, 2 vols.

Bréjon de Lavergnée, Jacques, 'Justice et Pouvoir municipal à Rennes aux XVIe et XVIIe siècles', *Bulletin et Mémoires de la Société Archèologique du Département D'Ile-et-Vilaine*, 86 (1984), 19–37.

Bremond, Alphonse, *Nobiliaire Toulousian, Inventaire Général des Titres Probants de Noblesse et de Dignités Nobiliaires*, Toulouse: Bonnal et Gibrac, 1863.

Briggs, Robin, *Early Modern France, 1560–1715*, Oxford: Oxford University Press, 1977.

Brunelle, Gayle, 'Kinship, Urban Alliances and the Meaning of *Etranger* in Sixteenth-

Bibliography

Century Toulouse', Unpublished paper given at the British Society for the Study of French History conference, Brighton, Sussex, England, April, 1996.

The New World Merchants of Rouen, 1559–1630, Kirksville, Missouri: Sixteenth Century Journal Publishers, 1991.

Brunet, Clovis, *Société des Antiquaires de Picardie, Bibliothèque Catalogue de Manuscrits*, Amiens, Yvert et Tellier, 1917.

Bryant Lawrence, *The King and the City in the Parisian Royal Entry Ceremony: Politics, Ritual, and Art in the Renaissance*, Geneva: Droz 1986.

'Parlementaire Political Theory in the Parisian Royal Entry Ceremony', *The Sixteenth Century Journal*, 7 (1976), 15–24.

Burnett, Ron, *Cultures of Vision, Images, Media and the Imaginary*, Bloomington: Indiana University Press, 1995.

Buffelan, Jean-Paul, *La Noblesse des Capitouls de Toulouse*, St Gaudens: L'Adret, 1985.

Buisseret, David, 'The communication of France during the reconstruction of Henry IV', *Economic History Review*, 18, 2nd series (1965), 267–77.

Henry IV, London: Unwin Hyman, 1984.

'The Legend of Sully', *The Historical Journal*, 5 (1962), 181–8.

'A Stage in the Development of the Intendant; the Reign of Henri IV', *The Historical Journal*, 9 (1966), 27–38.

Sully and the Growth of Centralized Government in France, 1598–1610, London: Eyre and Spottiswoode, 1968.

Busquet, Raoul, *Histoire de Marseille*, Paris: Editions Laffont,1945.

Callot, S., *Jean Guiton, Maire de La Rochelle et le siège de 1628*, La Rochelle: Quartier Latin, 1967.

Calonne, Baron A., *Histoire de la Ville d'Amiens*, Amiens: Piteux Frères, 1900, 3 vols.

Cameron, Keith, ed., *From Valois to Bourbon, Dynasty, State, and Society in Early Modern France*, Exeter: University of Exeter Press, 1989.

Camille Jullian, *Histoire de Bordeaux depuis les origines jusqu'en 1895*, Bordeaux: Feret et Fils, 1985.

Canault, Jean, ed., *Vie du Maréchal Alphonse d'Ornano, Lieutenant-Général en Dauphiné, Languedoc, et Guyenne et Maire de Bordeaux (1548–1610)*, Aubenas-en-Vivarais: Lienhart, 1975.

Canet, L., *L'Aunis et la Saintonge, de la guerre de cent ans à Henri IV*, La Rochelle: F. Pijollet, 1933, 2 vols.

Carmichael, Ann, 'Diseases of the Renaissance and Early Modern Europe', *The Cambridge World History of Human Disease*, ed. Kenneth Kiple, Cambridge: Cambridge University Press, 1993, 279–86.

'Infection, Hidden Hunger, and History', *Journal of Interdisciplinary History*, 14 (1983), 249–64.

Carré, Henri, *Recherches sur l'administration municipale de Rennes au temps de Henri IV*, Paris: Quantin, 1888; Geneva: Megariotis, 1978.

Carroll, Stuart, 'The Guise Affinity and Popular Protest during the Wars of Religion', *French History*, 9 (1995), 125–52.

Carsalade du Pont, Henri de, *La municipalité parisienne à l'epoque d'Henri IV*, Paris: Editions Guyas, 1971.

Bibliography

Cassan, Michel, 'Laics, ligue et reforme Catholique à Limoges', *Histoire Economie et Société*, 10 (1991), 159–75.

'Les Lendemains des Guerres de Religion', *Croyance, Pouvoirs, et Société des Limousins aux Français*, ed. Michel Cassan, Le Louvanel: Les Editions Cles Monedières,1988, 266–82.

'Mobilitié social et conflits religieux: L'exemple limousin (1550–1630)', *La Dynamique Sociale dans l'Europe du Nord-Ouest (XVIe-XVIIe siècles,) Actes du colloque de l'association des historiens modernistes des universités*, 12 (1987), Paris: L'Association des Historiens Modernistes, 1987, 71–92.

Le temps des guerres de religion, Le cas du Limousin (vers 1530–vers 1630), Paris: Publisud, 1996.

Cavalié, L., *Figeac: Monographie Institutions Civils, Administratives et Religieuses avant la Révolution*, Figeac: Imprimerie Moderne, 1914.

Cazaux, Yves, *Henri IV ou la Grand Victoire*, Paris: Michel, 1977.

Chamberland, A., 'Le Conseil des finances en 1596 et 1597 et les économies royales', *Revue Henri IV*, 1 (1905–6), 21–32, 152–63, 250–60, 274–84.

Chartrou, Josephe, *Les entrées solonnelles et triomphales à la renaissance (1484–1551)*, Paris: Presses Universitaires de France, 1928.

Chalande, Jules, *Histoires monumentales de l'hôtel de ville de Toulouse, tirage à part de la révue historique de Toulouse*, Toulouse: Imprimerie St Cyprien, 1922–5, 2 vols.

Chandler, Tertius and Gerald Fox, *Three-thousand Years of Urban Growth*, New York: Academic Press, 1974.

Charléty, Sébastien. *Histoire de Lyon depuis les origines jusqu'à nos jours*, Lyon: A. Rey et Cie, 1903.

Charronet, M, *Guerres de religion et la société protestantes dans les Alpes*, Gap: Charronet, 1861.

Chartier, Roger, Guy Chaussinand-Nogaret, and Emmanuel Le Roy Ladurie, eds., *Histoire de la France Urbaine 3: La Ville Classique de la Renaissance aux Révolutions*, Paris: Éditions du Seuil, 1981.

Chaussonat, Jean-Baptiste, *Armorial Consulaire de la Ville de Lyon*, Lyon: Bibliothèque de Lyon, s.d.

Chédevilles, André, Jacques Le Goff and Jacques Rossiaud, eds., *Histoire de la France Urbaine 2: La Ville Médiévale des Carolingiens à la Renaissance*, Paris: Editions du Seuil, 1980.

Chénon, Emile, *Histoire générale du droit français public et privé des origines à 1815 1: Période gallo-Romaine, période franke, période féodale et coutumière*, Paris: Société Anonyme du Recueil Sueiy, 1926,

Chevalier, Bernard *Les bonnes villes de France du XIVe au XVIIe siècle*, Paris: Aubier Montaigne, 1982.

Tours ville royale, 1356–1520, origine et développement d'une capitale à la fin du môyen age, Paris: Nauwelaerts, 1975.

Church, William Farr, *Constitutional Thought in Sixteenth-Century France, A Study in the Evolution of Ideas*, Cambridge, Massachusetts: Harvard University Press, 1941.

Clamageron, J. J., *Histoire de L'Impôts en France*, Paris: Libraire de Guillaume et Cie, 1868, 3 vols.

Bibliography

Clark, Peter, ed., *The European Crisis of the 1590s, Essays in Comparative History*, London: George Allen and Unwin, 1985.

Cohen, Ronald and Judith Toland, eds., *State Formation and Political Legitimacy 7: Political Anthropology*, New Brunswick, New Jersey: Transactions Books, 1988.

Cohen, Ronald and John Middleman, *Comparative Political Systems, Studies in the Politics of Preindustrial Societies*, Austin: University of Texas Press, 1967.

Coissac, A., *Le Consulat à Limoges au XVIe siècle*, Limoges: F. Plagnes, 1937.

Collins, James B., *Fiscal Limits of Absolutism, Direct Taxation in Early Seventeenth-Century France*, Berkeley: University of California Press, 1988.

'Un problème toujours mal connu: Les finances d'Henri IV' *Henri IV, le Roi et la Reconstruction du Royaume*, Pau: L'Association Henri IV, 1989; J. and D. Editions, 1990, 145–64.

The State in Early Modern France, Cambridge: Cambridge University Press, 1995.

Connolly, William, ed., *Legitimacy and the State*, New York: New York University Press, 1984.

Corbier, Baron, de *La vicomté de Limoges et le comté du Périgord: Leur réunion à la couronne à l'avènement de Henri IV, étude historique sur le domaine royal en Limousin*, Limoges: Ducourtieux et Gout, 1913.

Cornette, Joël, *Histoire de France: L'affirmation de l'état absolu 1515–1652*, Paris: Hachette, 1993.

Coston, Baron de, *Histoire de Montélimar et des Familles Principales qui ont habités cette ville*, Paris: Editions du Palais Royale, 1973, 2 vols.

Cressey, David, 'Kinship and Kin Interaction in Early Modern England', *Past and Present*, 113 (1986), 38–69.

Crouzet, Denis, *Les guerriers de dieu, la violence au temps des troubles de religion vers 1525–vers 1610*, Paris: Champ Vallon, 1990, 2 vols.

Curtin, Philip, *Cross-Cultural Trade in World History*, Cambridge: Cambridge University Press, 1984.

Daire, Rév. Père, *Histoire de la Ville d'Amiens depuis son origine jusqu'à present*, Paris: Chez-Le Veuve de Laguette, 1757.

Daullé, Alfred, *La Réforme à Saint-Quentin et aux environs du 16e à la fin du 18e siècle*, Le Chateau: J. Roland, 1901.

Davis, Natalie, *Society and Culture in Early Modern France*, Stanford: Stanford University Press, 1975.

Descimon, Robert, 'L'échevinage parisien sous Henri IV (1594–1610). Autonomie urbaine, conflits politiques et exclusives sociales', in *La Ville, La Bourgeoisie et la Genèse de l'Etat Moderne (XIIe-XVIIIe siècle)*, Paris: Editions du Centre National de la Recherche Scientifique, 1988, 113–50.

'La ligue à Paris', *Annales, économies, sociétés, civilisations*, 37 (1982), 72–111.

'Milice bourgeoise et identité citadine à Paris au temps de la ligue', *Annales économies Sociétés Civilisations*, 48 (1993), 885–906.

Qui étaient les seize? Mythes et réalités de la ligue parisienne (1585–1594), Paris: Klincksieck, 1983).

Dessert, Daniel, *Argent, pouvoir et société au grand siècle*, Paris: Fayard, 1984.

Dewald, Jonathan, *The Formation of a Provincial Nobility: The Magistrates of the Parlement of*

Rouen, 14999–1610, Princeton: Princeton Unversity Press, 1980.

Deyon, Pierre, *Amiens, capitale provinciale, étude sur la société urbaine au 17e siècle*, Paris: Mouton, 1967.

Dickerman, Edmund, *Bellièvre and Villeroy: Power in France under Henry III et Henry IV*, Providence, Rhode Island: Brown University Press, 1971.

Diefendorf, Barbara, *Beneath the Cross, Catholics and Huguenots in Sixteenth-Century Paris*, New York: Oxford University Press, 1991.

'The Catholic League: Social Crisis or Apocalypse Now?', *French Historical Studies*, 15 (1987), 332–44.

Paris City Councilors in the Sixteenth-Century: The Politics of Patrimony, Princeton, New Jersey: Princeton University Press, 1983.

'Prologue to a Massacre: Popular Unrest in Paris: 1557–1572', *American Historical Review*, 90 (1985), 1067–91.

'Recent Literature on the Religious Conflicts in Sixteenth-Century France', *Religious Studies Review*, 10 (1984), 32–67.

Dognon, Paul, *Les institutions politiques et administratives du pays de Languedoc du XIIIe siècle aux guerres de religion*, Toulouse: Privat, 1895.

Doucet, Roger, *Finance Municipales et Crédit Public à Lyon au XVIe siècle*, Paris: Librairie des Sciences Politiques et Sociales, 1937.

'Le Grand Parti de Lyon au XVIᵉ siècle', *Revue Historique*, 172 (1933), 473–513; 173 (1934), 1–41.

Les Institutions de la France au XVIᵉ siècle, Paris: A. and J. Picard, 1948, 2 vols.

Drouot, Henri, 'Autorité royale et Privilèges communaux, Henri IV et les officiers de la Milice Dijonnaise 1595', *Esquisses, 1573–1600, études bourguignonnes sur le XVIe siècle*, ed. Henri Drouot, Dijon: Bernigaud et Privat, 1937, 59–72.

'Les Conseils Provinciaux de la Sainte-Union (1589–1595)', *Annales du Midi*, 65 (1953), 415–33.

Un épisode de la ligue à Dijon, L'affaire La Verne (1594), Paris: Champion, 1910.

Mayenne et la Bourgogne, étude sur la Ligue (1587–1596), Paris: A. Picard, 1937, 2 vols.

'Le serment de fidélité des dijonnais à Henri IV', in *Esquisses, 1573–1600, études bourguignonnes sur le XVI siècle*, ed. Henri Drouot, Dijon: Bernigaud et Privat, 1937, 269–74.

Dubédat, M., *Histoire du Parlement de Toulouse*, Paris: Libraire Nouvelle de Droit, 1885.

Du Courtieux, Paul, *Histoire de Limoges*, Limoges: Librairie Limousine, 1925.

Dumège, Alexandre, *Histoires des institutions religieuses politiques, judiciaires et littéraires de la Ville de Toulouse*, Toulouse: L. Chapelle, 1844–6, 4 vols.

Dupré, Alexandre, 'Etude sur les institutions municipales de Blois', *Mémoires de la Société archèologique et historique Orléanais*, 14 (1875), 441–550.

Histoire de Blois, Marseille: Laffitte Reprints, 1977, 2 vols.

Durand, Yves, ed., *Hommage à Roland Mounsier: Clientèles et fidélités en Europe à l'époque modern*, Paris: Presses Universitaire de France, 1981.

'Les républicans urbaines en France à la fin du XVIᵉ siècle', *Société d'Histoire et d'Archéologie de l'arrondissement de Saint-Malo, Annales 1990* (1990), 205–44.

Durkheim, Emile, *The Elementary Forms of the Religious Life*, trans. Joseph Swain: New York: Free Press, 1965.

Dyer, Alan, 'Influence of Bubonic Plague in England, 1500–1667', *Medical History*, 22

(1978), 308–36.

Eurich, Amanda, *The Economics of Power: The Private Finances of the House of Foix-Navarre-Albret, 1517–1610*, Kirksville, Missouri: Sixteenth Century Journal Publishers, 1994.

Fagniez, Gustave, *L'Economie sociale de la France sous Henri IV, 1589–1610*, Paris: Hachette, 1897.

Farr, James R., *Authority and Sexuality in Early Modern Burgundy (1550–1730)*, Cambridge: Cambridge University Press, 1995.

Hands of Honor Artisans and Their World in Dijon 1550–1650, Ithaca: Cornell University Press, 1988.

Favatier, 'La Vie Municipale à Narbonne au xviie siècle', *Bulletin de la Commission Archéologique de Narbonne*, 2 (1892–3), 241–72, 355–72.

Favreau, Robert, ed., *Histoire de Poitiers*, Toulouse: Privat, 1985.

Finley-Croswhite, Annette, 'Absolutism and Municipal Autonomy: Henry IV and the 1602 Pancarte Revolt in Limoges', in *Society and Institutions in Early Modern France*, ed. Mack P. Holt, Athens: University of Georgia Press, 1991, 80–97.

'Ceremonial Reconciliation: Henry IV's Royal Entry into Abbeville, 18 December 1594', *Proceedings of the Western Society for French History*, 17 (1990), 96–105.

'Confederates and Rivals: Picard Urban Alliances during the Catholic League, 1588–1594', *Canadian Journal of History Annales Canadiennes d'Histoire*, 31 (1996), 359–76.

'Engendering the Wars of Religion: Female Agency during the Catholic League in Dijon', *French Historical Studies*, 20 (1997), 127–54.

'Henri IV et les Villes', *Henri IV, le Roi et la Reconstruction du Royaume*, Pau: L'Association Henri IV 1989 and J. and D. Editions, 1990, 195–205.

'Urban Identity and Transitional Politics: The Transformation of Political Allegiance Inside Amiens Before and After the City's 1594 Capitulation to Henry IV', *Proceedings of the Western Society for French History*, 20(1993), 53–61.

Flathman, Richard, *The Practice of Political Authority, Authority and the Authoritative*, Chicago: University of Chicago Press, 1980.

Fons, Victor, 'L'Organisation Municipale à Toulouse du temps des Capitouls', *Recueil de L'Académie de Legislation de Toulouse*, 26 (1877), 19–29.

Foucault, Michel, 'The Juridical Apparatus', *Legitimacy and the State*, ed. William Connolly, New York: New York University Press, 1984, 201–21.

Fouque, Victor, *Histoire de Chalon-sur-Saône*, Marseille, Laffitte Reprints, 1975.

Fradenburg, Louise Olga, *City, Marriage, Tournament, Arts of Rule in Late Medieval Scotland*, Madison: University of Wisconsin Press, 1991.

Friedrich, Carl J., *Tradition and Authority*, New York: Praeger, 1972.

Friedrichs, Christopher, 'Urban Politics and Urban Social Struggle in Seventeenth-Century Germany', *European History Quarterly* 22 (1992), 187–216.

Gaillard, Jean, *Les derniers temps de la ligue à Beauvais*, Beauvais: Imprimerie du Moniteur de l'Oise, 1900.

Galpern, A. N., *The Religions of the People in Sixteenth-Century Champagne*, Cambridge, Massachusetts: Harvard University Press, 1976.

Garrisson, Janine, *L'Edit de Nantes de sa révocation, Histoire d'une intolérance*, Paris: Editions du Seuil, 1985.

Henri IV, Paris: Editions du Seuil, 1984.

'La reconquête catholique (17e siècle)', *Histoire de Montauban*, ed. Daniel Ligou, Toulouse: Privat, 131–66.

Gasçon, Richard, *Grand commerce et vie urbaine au XVIe siècle, Lyon et ses marchands*, Paris: Mouton, 1971, 2 vols.

Gilsenan, Michael, 'Against Patron–Client Relations', in *Patrons and Clients in Mediterranean Societies*, ed. Ernest Gellner and John Waterbury, London: Gerald Duckworth and Company, 1977, 167–83.

Giry, A., *Les etablissements de Rouen, études sur l'histoire des Institutions Municipales*, Paris: Vieweg, 1883.

Goubert, Pierre, *Beauvais et le Beauvaisis de 1600 à 1730. Constribution à l'histoire sociale de la France au XVIIe siècle*, Paris: SEVPEN, 1960.

Gras, Pierre, ed., *Histoire de Dijon*, Toulouse: Privat, 1987.

Greengrass, Mark, 'The Anatomy of a Religious Riot in Toulouse in May 1562', *Journal of Ecclesiastical History*, 34 (1983), 367–91.

'Conquest and Coalescence', *Conquest and Coalescence The Shaping of the State in Early Modern Europe*, ed. Mark Greengrass, London: Edward Arnold, 1991, 1–24.

France in the Age of Henri IV; the Struggle for Stability, London: Longman Group Ltd, 1984, 1995.

'The Later Wars of Religion in the French Midi', in *The European Crisis of the 1590s Essays in Comparative History*, ed. Peter Clark, London: George Allen and Unwin, 1985, 106–34.

'Noble Affinities in Early Modern France: The Case of Henri I de Montmorency, Constable of France', *European History Quarterly*, 16 (1986), 275–311.

'The Saint Union in the Province: The Case of Toulouse', *The Sixteenth Century Journal*, 14 (1983), 469–96.

'The Sixteen, Radical Politics in Paris during the League', *History*, 69 (1984), 432–9.

Grosley, M., *Vie de Pierre Pithou*, Paris: G. Cavelier 1756, 2 vols.

Guenée, Bernard and Françoise Lehoux, *Les entrées royales françaises de 1328 à 1515*, Paris: Editions du Centre Nationale de la Recherche Scientifique, 1968.

Guenée, Simonne, Philippe Dollinger, and Philippe Wolff, eds., *Bibliographie d'Histoire des Villes de France*, Paris: Klincksieck, 1967.

Guggenheim, Anne, 'The Calvinist Notables of Nîmes during the Era of the Religious Wars', *The Sixteenth Century Journal*, 3 (1972), 80–96.

Guibert, Louis, *La Ligue à Limoges*, Limoges: Imprimerie-Libraire Ducourtieux, 1884.

Guillemin, P., *Saint-Dizier d'après les registres de l'echevinage, 1573–1789*, Saint-Dizier, Société archéologique et historique de Saint-Dizier, 1891.

Gutmann, Myron, *War and Rural Life in the Early Modern Low Countries*, Princeton: Princeton University Press, 1980.

Guyaz, Marc, *Histoire des Institutions Municipales de Lyon*, Paris: Dentu, 1884.

Hanley, Sarah, 'Engendering the State: Family Formation and State Building in Early Modern France', *French Historical Studies*, 16 (1989), 4–27.

Hanotaux, Gabriel, *Sur les Chemins de l'Histoire*, Paris: Champion, 1924.

Harding, Robert, *The Anatomy of a Power Elite: The Provincial Governors of Early Modern France*, New Haven, Connecticut: Yale University Press, 1978.

'Corruption and the Moral Boundaries of Patronage in the Renaissance', in *Patronage in the Renaissance*, ed. Guy Fitch Lytle and Stephen Orgel, Princeton: Princeton University Press, 47–64.

Hauser, Henri, *Recherches et documents sur l'histoire des prix en France de 1500–1800*, Paris: Les Presses Modernes, 1936.

Heers, Jacques, *Le clan familial au Moyen Age*, Paris: Presses Universitaires de France, 1974.

Heller, Henry, *Iron and Blood Civil Wars in Sixteenth-Century France*, Montreal: McGill-Queen's University Press, 1991.

Heller, Henry, 'Putting History Back in the Religious Wars: A Reply to Mack P. Holt', *French Historical Studies*, 19 (1996), 853–61.

Henshall, Nicholas, *The Myth of Absolutism: Change and Continuity in Early Modern European History*, London: Longman, 1992.

Holt, Mack P., *The Duke of Anjou and the Politique Struggle during the Wars of Religion*, Cambridge: Cambridge University Press, 1986.

The French Wars of Religion, 1562–1629, Cambridge: Cambridge University Press, 1995.

'Historical Method, and Historical Forces: A Rejoinder', *French Historical Studies*, 19 (1996), 863–73.

'Patterns of *Clientèle* and Economic Opportunity at Court during the Wars of Religion: The Household of François duke of Anjou', *French Historical Studies*, 13 (1984), 305–22.

'Popular Political Culture and Mayoral Elections', in *Society and Institutions in Early Modern France*, ed. Mack P. Holt, Athens: University of Georgia Press, 98–116.

'Putting Religion Back into the Wars of Religion', *French Historical Studies*, 18 (1993), 524–51.

ed., *Society and Institutions in Early Modern France*, Athens: University of Georgia Press, 1991.

Hodge, Robert and Gunther Kress, *Social Semiotics*, Ithatca: Cornell University Press, 1988.

Huizinga, Johann, *The Waning of the Middle Ages*, New York: Double Day Anchor Books, 1954.

Hugues, E., *Histoire de Langres au début du* XVIIe *siècle, 1610–1660*, Langres: Gueniot, 1978.

Jackson, Richard A., 'Elective Kingship and Consensus Populi in Sixteenth-Century France', *Journal of Modern History*, 44, (1972), 155–71.

Vive le Roi! A History of the French Coronation from Charles V to Charles X, Chapel Hill: University of North Carolina, 1984.

Jacquart, Jean, *La Crise Rurale en Ile-de-France 1550–1670*, Paris: Armand Colin, 1974.

Janvier, A., *Livre D'Or de la Municipalité Amiénoise*, Paris: Picard, 1893.

Jouanna Arlette, *Le devoir de révolte: La noblesse française et la gestation de l'Etat moderne, 1559–1661*, Paris: Fayard, 1989.

Kaiser, Wolfgang, *Marseille au Temps des Troubles, Morphologie social et luttes de factions 1558–1596*, trans. Florence Chaix, Paris: Ecole des Hautes Etudes, 1992.

Kamen, Henry, *European Society 1500–1700*, London and New York: Routledge, 1984, 1996.

Kaufman, Ruth, 'François Gérard's Entry of Henry IV into Paris', *The Burlington Magazine*, 117 (1975), 790–802.

Kertzer, David, *Ritual, Politics, and Power*, New Haven: Yale University Press, 1988.

Kettering Sharon, 'Brokerage at the Court of Louis XIV', *The Historical Journal*, 36, 1

(1993), 69–87.

'Clientage during the French Wars of Religion', *Sixteenth Century Journal*, 20 (1989), 68–87.

'Friendship and Clientage in Early Modern France', *French History*, 6 (1992), 139–58.

'The Historical Development of Political Clientelism', *Journal of Interdisciplinary History*, 18 (1988), 419–47.

Judicial Politics and Urban Revolt in Seventeenth-Century France: the Parlement of Aix, 1629–1659, Princeton, New Jersey: Princeton University Press, 1978.

'Patronage in Early Modern Europe', *French Historical Studies*, 17 (1992), 839–62.

Patrons, Brokers and Clients in Seventeenth-Century France, Oxford: Oxford University Press, 1986.

'Political Parties at Aix-en-Provence in 1589', *European History Quarterly*, 24 (1994), 181–211.

'Red Robes and Barricades: The Parlement of Aix-en-Provence in a Period of Popular Revolt, 1629–1649', Ph.D. diss. Stanford University, 1969.

'State Control and Municipal Authority in France', *Edo and Paris: Urban Life and the State in the Early Modern Era*, eds. James McClain, John Merriman, and Ugawa Kaoru, Ithaca, Cornell University Press, 1994, 86–101.

Kleinclauz, A., *Histoire de Lyon*, Paris: Masson, 1939, 2 vols.

Knecht, R. J. *The French Wars of Religion, 1559–1598*, London and New York: Longman, 1989, 1996.

Konnart, Mark, 'Civic Rivalry and the Boundaries of Civic Identity in the French Wars of Religion: Châlons-sur-Marne and the Towns of Champagne', *Renaissance and Reformation / Renaissance et Réforme*, 21, 1 (1997), 19–33.

'Provincal Governors and their Regimes during the French Wars of Religon: the Duke of Guise and the City Council of Châlons-sur-Marne', *Sixteenth Century Journal*, 25 (1994), 832–40.

'Urban Values Versus Religious Passion: Châlons-sur-Marne During the Wars of Religion', *Sixteenth Century Journal*, 20 (1989), 387–405.

Kuhrt, Amélie, 'Usurpation, conquest and ceremonial: From Babylon to Persia', in *Rituals of Royalty Power and Ceremonial in Traditional Societies*, ed. David Cannadine and Simon Price, Cambridge: Cambridge University Press, 20–55.

Lachiver, Marcel, *La population de Meulan du xviIème au xixème siècle (vers 1600–1870) Etude de démographie historique*, Paris: SEVPEN, 1969.

La Cuisine, M. de, *Le Parlement de Bourgogne depuis son Origine jusqu'à sa Chute*, Dijon: Rabutot. 1864, 2 vols.

LaForest, M. P. *Etudes sur les Anciennes Provinces de France, Limoges au xviIe siècle*, Limoges: LeBlanc, 1862.

Laronze, C., *Essai sur le régime municipal en Bretagne pendant les guerres de religion*, Paris: Hachette, 1890.

La Roque, Louis de, *Armorial de la Noblesse de Languedoc*, Montpellier: Félix Seguin, 1860.

Leach, Edmund, *Culture and communication, the Logic by which Symbols are Connected*, Cambridge: Cambridge University Press, 1976.

Political Systems of Highland Burma: A Study of Kachin Social Structure, Boston: Beacon Press, 1965.

Lebret, Henri, *Histoire de Montauban*, Montauban: Chez-Réthone, 1841, 2 vols.

Lecocq, Georges, *Histoire de la Ville de Saint-Quentin*, Marseille: Laffitte, 1977.

Ledain, Belisaire, *Histoire sommaire de la ville de Poitiers*, Fontenay: Auguste Baud, 1889.

'Les maires de Poitiers', *Bulletin et Mémoires de la Société des Antiquaires de L'Ouest*, 20 (1897), 215–74.

Ledieu, Alcius, 'Livres de Raison de Deux Seigneurs Picards (1559–1692)', *Le Cabinet Historique de l'Artois et de la Picardie*, 7 (1982), 321–28, 8 (1893), 11–20, 82–86.

Le Picard, Charles, *Catalogue des maires et échevins de la Ville de Rouen*, Louviers: Izambert, 1895.

Le Roy Ladurie, Emmanuel, *Carnival in Romans*, trans. Mary Feeney, New York: George Braziller, 1979.

L'Etat Royal de Louis XI à Henri IV 1460–1610, Paris: Hachette, 1987.

The Peasants of Languedoc, trans. John Day: Chicago, University of Illinois Press, 1974.

Levet, Jean, *Histoire de Limoges*, Limoges: Desagne, 1974, 2. vols.

Limouzin-Lamothe, Roger, *Bibliographie critique de l' histoire municipale de Toulouse, des origines à 1789*, Toulouse: Privat, 1932.

L'Orgnier, Louis, *Un homme à la mode, François de Louvencourt, siegneur de vauchelles et de Bourseville, poète, romancier et historien, Président-Trésorier de France en Picardie, Premier Echevin d'Amiens: La vie amiénoise à l'époque de la Ligue d'Henri IV et de Louis XIII*, Amiens: Société des Antiquaires de Picardie, 1942.

Lotman, Yuri, *Universe of the Mind, A Semiotic Theory of Culture*, trans. Ann Shukman, Bloomington: Indiana University Press, 1990.

Louandre, F. C., *Les Mayeurs et les Maires d'Abbeville, 1184–1847*, Abbeville: Jeuret, 1851.

Lukes, Steven, *Power A Radical View*, London: Macmillian, 1974.

Lynch, J., *Godparents and Kinship in Early Modern Europe*, Princeton, New Jersey: Princeton University Press, 1986.

Major, J. Russell, *Bellièvre, Sully and the Assembly of Notables of 1596*, Transactions of the American Philosophical Society, vol. 64, part 2, Philadelphia: The American Philosophical Society, 1974.

From Renaissance Monarchy to Absolute Monarchy, French Kings, Nobles, and Estates, Baltimore: The Johns Hopkins University Press, 1994.

'Henri IV and Guyenne: A Study Concerning the Origins of Royal Absolutism', *French Historical Studies*, 4 (1966), 363–83.

Representative Government in Early Modern France, New Haven, Connecticut: Yale University Press, 1980.

'Vertical Ties through Time', *French Historical Studies*, 17 (1992), 863–71.

Mandrou, Robert, *Introduction à la France moderne: 1500–1640, éssai de psychologie, historique*, Paris: Michel, 1973.

Manry, A. G., *Histoire de Clermont-Ferrand*, Clermont-Ferrand: Mont-Louis, 1975.

Margadant, Ted W., *Urban Rivalries in the French Revolution*, Princeton: Princeton University Press, 1992.

Mariéjol, Jean H., *Charles-Emmanuel de Savoie duc de Nemours, Gouverneur du Lyonnais, Beaujolais et Forez (1567–1595)*, Hachette: Paris, 1935.

Marvaud, F., *Histoire des Vîcomtes et de la Vîcomté de Limoges*, Paris: Dumoulin, 1873. 2 vols.

Mateu, André, 'Les émotions populaires au temps d'Henri IV: Un Exemple Layrac [Lot-et-

Garonne]', *Revue Agenais* (1981), 87–104, 255–68.

Maugis, Edouard, *Recherches sur les transformations du régimes politque et social de la ville d'Amiens, des origines de la Commune à la fin du* XVIe *siècle*, Paris: Picard, 1907.

Medick, Hans and David Warren Sabean, *Interest and Emotion, Essays on the Study of Family and Kinship*, Cambridge: Cambridge University Press, 1984.

Melleville, Maximilien, *Histoire de la Ville de Laon*, Paris: Dumoulin, 1846, 2 vols.

Ménard, Léon, *Histoire civile, ecclésiastique et literaire de la ville de Nismes*, Marseille: Laffitte Reprints, 7 vols.

Mercier de la Combe, Charles, *Henri IV et sa Politique*, Paris: Didier, 1877.

Mettam, Roger, *Power and Faction in Louis XIV's France*, Oxford: Basil Blackwell, 1988.

Meyer, Jean, ed., *Histoire de Rennes*, Toulouse: Privat, 1972.

'Quelques vues sur l'histoire des villes à l'époque modern', *Annales, économies, sociétés, civilisations* (1974), 1551–68.

Miron de l'Espinay, A., *François Miron et l'administration Municipales de Paris sous Henri IV, 1604 à 1606*, Paris: Plon, 1885.

Molho, Anthony, 'Il padronato a Firenze nella storiografia anglofona', *Ricerche Storiche*, 15 (1985), 5–16.

Monfaulcon, Jean-Baptiste, *Histoire Monumentale de la Ville de Lyon*, Lyon: privately printed, 1851.

Mousnier, Roland, *The Assassination of Henry IV, The Tyrannicide Problem and the Consolidation of the French Absolute Monarchy in the Early Seventeenth Century*, trans. Joan Spencer, New York: Charles Scribner's Sons, 1973.

Les Institutions de la France sous la Monarchie Absolue, 1498–1789 1: Société et Etat, trans. Brian Pearce, Paris: Presses Universitaire de France, 1974.

'Sully et le council d'état et des finances', *Revue Historique*, 192 (1941), 68–86.

La Vénalité des Offices sous Henri IV et Louis XIII, Paris: Presses Universitaires de France, 1971.

Neuschel, Kristen, *Word of Honor Interpreting Noble Culture in Sixteenth-Century France*, Ithaca: Cornell University Press, 1993.

Nichols, David, 'Protestants, Catholics, and Magistrates in Tours, 1562–1572: The Making of a Catholic City during the Religious Wars', *French History*, 8 (1994), 14–33.

Normand, Charles, *Etude sur les relations de l'état et des communautés au XVIIe et XVIIIe siècles*, Paris: Champion, 1881.

Nouaillac, Joseph, 'La Fin de la Ligue, Villeroy négociateur des politics. Essai d'histoire des négociations de 1589 à 1594', *Revue Henri IV*, 1 (1905), 69–81.

Nussdorfer, Laurie, *Civic Politics in the Rome of Urban VIII*, Princeton: Princeton University Press, 1992.

Orr, John, *Cinema and Modernity*, Cambridge, Massachusetts: Polity Press, 1993.

Ourliac, Paul, *Etude d'histoire du droit médiéval*, Paris: Picard, 1979.

Ouvré, Henri, *Essai sur l'histoire de Poitiers depuis la fin de la Ligue jusqu'à la pris de La Rochelle*, Poitiers: A. Dupré, 1856.

Pagès, Georges, *La Monarchie d'Ancien Régime en France de Henri IV à Louis XIV*, Paris: Colin, 1928.

Le Règne de Henri IV, Paris: Centre de documentation universitaire, 1934.

Parker, David, *La Rochelle and the French Monarchy: Conflict and Order in Seventeenth-*

Century France, London: Royal Historical Society, 1980.

The Making of French Absolutism, London: E. Arnold, 1983.

'Sovereignty, Absolutism, and the Function of Law in Seventeenth-Century France', *Past and Present*, 122 (1989), 36–74.

Parrow, Kathleen, *From Defense to Resistance: Justification of Violence during the French Wars of Religion*, Transactions of the American Philosophical Society, vol. 83, part 6, Philadelphia: The American Philosophical Society, 1993.

Partridge, P. H. *Consent and Consensus*, New York: Praeger, 1971.

Paton, Jacques, *Le Corps de Ville de Troyes (1470–1790)*, Troyes: J-L Paton Imprimeur-Editeur, 1939.

Patterson, Orlando, *Slavery and Social Death A Comparative Study*, Cambridge, Massachusetts: Harvard University Press, 1982.

Pèlus, Marie-Louis, 'Marchands et échevins d'Amiens dans la séconde moitié du XVIe siècle: crise de subsistances, commerces et profits en 1586–1587', *Revue du Nord* (1982), 51–71.

Peremezel, Jacques, *La Politique Financière de Sully dans la Généralité de Lyon*, Lyons: Audin, 1935.

Perrot, Jean-Claude, *Genèse d'une ville moderne: Caen au XVIIIe siècle*, Paris: Mouton, 1975.

Petit-Dutaillis, Charles, *Les communes françaises, caractères et evolution des origines au XVIIIe siècle*, Paris: Michel, 1947.

Picot, Georges, 'Recherches sur les quarteniers, cinquanteniers et dizianiers de la ville de Paris', *Mémoires de la Société de la Ville de Paris et L'Ile de France*, 1 (1874), 132–66.

Pigafetta, Filippo, 'Relations du Siège de Paris par Henri IV', *Mémoires de la Société de l'Histoire de la Ville de Paris et L'Ile de France*, 2 (1876), 1–105.

Pillorget, René, 'Luttes de factions et intérêts économiques à Marseille de 1598–1618', *Annales, économies, sociétés, civilisations*, 27 (1972), 705–30.

Les mouvements insurrectionnels de Provence entre 1596 et 1715, Paris: Pedone, 1975.

Pirenne, Henri, *Les villes et les institutions urbaines*, Paris: Alcan, 1939.

Plakans, Andrejs, *Kinship in the Past. An Anthropology of European Family Life 1500–1900*, London: Basil Blackwell, 1984.

Poirson, Auguste *Histoire du règne de Henri IV*, Paris: Didier, 1865, 4 vols.

Potter, David, *War and Government in the French Provinces, 1470–1560*, New York: Cambridge University Press, 1993.

Pouy, F., *La chambre du conseil des etats de Picardie pendant la ligue*, Amiens: Delatte, 1882.

Prarond, Ernest, *Les convivialités de l'échevinage ou l'histoire à table*, Paris: Champion, 1886.

La ligue à Abbeville, 1576–1594, Paris: Dumoulin, 1873, 3 vols.

Puget, Baron de, 'Le Capitoul Jacques de Puget (1544–1626)', *Revue Historique de Toulouse*, 22 (1935), 192–202.

Ranum, 'Courtesy, Absolutism, and the Rise of the French State, 1630–1660', *Journal of Modern History*, 52 (1980), 426–51.

Paris in the Age of Absolutism; An Essay, New York: John Wiley and Sons, 1968.

Raynal, Louis, *Histoire du Berry depuis les temps les plus anciens jusqu'en 1789*, Bourges: DeVermeil, 1847.

Ramet, Henri, *Le Capitoule et le Parlement de Toulouse*, Toulouse: Imprimerie Régionale, 1926.

Raz, Joseph, ed., *Authority*, New York: New York University Press, 1990.

Richard, Anthoine, *Mémoires sur la Ligue dans le Laonnais*, Paris: Didron-Neveu, 1869.

Richet, Denis, 'Aspects of Religious Conflicts in Paris in the Second Half of the Sixteenth Century', in *Ritual Religion, and the Sacred: Selections from the Annales*, ed. Robert Forster and Orest Ranum, Baltimore: The Johns Hopkins University Press, 1982, 182–212.

'Aspects socioculturels des conflits religieux à Paris dans la seconde moitié du 16e siècle', *Annales, economies, sociétés civilisations*, 32 (1977), 764–89.

Robbins, Kevin, 'The Families and Politics of La Rochelle, 1550–1650', Ph.D. diss. The Johns Hopkins University. 1990.

'The Social Mechanisms of Urban Rebellion: A Case Study of Leadership in the 1614 Revolt of La Rochelle', *French Historical Studies*, 19 (1995), 559–90.

Roberts, Penny, *A City in conflict Troyes during the French Wars of Religion*, Manchester: Manchester University Press, 1996.

'Religious Conflict and the Urban Setting: Troyes during the French Wars of Religion', *French History*, 6 (1992), 259–78.

Robiquet, Paul, *Histoire municipale de Paris*, Paris: Hachette, 1904, 3 vols.

Roelker, Nancy Lyman, *One King, One Faith, The Parlement of Paris and the Religious Reformations of the Sixteenth Century*, Berkeley: University of California Press, 1996.

Romier, M., 'Les députés des villes en cour au XVIe siècle', *Bulletin Historique et Philologique* (1909), 510–11.

Roney, Charles Patrick, *Commentary of the Harmony of the Gospels*, Grand Rapids, Michigan: Eerdmans Publishing, 1948.

Roschach, Ernest, *Des douze livres de l'histoire de Toulouse*, Toulouse: Publié par la ville de Toulouse, 1887.

Rosenberg, David Lee, 'Social Experience and Religious Choice: A Case Study, The Protestant Weavers and Woolcombers of Amiens in the Sixteenth Century', Ph. D. diss. Yale University, 1978.

Rossier, L., *Histoire des Protestants de Picardie*, Paris: Res Universis, 1990.

Rotberg, Robert and Theodore Rabb, *Hunger and History, The Impact of Changing Food Production and Consumption Patterns in Society*, New York: Cambridge University Press, 1983.

Roupnel, Gaston, *La Ville et la campagne au XVIIe siècle: étude sur les populations du pays dijonnais*, Paris: Colin, 1955.

Ruben, Emile, Félix Archard and Paul Ducourtieux, eds., *Annales Manuscrites de Limoges dites Manuscrit de 1638*, Limoges: Ducourtieux, 1867.

'Changements Introduits en 1602 par Henri IV dans le mode d'élection et le nombre des consuls de Limoges', *Bulletin de la Société archéologique et historique du Limousin*, 3 (1857), 147–51.

Sachy de Fourdrinoy, Gabriel de, *Historique de la Famille de Sachy de Fourdrinoy*, Blois: Editions Lignages, 1991.

Sacks, David Harris, *The Widening Gate, Bristol and the Atlantic Economy, 1450–1700*, Berkeley: University of California Press, 1991.

Salmon, J. H. M., 'Justice, Finance, and Administrative Revolution: Comments on Bernard

Bibliography

Barbiche's Henri IV, Sully et la Première Monarchie Administrative', *Proceedings of the Annual Meeting of the Western Society for French History*, 17 (1990), 24–9.

'The Paris Sixteen, 1584–94: The Social Analyse of A Revolutionary Movement', *Journal of Modern History*, 46 (1972), 540–76.

Renaissance and Revolt Essays in the Intellectual and Social History of Early Modern Europe, New York: Cambridge University Press, 1987.

Society in Crisis: France in the Sixteenth Century, New York: St Martin's Press, 1975.

Saudau, Louis-Claude, *Saint-Jean d'Angély, d'après les Archives de l'échevinage et les sources directes des son histoire*, Marseille: Laffitte Reprints, 1986.

Saupin, Guy, 'Les élections municipales à Nantes sous l'ancien régime, 1565–1789', *Annales Bretagne et de Pays de l'Ouest*, 90 (1983), 429–50.

'Les habitants et l'élaboration de la politique municipale à Nantes sous l'Ancien Régime', *Annales de Bretagne et de Pays de l'Ouest*, 91 (1984), 319–50.

Schabert, Tilo, 'Power, Legitimacy and Truth: Reflections on the Impossibility to Legitimise Legitimations of Political Order', in *Legitimacy/Légitimité Proceedings of the Conference held in Florence June 3–4, 1982*, Berlin: Walter de Gruyter, 1986, 96–104.

Schalk, Ellery, *From Valor to Pedigree Ideas of Nobility in France in the Sixteenth and Seventeenth Centuries*, Princeton: Princeton University Press, 1986.

Schneider, Robert, 'Crown and Capitoulat: Municipal Government in Toulouse 1500–1789', in *Cities and Social Change in Early Modern France*, ed. Philip Benedict, London: Unwin Hyman, 195–220.

Public Life in Toulouse, 1463–1789: From Municipal Republic to Cosmopolitan City, Ithaca: Cornell University Press, 1989.

Sèe, Henri, *Louis XI et les Villes*, Paris: Hachette, 1891.

Serret, Jules, *Préfets et Magistrates Municipaux d'Agen depuis les temps anciens jusqu'à nos jours*, Agen: Bonnet et Fils, 1886.

Soyer, Jacques, *Etudes sur la communauté des habitants de Blois jusqu'au commencement du XVIe siècle*, Paris: Picard, 1894.

Strong, Roy, *Art and Power, Renaissance Festivals 1450–1550*, Berkeley: University of California Press, 1973.

Sutherland, N. M., *The Huguenot Struggle for Recognition*, New Haven: Yale University Press, 1980.

Tardieu, Ambroise, *Histoire de la ville de Clermont-Ferrand depuis les temps les plus récules jusqu'à nos jours*, Moulins: Desrosiers, 1872.

Temple, Nora, 'The Control and Exploitation of French Towns during the Ancien Regime', *History*, 51 (1966), 16–34.

Testaud, Georges, *Des Juridictions muncipales en France, des origines jusqu'à l'ordonnance de Moulins*, Paris: Larose, 1901.

Tholin, Georges, 'Apèrcus Généraux sur le Régime municipales de la ville d'Agen au XVIe siècle', *Recueil des Travaux de la Société d'Agriculture Sciences et Arts d'Agen*, 5 (1877), 1–33.

'Des Tailles et des impositions au pays d'Agenais durant le XVe siècle jusqu'aux réformes de Sully', *Recueil des Travaux de la Société d'Agriculture, Sciences et Arts d'Agen*, 3 (1875), 91–135.

Travers, L'Abbé, *Histoire Civile, Politique et Religieuses de la Ville du Comté de Nantes*,

Nantes: Forest, 1841.

Tremblay, Victor, 'Nicolas Godin, Maire de Beauvais sous la Ligue, 1560 à 1628', *L'Annuaire de L'Oise* (1859), 447–69.

Trocmé, Etienne, 'Du Gouverneur à l'Intendant, l'Autonomié Rochelaise de Charles IX à Louis XIII', *Recueil de Traveaux Offerts à M. Brunel*, 11 (1955), 616–32.

'La Rochelle de 1560–1628. Tableau d'une société reformée du temps de guerres de religion', Thesis Bachelier en Thèologie, Faculté Libre de Thèologie Protestante, Paris: 1950.

'Réflexions sur le séparatisme rochelais (1568–1628)', *Bulletin de la Société de l' Histoire du Protestantism Français*, 122 (1976), 203–10.

Trullinger, Robert, 'Le Grand Voyer as an Instrument of Royal Centralization in Brittany under Henry IV', *Proceedings of the Western Society for French History*, 3 (1975), 26–34.

'The Royal Administration of Bretagne under Henri IV (1598–1602)', Ph.D. diss. Vanderbilt University, 1972.

Turner, Victor, *The Ritual Process Structure and Anti-Structure*, Chicago: University of Chicago Press, 1969.

Valensise, Marina, 'Le Sacre du Roi: Stratégie Symbolique et Doctrine Politique de la Monarchie Française', *Annales, Économies, Sociétés, Civilisations*, 41 (1986), 543–77.

Van Doren, Llewain Scott, 'Civil War Taxation and the Foundation of French Absolutism: The Royal Taille in Dauphiné, 1560–1610', *Proceedings of the Western Society for French History*, 3 (1975), 35–53.

'Revolt and Reaction in the City of Romans, Dauphiné, (1579–80)', *Sixteenth Century Journal*, 5 (1974), 71–100.

Vial, E., *Costumes Consulaires*, Lyons, Louis Brun, 1904.

Vic, Claude de and J. Vaissete, eds., *Histoire générale de Languedoc, avec des notes et les pièces justificatives*, Toulouse: Privat,1872–89, 15 vols.

Vries, Jan de, *European Urbanization, 1500–1800*, Cambridge, Massachusetts: Harvard University Press, 1984.

Waele de, Michel, 'Une question de confiance? Le Parlement de Paris et Henri IV, 1589–99', Ph.D. diss., McGill University, 1995.

Wartenburg, Thomas E., *The Forms of Power From Domination to Transformation*, Philadelphia: Temple University Press, 1990.

Weber, Max, *Economy and Society*, ed. Guenther Roth and Claus Wittich, Berkeley: University of California Press, 1978.

Weingrod, Alex, 'Patronage and Power', in *Patrons and Clients in Mediterranean Societies*, ed. Ernest Gellner and John Waterbury, London: Duckworth and Company, 41–52.

Wolfe, Martin, *The Fiscal System of Renaissance France*, New Haven, Connecticut: Yale University Press, 1972.

Wolfe, Michael, *The Conversion of Henri IV Politics, Power and Religious Belief in Early Modern France*, Cambridge, Massachusetts: Harvard University Press, 1993.

'"Paris is Worth a Mass" Reconsidered: Henri IV and the Leaguer Capital, March, 1594', unpublished paper presented at the Society for French Historical Studies conference, Wilmington, Deleware, March, 1994.

Zagorin, *Rebels and Rulers, 1590–1660*, Cambridge: Cambridge University Press, 1982, 2 vols.

Bibliography

Zeller, Gaston, 'L'Administration monarchique avant les Intendants', *Revue Historique*, 97 (1947), 180–215.

Les Institutions de la France au XVI*e siècle*, Paris: Presses Universitaires de France, 1949.

Index

Index

Lyons, 8, 12, 124, 136, 163
  Catholic League, defeat of, 71
  capitulation, 19
  centre of finance, 170–1
  conflict over elections, 72
  debt liquidation, 167–81
  Grande parti, 170
  Henry IV's entry into, 56–7, 58, 59
  size of town government, 80
  social composition of town government, 126–7

Mâcon, 78
magisterial dress, 48, 84, 98
Major, J. Russell, 7, 11
Mansfeld, Charles de 39
Mantes, 124, 127
Marcel, Louis de, 113
Mariéjol, Jean 6
Maroeuil, Adrien de 136–7
Marseilles, 11, 12, 16–17, 170
  conflict over elections, 74, 133
Martin, Jacques, 154
Mauple, Jean de 150
Maupin, Jean de, 49, 50, 51
Mayenne, *see* Lorraine
Meaux, 21, 78
Medici, Marie de, 136, 146
Mercoeur, duke of, 69
Mettam, Roger, 183
Montauban, 103, 110, 127
  consulate, 111–12, 128
  Edict of Nantes, 108
Montbarot, Marec de, 92, 96
Montbazon, Hercule de Rohan, duke of, 113
Montélimar, 103, 110, 113
Montpellier, 103, 108
Morlaix, 12
Moulceau, Jean de, 176–8
Moulins, Ordonnance of, 10
Mousnier, Roland, 3, 124, 130
Muir, Edward, 47
municipalities, 10
  size of, 8
  terminology for, 8

Nantes, 11, 12, 127,
  capitulation, 66
  government, social composition of, 129
  Henry IV's entry into, 61
  Henry IV's intervention in elections, 66–70
  indebtedness, 169
  liart pour livre, 164–5
Nantes, Edict of, 88, 99, 102, 103–11, 167, 182
  La Rochelle, resistance of 106–8, *see also* La Rochelle

Narbonne, 8
Nemours, duke of, 21
Neufville, Nicholas de, sieur de Villeroy, 178
Nîmes, 103, 110, 127
  Edict of Nantes, 108
Nogeret, Jean-Louis de, duke of Epernon, 154
noblesse de la cloche, 125

octrois, 171
Origny, Loys de, 96
Orléans, 11
Orléans, Henry de, duke of Longueville, 21, 49,
  95, 92
Orléans, Ordonnance of, 10
Ornano, Alphonse d', 133

Pagès, Georges, 6
Paillot, Jean, 20
Pamiers, 109
Paris, 8, 11, 12, 13, 14, 17, 19, 21, 91, 99, 105,
  164, 167
  èchevinage, 138
  elections, 70–1, 135–6
  Henry IV's entry into, 60
  as ideal town government, 138
  indebtedness, 170
  parlements, 105, 109
    Bordeaux, 124
    Grenoble, 109
    Paris, 80, 124
    Rouen, 79
    Toulouse, 109, 124
  partisans, 175–9
Patte, Jean 37
Patterson, Orlando, 1
Pécoul, Claude, 31, 42
Péronne, 17
Petiot, Martial, 153
patrons at court, 163
Petiot, Joseph de, 150
Picardy, 44, *see* Amiens
Pingré Antoine, 28, 37, 42, 46, 85
Poitiers, 12, 139, 142
  conflict over elections, 72
  government, social composition of, 129
  offices sold, 124
  Protestants, 147–8
  reduction of town government by Henry IV,
    148
Privas, 103
privileges of towns, 6, 10, 11, 12, 38, 63, 83,
  86–7, 115–18, 182, *see* autonomy, municipal
  Protestant towns, 101–3
    monitored by Henry IV 111–15
Prunier, Arthur, sieur de Saint-André, 113

218

CAMBRIDGE STUDIES IN EARLY MODERN HISTORY

*The Old World and the New**
J. H. ELLIOTT
*The Army of Flanders and the Spanish Road, 1567–1659: The Logistics of Spanish Victory and Defeat in the Low Countries Wars**
GEOFFREY PARKER
*Richelieu and Olivares**
J. H. ELLIOTT
*Absolutism and Society in Seventeenth-Century France: State Power and Provincial Aristocracy in Languedoc**
WILLIAM BEIK
*The Princes of Orange: The Stadholders in the Dutch Republic**
HERBERT H. ROWEN
The Nobility of Holland: From Knights to Regents, 1500–1650
H. F. K. VAN NIEROP
Classes, Estates and Order in Early Modern Brittany
JAMES B. COLLINS
Early Modern Democracy in the Grisons: Social Order and Political Language in a Swiss Mountain Canton, 1470–1620
RANDOLPH C. HEAD
*War, State and Society in Württemberg, 1677–1793**
PETER H. WILSON
From Madrid to Purgatory: The Art and Craft of Dying in Sixteenth-Century Spain
CARLOS M. N. EIRE
The Reformation and Rural Society: The Parishes of Brandenburg-Ansbach-Kulmbach, 1528–1603
C. SCOTT DIXON
Labour, Science and Technology in France, 1500–1620
HENRY HELLER
The King's Army: Warfare, Soldiers, and Society During the Wars of Religion in France, 1562–1576
JAMES B. WOOD
Spanish Naval Power, 1589–1665: Reconstruction and Defeat
DAVID GOODMAN
State and Nobility in Early Modern Germany: The Knightly Feud in Franconia, 1440–1567
HILLAY ZMORA
The Quest for Compromise: Peace-Makers in Counter-Reformation Vienna
HOWARD LOUTHAN
Charles XI and Swedish Absolutism, 1660–1697
A. F. UPTON
Noble Power During the French Wars of Religion: The Guise Affinity and the Catholic Cause in Normandy
STUART CARROLL

The Reformation of Community: Social Welfare and Calvinist Charity in Holland, 1572–1620
CHARLES H. PARKER

Titles available in paperback marked with an asterisk*

The following titles are now out of print:
French Finances, 1770–1795: From Business to Bureaucracy
J. F. BOSHER
Chronicle into History: An Essay in the Interpretation of History in Florentine Fourteenth-Century Chronicles
LOUIS GREEN
France and the Estates General of 1614
J. MICHAEL HAYDEN
Reform and Revolution in Mainz, 1743–1803
T. C. W. BLANNING
Altopascio: A Study in Tuscan Society 1587–1784
FRANK MCARDLE
Gunpowder and Galleys: Changing Technology and Mediterranean Warfare at Sea in the Sixteenth Century
JOHN FRANCIS GUILMARTIN JR
The State, War and Peace: Spanish Political Thought in the Renaissance 1516–1559
J. A. FERNÁNDEZ-SANTAMARIA
Calvinist Preaching and Iconoclasm in the Netherlands, 1544–1569
PHYLLIS MACK CREW
The Kingdom of Valencia in the Seventeenth Century
JAMES CASEY
Filippo Strozzi and the Medici: Favor and Finance in Sixteenth-Century Florence and Rome
MELISSA MERIAM BULLARD
Rouen During the Wars of Religion
PHILIP BENEDICT
The Emperor and His Chancellor: A Study of the Imperial Chancellery Under Gattinara
JOHN M. HEADLEY
The Military Organisation of a Renaissance State: Venice c. 1400–1617
M. E. MALLETT AND J. R. HALE
Neostoicism and the Early Modern State
GERHARD OESTREICH
Prussian Society and the German Order: An Aristocratic Corporation in Crisis c. 1410–1466
MICHAEL BURLEIGH
The Changing Face of Empire: Charles V, Philip II and Habsburg Authority, 1552–1559
M. J. RODRÍGUEZ-SALGADO
Turning Swiss: Cities and Empire 1450–1550
THOMAS A. BRADY JR
Neighbourhood and Community in Paris
DAVID GARRIOCH